The
Tender
Hour of
Twilight

The
Tender
Hour of
Twilight

Paris in the '50s,
New York in the '60s:
A Memoir of Publishing's
Golden Age

Richard Seaver

Edited by Jeannette Seaver

Farrar, Straus and Giroux ❧ New York

FARRAR, STRAUS AND GIROUX
18 West 18th Street, New York 10011

Photographs on title page and page xxii (right), copyright © H. Riemens. Photograph on page 220 (left), copyright © Alain Resnais. Photograph on page 221 (right), copyright © Mary Ellen Mark. All other photographs courtesy of Jeannette Seaver.

Library of Congress Cataloging-in-Publication Data
Seaver, Richard.
    The tender hour of twilight : Paris in the '50s, New York in the '60s: a memoir of publishing's golden age / Richard Seaver ; edited by Jeannette Seaver.
        p.   cm.
    Includes index.
    ISBN 978-0-374-27378-1 (alk. paper)
    1. Seaver, Richard.   2. Publishers and publishing—United States—Biography.
    3. Book editors—United States—Biography.   4. Translators—United States—Biography.
    I. Seaver, Jeannette.   II. Title.

Z473.S426 S43 2012
070.5092—dc23
[B]

                                                                        2011024951

Designed by Abby Kagan

www.fsgbooks.com

10 9 8 7 6 5 4 3 2 1

Photograph on title page: Back row, left to right: George Plimpton, Richard Seaver, Corneille, Mary Smith, Patrick Bowles, Gaït Frogé, Jane Lougee; front row, left to right: Christopher Logue, Austryn Wainhouse, Christopher Middleton

To Jeannette, my beloved,
without whose persistence, encouragement, patience,
resistance to my resistance,
and enduring love
this book would never have been

and

To Nathalie, Alexander, and Nicholas,
the lights of my life

Certain things I remember exactly as they were. They are merely discolored a bit by time, like coins in the pocket of a forgotten suit . . . The myriad past, it enters us and disappears. Except that within it, somewhere, like diamonds, exist the fragments that refuse to be consumed. Sifting through, if one dares, and collecting them, one discovers the true design.

—James Salter, *A Sport and a Pastime*

Contents

Part One ❧ Paris, 1950s

Part Two ❧ New York, 1960s

◥◥

Introduction

ICHARD SEAVER, EMINENT EDITOR, publisher, and translator, belongs to what is now thought of as a better time in American publishing, a period from, say, 1920 to 1950. Though he followed it by a decade or more, he personally carried on the legacy of a number of houses founded in that earlier time that reflected the tastes and character of individual owners. Writers might find a place to sleep, if necessary, in their publisher's offices, and some might be given a monthly stipend.

Seaver had graduated from the University of North Carolina, taught Latin at a prep school in Connecticut, and then gone to Paris to study at the Sorbonne in the years just after the war. There he edited with some friends a literary magazine called *Merlin*, and on his own, reading him in the original French and being overwhelmed by the simplicity and terror, discovered Samuel Beckett, whom he later met, published, and remained good friends with for the rest of Beckett's life.

In 1953, toward the end of the Korean War, he was called into the navy and served a tour as an engineering officer on a cruiser. When I first met him in Paris in 1961, he was a senior editor at Grove but still looked like a naval officer, capable and tough. I asked him once, out of curiosity, what he had known about engineering.

"Nothing," he said simply.

In Paris, he and his wife were glamorous *sans effort*. They knew everyone in town, it seemed.

In New York, he started his publishing career working at George Braziller and soon afterward went to Grove Press, where he remained for eleven years, from 1959 to 1970, years of great turbulence and importance. He became editor in chief.

Grove Press began publishing European avant-garde writers and political thinkers, Beckett among them. American literature, not uniquely, had for a long time been under moral constraints, as exemplified by Theodore Dreiser's realistic novel *Sister Carrie* being quickly withdrawn from circulation in 1900 by Doubleday when Mrs. Doubleday found it distasteful— the heroine lived in sin with a man and then repeated the offense. Books considered actually obscene could not be published in or brought into the United States. This included D. H. Lawrence's *Lady Chatterley's Lover*, first published in 1928, privately printed in Florence, Italy, and banned in England and the United States. Its theme, that the individual is fully realized only when both body and mind flourish, was not sensational, but its sex scenes, with their candor and the use of the forbidden word "fuck," kept the book underground.

There was an invisible fault line growing, however. Six years after *Lady Chatterley*, in 1934, Henry Miller's remarkable *Tropic of Cancer* was published by the Obelisk Press in France. Written in the Paris of the Depression years, when the franc had fallen to almost nothing and a dinner with wine could be bought for a dollar, it was a view from the depths, seething with sex and life, and it gradually acquired a legendary reputation. It had even greater cachet after the war, and college girls returning from France smuggled it in, hidden among their underclothes. Customs would confiscate it or worse; in the case of publishers, far worse: Jacob Brussel, who dared to publish it in New York in 1940, went to prison for three years.

Soon after Seaver arrived, Grove Press boldly published *Lady Chatterley*, followed by *Tropic of Cancer*. They were not the first books to challenge, in whatever form, the prevailing laws, but they were the ones, along with *Fanny Hill*, to spearhead the court battles. The decade of cultural and sexual revolution was at hand, and the verdict of a federal appeals court that *Lady Chatterley* was not obscene marked a decisive moment.

With Seaver, a new wave swept in: William Burroughs's *Naked Lunch* in 1962, Jean Genet's *Our Lady of the Flowers* in 1963, Hubert Selby's *Last*

Exit to Brooklyn in 1964, and in 1965 *Story of O* may be said to have contributed significantly to shaping the modern sensibility toward art and sex. Soon after, Grove published important political writers like Malcolm X, Frantz Fanon, and Régis Debray. Over the years, Seaver himself translated more than fifty books from French into English, including works by Marguerite Duras, André Breton, and the Marquis de Sade. Present-day painting, sculpture, and even dance would not exist without the literature that foretold them.

A publisher is known by his writers, and at Grove, then at Viking and Holt, Rinehart and Winston, and for the last twenty years of his life at Arcade, which he founded and ran with his wife, Jeannette, Seaver's writers were generally distinguished and significant, often foreign and sometimes lesser known, for example Andreï Makine and Ismail Kadare, though they included Harold Pinter, Octavio Paz, and John Berger. There were possible Nobel laureates but modest sales.

As befits an editor and translator, Seaver had an even temperament and was low-key—although anyone would seem to be, compared to Brendan Behan, who literally barged into Seaver's life in Paris—and it was better to be low-key at the violent 1968 Democratic Convention in Chicago, where Seaver and his wife were trying to shepherd an illegal Jean Genet through the police charges and general chaos.

There has been a lot that has changed dramatically in American culture since 1950, when Lady Chatterley was thought to be a moral danger to society and Burroughs and Allen Ginsberg were lepers. All this and more is in these revealing pages, as well as the character, charm, and New England–bred integrity of Richard Seaver in his long, distinguished literary—and also personal—life.

JAMES SALTER

Foreword

NYONE WHO KNEW DICK SEAVER will know that he was a man of exceptional modesty, in spite of his stature as a giant of the publishing and literary world. I have to admit that it took relentless hounding from his family to get him to record for literary history his remarkable years in Paris and New York in the 1950s and 1960s. When Dick finally started writing his memoir, he did so in the stolen interstices of a busy life, late at night, or on weekends now and then. He wrote for himself, he insisted, never intending it for publication. My extraordinary husband of many decades devoted his long career to discovering, reading, editing, and nurturing new voices. He loved his work. I noticed, however, that as he got down to the serious business of writing his memoir, each time he emerged from the privacy of his study, he would repeatedly declare how happy and energized he was to be going back to writing. Writing seemed to fulfill him in a way I had not seen before. Early on, back in Paris in the 1950s, Dick had written novels and poetry, not to mention his three-hundred-page thesis on James Joyce and the interior monologue. Discovering Beckett, however, was for Dick an overwhelming event, a kind of intellectual explosion. It stopped him short. From then on, it seemed, Dick felt unable to pursue his own writing. His muse turned silent.

So, all those years later, when he finally sat typing on his old Royal Standard, the joy triggered by his return to writing were wonderful for me to witness. I had a chance at the time to show Dick my edits, as he passed me page after page that flowed from his memory. He approved, encouraged me to do more. He would polish later, he said.

A few days before his untimely death, he and I were at a van Gogh exhibit at the Museum of Modern Art in New York City, and Dick happened to come upon a letter from van Gogh to his brother Theo. In that letter, van Gogh quoted Émile Zola's poetic phrase "the tender hour of twilight" as it pertained to the paintings he was working on. Dick announced he had found his title. In my trauma after losing him, I somehow could not recall those words. I searched high and low and had nearly given up hope when our daughter, Nathalie, discovered Dick's scribbles in his checkbook, in the jacket he had worn that day at MoMA.

Meanwhile, on Dick's desk, I stared at nine hundred manuscript pages he was never given the chance to polish. After reading the precious pages, reliving so many memories, and with my head spinning, I shared the manuscript with a few trusted literary friends who generously took the time to read it and offer constructive ideas. We all agreed: the manuscript needed to be cut. A daunting task. This is where I came in, tiptoeing.

In the course of the following many months, I set out to honor my husband's wishes, giving myself permission to perform light editorial surgery on his manuscript. Dick's voice, with its humor, modesty, and tenderness, led the way and guided me through.

It was only when Jonathan Galassi, the publisher of Farrar, Straus and Giroux and someone Dick liked and admired greatly, enthusiastically acquired the book for publication that I breathed more easily. That Jonathan liked Dick's writing and was eager to publish his memoir would have given Dick personal validation and profound joy. As for FSG's editor Sean McDonald, it was all back in the family. Sean had come to work for our publishing house, Arcade, straight from college. Dick had the highest regard for him, and Sean spent several years as one of Arcade's star editors. It is with a broad smile today that Dick would welcome Sean as his personal editor. Together we made it all fall into place.

I hope the reader will be transported back to a magical time of literary discovery, a time when major voices appeared both here and in France. And I hope Dick's voice, in its tender hour of twilight, can resonate with all of you as it did for me for fifty-five extraordinary years together.

JEANNETTE SEAVER

Preface

THE TERM "MEMOIR" is today of somewhat dubious distinction, a genre tinged with accusations of exaggeration, manipulation, un- or semi-truth, if not downright fraud, especially since the exposure a few years ago of James Frey's blatantly fictional *A Million Little Pieces*. Frey's basic sin, perhaps his only one, was failing to say up front that for the sake of pace, plot, dramatic tension, whatever, he had compressed here, combined there, fabricated in several places, the better to entice and please the reader. Presented as fiction, the book would not have raised an eyebrow, much less a storm. But would it have sold as fiction? A major part of its attraction was the palpable presence of the author, fallen and risen, the sinner redeemed. In all probability, had the book not been such a phenomenal success, the author's conscious concoctions would never have been brought to light. He was wrong, true, but I wonder if the punishment fit the crime. Still, let the reader not conclude that this tepid defense of Mr. Frey—whom I do not know—is to be taken as an excuse for any failings in my own book. It is simply that his opus, coming when I was well into mine, prompted me to reconsider the whole concept of memoir.

A memoir is a look back upon one's life and times through the inevitably refracted lens of the past. These are stories I have told many times over the years, and I warrant the latest versions differ in myriad ways from the original. Even from telling to telling, separated by only a few weeks or months, the tales change, subtly influenced by the reaction of the listeners, if not by one's own dimming memory.

I remember in the 1960s going to a play adapted from Joyce's *Ulysses* starring Zero Mostel. Having read the piece beforehand, I went to opening night and marveled at how closely, and beautifully, the actor adhered to the text. A few weeks later I went again, and this time noticed that there were a number of deviations, for the most part intriguingly seductive but clearly not Joyce. The audience that night was even more enthusiastic than it had been at the earlier performance. Doubting myself, I went home and reread the Joyce text, which confirmed that Zero was indeed improvising. I saw the play a third time, near its announced closing, and now Joyce had been virtually replaced by Mostel. If confronted, the actor, I'm sure, would have professed ignorance: of course he was still playing Joyce. What had happened, I suspect, was that he was responding to the audience's reactions night after night, and where they laughed or applauded an impromptu word or phrase, he inserted and embellished it. I understand Zero.

If all this sounds like an apologia for sins to come, it doubtless is. True, one can verify facts and figures from old records, one can consult colleagues and friends who were there, who can confirm, clarify, or deny your version. But they are as far removed from the event as you, and their memories often as imperfect as yours. Time is not kind to the harried mind, filling it each passing day with the detritus of the moment, like silt at a river's mouth slowly covering the earlier levels and slyly reconstituting the terrain.

Let me say, therefore, not by way of excuse but as fair warning, I have tried to tell these tales as they were, accurately and fairly, and if I have erred or memory has betrayed, blame it on those Irish genes my wife has encountered over the years. The reader should know, too, that in some rare instances I have changed the name of a character, either to protect privacy or because neither I nor anyone I knew could remember a person's name. There are in the book two lengthy episodes that were dreamed, not lived, and I leave it to the reader to detect them. The reasons will, I trust, be self-evident.

The reader should be forewarned as well that I have throughout resorted to dialogue. Dialogues are approximate, though accurate in tone and tenor, and verified whenever possible with those involved.

———

I had never intended to make this work public. In fact, I resisted it for a long time, even when, after hearing a fragment, a presumably amusing anecdote surging from the past, an incident revealing an added facet to a person or personage already known, my patient listener would react by saying, "You must really write about that." When I would protest that my life was ordinary compared with that of so many others, the high livers and high-profile lovers and achievers who daily grace the front pages of the world's press, the response often was: "But Paris in the fifties was special, and your years at Grove in the sixties changed the world." Jeannette was the first to agree, but she was clearly biased. When over the years others echoed her insistence, including the man I admired most at the time in British publishing, my friend Matthew Evans, former chairman of Faber and Faber and now Lord Evans of Temple Guiting, a Labour peer, I decided to set forth, give it a shot. It would not, I told myself, be too long a journey. A year perhaps, no more.

Now, eight years later, I realized how unrealistic I had been. In fairness, I had other concerns, other demands. A dozen years earlier, Jeannette and I had started our own publishing house, a folly in the eyes of most. A daunting venture. Each day had its challenges, often seemingly overwhelming; each its rewards. We made our share of mistakes—more than our share, no doubt—for while we initially focused to a large extent on works abroad, this country was turning increasingly inward, largely oblivious to what the world outside our borders was doing, thinking, and writing. Still, we published dozens of fine writers, many little known at the time, formed friendships around the world, managed against all odds to survive. But the struggle left little time to write: evenings and weekends, the odd morning. When, discouraged, I would flag, Jeannette would quickly cite a dozen instances of people with full-time jobs who wrote *and* published. Then, like an old dray horse, I would reharness and plow forward. Whenever I did, I found I loved it. Most rewarding was the mind's response to the constant probes: memories delved for did resurface, often with surprising clarity and color. From the dark inchoate mass of stored material, filed and forgotten, I relived moments, many cherished, that otherwise would have been lost forever.

But I digress.

The first time, I fear, of many.

RWS

NEW YORK CITY, 2008

Part One

Paris, 1950s

Photographs on preceding pages, left to right: Richard and Jeannette Seaver;
Alexander Trocchi and Richard Seaver; Richard Seaver; Richard Seaver,
James Baldwin, and Herbert Gold

1 ∾

Café Sitting at St. Germain

ONE SPARKLING LATE MAY MORNING in 1952 when, after endless weeks of dreary, unrelenting winterlike weather, the sun had finally wormed its way through the stubborn gray blanket that had been clinging to Paris, I was sitting on the terrace of the Café Royal at St. Germain des Prés, pretending to read the paper but really watching the world go by, a constant stream of locals and a trickle of tourists—the latter so obvious they could have been picked from the crowd even by the familiar cyclopean beggar who went, appropriately, by the name Petit Jésus, bowing scrapingly low at the church door across the square, his floppy beret extended to welcome the occasional oblation—the Parisian girls suddenly out in full force, piquant and pert in their flowered smocks and blouses, their swirling skirts, their high-toned legs. After seven drab months of hibernation, they had, seemingly overnight, emerged in full flower, a medley of primary colors, proclaiming that winter was finally, irrevocably over. Each colorful passerby, floozy or Flora, just waiting to be plucked.

I was enjoying my café crème when I heard a male voice, melodious with its South African lilt. "Why are you shaking your head?"

"Patrick!" I said, motioning to the empty chair across from me. "You caught me ruminating."

"Ruminating, my arse! You were ogling every Parisian lass passing by. I've been watching you for several minutes.

"Anyway, I wanted to see you. There is somebody I want you to meet. A writer friend of mine named Alex Trocchi. He has a new magazine."

"*Merlin*," I said. "I saw it at the kiosk across the street."

"Trocchi read your piece in *Points* and wants to meet you. When is a good time?"

I shrugged and glanced at my watch. Eleven thirty. "How about now?"

"I am not sure they'll be up," he said.

"They?"

"He lives with a smashing girl. An American named Jane Lougee. A banker's daughter from Limerick, Maine."

"Ah," I said. "Where do Sir Trocchi and Miss Limerick live?"

"About twenty minutes from here. At the Hôtel Verneuil."

Patrick Bowles, a white South African who could not bear to live in his tortured, apartheid-ridden homeland, had fled a year or so before to London. Appalled by its weather, he had quickly crossed the Channel to Paris, only to discover that the weather here was not all that much better, though the general climate was far more exciting. In his mid-twenties, Patrick was classically handsome: beneath a rich shock of chestnut hair lay a high prominent forehead, an arrow-straight nose, full sensuous lips, and a firm chin. There was a calmness, a gentleness about him that sprang from an inner balance few possessed—or at least few I knew. Like most of us on the Left Bank, he cobbled together an existence by placing a newspaper article here, a book review there, a story or poem in one of the literary mags (payment for which might get you a lunch or dinner at Raffy's around the corner), or, more lucratively, by teaching English at Berlitz (hey! if it was good enough for Joyce, it's good enough for us!) or, even better, teaching English to well-to-do young Parisian ladies, whose parents sensed that in this brave new postwar world their beloved mother tongue would have to yield, if only a tad, to the invasive English, if their offspring were to survive and prosper. Then there was a small supplement from home, wherever home was, a tentative gift from worried parents who pictured their wayward offspring down-and-out in Paris, living just above, or even slightly below, the imagined starvation line. Patrick and I shared another common trait: we both used, as our only means of transportation, the trusty bicycle and in our Paris years had logged thousands of kilometers, not only in Paris itself, but to and from our respective jobs. For a year or so I had earned a share of my daily bread by teaching English to Air France stewardesses twice a week. The pleasure was all mine, since most of them had been picked as much for their stunning looks and shapely forms as for their personalities or amiability. Until these postwar years, the French had never quite admitted to themselves that theirs was not the premier language of the planet and had eschewed all others, including the obtrusive English. But some prescient Air France administrator had doubtless faced up to the dismal fact that in the competitive new aviation world, a place would have to be made for *zee Eenglessh*. Thus to my Berlitz teaching load was added the more pleasurable, slightly more lucrative, but more demanding post at Air France. Demanding because, twice a week, I had to straddle Big Blue—for such had I dubbed my battered, thin-tired Peugeot bike—and head from the rue du Sabot to Orly Airport, a ride of an hour and a half most days. One way. Thus for an hour-and-a-half teaching twice a week I had to carve out close to six hours of my Paris life. Good for the legs, I kept telling myself. Think wrestling. Think Maurice Goudeket—Olympic athlete, Colette's husband. Think Tour de France. Go, Coppi, go! I would whisper to myself on especially dark or difficult rain-spattered days. But Patrick's gig was far worse: in January he had started teaching English at a school in Le Havre, a good two hundred kilometers from Paris, and lacking the desire— or the wherewithal—to take the train, he bicycled in every weekend. True, he had arranged with the school to have no classes on Friday or Monday, but still, it took him most of those two days to-ing and fro-ing for the pleasure of spending Saturday and Sunday here. But we were young and in Paris, and these presumably daunting mountains were as molehills to us.

Both the Deux Magots and the Flore were already famous from before the war, and older writers—Jean-Paul Sartre, Simone de Beauvoir, Jacques Prévert—were known to hang out there, lending those starched-waiter places a tone of slight, if not considerable, superiority generally lacking at the Royal. Basking on the terrace there, at what seemed to us both the center of the universe, we felt that there was nowhere else on earth we would rather be. So it wasn't the world of Joyce and Sylvia Beach, of Hemingway and Scott Fitzgerald, or even of Henry Miller and Brassaï's haunting *Paris by Night*. Nor were we, however long their shadows, trying to emulate them. Paris had been their mentor or mistress; now she was ours, to do with what we would.

The city had been humbled by the war. Class distinctions had been, no, not eliminated, but certainly greatly leveled—whether permanently or not only time would tell. Virtually everyone was poor. Rationing had been lifted, but luxury goods were still almost nonexistent. And the Parisians, with

their reputation as acerbic, arrogant, and disputatious, were actually often-
times pleasant, not only with one another, but now even with foreigners.
That's not quite fair: France, and especially Paris, had long welcomed foreigners, especially those fleeing their own countries in times of repression,
war, or revolution. Even in 1952, thirty-five years after the Russian Revolution, a fair share of Paris taxi drivers were Russian. You never knew when
you'd be driven home by a prince or a count. There were many new divi-
sions among the French, but today they were more along political than
class lines. French politics had always been driven and strident, for, on the
one hand, every Frenchman—and woman—had a lock on the truth and, on
the other, the French yield uncomfortably, if at all, to any law ever passed,
no matter what the regime. But their brutal, unexpected defeat in 1940
had humiliated the country, stripped it bare. And the war years had only
humbled it further, as political lines hardened. The occupation brought
out the worst in many—as it brought out the best in some—and for those
who survived with their lives, if not their consciences, intact, a whole new
world of hardship and deprivation awaited them after the momentary euphoria of the liberation had worn off. During my first years here I had
stood in line for all the essentials, from bread to wine, milk to meat, sugar
to the heating alcohol needed for your two-burner stove. So had everyone.
The miracle was that the French handed us *étrangers* a ration card equal in
all respects to those given to their own citizens. As long as you had a valid
local address, you had a valid ration card. And—one of the attractions for
fledgling artists and writers—life was so incredibly cheap. Thirty cents a
day would get you a hotel room—not with bath, mind you, but with *eau
courante*, "running water," as the street-level hotel sign proudly proclaimed.
The room had a bed, a basin, a table, and a chair. Around the corner were
the public baths, where for a few francs you could take a scalding-hot
shower. Payment by the quarter hour. Up to your conscience how clean
you came out. If your budget was really tight, you could take a *douche
double*, two for the price of one, the sex of your co-showerer up to you, no
questions asked by the management. As for food, while there were still
shortages, the indomitable French culinary spirit, which had been all but
crushed by the Germans for five long years, was slowly reasserting itself,
stymied only by the recurrent lack of this or that basic ingredient. American aid helped but also led to unfortunate misunderstandings, among them
corn flour: there was no way on earth that corn flour could be transmuted
into French bread, the country's pride (and rightly so; I could not understand how the United States had lasted all these years with, as its presumed

staple, the tasteless white nonsense that passed for bread). The point was, for those lucky enough to be dealing, even partially, in pounds or dollars, one could live for a third of the cost back home. Not well, mind you. I speak only of the Left Bank and the young. There was, we knew, a whole other world across the river, the world of diplomats and businessmen, of journalists and politicians, who lived high on the hog and experienced a whole other Paris than ours. We were here to find ourselves and save the world, presumably in that order, and we were ready to do it on a shoestring. If any of us had come here with false illusions, romantically drawn by the towering figures of past generations, we soon lost them. Not only had Paris changed, so had the world. Politically and artistically, it seemed to us far more complex and challenging than the one in which those two disparate birds—the sovereignly solipsistic Joyce and the hedonistic Hemingway—had lived twenty or thirty years before. The scars of World War II were fresh, unhealed, and, as we would later learn, too often buried. Close beneath the surface, resentments still lingered, as did guilt for those with a conscience. The trials of the French who had actively compromised themselves under the Germans were by now a thing of the past, but few felt that justice had really been done. If "compromise" was an ugly word, it was far less offensive than "collaboration." The French knew that their record under the occupation was less than impeccable. But there was a difference between passivity, of survival at (almost) any cost, and active collaboration, of doing the Germans' bidding in rooting out the Jews, the Gypsies, the homosexuals, and the politically undesirables, rounding them up, and herding them to Drancy, a city just north of Paris, which the Vichy government in 1941 converted from a projected public-housing project to a prison camp, a holding pen from which over the next three years some sixty-five thousand Jews were herded into the cattle cars of death and shipped to Auschwitz and other concentration camps. The profound revelations of the Holocaust, and all it implied, were just beginning to emerge. In a recent issue of *Les temps modernes* I had read a document that overwhelmed me, written by a Hungarian Jewish doctor, Miklos Nyiszli, who had been deported to Auschwitz in 1944 and survived to tell the tale.* Other revelations of Nazi atrocities—not just the horrors of war, of any war, but bestial

---

*But at what cost? A pathologist, he had upon arrival been "selected" by the infamous Dr. Mengele to assist him in his mad experiments on dozens of inmates. In so doing, however, he saved not only himself but his wife and daughter. A complex case of the will to live versus morality. Easy to condemn the good doctor, but what would *you* have done?

tales of death camps and genocide, murder on a scale never seen before in human history—were emerging, tentatively at first, and with them the need for the French to do some serious soul-searching: How clean was my wartime record? To what degree did *I* collaborate?

Meanwhile, on a whole other level, a thousand miles to the east but seemingly almost next door, the Soviet Union, our erstwhile ally, suddenly loomed as the ultimate solution to some, the ultimate menace to others. No in-between. For many French, an innately conservative people, Communism was strangely the answer, in part because the Communist record for resistance during the war was among the best, and also because the memory of the French right wing's collaboration with the Germans was still embarrassingly fresh. The conservative French often saw Germany as the buffer between them, their goods and possessions, their way of life, and Stalin's barbarian hordes to the east. For much of the war, almost to the very end, these people had lived a life free from fear: their dinner parties, their dances and entertainments, their visits to the nightclubs and concerts virtually unchanged. By late 1943, however, and more certainly with the dawn of 1944, these privileged few knew that the game was up: the invincible führer's brief but devastating stint as emperor of the Western world was coming to a cataclysmic end.

But good and evil are rarely as clear-cut as people would like to believe, and for the French there was now almost as great a fear of Uncle Sam, with his frightening new weapon of ultimate destruction and paranoid politics, as there was of Uncle Joe. The scare stories coming out of Washington almost daily left us perplexed and distraught. The other Joe, the bejowled McCarthy, struck fear in our expatriate hearts, and whenever two or three Americans met—I speak still of the Left Bank—sooner or later the conversation would turn not only to the coldly self-serving machinations of the maverick senator who, thank God, was three thousand miles away but, more immediately, to his two swashbuckling sidekicks, Roy Cohn and David Schine, the not-so-funny comedy team traipsing through Europe, wreaking havoc at every embassy and consulate along the way, turning over stone after spurious stone, hoping to find a Communist, or at least a fellow traveler, cowering underneath. The French regarded these two stooges with a mixture of ridicule and disdain, wondering how we Americans could grant them—long before the phrase was born—even fifteen minutes of fame. But the French could look at the McCarthy phenomenon with distant objectivity; as far as they could tell, it did not affect them directly. We Americans, despite the watery distance between us, felt personally threatened. What had happened to the world in so short a time? With Germany and Japan defeated, wasn't there supposed to be a respite? A time to relax and recoup, to enjoy our presumed triumph over evil? After World War I, our elders had mistakenly believed, with the world made safe for democracy now and forever, it was a time to play. Drink and dance the nights away. And Paris had indulged them. Not so our generation: rightly or wrongly, we felt we had awakened from one nightmare only to find another looming. The bomb may have won the war, but it now posed a problem such as the world had never faced before. Existentialism, not hedonism, was the order of the day. Still, on this radiant spring day, it was easy to put all that behind us.

2 ∿

Meeting Alex Trocchi

WENDING OUR WAY THROUGH the narrow, bustling streets from St. Germain des Prés across the welcoming carrefour de Buci, thronged now as hungry Parisians bought their meats and gleaming fruits and vegetables from the dozens of stands that ringed the square, we crossed the boul' Mich and entered Elliot Paul's old domain.* He would not have recognized it. Now the Algerian rug merchants reigned, their heavy wares slung over their shoulders, their hands either full of baubles they were trying to hawk to unwary tourists or, more than half the time, it seemed, nervously fingering prayer beads. As for the hotel itself, it reeked of cabbage and urine—cause and effect?—and, oddly, no one sat at the ill-lit desk to query our purpose or destination. From the looks of two of its presumed lodgers lounging in the murky lobby, prostitution must have been the mainstay of the establishment. The only reassuring aspect—at the end of the street, literally facing Notre Dame across the Seine—was George Whitman's tiny but welcoming bookstore, the Librairie Mistral.

Up we climbed the four flights of rickety stairs, mostly in the dark

---

*Elliot Paul was an American writer and journalist, a friend of Joyce's and Gertrude Stein's, who lived in Paris after World War I. He was the author of many books, and his *Last Time I Saw Paris* became a must-read for anyone traveling to Paris.

because that great electricity-saving convention the French had devised, the *minuterie*—literally "the minute-long light switch"—here lasted at most ten seconds before plunging the climber once again into Stygian darkness. We finally reached a landing into which a sliver of light had somehow managed to slip. Pat knocked, and the door opened to a tall, hawk-nosed man, who I judged was in his mid- to late twenties, with thick, tousled light brown hair. Barefoot, he was dressed in khaki trousers and an open-neck light blue shirt that matched his deep-set, laughing eyes.

"Patrick! What brings you here in the wee hours of the morning?"

Nearby, the bells of a church, probably St. Julien le Pauvre, were just tolling noon.

"This is the American friend I was telling you about." Patrick nodded in my direction. "Dick Seaver, Alex Trocchi."

Alex thrust out his hand, grasped mine in a firm grip, and said, "Welcome to our humble abode," and with a sweeping gesture of his right arm invited us in.

It was a typical Left Bank hotel room of the time, small and dimly lit, with hideous flowered wallpaper scuffed and peeling in a dozen places. Its only window looked onto an oversized air shaft that made a vague claim to courtyard status with a scrawny tree that had managed, against all reason, to push its fragile branches as high as this floor. A hesitant handful of lance-shaped leaves fluttered just outside the window. It turned out to be a sumac, waywardly spawned no doubt by some chance seed from the West.

A four-poster bed occupied a goodly portion of the room, whose only other furnishings were a bulky armoire separated from the bed by a scant three feet and, in front of the window, which from all appearances had last been washed just before the war, a small wooden table bare except for a vintage typewriter and, parked precariously on the far-left corner, a hot plate. Majestically curled into a near-perfect ball on the center pillow of the bed lay a Siamese cat, its blue eyes taking in our every move.

"Can I offer you some tea?" Alex said. "Or coffee? Or perhaps a bit of fine Scotch?" He paused. "Or is it too early for that?"

I found myself mesmerized by the—for me—enchanting Scottish lilt of Trocchi's speech, at once musical and clipped. His voice was soft as silk, punctuated every sentence or two with a broad smile. I declined, but Patrick said tea would be fine. It seemed like a strange chaser for the morning beer, but who was I to judge? Perhaps beer plus tea was the national drink of South Africa.

"Pat's told me a bit about *Merlin*," I said. "He assures me it's the only serious literary magazine in Paris—"

"The most serious," Pat corrected. "*Points* has had some good material—"

"Maybe 'serious' is the wrong word," Trocchi said. "But we do intend to be good. My feeling is that we can't just emulate the literary magazines of the twenties and thirties. These are parlous times, mon, what with the Russians on the one hand and the ugly Americans on the other rattling their apocalyptic bomb. It's frightening, mon, damn frightening."

Jane Lougee, *Merlin's* benefactor and publisher, just entered. She had silken dark brown hair that she wore with schoolgirl bangs, china white skin, into which were set dark flashing eyes, an easy smile, and, it turned out, a sunny disposition that nothing seemed to faze. Besides, she had the good sense to have a banker for a father. Whether she was truly rich or not I had no idea, but I suspected—despite the dreary room—that she had enough to back Trocchi's immediate literary ambitions, for in glancing at the magazine the day before at the kiosk, I had noted that her role was listed as "Alice Jane Lougee (Publisher), Limerick, Maine"—the geographical attribution striking me as more than a bit strange for a Paris-based magazine. Maybe it had to do with taxes, I thought. Her father was apparently underwriting *Merlin*, so he couldn't be all bad. Alex introduced me to Jane, and when we shook hands, I noticed her grip was as firm as Trocchi's.

"Please stay for lunch," she said. And she pulled from her magic *filet*— I could never bring myself to say "string bag" or "net bag," which my dictionary assured me was the proper translation—some pâté and cheese and rillettes, plus a half kilo of butter and two freshly baked baguettes, and, presto, a liter of red wine. No label, but what the hell. *Gros rouge*: at Buci, as at most wineshops in the area, you could, if you brought your own empty bottle, buy a liter of wine for a hundred francs—roughly twenty-five cents—poured from the vast oaken casks in the back. Mostly Algerian, not smooth by any means, but eminently drinkable, especially for our untutored palates.

Over lunch Trocchi talked about the magazine he envisioned. Tapping his finger on a copy of issue number 1, which had just appeared, he said with the authority born of true conviction: "No writer today can afford to be *non-engagé*—uncommitted. No matter how good some of the magazines published here were before the war—and some were very good—art for art's sake is a thing of the past."

"Some extraordinary writing came out of that period, though," I said. "Start with Joyce. Total self-indulgence. Epitome of literary arrogance. But, by God, look what resulted!"

"Of course, mon. I'm simply saying that today historical conditions are different. We can't pretend the world we've been handed doesn't exist."

Pat laughed. "You sound like a Scottish Sartre."

"To a degree," Alex said, "to a degree. It's a question of being aware, that's all."

"So where does that leave poetry?" Pat asked. "Does poetry have to be politically aware? God forbid! One step further and you have the socialist drivel of the Soviets."

"Don't be daft, mon," Trocchi thundered, pouring another round of wine into the yogurt jars that served as glasses. "But part of an artist's task today is to address—at least not ignore—the problems we have to face. Picasso was able to be political without compromising his art. Ditto Malraux. And, yes, Sartre."

Trocchi turned to the typewriter and, unscrolling a page, added it to a couple of others on the table. "Here's the editorial I've written for issue number two," he said. "Still needs a bit of fine-tuning, but it expresses what I feel the magazine should be. We want to find new writers. And not just English language. After all, we're based in Paris. Patrick says you know the French scene better than anyone here—"

"More important, he speaks French like a Frenchman," Patrick said.

"I spent my first couple of years here avoiding my compatriots, I'm afraid. Pretty stupid when I look back, but I really was determined to learn the language, immerse myself in French culture. I've come across some pretty interesting French writers. A girl I met my first summer here gave me a list of those I *had* to read. Barely halfway through it. But you're not interested in known quantities, I assume. Oddly today, the most original new writers aren't French, though they're writing in the language. One or two in particular."

The nearby church bells tolled two o'clock, and suddenly I remembered that I had to be at Berlitz at three sharp. My livelihood still depended on it. Earlier in my Paris stay I had taught three, even four times a week, sometimes as many as five lessons a day. The Berlitz book was entirely practical: no room or time for literary or philosophical nonsense. At the end of a one-hour lesson, the student who was *doué*—"talented"—might even manage to take the train or bus in English, pay the fare, engage in conversation with an amiable neighbor ("What a nice day eet is, *non*? Are you going far? I am going to Chee-ca-gó, where eet is very windy, is it not? Especially in winter, *non*?"), and even alight at the proper stop. Not much more. But five stints in my one-on-one cubicle—3:00 p.m. to dinnertime—brought in a cool thousand francs—two and a half dollars—sufficient to keep the wolf from the door for hours on end. To be sure, at the end of four or five such sessions, with ten minutes off for good behavior between classes, we *professeurs* were so linguistically stupefied that it took a good three glasses of wine to restore us to normalcy, or the semblance thereof. Still, the choices were not many, and we were grateful for small Parisian favors. As time went on, I kept wondering how Joyce had done it without going mad. I suspected that with his powers of concentration, he could teach by subconscious rote while his creative mind, far beyond the cubicle, was forging new words, new combinations, new images that would later surface on the pristine page. Emulating the master, I tried that one day, letting my subconscious take over, and almost immediately found my pupil looking at me as if *I* had gone mad, for my conscious mind was all of a sudden spouting T. S. Eliot–like poems of my own concoction whereas my subconscious, which should have been rattling its way mechanically through the Berlitz teaching manual, had apparently gone inoperative. I gazed at the little black box in the far corner, which no teacher could ignore, for a microphone implanted there led into the office of Mr. Watson, who ran the school with a kindly hand but could not, would not, tolerate the least deviation from the cherished manual.

Shaking hands at the door, Trocchi and Patrick and I agreed to meet the following Tuesday. One o'clock on the terrace of the Royal. As we made our way darkly down the four flights, Patrick asked me what I thought of Trocchi. Groping for the third time for the elusive *minuterie*, I said: "I liked him. Bright as hell, clearly. But I tend to beware of first impressions. At least half the time I've been wrong."

We were again plunged into darkness, but if I had not lost count, there was only one more flight to go.

"Read the first issue," Pat said. "Then let's talk."

As we descended the final steps into the sun-splashed lobby, almost blinded by the sudden change, I saw that a concierge, a birdlike woman of indeterminate age dressed all in black, was now perched on a chair before a warren of boxes above which dangled a dozen or so heavy keys to her kingdom. I nodded to her. She nodded back, but her suspicious scowl told me hers was not a friendly greeting. For all she knew, we were interlopers, maybe even foreigners, freeloading off one of her paying guests. I gave her

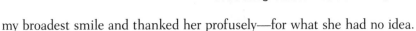

my broadest smile and thanked her profusely—for what she had no idea. But then, neither had I.

The next day I bought and devoured the first issue of *Merlin*, every last word. I was impressed. The best piece was Trocchi's, a story called "A Meeting," but there was another piece of fiction by an American, Eugene Walter, of whom I had never heard, that was almost as good. In both, the writing was crisp and personal. Nobody's acolyte, they. And it included five poets, also all good, three English, one Canadian, and an American, who to my mind was the best of the lot. How different the American's aesthetic from that of the others, even from that of our northern neighbor, who was clearly talented but given to a pretentious use of line organization and wrong-legged commas. Still, he was better than I would ever be. My poetry was sorely lacking in obscurity. The best of the English poets in the issue was someone named Christopher Logue. In love with fancy words but not always sure of their use, I noted condescendingly. How could he have so massacred Trebizond? Still, remembering Sylvia Beach and the Paris publication of *Ulysses*, one had to make allowance for the spelling and punctuation errors introduced by the French printers, most of whom did not speak a word of English. I had no idea how old this Christopher Logue was, but his tone was classical and contemporary at the same time. All I knew was the bio blurb at the end of the issue: "English poet and falconer, lives in Paris. Is writing a book on the idea of the castle in Europe." That I liked. Pat had spoken highly of Christopher as a person and poet, and I was eager to meet him. I closed the issue with a feeling that if I could, this was a magazine, an environment, I'd like to be part of.

After digesting the first issue of *Merlin*, I also read Trocchi's proposed editorial for the next, which he had handed me as we left his hotel that first day. He had announced *Merlin* as a "quarterly magazine of literature," with the prophetic caveat that "the size of the magazine and its continued appearance will be determined by the amount of suitable material received and the response of subscribers." About the forthcoming editorial I was less sure. Intelligent, yes. Probing, yes. Convoluted, to a large degree. Pretentious, absolutely. I reread some of the lines that both impressed and grated: "It is not enough to deplore the state of modern writing in general. Who is bad, and why? Generalized obloquy is not enough." If generalized obloquy was not enough, then who specifically was censured, who praised? Tell me who your enemies are and I'll tell you whether I agree.

3 ∿

Meeting *Merlin*

THE NEXT TUESDAY, Pat came to pick me up at my own humble abode on the rue du Sabot—the Street of the Wooden Shoe—hard behind St. Germain des Prés. I lived on the ground floor, a kind of storage depot behind and contiguous to an antiques store specializing in primitive art. In contrast to my former quarters at 21, rue Jacob, at most a couple hundred square feet, probably less, the depot was more than a thousand. Light came from a generous skylight over the area nearest the street and was sufficient during bright days to obviate the need for electricity. The building, probably fifteenth century, had formerly been the windmill of St. Germain and consisted of two parts: two stories set directly on the rue du Sabot, and then, behind, four stories that had housed the windmill itself. One crossed from the front building to the back over a narrow bridge. Upstairs, beyond that bridge, lay a bevy of rented rooms—squalid, I was sure, judging from the only one I had seen. The occupants, of uncertain number, for one could never tell who was the renter and who the guest or passerby or lady for the night, ascended to their quarters by a stairway we never, or rarely, used.

But I lived there rent-free, in return for tending the shop for an hour or two a day and, when the owner was absent, sometimes for two or three days running. The shopkeeper was a dapper Swiss, Oscar Mayer—no relation to the American purveyor of meat by the same name—a man in his late thirties or early forties with a true passion for primitive art. He spoke perfect mid-Atlantic English, part American, part British, but clipped with sharp Swiss shears and interspersed with slang that rarely hit the mark. He wore dark, impeccably cut suits and starched white shirts, more often with an ascot than a four-in-hand tie, and in the evening, winter and summer, he sported a flowing black cape. His jet-black hair, neatly swept back into a mini-mane, and his equally impressive mustache made him look more serious than he really was. But the silver-tipped cane he carried, more a personal swagger stick, was dead serious: when triggered, a tiny switch on the cane head turned the tip into a sword. He carried it with him whenever he went out. Was it legal? I asked, the first time I saw him trigger it. "Of course not," he said. Wasn't he worried that someone might notice it and tell the cops? As for the cops, he would take his chances. Besides, he added, he had friends in high places. During my years in France, I had heard dozens of people claiming to have "friends in high places." Given the rapid turnover of French governments during the Third Republic, I wondered if, when those suddenly in dire need called their "friends," anyone answered. In any event, Oscar's cane gave me pause, but also new respect.

I had moved there a year earlier from my crow's nest room at 21, rue Jacob, a *pension de famille* (now a chic hotel, Les Marronniers), where I had lived for a couple of years, a former maid's room that suited me fine, for those who lived on the top floor were not obliged to take meals as were the other lodgers. Though the steep eight-story climb was tough, the legs were young and bicycle-strong, and the view over St. Germain well worth the eleven-dollars-a-month rent. The only inconvenience—unless you counted the tiny Turkish toilet tucked halfway down the stairs to the next floor, which demanded a certain acrobatic prowess to enter, employ, and emerge from unbowed and unscathed—was that the ancient red-tiled floor was roughly twenty degrees off the horizontal. Bricks liberated from a nearby construction site propped up both bed and table, while the armoire was wedged neatly in the lower inside corner, never to be budged. As for the wooden chair that was meant to go with the table, I had solved that minor problem by sawing two inches off the front legs, unbeknownst to my often scowling, never-smiling 250-pound landlady (a guess, to be sure; I had never seen her on a scale, much less scaled her, but I knew I was not far off the mark). Surely, Madame Germaine, for that was her name, would one day thank me for the fine leveling work I had done.

I had moved for several reasons. First, after almost two years' lopsided residence I was being increasingly pressured to join the pensioners downstairs for meals and, having once or twice sampled the local fare at dinnertime, decided that survival was in question. Despite all the food shortages, the cook at the *pension*, whom I had only glimpsed but, I concluded, could not have been French, regularly brought forth to table culinary concoctions as unrecognizable as they were inedible: meat there was, but from its taste and consistency, not to mention its disconcerting toughness, I had come to the conclusion that the unfortunate and unsavory Parisian habit acquired during the war of cooking meat of dubious origin had been perpetuated during these halcyon postwar days. Second, it was rumored that fellow pensioners were complaining that my girlfriend and I made too much noise late at night, which was doubtless true. (In our defense, we were forever fighting a twenty-degree angle in everything we said and did there.) And, finally, I determined that if I stayed on much longer, pacing the floor as I did in search of a cogent thought, I'd end up gimpy, for though my uphill leg, my right on the trip across from east to west, showed signs of shortening, it loosened nicely on the return journey from west to east. But since I inevitably ended up at the skylight, on the western side overlooking the church, that final trip, multiplied by hundreds if not thousands, would surely have its effects.

On the last day of October, I announced my impending departure to Madame Germaine. She took it very hard. And here I thought she had never cared!

"You're really *leaving*?" she said, conveniently forgetting my downstairs neighbors' complaints. "Good tenant. Always pay on time." Ah, that was it. I actually did, carefully adding a couple hundred francs to each month's envelope, which I meant as atonement for the presumed noise factor. She took it as a tip for her many kindnesses.

"You can always come back, you know!"

I shuddered at the thought. Still, it was heartwarming to know that somewhere in this teeming Gallic city of two and a half million I would always have a home. Sort of.

We met at the Royal under a still-serene pale blue sky when everything in Paris is bathed in magic; the four of us—Alex, Jane, Patrick, and I—were joined by a newcomer, Christopher Logue. A slight young man with a sallow complexion, a nervous smile that revealed a sorry set of teeth, and eyes flashing as one imagines a falconer's would, he had a deeply resonant voice and perfect diction, as if he were not speaking to us common mortals but reciting, doubtless to the gods. His unusually high forehead was topped by unruly dark tufts that sprouted like weeds from the mass below. I had expected a larger, older man, for the poems had both body and erudition, a maturity ill suited to this too slender soul—the result of a chary diet born not of self-imposed restriction but of constant lack of funds. Only his voice befitted his lines, one of which came back to me: "Close to the sea I live with weather cock to catch all winds." I shook Logue's hand and told him how much I had liked his *Merlin* poems, reciting a couple more lines as if to prove it. Had I waited till later, it might have seemed perfunctory, lip service, but because they were literally my words of greeting, I think I made a friend for life. Christopher was dressed suitably, not for the occasion, which was informal, but for the role he had chosen in life: the Poet. Even on this glorious spring day, he was dressed in black: trousers, a white shirt only slightly the worse for wear, a tie, and a cape of which the Count of Monte Cristo would not have been ashamed. Christopher, I promptly learned, was neither reticent nor retiring. His response to my heartfelt compliment was: "Yes, they're quite good, aren't they? It's part of a long poem I'm writing. Another section will appear in the next issue, right, Alex?"

"Absolutely, old man, absolutely," Alex said.

"You mentioned you know some French writers we might want to publish," Alex said, turning to me. "One in particular," I said, fixing Trocchi's inquiring gaze. "Extraordinary. Like nothing I've ever read. And another who's also very good, though he might not fit into the magazine, since he's a playwright. Anyway, the curious thing is, neither is French."

"I'm afraid you lost me, mon," Alex said. "I was asking about *French* writers."

"One is Irish, the other Romanian. But both *write* in French," I explained. "And both live here in Paris."

"Who's the Irishman?"

"His name is Samuel Beckett. I came upon him several months ago, and I've read everything he's written, or at least everything available. Some of his early works are out of print."

"Wasn't he somehow involved with Joyce?" Trocchi asked.

"Right. In fact, I've seen more than one reference to him as Joyce's secretary," I said. "Apparently, he wasn't, but he was part of that whole coterie around Joyce—Irish, English, French, God knows who—in the late twenties and thirties, after *Ulysses*."

"What about Beckett?"

"He wrote the lead piece in the critical volume on Joyce that Sylvia

Beach published, I think in 1929 or '30, about that mysterious work in progress . . . Also translated, or helped translate, 'Anna Livia Plurabelle' into French."

"But what has he *written*?" Trocchi wanted to know.

"Three novels, at least one play, and a couple of short stories, all in French. There's also apparently a slim volume of poems, an earlier volume of stories called *More Pricks Than Kicks*, both in English. All I know about those last two are their titles. I've read the three French novels and both stories. Incredible. And last year I heard a portion of his play *En attendant Godot*—*Waiting for Godot*—done at the French radio, by an actor-director, Roger Blin . . ."

"Never heard of him," Trocchi said.

"Very important," I averred, "totally committed to the theater, especially the avant-garde. And the portions of *Godot* they performed were extraordinary."

"What about the novels?" Trocchi asked.

"Three *M*s," I said. "The first is called *Murphy*, the second *Molloy*, the third, which has just come out, *Malone meurt*—*Malone Dies*."

"All these written in French?" Patrick asked. "With such Irish titles?"

"No, *Murphy* was written in English. Published just before the war, I think. Not available. But a French translation came out four or five years ago." I didn't know it at the time, but it was Beckett himself who had done this translation during the war, to try, as he put it, to keep from going insane. "The novel is good, not great. Still under the Joycean influence, I suspect. As for *Molloy* and *Malone*, absolute pure masterpieces."

"Dick put me on to *Molloy*," Patrick said. "He is right. It's like nothing I ever read before."

"How did you come upon him?" Trocchi wondered. I thought I detected a shadow of annoyance, as if to say: If he's so special, why haven't I heard of him?

"Do you want the long version or the short?"

"Short," Christopher said.

"Is there a medium?" Trocchi asked.

"Chance," I said. "Chance and geography. I live on the rue du Sabot, and to get to St. Germain, I usually go by the rue Bernard Palissy, where there is a young French publishing house, Les Éditions de Minuit.

"Last year, in the window of Minuit I saw two books displayed, *Molloy* and *Malone*, by one Samuel Beckett. The name rang a Joycean bell, but for the life of me I couldn't figure what an Irishman was doing chez Minuit. I assumed they were translations, so I asked both Gaït Frogé at the English Bookshop and George Whitman at the Mistral if they had the originals, and both said no, never heard of them. So, my curiosity piqued, I went into the Minuit offices and bought both books. Turned out they were in fact written in French. And what French, I might add. They knocked me out. At Minuit they told me a further novel, *L'innommable—The Unnamable*—was coming next year. If you want my opinion, he's as remarkable as Joyce. Totally different, but remarkable."

"If that's the case," Trocchi interrupted, "why don't you write a piece about him, Dick? For the next issue."

"I don't know," I said. "That's a tall order."

"Give it a try, mon. If he's that important—"

"When do you need it?" I asked, already knowing the answer.

"Three weeks," Trocchi said.

I shook my head. "Okay," I said, "I'll give it a shot."

"And who is the second?" Trocchi asked. "You said there was a Romanian . . ."

"Ah, yes. Ionesco," I said. "Eugène Ionesco. A playwright. Romanian, but he also writes in French. He has a new play just on you should see, *Les chaises*. At the Théâtre Lancry. Different. And very funny. You'd better hurry. It might be closing soon."*

"In French," Alex said. "I'm not sure ours"—nodding to Jane—"is good enough."

"Pat or I will go with you," I said. "Really worth it."

We all agreed to meet the following week.

---

*As for closing soon, as of 2009 it was still running at the Théâtre de la Huchette, to which it transferred soon after it opened, fifty-six years later!

4 ❧

Tracking Down the Work

THAT AFTERNOON I sat down and began rereading *Molloy*; again I fell totally under the spell. It *was* a masterpiece. *Malone*, too. How do you write a meaningful comment on such rich, complex, still-undiscovered work without making a critical fool of yourself? So make a fool of yourself. Tentatively, I picked up my pen and wrote:

SAMUEL BECKETT: AN INTRODUCTION

It could be no more than that. Exegesis was not my forte. To write more than an "introduction" would be pretentious, for I knew that, however great my visceral admiration, cerebrally I had not begun to plumb the depths of these two works. But what puzzled me most was why Beckett had not been recognized before, in England, if not yet in France. Yes, "introduction" was the proper term, and doubtless the right approach. Out, damned modesty: if conviction means anything, then write from the heart. Slightly less tentatively, I wrote:

> Samuel Beckett, an Irish writer long established in France, has recently published two novels which, although they defy all commentary, merit the attention of anyone interested in this century's literature.

Off and running? Well, walking at least. It took me two full weeks to write the piece, and when I was finished, I thought I had barely reached the starting point. I wanted to tear it up and begin again. I had at most scraped the surface. All I was sure of was that I had had the great good fortune of coming upon—"discovering" was far too pretentious—a genius; the term is not too strong. What impressed me most was the deadpan humor, the self-doubt and self-deprecation layered on a bed of rock-hard erudition, worn gossamer light. At the same time, from book to book there was a successive stripping away of the extraneous: what had sometimes glittered but cluttered in *Murphy* had virtually disappeared in *Molloy* and *Malone*. The movement seemed inexorably toward minimalism, perhaps ultimately toward silence. But one thing, it seemed to me, was sure: any influences that might have affected or tainted the earlier voice had gone, been discarded or fully integrated. From *Molloy* on, Beckett was his own man.

It was still with tentative pen that, on June 14, I wrote the final paragraph:

> Is it possible for Mr. Beckett to progress further without succumbing to the complete incoherence of inarticulate sound, to the silence of nothingness where mud and Molloy, where object and being, are not only contiguous but one? Mr. Beckett's next book, announced for publication early this winter, will have to reply. Perhaps the name is significant. It is called *L'innommable—The Unnamable*.

That evening I showed the piece to Patrick. He sank into my one easy chair, a street relic I had recuperated one early morning, when in the dim light of predawn it had struck me as an appropriate, indeed necessary, addition to the rue du Sabot's underfurnished salon. Hailing a nearby clochard, bedded down in the doorway of a recently closed café, now his domain till dawn, a well-worn gray blanket pulled tight around him, empty bottle of red to his right, he too waiting for the sun also to rise, convinced his luck would turn with its arrival, I nudged him and promised fifty francs if he would help me tote the chair the twenty or so blocks to my modest lodging. "A hundred," he said without a blink. We settled on seventy-five and began our struggle. We were obliged to stop every few meters to rest, so that in due course the sun, having no alternative, finally did heave into view with us still half a dozen blocks from the Wooden Shoe. I was ready to give up, to abandon the precious antique to its morning-after fate, for the clochard, despite our nascent friendship, was menacing to re-demand the hundred, and both of us had such a thirst as only a long white night can instill. We had passed dozens of cafés, but all were dark and shuttered, their chairs reversed onto the tables and entwined in chains that gave witness to the faith the café owners placed in their fellow man. Then suddenly a light shot on in a café half a block away, which we reached, bearing our burden, in a flat sixty seconds. Nothing like a crying need to spur the carcass on. Once there, we parked our elephant by the curb, thoughtfully leaving enough room for the passersby to inch around without stepping into the street, then parked ourselves at the bar and drank a house red, harsh to the palate but healing to the body.

That evening, when I fell awake, I looked at the chair in the corner and wondered where the hell it had come from. Ah, yes . . . Gingerly, I stole toward it, the better to assess its merits, only to discover that its innards were bare. Only springs, coiled and menacing. For a moment I thought of throwing it out, then recalled my night's labors. No, it was mine now, for better or worse. To have and to hold. To stuff and repair. A few old towels spread carefully over the coils, then a throw thrown over them, *et voilà*, just like new! Well, almost . . .

It was into this chair that the unwary Patrick had sunk and started to read my Beckett piece. I felt more and more uncomfortable watching his eyes skim the page, pausing here with a frown, there a faint smile. I headed for the door.

"Where are you going?" Patrick asked, lifting his eyes.

"I'll be right back," I lied. "I have an errand to run." No author, I realized, should be present when someone is perusing his work, however modest.

I decided to go have a glass of predinner red wine at the Royal. There were two more or less direct routes from my former banana-drying-warehouse-primitive-antiques-boutique home to St. Germain, one by the rue du Dragon, past the tempting, garlic-impregnated odors of Raffy's restaurant, the other via the rue Bernard Palissy. The latter, my favorite by far, passed the offices of Les Éditions de Minuit, Beckett's new publisher, in whose window at number 7 I had, the year before, seen the pristine copies of first *Molloy* and then *Malone meurt. Molloy*, which came out in January, caught my eye by its seeming disparity: so Irish a title and author in so French a cover? It was not until my fifth or sixth passage that I finally made the connection. I was deeply into Joyce at the time. Suddenly the light went on: of course, the man who had written that intelligent, perceptive, and God knows erudite piece in the collection of twelve odes to Joyce entitled, only half facetiously, *Our Exagmination Round His Factification for In-camination of Work in Progress*, which Sylvia Beach had published a decade before the war.

Number 7 of rue Bernard Palissy, I was told early on, had until fairly recently been the neighborhood bordello. Just after the war, the puritanical wrath of a famous Gallic zealot, a woman named Marthe Robert, had induced the authorities to remove this prostitution blot on France's escutcheon, close down its clean, well-regulated, if not well-lit whorehouses, and return the country to the path of moral rectitude. Marthe Robert was not alone, of course, there were other voices and other pressures, but she was the standard-bearer, and the law eventually passed bore her name. Like the work of most zealots, however, her "solution" accomplished little: How can one legislate sex out of business? All she did was chase it out of doors, so that the postwar prostitutes, instead of having shelter, medical supervision, and in most places a madam on whose motherly shoulder the girls could lay their dreams and dramas, were driven into the harsh, cold streets. Gaze as I did, when I first entered the premises, at the few desks and tables, the walls of shelves and files, I could not envision the place as a dim-lit den of iniquity. The only vestige was the grilled peephole on the thick wooden outside door. "What's the password?" *"Poisson."* "Okay, you can come in." Now above the slightly rusted grille the sign read: ENTREZ SANS SONNER—COME IN WITHOUT RINGING. A bordello replaced by a publisher. Was that progress? I wasn't sure.

Anyway, I had finally entered number 7, mounted the ancient staircase, and purchased both books. (My God! Can that have been a year ago?) Later that day I opened *Molloy* and began to read: *"Je suis dans la chambre de ma mère. C'est moi qui y vis maintenant. Je ne sais comment j'y suis arrivé."* "I am in my mother's room. It's I who live there now. I don't know how I got there. Perhaps in an ambulance, certainly a vehicle of some kind." Before nightfall I had finished the book. I will not say that I understood all I had read, but if there is such a thing as a shock of discovery, an illumination, I experienced it that day. I was, quite literally, overwhelmed. The utter simplicity, the beauty, yes, and the terror of the words shook me as little had before. And the man's vision of the world, his painfully honest portrayal thereof, his anti-illusionist stance, tearing down what he had carefully wrought, stating fact, and then questioning it almost before the ink was dry . . . And the humor; my God, the humor . . . Page after page, I found myself laughing out loud. If I was not quite Molloy—there was already a profound bicycle affinity—I knew I would doubtless be one day. Or such was my fond hope: to have, in the midst of the utter confusion and despair, one moment of truth and light.

I had waited a day or two, then reread *Molloy*, tempted to plunge into *Malone meurt*, which was sitting on the shelf two feet away, pages uncut (in those days the pages of French books, while folded, gathered, and bound, were not cut along the outer edge, which meant the reader needed a knife or letter opener at his side as he advanced. The practice, which I somehow felt was romantic—perhaps I was romanticizing everything about Paris, about France—has, alas, since been largely abandoned) but resisting the temptation, as one resists the seductive sweet. The second reading was even more exhilarating than the first, more rewarding as well, for further glimmers of understanding began to penetrate my brain. Next day I had gone on to *Malone*. Full worthy of the first. Two stunning works. Miracles. Like a druggie, I had to have more.

The following morning I had walked around the corner and again entered number 7, without ringing. This time there was a blue-clad employee downstairs in the entranceway. We exchanged *bonjours*—without which nothing progresses in France—upon which I asked him if Minuit had published other works by Beckett. "Who?" he wanted to know. "Samuel Beckett," I said, "the man who wrote *Molloy* and *Malone meurt*—there!" and I pointed to the back of the unassuming display case in which the two unheralded masterpieces were still standing, only slightly off the vertical. The man shrugged—"*Je ne sais pas, monsieur,*" he said prophetically—and gestured me upstairs.

The door to the office at the top of the stairs was wide open, so I tapped gently and entered, repeating my downstairs question to a handsome, imposing woman seated before a bulky typewriter, vintage 1930s, I judged. "I don't think so," she said, "but let me check." She picked up the receiver of her antiquated cradle phone and dialed. The person she called, I later learned, was Jérôme Lindon, owner, publisher, and editor of Minuit, a man I would soon meet and come to admire beyond measure. His end of the conversation, which went on for a good two or three minutes, must have been detailed, since hers consisted only of "Yes, yes . . . I see . . . Uh-huh . . . All right. I'll tell him that."

"No," the secretary informed me as she hung up, "those are the only two works by Monsieur Beckett that we have, although another work is in preparation. But there is another, earlier Beckett novel available from another publisher, Bordas, which Monsieur Lindon says is still in print. It is called *Murphy.*"

Thanking her, I had dashed down the stairs three at a time, nipped around the corner, hopped on Big Blue, and pedaled over to Bordas, a long stone's throw away on the rue de Tournon. *Murphy*, I knew, had been published just before the war by the London firm of Routledge, to little success. But how and when—not to mention why—it had reached French shores, I had no idea. And why it had been published by Bordas, whereas the other works were clearly the coveted domain of Minuit, was another mystery to explore. But the immediate task was to see if *Murphy* truly existed in whatever format or language.

Bordas was an unassuming place, a narrow little shop that, from the window display, looked to be a general bookseller, offering the latest in fiction and nonfiction from all the Paris publishers. Nary a sign of *Murphy*, nor any other visible manifestation that Bordas was a publisher in his own right. Tentatively, I pushed open the door. The only sign of life inside was a slightly stooped fellow clad in a shopworn gray tunic, his pate awash with gray-white hair, unkempt, uncombed, and doubtless unwashed, its front, back, and sides battling one another chaotically for cranial supremacy. Over his frontal area, the unruly mop descended well into his eyes, which he did not seem to mind in the least. He reminded me of my boyhood dog, a smaller, bastardized version of the English sheepdog, whose bangs completely covered the poor pup's eyes, to no apparent impairment of her sight. The only problem was, with her fluffy upturned tail that looked for all the world like her bangs, people were as wont to pet her tail as her head. "Nice doggie," they would say, petting her rear. "The other end," I would say, "unless you prefer the ass." Upon which most would recoil and hastily retreat.

In his left hand, the clerk was carrying three copies of some title, apparently moving them from one side of the store to the other.

"*Bonjour*," I tried. "I'm looking for a particular title . . ."

He lowered his head, the better to see through the tangle who the intruder might be, then turned it inquisitively to one side, waiting.

"This *is* the Maison Bordas?" I ventured.

"*Bonjour*," he finally responded. "Yes, it is. Are you looking for a particular title?"

"A book called *Murphy*," I said. "By Samuel Beckett."

His free hand quickly brushed his hair back, revealing pale blue vitreous eyes filled with surprise or consternation. "We don't get many calls for that title," he said.

"But you do have it in stock?"

He nodded. "Oh, yes," and, setting down the three copies—which turned out to be the latest issue of Jean-Paul Sartre's *Les temps modernes*—he opened a door at the back of the shop and approached a ceiling-high stack of books just inside. He pulled from the corner a short stepladder, up which he clambered with surprising speed, and from the top of the pile neatly plucked a copy. Dusting it lovingly with the sleeve of his tunic, he handed it to me. "Monsieur Bordas will be pleased," he murmured, so quietly I could barely hear him.

I reached into my pocket and pulled out the three hundred francs— which in those days translated into roughly seventy-five cents—listed as the price on the cover. "Thank you," I said, "thank you a thousand times," for I had convinced myself that the object of my desire would not be found here.

"*C'est moi*," he said, "*c'est moi qui vous remercie.*" No, it's I who thank you. I thought I detected a trace of emotion.

Many years later, A. Alvarez, writing on Beckett, reported that by 1951— the year in which I made my precious acquisition—only ninety-five copies of the French edition of *Murphy* had been sold. I had to assume, from the surprise and barely suppressed delight of the Bordas clerk, that mine had been number ninety-six. And that out of a printing of thirty-five hundred copies five years before. What was wrong with the world?

I took my copy home and read *Murphy* well into the night, lovingly slitting the pages as I went. I fell asleep and dreamed of West Brompton, where I had never been. Early next morning I repaired to St. Germain des Prés, taking the Bernard Palissy route, blowing a kiss to number 7 as I passed. For the next two hours I read—no, savored—the balance of *Murphy*, loving and suffering with him as he labored from mishap to mishap. Incapable of working, the ultimate degradation. Not even the love of Celia—*sail y a*—could move him to action, much less a job, into whose mindless maw he refused to be swallowed, Murphy stoutly—if such a term can be applied to this Irish Oblomov—defending his myriad courses of inaction. I could relate to that. *Murphy* had neither the polish nor the profundity of *Molloy* and *Malone*, which were transcendental, but it was still like nothing I had ever read: funny, bawdy, irreverent, skewering, self-deprecating. Smarting with language. Like difficult music heard for the first time. A bit too clever for its own good, perhaps. Joyce lurking not too far, not far enough. Erudition, obvious erudition, bursting through at times like mushrooms in the night (is it then they do it?) to intrude on the hilarious ebb and flow.

"But betray me," said Neary, "and you go the way of Hippasos."

"The Akousmatic, I presume," said Wylie. "His retribution slips my mind."

Murphy, willfully inept, was one of literature's major disasters, a man whose mind and body are so at war that he binds himself to a chair with scarves. A portrait of human loneliness. Sidesplittingly pathetic. It was a one-person ride: all the other characters were Murphy's puppets, with little or no sign of flesh and blood. Figments of his demented mind. The asylum where he worked should have kept him and never let him go: he was more at home there than anywhere else. But then, so was I. For five or six hours, I *was* Murphy.

Though not as grimly comedic, as masterfully controlled as the two later novels, it was still pure pleasure. It was a young man's novel—Beckett, a relatively late bloomer, was roughly thirty when he wrote it, still striving to find his own voice or rid himself of influences, especially that of Joyce, omnipotent and overpowering. Recondite, full of wordplay, jam-packed with allusions and references, most of which, Dante aside, I feared I had missed but was determined to nail down sooner or later. Despite those reservations, *Murphy* only confirmed for me what I already felt: Samuel Beckett was the most exciting writer I had read since I'd come to Paris. Since Joyce, certainly. But why was he so little known? I glanced at the copyright page: first published by Routledge in 1938. French edition 1947. My God! Thirteen years ago! And the translation coming up to five. Beckett had been born in 1906, his bio notes had told me, which meant he had just turned forty-five. Forty-five, for God's sake, and nobody was reading him!

For the past year, I had buttonholed friends and acquaintances, mostly French, about Beckett, not so much to proselytize, though that was part of it, as in the vain hope that something more he had written might turn up. There is a point in persistent pursuit, even of lost causes, for one night over dinner at the Dôme—a radical change of locale, but many of my French friends preferred Montparnasse to St. Germain—a young French writer, Daniel Mauroc, also published by Minuit, expressed surprise that I had not read the stories.

What stories? I wanted to know.

"I know of at least two," he said, "one published in *Les temps modernes*, the other in *Fontaine*. One is called 'Suite,' the other 'L'expulsé,' I believe."

"Continued" and "The Expelled." I especially liked the sound of the first, for it promised more to come. That surmise proved correct, though not quite as I had suspected. I went by the office of *Les temps modernes* and asked if they had any copies left of the issue containing "Suite." Checking the contents of an oversized ledger, the young woman started her backward pursuit in time, her dainty forefinger scrolling slowly down page after page. She licked her forefinger each time she turned the page, a gesture slightly lubricious, at least in the first sense of the term, hopefully the third. When she reached 1948 with no luck, she glanced up, removing her oversized horn-rimmed glasses to reveal a pair of azure eyes that might have tempted even Murphy to cast off his seven scarves and charge from his hideaway in search of gainful employment, for the face in which those soulful eyes were embedded was a Botticelli at the very least. Rising. I could feel myself falling hopelessly in love in that grim, Marxist-spare office.

"No luck," she said, shaking her pretty head. "Unless you know the year."

I remembered Mauroc saying it was shortly after the war. "Nineteen forty-six?" I ventured. "Maybe forty-seven?"

She fluttered the pages further backward in time, perused each carefully, with a patience I thought was rare, for the Gallic mind is as swift as it is dismissive, till a slow smile broke like early sunlight over her face. A look of triumphant gravity. Archimedes in his bath. "Here it is," she said. "You were right. July 1946 issue." She pushed back her chair, rose, and headed for a back room. Five years ago. Could there be any copies left?

Within minutes she was back carrying a pristine copy. I thanked her a thousand times (in French), counted out the money, gazed at her steadfastly, and asked if, to thank her more concretely, I might ask her out for a drink.

"That would be lovely," she said, and my heart leaped. We agreed to meet the following afternoon at six at the Flore, Sartre's hangout. It seemed appropriate.

"What is this 'Suite' you are looking for in that issue?" she asked.

"A story by Samuel Beckett," I said.

"Never heard of him," she said. "That's a strange name. Is he French?"

"No, Irish."

"Ah," she said, as if that explained everything.

"May I ask you *your* name?" I said.

"Cecile," she said. Another coincidence. My Celia. My soon-to-be Celia.

"And my name's Richard," I said, "though most people call me Dick."

"Ah," she said, "Deek. In France, you know, that's mostly a name they give to dogs."

For a fleeting moment I considered canceling the morrow's drink but thought better of it.

"Suite" was a marvel, on a par with *Molloy* and *Malone*. Like the later novels, it was reality stripped bare of inessentials. A desolate song, mournful yet stunning, its protagonist bent but unbowed—or, rather, bent only by the ultimate knowledge that springs from being born. "Don't pity me," he seemed to be saying, "I am beyond pity." Maybe yes, maybe no. Still, the story felt strangely incomplete. With Beckett, I reasoned, his ideas of complete or incomplete doubtless had little to do with those with which I had been inculcated. It was only later that I learned, from Beckett himself, that my surmise had not been amiss: "Suite" represented only the first half of a novella. In sending it to *Les temps modernes*, Beckett assumed, rightly or wrongly, that at some later date, hopefully the next issue, the magazine would publish the second half. But when he sent the second half, Sartre's co-editor Simone de Beauvoir returned it with a note indicating that it was not the magazine's policy to publish sequels. Didn't the title clearly imply there was more to come, for God's sake? She, or Sartre, had presumably thought that what Beckett had sent them in the first place was the complete work. Or perhaps they thought Beckett was putting them on, testing whether they could distinguish a part from a whole. In any event, the incident angered Beckett—a man very slow to anger. With some reluctance but obvious emotion, he sent de Beauvoir an imploring letter, saying that the magazine's rejection "was the stuff of nightmares," for by not publishing the entire story, she was mutilating his work, "cutting me off before my voice has time to mean something." Petulance? It may have appeared so to Sartre and de Beauvoir at the time, but in the light of the total integrity for which Beckett would later become legendary, and the brilliance of the story itself when read as a whole, his distress certainly seems justified. In all fairness to Sartre and de Beauvoir, Beckett's go-between, Tony Clerx, had failed to mention to the two editors that "Suite" was only the first part of the story. In any event, perhaps to make amends, *Les temps modernes* had published in their November 1946 issue a dozen of Beckett's poems in French. Still, I'm not sure he ever forgave them for what he deemed their literary myopia.

Finding a copy of "L'expulsé" was much easier. This time I knew the date, 1947, and the austere clerk who took my request was back in under two minutes with the issue, no questions asked, cash on the barrelhead, *au revoir et merci.*

The results of the second search were even more rewarding than the first, for "The Expelled," aside from not being truncated, was, to my mind, even better. To weep over, it was so poignant; to laugh over, it was so darkly hilarious. The protagonist was here again a Thomas doubting not of his Lord or master but of himself, groping to make sense of the world, of the meanest of acts, the most basic of situations, in the instance trying to cope with the fact of being literally thrown out, expelled from wherever he had been living—his asylum, his hospice—by focusing on, calculating in his mind, how many steps down "they" had thrown him:

> There were not many steps. I had counted them a thousand times, both going up and coming down, but the figure has gone from my mind. I have never known whether you should say one with your foot on the sidewalk, two with the following foot on the first step, and so on, or whether the side-walk shouldn't count. At the top of the steps I fell foul of the same dilemma. In the other direction, I mean from top to bottom, it was the same, the word is not too strong. I did not know where to begin nor where to end, that's the truth of the matter.

The body battered and beleaguered. The narrator humiliated and bereft, but the rational mind still works, still theorizes in absurd wonderment.

Both stories just as brilliant as *Molloy* and *Malone.*

Having read and reread both stories, like a druggie I needed a further Beckett fix, but none was to be found. Then, as often happens in life, enter serendipity. A few years before, I had met an aspiring young dark-haired, fine-featured Garbo-look-alike budding actress, Delphine Seyrig, as bright as she was young. She was a drama student and also a close friend of the famed actor and avant-garde director Roger Blin, who would probably be directing a Beckett play early next year, she said, either a long play entitled *Eleuthéria* or the shorter one *Waiting for Godot*, a portion of which we had heard together the year before at the French radio's Club d'Essai. More likely the latter play, she said, because it had fewer actors and would be far less expensive to produce. And money for plays, like money for magazines, was hard to come by in those days. (In those days?)

Delphine was an unexpected benefit of my stint at Le Collège Cévenol, a secondary school in the Cévennes Mountains where I had spent my first summer in France as a work camper. She had been a student there, and our paths had crossed briefly: as the work campers arrived, the students were packing to leave. Frank Manchon, member of the Collège Cévenol, and in charge of welcoming American students, who had greeted me upon my arrival in Paris, had given me her name, and a day or two before she departed for Paris, I had made a point of introducing myself. To my great surprise, she spoke perfect English, or rather American, and my first reaction was that I had been led to the wrong young lady, for I knew at the school there were a few English and Americans. But, no, it was indeed Delphine. Her father, a leading archaeologist, had gone to New York as the French cultural attaché of the Free French government during the war, and she had spent several formative years in middle school there. Her heart was set on the theater. Despite her tender age—she was fifteen or sixteen at the time—with her deep, melodious voice, and with her ravishing good looks, she would, I was certain, make her mark. Back in Paris I saw her little, for she ultimately did continue her studies, not at Collège Cévenol in Chambon, but at a Paris lycée. But the minute she had her *bac*, she began her theater studies at one of the leading drama schools, at which point fate brought us again into contact. The intervening three years had only added to her beauty, and that very special voice had either matured on its own or been enriched by her lessons. An avid theatergoer, she invited me to join her every week or two, never allowing me to pay for her ticket no matter how greatly I insisted, though she let me invite her to an occasional dinner before or after the theater. Through her, I had seen more plays than I had during my previous years in Paris, some of little interest (to me, not to her, for whom every work was fascinating, if not for its inherent worth, then for the direction, the settings, the costumes, the technique of one or more of the actors or actresses), but several utterly compelling: Eugène Ionesco's *Les chaises*, *La leçon*, and *La cantatrice chauve*; Arthur Adamov's *La grande et la petite manoeuvre*; August Strindberg's *Ghost Sonata*, which Blin directed at the Gaîté-Montparnasse; Jean Anouilh's *La valse des toréadors* and *L'alouette*. I was fascinated—"mesmerized" would be a fairer term—by Delphine, tempted as well, but I confess, too, that Delphine irritated me a tad. More than once, when I was enjoined to pick her up either at school or, more often, at the nearby Luxembourg Gardens, she was surrounded by a gaggle of fellow drama students, all of whom looked to be twelve and seemed bent on out-gesticulating one another, as if already in performance. Delphine—already an actress on- and offstage—would acknowledge my presence, smile, and turn back to the young yakking colleagues, to finish her nontext. I would tap my watch to remind her that a curtain lay ahead if she was still interested, and finally she would break away with a smile that won her instant forgiveness.

It was Delphine who, as noted, had roughly a year before provided me with the latest and most intriguing clue to the Beckett enigma. One night on our way to the theater she casually mentioned that the French radio was going to record and broadcast part of *Godot* in a couple weeks. "Would you like to go to the recording session?" she said. "Roger told me that Monsieur Beckett will doubtless be there."

A chance to meet the man. "Of course," I said, "just tell me when and where."

"We'll go together," she said. "Pick me up at my mother's on the rue Vaneau."

Promptly at two, I rang her doorbell; the broadcast, which was close by in a Left Bank studio, Le Club d'Essai de la Radio, was scheduled for 3:15. On our way over, I asked Delphine if she had read the play or knew anything about it. She shook her head. "All I know is that Roger thinks it's wonderful. Different. Like nothing he's ever directed."

"Having read Beckett's fiction," I said, "I'm having trouble trying to imagine what one of his plays might be like."

When we arrived, there were at least two or three dozen people in the studio, including the actors. Technicians were scurrying to and fro, pulling on electric cords, checking mikes, studying boards. I recognized Blin, whom I had seen in two or three plays, but none of the other three actors, who were huddled in one corner, script in hand. I looked carefully from face to face, but at least at this juncture no sign of the author. Delphine introduced me to Blin, who stood politely, shook my hand, and smiled, obviously having other matters on his mind.

"Will Monsieur Beckett be coming?" Delphine asked.

"In principle," Blin said. "But who knows? He's shy to a fault. Still, he said he was anxious to hear this."

I thought Blin was being more than polite, solicitous, to a very young lady, his student, at a time when he should have been communing with himself minutes before a performance. I later learned, however, that Miss Seyrig was more involved in the Blin production than she let on. She had recently received a small sum of money from an uncle, the purpose of which he had stipulated was for travel and to broaden her young horizons. But when

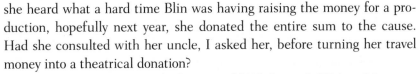

she heard what a hard time Blin was having raising the money for a production, hopefully next year, she donated the entire sum to the cause.
Had she consulted with her uncle, I asked her, before turning her travel
money into a theatrical donation?

She looked at me strangely. "How could I?" she said. "He's in Montparnasse."

"So," I insisted, "that's not exactly at the other end of the world."

"Cemetery," she said. "Montparnasse *cemetery*."

Only then did I realize the money given was not a modest avuncular
gift but an inheritance of some substance. My estimation for the young
lady, already considerable, increased even more.

The technicians appeared ready, to judge by their sudden lack of movement, which a minute before had been frenetic, and the actors took their
places before five full-length mikes. In addition to Delphine and me, there
were a few people, none of whom we knew. But no Beckett. I was sorely
disappointed, for I badly wanted to meet him. Maybe he was simply a little late. In retrospect, that was one of the most outlandish thoughts ever to
cross my mind. For when finally we did meet, and in all subsequent encounters, you could set your watch by his arrival. The most punctual man
I had ever known. I learned painfully how much he judged tardiness a
cardinal sin, for, a year and a half later, when we were to meet at a café in
Montparnasse to go over my draft translation of one of his stories, I was a
few minutes late. He was seated at a table in the back, a short glass of beer
called bock set primly before him, clearly untouched, his only sign of irritation the beat of his long, already slightly arthritic fingers in a noticeably
loud tattoo on the tabletop. Not a word of reproach. Never. From then over
the next almost forty years, whenever we met, I made sure I arrived several
minutes *before* the appointed hour.

"Do you think he's coming?" I whispered to Delphine.

She glanced around the room and shrugged.

Our answer came almost immediately as Monsieur Blin made an announcement.

"Monsieur Beckett had hoped to be here but has sent word that he
cannot come. In his note he says that since he knows little or nothing about
the theater, he thought his presence would in any event be superfluous."

That settled that.

We had been told upon arrival that only a segment of the play was to
be recorded, and in all fairness one couldn't judge the whole from only a

part, but what we heard was so extraordinary that we didn't know whether to laugh or cry. For me, having read his stories and novels, it was not unknown territory. But this was different, even more spare than the prose. Before the recording began, Blin had announced the setting: a barren stage, with a rock in the foreground and a tree, equally barren, right rear.

At the end of the broadcast, Delphine and I emerged into the bone-chilling gray of late-afternoon Paris.

"What did you think?" Delphine asked as she sipped her hot tea on the indoor terrace of the place into which we had slipped to get warm.

"I'm fascinated but frustrated," I said. "How can I get my hand on the whole play?"

"You can't," she said. "Blin says Beckett and he are still working on it."

"But I assume Minuit will publish it," I said.

"After it's put on," she said. "Not before."

"Any idea when that will be?"

She shrugged.

I glanced across the square and saw by the church clock, in which one could surely trust, that it was well past nine. My God! Miserable cur that I was, I had left Patrick alone for well over an hour. Surely by now he was long gone. I paid and walked quickly back to the rue du Sabot, where I opened the door not to emptiness but to Patrick, fast asleep in Big Bear's torture chair. Utterly and completely in repose—how it was possible on that chair I still can't fathom—my precious pages lying primly beside him. He opened one bloodshot eye.

"Smashing," he said. "It's really excellent."

He struggled to his feet. "Anyway," he said, "I'm sure your piece will make people want to read Beckett."

"I hope so," I said, picking up my pages. Patrick had more than returned the favor; his marginalia, I could see, were pointed and intelligent. One way to tell true friends is by their critical comments: false friends put down or procrastinate; real friends are always constructive, even when they're critical.

5 ⤸

From Dublin to Galway

DESPITE MY GROWING OBSESSION with the elusive Irishman named Beckett, I was still deeply involved with another writer from the Old Sod, Mr. Joyce himself. The more I learned about him, the more I delved into his complex past, the more I felt that perhaps, after all, Mr. Beckett was on the right track. Same purity. Same absolute dedication to his art and—here I could relate to some degree— same impecuniosity. In his earlier years, Joyce had often been on the edge of bankruptcy, bailed out by his younger, far more practical brother Stanislaus, but even as he was nearing forty, Joyce was constantly hard-pressed to pay his many creditors. At one point things were so bad that Joyce's young son, Giorgio, happening upon his uncle Stanislaus one day in the streets of Trieste, testily informed him that he, and the rest of the family, had gone hungry that day. At which point Stanislaus, who generally disapproved of James's lifestyle, arranged to have a stipend in his hands next day. In his diary of the time, Stanislaus noted: "I have saved James and Nora six times from starvation." Not that poverty is a necessary virtue, but ranking money as low as possible in the list of one's priorities struck me in those bygone days as the basis for any serious artistic endeavor. As soon as that profound thought crossed my mind, a dozen examples of the contrary arrived to refute it. Ah, how hard it is to have a profound thought that sticks!

I had accumulated two or three hundred pages of notes, salient facts, and jottings of a manuscript about Joyce, not sure where it was going, but so fascinated by both the man and his work that I couldn't get enough. His *Portrait of the Artist*, which I knew had been badly received upon its publication, was to me a small gem. As for *Ulysses*, a masterpiece—no other word would do—which I had read and reread, each time rewarded further.

Joyce's sisters were alive and well in Dublin. Why didn't I write and ask if I could talk with them about my subject? Some precious insights might be gleaned there. Two of them at least, Eva and Eileen, had spent time with their brother in Trieste, where Joyce had lived for a dozen years prior to World War I.

Why Trieste? Having made up his mind to leave Ireland for fairer shores and having responded to news of an opening to teach English in Ravenna, Joyce had convinced pretty, auburn-haired Nora Barnacle to share his life abroad. He arrived almost penniless, to find the teaching post had been filled. But, he learned, there was an opening at the Berlitz School in Trieste, which he was quick to seize.

One of the addresses was a nunnery, and knowing Joyce's uncompromising hatred of the Church, I was sure I'd never hear from that lady. To my great surprise, however, both responded: Eileen was warm, her sister perfunctory, but what the hell. The idea of hearing firsthand from Joyce family members set my heart beating fast.

The following morning I set out to find the two ladies. First, the nunnery, a neat redbrick building whose windowed flower boxes were a riot of color but whose imposing large black door looked forbidding. I pulled the cord and heard a tinkle within, and the door was opened by a starchly coiffed lady, who looked at me sternly, no, with scarcely concealed distrust. I announced myself (meself?) and the purpose of my visit. The level of distrust increased measurably. "And is she expecting you?" I confessed she was, and with a further withering glance she turned and disappeared, leaving the door slightly ajar. A minute or so later, a similarly clad lady arrived— "diminutive" is the word that came to mind—to fill the lower-half void of the now-open door. I reminded her of my letter and hers in reply. She frowned. Yes, she had a vague memory. Could I ask her a few questions about her brother James? No reaction. Had she indeed been with him in Trieste? A nod. "I didn't stay long," she said. I asked if I might come inside, for I felt awkward here on the top step. There were four steps up to the convent, if that is what it was called here. I have always had a problem with steps. I never knew whether to count the top step as one, or whether it was the stoop and didn't count at all. In which case there were three. No matter. She shook her head. "All right then . . . I understand," assuming the likes of me were not allowed into the outer sanctum, much less the inner. "Were you living with your brother and his wife?" "She wasn't his wife," she said in barely a whisper. Then: "I've nothing further to add." With which she stepped back and closed the door, I must say in all fairness, gently.

Well, Seaver, what did you expect?

Refreshed and revitalized from my morning's rebuff by a visit to a nearby pub, I set out to find sister Eileen. Again the three steps up—or was it four?—this time to a large green door, blessed with a large brass knocker. This time the door opened to a lady, small and wizened, but whose warm smile and twinkling blue eyes made me feel immediately at home. She led me into her parlor, which looked out onto the street, offered me tea, and settled down in a flowered easy chair across from me. First, she wanted to know my interest in her brother, and when I said, quite simply, I thought him the greatest writer of our time and was hoping to do a thesis on him and his work, she visibly relaxed.

For the next hour and a half Eileen talked of him, eloquently and lovingly, from his early years at Belvedere school, where he first embraced, almost fanatically, the Church, before he as fiercely repudiated it; their life in Dublin, a close family of ten children—four boys and six girls, whom (the latter) Jim, the eldest, referred to as "my twenty-three sisters"; her years in Trieste living with his family before World War II. Seven years younger than James, she was, she felt, the closest to him in many ways. Not as close as Stanny, she added, but theirs was a relationship of sibling rivalry. Dared I ask her about Nora, about their relationship? From what I had heard, she was totally disinterested in his work. "That's true," she said. "Nora was a simple lady, with little schooling. But James loved her, of that I am sure. Lost without her."

Did the name Beckett mean anything to her?

"*Samuel* Beckett? Of course. One of Jim's disciples. Came to Paris in the twenties, I believe, an exchange student from Trinity to the École Normale. Friend of Tom McGreevy's. Jim liked him, thought he had talent, though from all I've heard he's been totally unsuccessful as a writer. Jim read his *Murphy*, published just before the war, I believe, and thought it showed talent. It seemed to him, however, that Beckett was too much under his influence; he'd have to get out from under it to find his own voice.

"But there was a problem between them. Jim's daughter, Lucia, a most talented but troubled young lady, was quite taken with Beckett and assumed he came to the flat so often especially to see her. Fact was, he came to see my brother, but she was besotted, and Beckett's lack of response to her obvious overtures worsened her depression. So at one point, as I recall, Jim had to suggest that he keep away, which wounded Beckett deeply."

"I'd heard tell," I said, "that at one point he was your brother's secretary. Is that true?"

"Absolutely not. Jim had dozens of people around him all the time—he was very gregarious, y'know, though those who didn't know him apparently pictured him alone in his ivory tower—and Beckett was one. Remember, Jim, who'd always had eye trouble, was almost blind in those Paris years and needed help to transcribe his thoughts and writing. Read aloud to him. Run errands for him." She laughed. "He was good at that."

For the next three weeks I trekked—if that is the word, for I had no wagon or oxen, only wrestler-sturdy legs—across Ireland, opting for the back roads and byways, though even on the larger routes few cars or trucks broke my silence. At times it was as if I were alone in the world, with only birdsongs and bleatings to remind me I wasn't. Those I met were unfailingly pleasant, greeting me often with a tip of the hat or a "God bless!"

Ah, yes, the clouds. If there is one word that memory calls to mind of my Irish cross-island journey, it was "WET." It rained virtually every day, sometimes only a damning mist, but often a downpour. At times the sun struggled through, though not enough to dry me off. Every fourth or fifth day I'd give in and take refuge at a B&B, to take a warm bath, dry my clothes, and eat a hearty meal. I'd awake refreshed and ready to press on. One morning as I was leaving my room, a young man exiting his across the corridor greeted me cordially with "It's a smashing day! Absolutely smashing!" By which I assumed the tide had turned, the sun was out in full force, and my journey would not be further marred by the endless sloshing sound in my weary boots. Peeking out, however, I wondered if my neighbor was of sound mind, for to me it looked its usual gray—though a tad lighter than normal—but no sight of the sun. At breakfast I asked him why he thought the day was "smashing." "Look outside," he said, "don't you *see*? It's only a *drizzle!*"

It was only years later, when I read Flann O'Brien's Gaelic romp, *The Poor Mouth*, that I realized the full extent of the Irish weather problem: when the hapless hero of the novel wants to dry off, he simply jumps into the western sea!

6 ∾

Financing a Magazine

OVER THE NEXT SEVERAL WEEKS I saw Alex, Christopher, and Jane almost daily, with Patrick joining us on the weekends.

There were immediate practical issues to face. Arthur Fogg Lougee, Jane's father, our Maecenas, had underwritten *Merlin*, but, it turned out, only the first issue. As a businessman and (even local) banker, he was willing to launch the ship, but it was his firm opinion that once it set sail, it should pay for itself. Arthur had asked and been told what the print run of the first issue would be: three thousand copies. And the distribution? A thousand for France, mostly for the Left Bank kiosks and the half a dozen bookstores catering to English-language tourists; a thousand to England; and the last third to the States, that is to him. What he planned to do with his thousand copies was anyone's guess: Inundate the local Limerick bookstore? Sell them in the lobby of the bank? Give them as a gift to new customers? Sit and wait for the subscriptions to roll in? In any event, if he *could* sell out his copies, whose American cover price was sixty cents, he would have virtually recovered his investment. And if France and England performed even half as well, voilà, the magazine would be returning a tidy profit. Excellent business, as seen from the rocky shoreline of northern New England circa 1952.

The only problem with his arithmetic was that the chances of selling out were nil, of unloading half of them slim, and even a quarter unlikely. More, Alex and Jane had been steadily eating into Papa Lougee's largesse, what with the Hôtel Verneuil a heady fifty dollars a month and the prices of food and wine inevitably inching up, not to mention Alex's new obsession with pinball machines, which had lately sprung up in postwar Paris, a cultural gift from the West, precursor, alas, to many more.

"Stimulates the brain," Alex would explain if anyone, including Jane, dared question. "Relaxes and stimulates. I have some of my most creative ideas watching that little bouncing ball wend its way down the *piste*."

"How can that mindless machine inspire you?" Patrick said. He actually looked hurt.

"It does, old man, believe me it does," Alex said, his eyes on the wildly blinking lights, his hands nervously working the flippers. "The fact it's mindless is the whole point: leaves the brain free to soar." With which he would turn and break into a broad bad-boy grin that few could resist.

But while the brain was soaring, we had to strategize about our upcoming approach to the Imprimerie Mazarine, which had printed the first issue. Jane's father had paid for that first issue up front. Cash on the barrelhead.

Alex could charm most people out of their skins, but printers, I knew, were a no-nonsense breed. And we, let's not forget, were *sales étrangers*, "filthy furriners," whose bona fides were at best suspect. Approaching a new, unknown printer at this late stage struck me as folly, especially with the absentee month of August looming. So, dressed in our business best, which was dubious if you probed—frayed here, soup or wine spotted there (I speak of the males of the species; Jane was resplendent in a white dress bursting with sunflowers)—but which, for a short visit, at eleven in the morning, almost reeked of respectability, Alex, Jane, Christopher, and I paid a visit to 35, rue Mazarine, where we were cordially received by Monsieur Louis Lebon. Though the *patron*, he was dressed for the press, his well-endowed body covered from torso to toe with a sturdy blue canvas coverall. His hands were ink stained, and he bore dark smudges on both cheeks as well as on chin and forehead.

"Excuse me, *messieurs, dame*," he apologized, "let me wash up before we talk." He repaired to the washbasin at the far side of the room and scrubbed himself vigorously till he looked almost cherubic. Coming back to his desk, he shook hands all around—another Gallic custom without which nothing can begin—then sat down across from us and smiled benignly. A man of middle years, I judged, he was, once scrubbed, rather handsome, with sharply sculpted features, the most salient of which was an aquiline nose that, for prominence and curvature, rivaled that of Alex himself.

In the background the muted, rhythmic thunder of the printing presses made normal conversation difficult, so our voices were obliged to increase a dozen decibels, if I have my logarithm straight.

"Your first issue was a success?"

We all nodded, in deceptive unison. So far we had collected perhaps a couple of hundred dollars from issue number 1, virtually all from sales through the English Bookshop on the rue de Seine and the Librairie Mistral, plus a dozen or two well-intentioned subscriptions, including one astonishing Life Subscriber who had sent us a check for fifty dollars together with a letter wishing us a long and healthy life. No news from Limerick, Maine, on American sales, but we were hardly in a position to badger our benefactor. As for England, sales there had been confided to one A. L. Robertson, stationed not in London but, of all unlikely places, on the Isle of Man. Set tidily in the Irish Sea halfway between Northern Ireland and England, the Isle of Man struck me as one of the less enlightened business choices of mid-century, if sales success was a factor. When I mentioned this to Trocchi, he became immediately defensive. "Robertson is first-class," he declared, "completely committed to art and culture. That's what we sorely need, Dick. People who *believe*. If we give *Merlin* over to your normal big distributor, it will be lost in the shuffle, believe me." I believed. But when I asked if, so far, he—we—had received any report on sales, he seemed almost hurt that I should raise the question. "He's just received the first issue," he said.

"And we're about ready with the material for issue number two," Alex was saying.

"Excellent," said Lebon. "Have you brought the manuscript with you?"

"Not today," Alex said. "We thought we should discuss various matters first."

"Such as?"

I exchanged glances with Jane and thought I detected a like frown of concern on her forehead.

"Schedule," Alex said, and I saw *le patron* visibly relax. "Payment terms." And, visibly, he stiffened.

"You mentioned a schedule of September fifteenth," Lebon said, "and if you deliver the manuscript this week—or even next—that we can comfortably meet. As for payment, I assume Monsieur Lougee—a solid French name, no doubt—will be guaranteeing the bill as before."

Prior to meeting with Lebon, Alex, Jane, and I had discussed the matter of total honesty. "Candor" was the word I believe was bandied about. Should we or shouldn't we level with him, namely, that this time Papa wouldn't be footing the bill, *we* would.

"Don't be daft," Alex said, "of course we don't tell him. We've got his confidence now. He probably won't even ask about payment."

"I'm not so sure," Jane murmured. "He wanted Father to pay the full amount up front."

We had quickly calculated that with the savings Jane and Alex were making by moving out of the Hôtel Verneuil, living on only half of her father's monthly allowance, plus my own meager savings from having moved into the rue du Sabot rent-free, we could come up with roughly half the payment for issue number 2. "Half down and half on delivery, that sounds fair and reasonable to me," Alex concluded. "Who could refuse that?"

"We will bring you the first half tomorrow," Trocchi went on. "A hundred fifty thousand francs. Cash. We very much want to stay with you," he went on, "but you must be reasonable with us as well."

"I'm sorry," Lebon said. "I like to help young people, worthy endeavors. I, and my father before me, already have, as I said. But with those earlier American and British magazines, people always paid in advance. It was a rule they accepted and honored."

Alex shook his head. "I think you're making a mistake, monsieur, a grave mistake."

"Unless," Lebon tried, "Monsieur Lougee could guarantee the second-half payment."

"Perhaps," Alex said, "perhaps. We'll let you know tomorrow."

Outside, the pounding of the Mazarine presses fast becoming a fading memory, we repaired to one of the outdoor cafés at the nearby carrefour de Buci, bustling as always at this time of day, even in midsummer, awash with vendors crying their wares and black-clad women jostling with their market baskets and fondling the ripe, plump vegetables and fruits. The heady odor of the open street market—a mixture of piquant spices and crushed garlic, of *frites* frying merrily on the corner, of wine gurgling from huge casks into the empty bottles proffered by the soon-to-be thirsty, of meat cooking in the restaurant next door, of fresh-baked baguettes—

reminded us how close France was to recovering its prewar culinary splendor. It also reminded us how desperately hungry we were.

"So where does that leave us?" I said. "I don't see any way we can raise the full amount he wants. And we're running out of time."

Jane looked glum. Hitting up Daddy was out of the question.

"Don't worry," Alex said, "I have another printer all lined up."

We waited.

"Fontenay-aux-Roses," he continued enigmatically. "Name mean anything to you?"

"A Paris suburb, no?" I ventured, trying unsuccessfully to place it in the periphery: Neuilly? Issy-les-Moulineaux? Montreuil? Boulogne-Billancourt? So many suburbs, so little concrete knowledge of the world beyond the Left Bank. Even after four years. I made a resolution to explore the area sometime in the near future: the *proche banlieue*.

"You all make fun of my pinball prowess," Alex said. "Well, at the Mabillon the other day I was hard at it, racking up the best score of my life, when this man saunters over, clearly impressed, watches me finish the game, then challenges me to a match. Great big guy. Towers over me. An ox—a bull, rather. Anyway, to make a long story short, he wipes me out. Truly impressive body moves. After which he of course invites me for a beer, asks me what I do, and so forth. When I pull out a copy of *Merlin*, he laughs out loud. 'What's so funny?' I ask him. 'Fate,' he says, 'I believe in fate . . .'

"Turns out he's a printer." Alex pulled out his wallet, rummaged through it, and finally came up with a crumpled but still readable business card:

JEAN-LOUIS LECONTE

GÉRANT

IMPRIMERIE DE LA S.A.I.B.E.L. FONTENAY-AUX-ROSES (SEINE)

Monsieur Jean-Louis Leconte was, as Alex had described, a tall, strapping man. Though he was grizzled, I judged him to be only in his mid- to late thirties. I had met a number of Frenchmen over the previous four years who at first glance looked middle-aged—faces etched with deep lines, hair prematurely gray, shoulders slightly stooped—and inevitably each had a war story that explained the aging. Something we Americans had trouble understanding, even those who had known battle during the war. It was not just stress. It was a matter of duration. Four long years of occupation, of never knowing, each time you left your house, whether you would ever return, of living in constant fear of the knock on the door at 3:00 or 4:00 a.m.

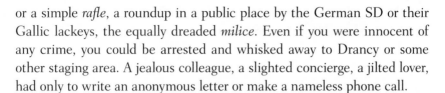

or a simple *rafle*, a roundup in a public place by the German SD or their Gallic lackeys, the equally dreaded *milice*. Even if you were innocent of any crime, you could be arrested and whisked away to Drancy or some other staging area. A jealous colleague, a slighted concierge, a jilted lover, had only to write an anonymous letter or make a nameless phone call.

If the war had turned Leconte's hair gray, there was no sign his body had suffered. He looked in the peak of condition. I wondered if he might not be one of Maurice Goudeket's wrestlers, though I had never seen him in the gym with the other Olympic wrestling hopefuls with whom for several months I had been working out, trying to adapt my American college wrestling skills to the *lutte gréco-romaine* that prevailed here. I was improving, I kept telling myself. It was taking longer every month for the French grapplers to pin me, which I construed as progress. The hardest thing for an American wrestler here was not to let the shoulders touch the mat for even a split second. In college, you had to hold your opponent's shoulders to the mat for a full three seconds to end the match. Here it was only the time it took for the referee to count *vingt-et-un*, *vingt-deux*, barely a second, and you were toast. Of course, it worked both ways: you just needed to twist your opponent in such a way that his shoulders grazed the mat, and he was gone. What's more, if one wrestler in *gréco-romaine* gained a six-point lead, the match was over, whereas in American collegiate wrestling many a man behind by ten points suddenly pinned his opponent in the last thirty seconds. It meant throwing every move and combination learned over a decade out the window and starting from scratch. I wondered how my charges at Pomfret School were doing, those I had left behind in a fledgling wrestling program when I hied myself off to Paris. And if ever I were to return, would I know how to coach freestyle again, or only *gréco-romaine*? Fleeting thoughts, begotten by the towering presence of our new printer.

His biceps, I noted, were roughly the size of my thighs, but it was not till he stood up that I realized the full extent of our potential problem: he was a good three inches taller than Trocchi's six feet two and had to weigh close to 250. Muscle-to-fat ratio: disconcerting. Whoever said the two world wars had sapped France of all its virility, leaving a nation of ninnies and the physically inept, had clearly never met Monsieur Leconte.

"Why didn't you pick a printer five feet five?" I muttered to Trocchi in English. "This guy looks like he could snap both our necks with one hand and toss our limp remains in the Seine."

"Don't worry," Alex said, "I have him in the palm of my hand."

Monsieur Leconte assured us that even with the place closed for part of August, he could meet our September 15 deadline if he had all the material in two weeks. That would give him time to typeset the issue before closing, and we could return the corrected proofs the first of September.

We shook hands all around. I had always thought I had a pretty solid grip, but when Leconte's hand encircled mine, I was Jack and he the giant.

Outside, we exchanged not a word until we were safely on the train. At which point we gave each other the 1952 equivalent of a high five and burst out laughing.

"What did I tell you?" Alex said, beaming.

"I have to hand it to you," I admitted. "And I swear I'll never bug you again about playing that goddamn pinball machine. There's only one thing . . ."

Alex sighed. "I hear a negative looming."

"Simply a question, nothing more. A simple pragmatic question."

"Namely?"

"Given the size, weight, and girth of torso and limb of our new printer, what happens if, come September 15, we can't come up with the second half of the payment?"

"Pish and bother," Trocchi responded derisively. "That, my dear Seaver, is a bridge we cross when we come to it."

Patrick was only vaguely interested in the finances of the enterprise, Christopher the falconer not at all. So Alex, Jane, and I sat down the next afternoon at the terrace of the Royal, pencil and paper in hand. Roughly 300,000 francs remained of Arthur Fogg Lougee's beneficence—$750. The printer needed 150,000 by mid-September—I speak of old francs, of course, of that postwar period when anyone with a decent job was a multimillionaire (in francs)—leaving Alex and Jane, if they funded the number from their personal kitty, $375 to live on for the next three months. Jane, usually imperturbable, seemed momentarily at a loss. "Can we really make it on $125 a month?" she wondered out loud. Since falling in love with Alex, she had measurably lowered her standard of living. Alex patted her hand reassuringly, but she was not finished. "No, the most we can put up is $150."

"Which means we still have to find 90,000 francs in the next three or four weeks," I said. "Daunting but not impossible."

Pooling our resources, including 50 quid that a benevolent relative had just sent Pat and $75 from me, a payment just received from the *New York Herald Tribune* for an article I had written on the actor Jean Gabin, we arrived at a grand total of 110,000 francs, which seemed a fortune until you divided by the current 400: roughly $275, a pitiful sum in the world's eyes, but not in postwar France, where the dollar was ace, king, and queen rolled into one. We all agreed to put our share in escrow—that is, in true French fashion, under the mattress, where it would remain inviolate until September 15. The remaining 40,000 francs due our Fontenay-aux-Roses Gargantua were sure to be found. For the next few weeks we would simply tighten our belts a notch. Another notch. Thus reassured, we signaled to the waiter to bring us another round of *gros rouge.*

When issue number 2 appeared, surprisingly on schedule, all five of us showed up at the office of Monsieur Leconte, on whose desk a dozen copies sat in proud array. Distributing one to each of us, Leconte took one himself, opened it, and, instead of pretending to read, brought it to his nose. It's true: there's a wonderful smell to newly printed books that fades within a day or two, which only printers and editors can fully appreciate. We all skimmed the pages: nothing seemed out of place, no blanks where pictures were intended, no missing passages. The black type was sharp and clear. Handshakes all around. I wondered if poor Jane's dainty right hand would disappear, wrist and all, but Leconte, a true, if gruff, gentleman, only grazed her outstretched fingers.

He handed us the invoice, duly stamped to make it official, and we in turn handed him the 150,000 francs due, in new, crisp 5,000-franc notes. The day before we had gone to the bank with our collection of badly wrinkled banknotes and exchanged them for these crisp, clean ones. Made a better impression, we all agreed. In any event, Leconte seemed pleased as he counted the stack, only occasionally licking his thumb.

"*Voilà, parfait!*" he said, looking up. He signed the invoice, stamped it with a hearty "*PAYÉ,*" and again we shook hands all around. He hoped we were pleased. We assured him we were and congratulated him on keeping to the difficult schedule. He wished the magazine success and, surprising us for someone so blunt and, from our limited experience, private, started reminiscing about the recent war. I began translating as quickly and accurately as I could.

"During the war, times were difficult," he began, "very difficult. We had to decide whether to close our business or print for the Germans. Early after they arrived in Paris, they sent SS people around to all the printers, in July and August, to check out what we were doing, who we were working for—which publishers, magazines, newspapers, private clients. They told us that henceforth we could print nothing without their authorization. Not an invitation, a broadsheet, nothing, under penalty of imprisonment. 'Collaboration' is a dirty word today. But it was invented by our leader, Marshal Pétain, a man much revered—don't forget he was remembered for saving France at Verdun, for defeating these same Germans in World War I—and most Frenchmen felt it was mandatory to continue business as usual. He kept reminding us that, though we had lost the war, the victors had granted the privileged status of having our own government. The other countries did not: they were under the administration of German officials. At first it seemed to make some sense: we had been defeated but, with Pétain as head of government, not dishonored. So for a few weeks we stayed open and fulfilled their demands: posters, official documents, some new magazines the collaborators were concocting. But seeing those swastika-laden documents coming off the presses made us sicker and sicker. Physically ill. So we began talking among ourselves about shutting down. However, to close down meant not only to lose your equipment, which the Germans would impound, but also to fire a dozen workers.

"We met and discussed the matter as early as October 1940, just four months after the Germans arrived in Paris. And, quite quickly, the decision was to not close down but appear to remain open. Two of our workers were Jewish—which of course the Germans didn't yet know—and by September it was already clear the Germans would treat our Jews the way they had treated theirs. Or worse. Oddly, it was our non-Jewish workers who were most adamant about not collaborating. So one day we began dismantling the equipment, a piece at a time so no one would notice, and taking it out by night. During the day we were still open, but over the next several weeks we kept taking the presses apart and carting them to safe places in the far suburbs. By early 1941, the Germans had stopped coming personally to deliver their material; they had Frenchmen taking their place. We had the good fortune of having as our contact a member of the Resistance, who covered for us until we were down to one press. Then one night we closed and shuttered the place—the same place where you are sitting now—and the next day we were in business again, but working now for the Resistance, underground. During the next three and a half years we had to move our presses half a dozen times, each time harder, for the German patrols were more and more prevalent. But somehow we managed. And, I am proud to say, we manufactured several thousand—somewhere I have the precise number—perfect ID cards, which I'm sure saved many, many precious lives.

"And here we are printing for you, the English. What a pleasure after those dark years. You know, before the war we printed some of the literary magazines of the English—not all their issues, but some—so for us your magazine is a kind of continuity." He paused. "But I spoke too much. I believe I have all your shipping instructions, do I not?"

Alex assured him he did, and again thanked him for his fine work. Another round of obligatory handshakes, and finally we headed for the door.

As we emerged onto the street, we all felt not only energized at having brought issue number 2 into the world but also moved. Never judge a printer by his size. Beneath the gnarled oak that was Monsieur Leconte lay a man of principle, courage, and, by God, sensitivity.

Still, I was greatly relieved we had paid the bill in full.

7 ∾

Waiting for Beckett

A WEEK OR SO LATER, I penned the following note to Beckett:

Dear Mr. Beckett:
Enclosed please find a copy of the second issue of Merlin, *an English-language quarterly printed in Paris. On page 73 you will find a brief essay on your work, which I have recently discovered and admire greatly. I am the first to realize how tentative and inadequate the piece is, for I know I have only begun to plumb the depths. But I hope nonetheless you will find some merit in its pages, if only to tell the readers of* Merlin—*too few in number, I fear, to make an immediate impact*—*to what degree we feel your work is of major importance.*
                                                                    Sincerely yours,
                                                                    Richard Seaver

Next day I walked around the corner, armed with a copy of the magazine and the enclosed letter, entered the sanctum sanctorum of Les Éditions de Minuit, mounted the now-familiar stairs, and asked the same buxom lady behind the desk if I could see Monsieur Lindon.

"Do you have an appointment?" she rightly wanted to know.

"Not really," I said, realizing immediately how asinine my response was. Either one had an appointment or one had not. "But," I added, trying to save the situation, "perhaps you might tell him it's about Monsieur Beckett."

Reluctantly, it seemed to me, she picked up the phone and dialed upstairs, explaining that there was a young man who had walked in off the street without an appointment, not very well dressed—no, in all honesty, she did not say that, I imagined that was what she was thinking and would have liked to report—who wanted to see him about Monsieur Beckett. Much to her surprise, and I must admit to mine, he apparently told her to send me right up.

The next flight was narrow and much steeper than the downstairs, what the French call *escalier en colimaçon*, a "spiral staircase," the kind of corkscrew staircase I associated with dungeons and keeps.

Tentatively, I knocked, a voice from inside cried, *"Entrez,"* and there I was face-to-face with Beckett's publisher. Tall, thin as a Gallic rail, his dark hair thinning both left and right, his dark eyes piercing, he sat stiffly behind an obscenely clean desk. In disturbing contrast to my war-surplus khakis, he wore a neatly tailored dark suit, a starched white shirt, and a somber tie. I judged him to be ten, maybe fifteen, years older than I. He rose to shake hands, then sat back down and gestured toward a chair in front of him. I began to stammer out the purpose of my visit, my French having suddenly deserted me. I pushed a copy of the magazine across the desk and, my language creeping back like a chastened hound, spent two or three reasonably eloquent minutes describing how much I, and the magazine, admired Monsieur Beckett's work, and how grateful I was personally to him, Lindon, for having discovered and published him. There is, I added, an essay in the issue expressing my strong opinion that Beckett's work is major, even seminal.

If I was hoping my words would generate a response, verbal or facial, I was disappointed. Lindon was as impassive as Buddha himself. But I later learned that my impassioned peroration about the author he, Lindon, admired above all others, a writer about whom he would one day say that publishing him alone justified his vocation, created an immediate bond between us that would last forever.

He promised to send the magazine and my note to Beckett. I was even more grateful when, having told him we'd like to publish something by Beckett in the next issue, he averred that Beckett had written a novel in English during the war called *Watt*. No, he had not read it. He did not read English. But as far as he knew, it had not been published.

Could we see it?

"I'll mention it in my covering note," he said. "The rest is up to him."

I thanked him warmly, and as I got up to leave, he stood and extended his hand. I had almost made the unpardonable error of not proffering my own hand, a gaffe in France almost as egregious as beginning a conversation with anyone—friend, foe, stranger—without first saying "*bonjour*" or "*bonsoir*," depending on the time of day. As we shook hands, he said: "*C'est bien que vous aimez Beckett. C'est un grand écrivain. Très grand.*"

By September, *Merlin* had moved its editorial office into the rue du Sabot ex-warehouse. My *patron*—now friend—Oscar had announced in late summer that he was going "for a few months to the States." My heart skipped the proverbial beat: after all that toting and lifting, all that cleaning and sweeping, was I to be kicked out as meanly and summarily as Beckett's beleaguered hero in the story I had tracked down "The Expelled"? I envisioned myself back at Madame Germaine's doorstep, begging for reinstatement. No, there would have to be another solution. Or—my mind was racing, at least moving at an unaccustomed pace—was he expecting me to run the shop full-time? I had neither the time nor the inclination, not to mention the antiquarian knowledge. Fearing the former, expulsion, I alluded to the latter.

"No, no," he assured me, "the shop will be closed. But there are a few clients who may call, like Monsieur de Mereille from the Musée de l'Homme, whom you know, and you should open up for them. I'll give you the full list. I've paid the rent for the next four months, and I'll leave you money for the phone and electricity."

Quickly pushing my luck, I asked nonchalantly: "What about the room upstairs?"

In front of the aforementioned rabbit warrens in the old mill itself, directly above and in front of my warehouse, one flight up, was Oscar's apartment. All right, room. It was no more than twenty-five square meters, but the bedroom itself was of decent size with a floor-to-ceiling window facing east, so that on fair summer days, though in the shadow of the old mill most of the time, it let in welcome light for several hours a day. It came with a generous double bed, a desk and chair, an overstuffed armchair of fading red velvet, and a floor lamp to read by. What's more, to the right of the entrance was a tiny kitchen with a sink and a two-burner gas—not alcohol—stove. In other words, pauper's heaven.

"Yours if you want it," he said, "till I come back."

With me upstairs, we could use the ground floor exclusively for the *Merlin* office, where we were preparing issue number 3.

Proof that copies had reached the far-distant shores of Maine and the Isle of Man came in the form of submissions from both the United States and England. Plus a trickle of subscriptions. More of the former than the latter, from which we surmised that there were more writers in the world than readers. The editorial premise in *Merlin* 2 was that "good writing was being written" and that the magazine intended to look for and publish it. From the early submissions received, however, we began seriously to question that premise.

For weeks we waited for some word from Beckett, either directly or through Lindon, but nothing came, to the point where I began to doubt that Lindon had ever sent the magazine on.

It was Delphine who again came to the rescue. Of course she knew where Beckett lived; Blin had sent her more than once to pick up corrected pages of *Godot*, which was going into rehearsal: 6, rue des Favorites in the fifteenth arrondissement, a working-class building off the rue de Vaugirard. I pedaled at top speed to the precious address, slaloming my way through traffic as if I were competing in the Winter Olympics. I was armed with a modest package containing issue number 2 and a covering note that said that if it were true that *Watt* was available, we'd be interested in publishing an extract in *Merlin*. I added that I was aware Monsieur Lindon had sent an earlier copy of the magazine, but I wanted to make sure it had not gone astray in the post.

What struck me most as I parked Big Blue was the impressive herd of bicycles huddled back behind the stairs. With *Molloy* still fresh in my mind, I tried to determine which might be his: I searched for one with crutches attached to the handlebars, but saw none.

I tapped on the glass window of the concierge's door—once, twice, discreet but insistent—and in due course a face peered through the partially frosted glass, which gave her the distinct advantage of seeing me clearly while shielding half her face. By the half look she gave me, she doubtless took me for the neighborhood rapist. I had never figured out what kept the Paris concierges so busy behind their closed doors, and why, when they reluctantly responded, they automatically assumed the worst of their callers. Especially a caller as clearly benign as me, dressed impeccably in cast-off army fatigues a size too big and sporting a two-day beard. I refer to male visitors of course. They—concierges—are slightly more indulgent to the distaff side, I had noted. Perhaps a holdover from the war, when they could, and often did, hold the life—or death—of their tenants in their hands. Many had thwarted the Germans and their local henchmen from laying hands on the suspected or wanted; others, though—I had heard the stories, and they were harrowing—had collaborated, out of weakness, out of fear for their own safety, or as an act of retribution against someone they felt had wronged or slighted them. Greed as well: I knew of cases where, having denounced a lodger, the concierge would quickly pillage the apartment of all its valuables before the seals were placed by the authorities. And if the unlucky lodger happened to be cleared, which did happen, and returned to his or her lodgings, no one could trace the theft to the putative guardian of the gate. And even if the victim did, through visual evidence (isn't that my polka-dot dress she's wearing?), to whom could you report the problem? That same authority under whose suspicion you still lived?

"Monsieur Beckett," I said through the glass. "I have a package for him."

She continued to stare at me.

"Shall I take it up to him?" I said in the gentlest tone I could muster, waving the thin packet across the dim horizon of her stare.

Slowly the door opened a crack, and a bony hand, followed by an equally bony wrist, snaked through. "*Septième étage*," she croaked. Seventh floor. "*Merci.*" I smiled and made for the stairway. "*Il n'est pas là*," she croaked again, her vocal cords having somehow returned. He isn't here. "*Revenez plus tard.*" Come back later.

"At what time?" I asked, plaintively, I'm sure. "What time will he be home?"

"*Je ne sais pas, monsieur.*"

"Then how will I know when I should come back?"

She shrugged. Clearly that was my problem, not hers.

"*A quelle heure rentre-t-il normalement?*" I ventured before giving up and declaring her the winner of this battle of wits. Or nonwits. What time does he usually come home?

Again she shrugged. "*Je ne sais pas, monsieur*," she said. "*Il n'a pas d'heures précises*," she allowed. I don't know. His schedule is erratic. She looked increasingly fatigued by all this pointless banter, but still managed to add: "*Parfois il ne sort pas du tout pendant des jours. Sa femme fait toutes les courses.*" Sometimes he doesn't go out for days at a time. His wife does all the errands.

Ah, a wife. I was making progress. A few more pointed questions and I might know the intimacies of their daily life.

"Then," I said, "is it possible he's up there now? Or she?"

The concierge shook her head, a long-accustomed gesture, I assumed. *"Absolument pas!"* No, absolutely not. *"A vrai dire, ils sont partis depuis des semaines,"* she added, as though the realization had just dawned. Actually, they've been away for several weeks.

The news reassured me. And exonerated Monsieur Lindon, who, I was now sure, had indeed sent my letter. "In that case," I said, producing a hundred-franc note, "can you give the package to him when he returns to Paris?"

She nodded, as if to say that that might be arranged.

It was October when I delivered the package, and as the days and weeks sped by without a response, we went about preparing the next issue sans an extract from *Watt*. As a quarterly, the next number should have appeared on December 15, a dubious date given the year-end holidays. More important, we did not have the down-payment money for Monsieur Leconte. Even pooling our latest resources, we were still sixty thousand francs short. At a high-level meeting—Alex, Jane, Christopher, Patrick, me, and a newcomer to the group, Austryn Wainhouse—we made the decision to push the next issue off a month or two.

By now I had become deeply involved with the venture, and Trocchi, to seal my commitment, conjured up the slightly bizarre title of advisory editor and director. My job, among other things, was to broaden the scope of the magazine into issues both social and political. *Merlin* 2 had provoked a fair amount of reaction for so limited a circulation. The praise we could savor and ignore; the attacks needed comment. The accusation that we had "a ludicrous faith in the very science that will destroy us" especially demanded a response. The next issue's editorial reiterated our commitment to hit at rigid or outdated categories, trying to separate the scientific from the metaphysical.

This new orientation of the magazine, dealing head-on with the issues of the day, had evolved from our discussions over the past several weeks, together with the growing awareness on all our parts, especially mine and Austryn's, that to ignore the pressing ideological and political pressures of the day was tantamount to moral suicide. *Merlin* would remain primarily literary, its focus on poetry and fiction, but in each succeeding issue we would address, or try to address, some aspect of the precarious—or, in Trocchi's word, "parlous"—world we had inherited.

When I had first come to Paris four years before, I felt that with the end of World War II we had entered a new, at last enlightened era in which we would all create, experiment, live in a climate free from hate and distrust. The loathsome Nazis and their fascist allies were disgraced and dishonored in the eyes of all mankind. The victorious Americans, British, and Russians, arm in arm, would march proudly and collectively into the brave new world. But now, only seven years after the brief idyll, armies embracing fraternally on the Elbe, the specter of apocalyptic war loomed large in all our minds. The West, and especially the Americans, had a new obsession: Communism, a disease as feared and dreaded as the Nazis had so recently been. It was Orwellian. And it could not be ignored. Back home, Joe McCarthy, the senator from Wisconsin, was still on a rampage, rooting out homegrown subversives—read Commies—in government, business, and entertainment, wherever they did or did not exist, it mattered little. Austryn had recently arrived in town, after spending the better part of a year touring Europe on a motor scooter with his charming young wife, Muffie. A Harvard graduate, Austryn had come to Paris to stretch his literary wings, write novels, translate—his French was good before he arrived—and presumably live the Left Bank life. Wainhouse *père*, we learned, was in the State Department, so when Austryn spoke out on American politics, we listened.

Austryn did not quite fit the heretofore slightly scruffy *Merlin* mold. He dressed smartly, was well-groomed, spoke in flowing sentences that never, as far as I can remember, revealed a grammatical error. And he carried, wherever he went, a handsome briefcase. Now, in my time I have seen briefcases put to a variety of uses. I have seen the homeless with such an appurtenance, inside which lay their every possession. In France, the briefcase is, I discovered, often used as a *baise-en-ville*, a polite translation of which would be "overnight bag"; a more accurate and literal rendering, "quick-fuck equipment kit." In Italy, at least in the 1950s, well-dressed "businessmen" would clutch them to their breasts as they hurried on their appointed rounds, but instead of holding state papers or business analyses for pending deals, they were often revealed to contain a ham-and-cheese sandwich and a flask of red wine. But Austryn's briefcase was a disconcertingly orderly file of his life, his writing, his appointments, his plans for today, tomorrow, next week, God knows when. I was suspicious. My father, only half-joking, had always said that an orderly desk was the sign of a disorderly mind. I assumed the same applied to briefcases.

In any event, meet we did, at Gaït's English Bookshop on the rue de Seine, together with Christopher and Alex. With George Whitman's Librairie Mistral, Gaït's was one of the two meaningful bookshops on the Left Bank that catered to an English-reading public, with an excellent selection of the classics and all the latest British and American fiction and nonfiction worth mentioning. Gaït Frogé was a tall, handsome woman in her mid-thirties, her pale skin in sharp contrast to her striking auburn hair. Always impeccably dressed, she ran the bookshop by herself, and whenever she had to step out for an errand or rendezvous, she invariably entrusted the shop to whichever of her clients happened to be there at the time. "You won't mind tending the shop for half an hour or so, will you, dear?" she'd say. "I won't be long. And if you need to make change, the money's in the middle drawer." Pause. "And, love, would you make note of anything you sell so I can reorder." Sometimes she wouldn't be back for an hour or two, but there was plenty to read or, if the muse descended, you could always use her desk to pen your masterpiece. If she was gone overly long—three or four hours on occasion—you could snare some other client you knew she trusted and pass on the job.

From the beginning, Gaït had been a friend of *Merlin* and the Merlinites, and there were always stacks of the magazine—current and back copies—on her counter. She also allowed us, if we wished, to use the shop as our mail drop. I have known personal bookshops in my time, but none on any continent quite equaled the happy informality of Gaït's, or the opera-learning-center, pay-as-you-can philosophy of George Whitman's a few blocks away.

Austryn had of course been quick to discover the rue de Seine emporium, and it was doubtless inevitable we meet. He had written a novel, entitled, Gaït informed us, *Hedyphagetica*.

"Any idea what the title means?" I asked Alex.

He looked irritated, as if he considered the very question unworthy of a response. I felt humbled. I wished I had taken Greek instead of Latin, for it sure as hell sounded Greek to me.

"How the fuck should I know?" Alex shook his head. "I'm Scots-Italian, not *Greek*, for Chrissake! Anyway, that's beside the point. Gaït hears that the man's translated the entire *Philosophy in the Bedroom*."

"The marquis de Sade?"

"None other . . . Don't you see, mon, what that could mean for us? Put two and two together."

"The marquis and who? The marquis and . . ."

"*Merlin!*"

"I'm missing a beat."

"We'll publish the Sade as the first volume of our Collection Merlin line. We've been talking about starting a book-publishing line: Christopher's *Wand and Quadrant*, Beckett's *Watt*, my *Young Adam* . . . But we always run up against the same damn problem: money. Won't Sade sell like hotcakes? And with the money we make from that, we finance the magazine. And the books. It's that simple. All this time we've been pinching pennies and worrying about a few thousand francs here, a few thousand francs there. Sade will bring in *hundreds* of thousands. It's a godsend, old man, a veritable godsend."

Rarely had I seen Trocchi so enthusiastic, so cheerful and upbeat, and I didn't want to puncture his euphoria with another dumb question. But swirling through my mind was one: Wasn't the marquis de Sade still forbidden in France? Banned? In which case, wouldn't those who published him risk prosecution? Or jail? At the very least, expulsion?

A few days later we walked over to rue de la Boucherie and met Austryn at George Whitman's bookshop, the Librairie Mistral.

"I understand you have translated Sade," Alex said, then laid out his villainous scheme.

Yes, Sade would sell, Austryn agreed. But there was one slight problem: Sade was, and almost always had been, banned here. There was a brief period after the Revolution, in 1790 to be exact, when Sade, newly released from the Charenton Asylum for the Insane, to which he had hurriedly been dispatched on the eve of the Revolution after having spent most of seventeen years in the prisons of Their Majesties Louis XIV and XV because of his scandalous life and even more scandalous works, was allowed to publish specifically the novels *Justine* and *Juliette*. But that freedom was short-lived, as are most postrevolutionary periods, when those new to power throw open all the once closed doors to prove real change has taken place, then quickly close them again to consolidate their power. In Sade's case, Austryn went on, in 1793 his works were again banned, and he was remanded to an even worse prison than those he had endured under the *ancien régime*. His works have been banned to this day. To be sure, some clandestine editions have appeared, privately printed but never sold above-board. So without question, Austryn concluded, if *Merlin* proceeded, it would surely be prosecuted.

"But they're banned in *French*," Alex protested. "We'd be publishing him in *English*. The French don't give a fuck about English, don't you think? They'd probably never even notice."

Oh, they'd notice all right, Austryn assured him. It might take them a bit longer to find out, but when the first copy hit England, the Foreign Office would be on the back of the French overnight. "What do you think they'd do?" Trocchi asked, clearly not yet ready to throw in the sponge.

"Prison probably," Christopher said dourly.

"No, not prison. As foreigners you would face immediate expulsion," Austryn guessed. "Most likely with the proviso that you never return to France. At least for the foreseeable future."

"Damn!" Alex said. "Another brilliant idea down the fucking drain."

We had all but given up hope of ever hearing from Beckett when, one dark and stormy early evening in late November, as we were preparing a spaghetti and meatballs dinner at the rue du Sabot culinary emporium, a knock came at the door. The noise of the rain on the glass roof above was so deafening we barely heard the knock. When finally I answered, there, outlined in the light, was a tall gaunt figure in a raincoat, water streaming down from the brim of the nondescript hat jammed onto the top of his head. From inside the folds of his raincoat he fished a package, not even wrapped against the downpour: a manuscript bound in a black imitation-leather binder.

"You asked me for this," he said, thrusting the package into my hand. "Here it is."

At which point I realized this was *Watt*, and the rain-soaked silhouette Mr. Beckett himself.

"Thank you," I managed. "You must be drenched. Won't you come in?"

"Can't," he said. "I must be off. Let me know what you think." He pronounced the last word as though it had no *h*—"t'ink." With which he turned and strode off into the night.

I turned back to the others, who had paid scant attention to the business at the door, and held my trophy aloft. "*Watt*," I declared. "The long-lost *Watt*!"

"What?" Patrick asked.

"I said, *Watt*."

"We know *what* you said," Trocchi mimicked. "We just don't know *what* you mean."

"Sounds to me like 'Who's on First,'" Charlie Hatcher murmured. Charlie was a Canadian poet, a rather loose member of the *Merlin* group, whose wonderfully inventive poem "Quintus Mucius Scaevola: IV" had appeared in the first issue. Obviously the only other member of the clan aware of the classic baseball routine.

Having carried that terrible punning as far as it would go, I cried, "Enough," opened the black binder, and glanced at the neatly typed first page.

> Mr Hackett turned the corner and saw, in the failing light, at some little distance, his seat. It seemed to be occupied. This seat, the property very likely of the municipality, or of the public, was of course not his, but he thought of it as his. This was Mr Hackett's attitude towards things that pleased him. He knew they were not his, but he thought of them as his. He knew they were not his, because they pleased him.

It was coming up to seven o'clock when I read those lines for the first time, and we quickly decided that the pleasure should be shared. We would read it aloud till we could no more. Eschewing dinner, literally turning our backs on the spaghetti and meatballs, I began to read aloud. Already by page 2 the assembled group—Trocchi, Jane, Patrick, Christopher, Charlie, and I—were smiling despite ourselves:

> Mr Hackett decided, after some moments, that if they [the people on the bench] were waiting for a tram they had been doing so for some time. For the lady held the gentleman by the ears, and the gentleman's hand was on the lady's thigh, and the lady's tongue was in the gentleman's mouth . . . The lady now removing her tongue from the gentleman's mouth, he put his into hers. Fair do, said Mr Hackett. Taking a pace forward, to satisfy himself that the gentleman's other hand was not going to waste, Mr Hackett was shocked to find it limply dangling over the back of the seat, with between its fingers the spent three quarters of a cigarette.

By the time I had got to page 15, well into the shenanigans of Tetty and Goff, we were all guffawing, if that is the proper term, for the laughter was now bordering on the loud and coarse. When my voice gave out about page 22 or 23, I passed the manuscript to Christopher, who, wiping his eyes on the back of his sleeve, took up the task, Mr. and Mrs. Nixon having made their departure into the gloaming, Mr. Hackett having scratched to satisfaction the crest of his hunch—for he was hunchbacked, in case I have failed to note that salient point—on the backboard of his beloved bench, and Watt, known at this point only by his bulbous red nose and the intriguing fact that, seven years before, he was seen in the street with one foot bare, which prompted Mr. Nixon to lend him five shillings with which to buy a boot, or a shoe, that sum now having ballooned to seven shillings— no, six and nine pence, for it is important to be precise—presumably the difference being explained by seven years of interest.

Christopher opened to Watt's first smile, at least the first known to the reader:

> Watt had watched people smile and thought he understood how it was done. And it was true that Watt's smile, when he smiled, resembled more a smile than a sneer, for example, or a yawn. But there was something wanting to Watt's smile, some little thing was lacking, and people who saw it for the first time, and most people who saw it saw it for the first time, were sometimes in doubt as to what expression exactly was intended. To many it seemed a simple sucking of the teeth.
>
> Watt used this smile sparingly.

Alternating around the room, we read well into the evening, some readers lasting up to twenty pages before voice or wit gave out, others no more than a round dozen. But as the church bells of St. Germain tolled ten, there was a pause as Patrick, the greatest appreciator of food, paused in mid-sentence and said: "I don't know about you, but I'm hungry."

The pasta we had been planning now lay thickly, heavily in its enormous pot. Could it be revived, or were we destined to repair to a restaurant nearby, a certain strain on our collective budget? I lit the burner and stirred. After five minutes, little or no sign of life. But soon the faint odor of basil and Parmesan gave a ray of hope. We poured red wine all around, into our odd mélange of glassware, ranging from two true crystal stem glasses, lifted from God knows where, to lowly yogurt jars. But the wine, as usual Buci's best, tasted good and warming in whatever its container. By the end of the second glass, with Jane now in charge at the burner, the pasta, definitely coaxed back to life, as surely as from the place of the skull two thousand years before—the comparison is unfair, but there you are— was dished out in generous proportions. Above, the late autumn rain still thundered. Undeterred, the reading went on. Incredibly, no one fell asleep or even nodded. A testimony to genius.

By the time we had reached the end, the mathematical byplay among Mr. Nolan, Mr. Case, and Mr. Gorman—presaging the sucking-stone sequence of *Molloy*, which my friends had not yet read—we were exhausted but exhilarated. Then we saw there was, on the page following the end, "Addenda." Footnoted as follows: "The following precious and illuminating material should be carefully studied. Only fatigue and disgust prevented its incorporation." The author's final self-inflicted comment. Consciously erudite, with commentary in four or five languages, not to be taken seriously, unless for some odd reason you cared to. We cared to. Our favorite note of the "Addenda": "for all the good that frequent departures out of Ireland had done him, he might just as well have stayed there."

"The author speaking of himself?" Trocchi wondered.

"One would presume," Charlie Hatcher said. "He seems to have had no recognition at home."

"You mean in the English language?" I asked.

"Not much more here in France," Patrick said.

"How does this compare with *Molloy* and *Malone*?" Alex wanted to know.

"There's a lot of *Watt* in *Molloy*," I said. "Same humor, same self-mockery. *Watt* is more specific: we're still clearly in Ireland, whereas in *Molloy* and *Malone* time and place are on a whole different plane. Anywhere. Cosmic."

"Big word," said Christopher.

"Not too big," I said. "This man's a genius."

"I loved it," Jane said. "I really loved it."

"How often do you spend eight hours laughing," Patrick murmured, as if in awe, "over a *novel*?"

"How do we feel about including a piece in the next issue?" I said, glancing at my watch as if, at 4:00 a.m., we could call the printer.

"We *must*," Jane declared.

"The problem is," Trocchi said slowly, "the full content is almost ready for the printer. We've no room. Number 3's already at sixty-four pages."

"Let's make room," Patrick said.

"Quiet down there, or we'll call the goddamn *flics*!" thundered from overhead. Cops were the last thing we wanted, what with our official papers not necessarily in impeccable order. "Do you know what fucking time it is!" Another angry voice from above. Unsure, we glanced collectively at our respective watches. "Five-oh-six," Hatcher asserted. "I m-make it oh-eight," Patrick corrected, barely suppressing a hiccup, "coming up to five-oh-nine." "Your watches are all friggin' fast," said Trocchi, laughing with the authority of the true drunken leader. "I make it four fifty-nine!" And, as if to end the argument, the pre-matins bells of St. Germain began to toll the hour. So it was, even though it was not as late as—or earlier than—our upstairs plaintiffs had thought, we shouted up our apologies and resumed debating among ourselves, more quietly now, whether we should, or financially could, interrupt the uncertain flow of the magazine and add an extra eight pages to the issue. The decision, by a unanimous vote, was to do so. The question of how to raise the money for the extra pages was adjourned until the morrow. In our state, to try to calculate the precise sum was beyond our poor power to add or subtract. But to have solved such an important, perhaps even historic, literary problem in less than twelve hours made us feel that the day, the night, had not been in vain.

Next morning—correction: at one o'clock the following afternoon, it only seemed like morning—we gathered at the Royal for breakfast, to read and ponder Beckett's choice of text, which I had managed to locate with one bloodshot eye (the other refused to open, even after a warming Bloody Mary).

I rescued the rain-spattered envelope from the detritus and tore it open. A spidery hand, not easy to read. But, indeed, the author made known his wishes:

> *Mr. Seaver:*
> *Here is the manuscript of* Watt *which you requested. In the event you wish to extract something from it for the magazine, it should be the passage beginning with the paragraph "Watt had little to say on the subject of the second or closing period of his stay in Mr Knott's house" and ending with the paragraph beginning*
> *"But he could not bear that we should part, never to meet again . . ."*
> *Please let me know if this is agreeable to you.*
> *Sincerely,*
> *Samuel Beckett*

The chosen passage was the second or closing period of Watt's stay in Mr. Knott's house, one of the funniest but also most reader-demanding in the entire novel. Almost two pages described, in endless, excruciating, hilarious, mathematical detail, the various accoutrements with which Mr. Knott clothed—or did not clothe—his feet:

> As for his feet, sometimes he wore on each a sock, or on the one a sock and on the other a stocking, or a boot, or a shoe, or a slipper, or a sock and boot, or a sock and shoe, or a sock and slipper, . . . or a stocking and slipper, or nothing at all.

And so on through every conceivable variant. Later the same passage offers a complete rundown of Mr. Knott's movements in the privacy of his own room:

> Here he stood. Here he sat. Here he knelt. Here he lay. Here he moved, to and fro, from the door to the window, from the window to the door; from the window to the door, from the door to the window; from the fire to the bed, from the bed to the fire; from the bed to the fire, from the fire to the bed; from the door to the fire, from the fire to the door . . .

And, to top it off, we are given an inventory of the furniture in Mr. Knott's room—"this solid and tasteful furniture"—which Mr. Knott, on different days of the week, rearranges according to some mysterious but presumably logical plan:

> Thus it was not rare to find, on the Sunday, the tallboy on its feet by the fire, and the dressing-table on its head by the bed, and the night-stool on its face by the door, and the washhand-stand on its back by the window; and, on the Monday, the tallboy on its back by the bed, and the dressing-table on its face by the door, and the night-stool on its back by the window, and the washhand-stand on its feet by the fire . . .

And so on for nineteen days, till "Friday fortnight." And, the author reminds us, that "inventory" fails to take into account the movement of the chairs in the room, which "were never still," and the corners of the room, which "were never empty."

Predating and presaging Molloy's sucking stones by several years, this same Wattian attention to detail was, in the context of the novel, as provocative as it was innovative. Beckett was turning not only the furniture on its head (or its face) but the modern novel, as Joyce had done before him. And, I realized, though Beckett had often been accused of emulating the master's erudite style in his early works, here he had taken one of Joyce's challenging precepts, which was to explore the ultimate possibilities of a given situation, and molded it to his own literary-comedic ends.

Brilliant, I thought, even more so in the light of day. But if the passage were taken out of context, and without the knowledge of the astute Joycean connection, would our readers get it or would they (more likely) consign *Merlin* to the nearest dustbin or wastebasket in anger or frustration? Christopher was of the latter bent.

"Put more than a *few* readers off," he muttered.

"No question," Charlie said somberly. We were already on our second cup of coffee, so there was still a good way to go before normalcy set in.

Alex shook his head, and I thought he was about to agree when he said, softly but firmly, "The man's amazing. We'll not only make room for it in number 3, we'll open the issue with it."

And so we did.

8 ~

Meeting Sartre

IN THAT DARK WINTER of 1952, the magazine moved to a new printer, a Monsieur Arrault, whose worthy establishment lay in Tours, some 150 miles southwest of Paris on the Loire. Trocchi had, several weeks before, burst into the rue du Sabot, Jane not far behind, beaming and waving a sheet of paper. "We have a printer who can give us two colors. We've just come from Tours. Two colors! My God, d'you know what this means?

"There's something else," Trocchi reported, as visibly proud as a marshal of France bringing news to Napoleon that the gates of Moscow were at hand. "*No* down payment. No advance. Payment only on delivery."

Suddenly the second color relegated itself to second place.

"How did you work *that*?" Patrick asked, clearly impressed.

"Charm," Alex said, modestly. "Charm and Jane. I think the printer's in love with Jane."

She laughed. "Tell the truth, Alex."

"All right." He smiled. "We heard about this printer, called him, hopped on the train this morning, and by mid-afternoon had a deal. He was dying to get some business, and the sight of our first two issues convinced him we were creditworthy. Down payment of 10 percent, that's all. And we get two colors . . ."

"Throughout?" Christopher asked.

"Not quite," Alex said. "There's a little nozzle at the end of each sheet coming through that gives a touch of color, a spray, at the end of the run."

"Hmmm," Patrick said, obviously less impressed.

"But that's not the point," Alex went on. "The point is the payment terms, don't you see? Gives us more time to raise the money to pay for the issue, more income flowing in from numbers 1 and 2, that sort of thing."

By its third issue, *Merlin* was a changed magazine, and not just because of the second color and a printer in the provinces. Not only had it become the voice of a future immortal; it had also become, by natural evolution, not so much politicized as, in the Sartrean sense, *engagé*—politically involved—through the inauguration of the Chronicles section. The first such offering was an extract from the work of a Hungarian doctor who had survived Auschwitz. It was the first, or one of the very first, eyewitness accounts of what had gone on in the KZ horror barracks during World War II. After the liberation of the camps, the author had returned to Hungary, where he had been reunited with his wife and daughter, both of whom had miraculously survived as well.

The revealing—and devastating—extract had appeared a year or so earlier in Jean-Paul Sartre's magazine, *Les temps modernes*, founded after the war but already generally considered the most influential French literary-political magazine of the day. Like Trocchi, Austryn and I both felt strongly that in Paris in the 1950s, one could not ignore the political situation, which had evolved so quickly and so radically over the past five years. That fall I had suggested to Trocchi that if we were politically committed—not to any policy or party, but simply recognizing the Realpolitik of our time, as the editorial of number 2 had clearly stated—we should not only editorialize about it but dedicate a Chronicles section of the magazine to it. We could find or commission articles on our own but also make an arrangement with some compatible, like-minded French magazine such as *Les temps modernes*.

Alex wasn't so sure the latter notion was practicable. "What makes you think Sartre would even give us the time of day?" he said. "He's known bloody worldwide. How do you get to him in the first place?"

"He lives right here on the rue Bonaparte," I said, pointing to a window directly across the square from where we were sitting. "Let's write him a note, enclose a copy of both issues, and tell him what we have in mind. What do we have to lose?"

This time the response was swift, if only partially positive. Within a week I received a note, on Sartre's letterhead, not from the great man himself but from someone named Jean Cau, who apparently was Sartre's assistant. He suggested we meet at the Flore the following week. I wanted Trocchi to join me, but he begged off, worried his poor command of French might be a deterrent.

"You make the first step, Dick," he suggested, "and we'll take it from there."

Jean Cau turned out to be young, perhaps half a dozen years older than I, a handsome man with an open expression and ready smile despite the fact that, working daily with Sartre, he bore a lot of the world's political burden on his shoulders.

"Monsieur Sartre was impressed with your magazine," he said as we sipped a beer, "and sympathetic to your idea. He wanted to know how such an arrangement would work and what, if any, articles from *Les temps modernes* you wanted to translate."

"We thought a reciprocal arrangement, formal or informal," I ventured, realizing as I said it that it would be more a one-way street than reciprocal. "You could use anything from our magazine and we from yours. You'd have to approve our choices, of course, and we yours. But on our end, I assure you approval would be a mere formality."

"Can you give me an example?" he said, perhaps testing whether we were actually au courant with the recent contents.

I gave him a couple, including Nyiszli's firsthand report from Auschwitz. "We can't pay much," I said, "though we can pay something, even if it's token."

"Let me get back to you," he said. "I know that Sartre's less interested in money than in getting ideas and events he feels are important more widely disseminated."

True to his word, Jean Cau sent me a note the following week asking if I would come and meet Sartre. This time Trocchi's resistance melted: seeing the Great Existentialist face-to-face was too good an opportunity to pass up.

Dressed in our pawnshop best, we arrived promptly at the appointed hour, passed muster with the concierge, who even went so far as to smile and tell us Monsieur Sartre was expecting us, and took the elevator to the top floor. Trocchi passed his hand admiringly over the polished wood as the elevator inched its way upward. We, like the majority of Parisians, were not used to elevators, especially on the Left Bank. Most that did exist were charmingly antiquated, too narrow for more than two or three people to squeeze into without committing unconscious sexual assault, and required agility to nip in before the folding doors sliced you vertically in two. But Sartre's, though slow, was reasonably large and elegantly appointed.

Jean Cau met us at the door and ushered us through the well-furnished apartment to Sartre's book-lined study. I was surprised to find such bourgeois taste in a man I associated with fiery left-wing politics; I had expected something more spartan. But I was fast learning that in France, a decidedly conservative country in so many ways, one's politics and one's lifestyle could be diametrically different. I remembered once, at a political rally of Sorbonne students, I had seen one of my friends arrive in a chauffeur-driven car. I knew he was not only a Communist but of Maoist bent, but when I asked him how he could accept these upper-class privileges from a society he was intent on destroying, he looked at me pityingly. "I expect you must think I sleep on a pallet and dine on nothing but boiled cabbage or potatoes," he said. "We're not trying to destroy the amenities of life, Dick, merely reworking the political system so they won't be reserved for the happy few. So I see absolutely no contradiction between that goal and using my father's chauffeur to drive me here." With which he raised his Maoist banner and plunged into the emotionally charged crowd. Years later I learned he was the recently appointed CFO of a major French business, living in a town house in Neuilly. I wondered if there were statistics on those who, radically left when they were young, became more and more conservative as they grew older. With Sartre, however, age seemed only to have made him increasingly radical.

He was seated poring over some handwritten pages on his desk. When he stood to greet us, we were both surprised by how short he was. His smile was warm and welcoming. Cau introduced us, and after the de rigueur handshakes Sartre gestured for us to have a seat in front of his desk. Cau sat off to one side. For us, used to the dim light of the rue du Sabot, Sartre's apartment was blindingly bright.

"Jean has talked to me about you and your request," he began, staring, I knew, directly at both of us. I say "I knew" because, although I had heard that Sartre was walleyed, it is one thing to hear it, another entirely to witness it firsthand: one eye looked straight ahead, the other off to the side. Although he was wearing glasses, they seemed only to magnify the problem. Alex, putting on his most stylish Scottish accent, went on at great length about *Merlin*, its hoped-for place in the English-language literary world. Sartre understood some English—more, I suspect, than he let on—but when his brow knitted at some especially recondite phrase, Cau or I would jump in to interpret. At one pause I added how much we admired *Les temps modernes*.

Sartre nodded, but then, proving he had more than glanced at the issues we had sent, said: "I thought Dr. Ayer's piece in your first issue was very interesting. I don't agree with a lot of it, of course, but he's a bright man and his take on existentialism provocative. I suspect you English will never succumb to it."

"I'm Scottish," Trocchi corrected.

Sartre smiled thinly. "I should have said Anglo-Saxon."

"What if we were to do the Nyiszli?" I offered. As I recalled the Ayer article, it was more to bury existentialism than to praise it. Still, Sartre was clearly interested in what Ayer had to say about his philosophy, but also impressed that *Merlin* had published it. "How would that work?"

"Powerful piece," Sartre said. "I fear we're just scraping the surface of what really went on in those camps. Anyway, ideally you should translate from the Hungarian. Do you have such a person?"

Trocchi and I looked at each other, nonplussed.

"Not really," I said. "What about translating from the French?"

"Perhaps," Sartre said, "but in that case I should put you in touch with our translator, Monsieur Tibère Kremer. He lives here in Paris, so you could either translate together or submit yours to him for vetting. Jean," he said, "do we have Tibère's address?"

Cau nodded and went over to the file cabinet to find it.

"Do we need some kind of formal arrangement?" I asked. "Some sort of letter between us?"

Sartre shook his head. "I see no reason. We can do this on a piece-by-piece basis. Simply remember to note, for anything you choose, that it's published by arrangement with *Les temps modernes*."

"How about payment?" Trocchi wanted to know.

"Work that out with Jean," Sartre said. "Whatever you agree to is fine with me."

I had wanted to tell him how much I admired his work, especially the theater—but somehow couldn't bring myself to do so. He had received us as equals, and it was better, I decided, to keep it that way. We shook hands and took our leave.

At the door, Jean Cau said: "As for the money, what Sartre meant by leaving it up to me is that you should pay what you can. Whatever you pay your other contributors. We know from publishing literary magazines in our own language how difficult a proposition it is. For the Nyiszli, work it out with Monsieur Kremer. He should have a fee, but we won't ask for anything beyond that."

Downstairs, Trocchi said: "Now, there's a true gentleman. If only there were a few more of his kind about."

"How about the eye business?" I asked as we hastened back toward the rue du Sabot with our good news.

"Ah, yes, that was a trial, wasn't it?" Trocchi said. "But d'you know, by the end of the meeting I wasn't even noticing it, were you?"

"No, but I now understand for the first time a line he wrote, I can't remember where: 'L'enfer, c'est les autres,' which roughly translates as 'Hell is other people.' He must be acutely aware that 'the others' are always trying to cope with his walleye problem."

9

American in Paris

TILL NOW Austryn had been a *Merlin* "outsider," interested in but not yet part of the magazine. He and his wife, Muffie, had recently set up housekeeping a few blocks away on the rue des Ciseaux, a virtual alleyway so narrow you could reach out and almost touch the buildings on both sides, which ran between St. Germain des Prés and the rue du Four. One of the exotic but also comforting aspects of living in Paris was these ancient streets with endearing names: the rue du Chat Qui Pêche (the Cat That Fishes Street); the rue des Bons Vivants (no translation necessary).

Like me, Austryn was fluent in French, but his was an exquisitely mellifluous version that, according to the French themselves when exposed to it, dated "mid- to late eighteenth century." Quite rightly and courageously, he was interested in the authentic works, those that had made Sade the scourge of his time and had landed him in prison under no fewer than four regimes: the monarchy (two kings), the Revolution, the Terror, and the empire. Austryn was working on, or perhaps had already finished, the unexpurgated version of Sade's *Justine*, though what he planned to do with it only he knew, since the work was still banned 140 years after Sade's death.

As for Austryn's novel, *Hedyphagetica*, only Christopher had seen it—or, actually, patches of it. I asked Christopher how it was, and he frowned, thought for a minute, then said: "Interesting. Quite interesting."

We scheduled a dinner for the following night, to which we invited Austryn and Muffie.

"You have no idea of the political climate over there right now," Austryn assured us. He was referring to the witch hunts led by the jowly, balding, ferret-eyed Joe McCarthy, who was making political hay, daily, it would seem, by preying on the growing fears in the States about Uncle Joe Stalin and the Communist threat to the American Way of Life.

"We *do* read the papers," Trocchi said, a bit defensively. "What's going on over there is pretty bloody awful."

"And getting worse," Austryn said. Then he wagged a finger: "And don't think you're safe over here. Europe is crawling with CIA agents. Especially Paris.

"I can tell you that in this very innocent-looking Left Bank restaurant, there are people listening to what we say."

"That's because we're talking too loud," Patrick suggested.

"You really mean *here*?" Trocchi asked incredulously, nodding around the smoke-filled room. We were in a small restaurant on the rue Bonaparte almost directly across from the École des Beaux-Arts. I'd eaten here dozens of times. The place couldn't hold more than thirty-five or forty people elbow to elbow, and from my experience most of them, especially at lunch but also like tonight at dinner, were Beaux-Arts students, as one could tell from their provocative clothing and compulsively rowdy behavior. After all, they had a reputation to uphold. At the annual Beaux-Arts ball, known locally as the Bal des Quat'z'Arts, which had been revived after the war, each atelier was tradition-bound to outdo not only the others but also the preceding year's shenanigans. "More outrageous than last year" was the order of the day, both during the parade through the streets and later into the predawn hours at the Salle Wagram, where the fete ended up. The police were not only indulgent but overtly supportive, and it took excesses well beyond the norm for them to move in and restore order. This was the one night of the year when the young Beaux-Arts students—who would go on to be artists, sculptors, architects, teachers—could loose their libidos with no fear of reproach or recrimination. Tonight as usual the Beaux-Arts restaurant was jam-packed. Yes, the place *was* noisy as hell and, yes, the clientele was a mixture of students and their elders—Beaux-Arts teachers and outsiders like ourselves. But glancing quickly around, trying to spy an American—and in these postwar days it was relatively easy to pick out tourists, both by their look and by their dress—I saw none. And heard nothing but French from one end of the restaurant to the other.

"Yes," Austryn said, "I mean right here." He lowered his voice almost to a whisper. "You see those two chaps over there?" Austryn, I had noted, used Anglicisms—more often than Alex or Christopher, actually—but somehow they didn't seem out of place. He nodded toward the far corner, directly behind me, where two men, quite young, were dining quietly with a stunning blonde. Shifting my chair, I saw whom he meant. They had completely eluded my earlier sweep. One point for master counterspy Wainhouse. "They're both CIA," he declared.

"Come off it, mon," Trocchi said, smiling a bit indulgently. "Why in Christ's name would the CIA be wasting its time in a low-down restaurant like this?"

"I assure you," paranoid Austryn continued, "they're CIA. You can't believe how many agents they have abroad these days. London. Paris. Rome. All over Germany. They don't trust any of these countries, especially France and Italy with their strong Communist parties. And, believe me, they do send people into just such places. To find out what the students are really thinking. And to see what people like ourselves—deserters, if you will—are fomenting."

I'm not sure how much of what struck me as a bad case of incipient paranoia anyone did buy that night or in the months and years to come. I certainly didn't. Nor did I feel inclined to look over my shoulder or lower my voice. But I was intrigued enough to feign a trip to the WC at the back of the restaurant, which enabled me to pass the table Austryn had pointed out.

"So," Austryn said, having divined the purpose of my trek, "am I right or not?"

"They *are* Americans," I admitted.

I—we—saw a look of triumph on Austryn's face.

"But that's all I can say. What their occupation or profession might be, I haven't a clue."

"You see, I can spot them a mile away."

However I tried to refute his claims in my mind, I found during the following weeks that I did take a closer look at my compatriots in public places, did try to overhear a snatch of conversation that would reveal the spy behind the mask.

America seemed like a distant memory. On my glorious graduation day back in Chapel Hill, I had begun to ask myself: What *do* you want to do with your life? I was aching to go out and see the world. France was a romantic notion, of course, and to some degree Hemingway and Fitzgerald were responsible, doubtless Henry Miller too, but more to the point, my former roommate at UNC, Jack Youngerman, was already there, extolling in letters Paris's many virtues. But two or three of my professors had urged me to teach, and I had paid three or four visits to Pomfret School in Connecticut, near where my parents lived. I had met some of the teachers and was much impressed by the headmaster, a tall, sturdy, patrician-looking man in his mid-forties with the equally patrician name Dexter Strong.

I was hired to teach English and Latin, but within weeks of my arrival the real Mr. Chips of the school, the oldest teacher at Pomfret and the long-time head of the math department, fell ill. Dexter Strong, poking through my college records, noted that I had taken a number of math courses. Indeed I had, for at one point, urged by my father to learn something practical, I had briefly considered becoming an engineer. Plus the navy's V-12 program—of that, more later—had required me to take some math courses as well. And so I began my career as a professor of mathematics, may all the poor children to whom I was bequeathed forgive me. I worked out a method whereby I stayed at least half a dozen pages in the assigned textbook ahead of the students, and for the better part of the first semester that worked reasonably well. But I knew I was skating on thin ice. The smartest kid by far in the class was the son of the dean of Barnard College in New York, a slight blue-eyed young man of fair skin and fairer hair who looked as though no ray of sunlight had ever touched him. He wasn't a bad lad; he was simply too smart for his own good, certainly for the likes of me, and clearly math was his favorite subject. One day he asked a question that stumped me completely. I cleared my throat and murmured that I wasn't inclined to deviate from the morning's assignment but would happily talk to him later. Fortunately, I had other classes scheduled, so I could not see him till after lunch, which gave me time to repair to my room and look up the answer—thirty or forty pages beyond the math I had mastered till then. During my afternoon meeting with the cherub, I pontificated as I cleared up the question, but in my heart I knew the jig was up: Christopher— for that was my diminutive nemesis's name—Christopher the Christ-bearing boy, had somehow figured out my strategy of staying just ahead of my wards, so he had diabolically made the great leap forward to a place in the book he guessed I would not have reached. I had no choice: over the next few days—and nights—I moved far ahead of the little bastard, in fact studied page after page, equation after equation, till I reached the end of the hated tome.

Through the end of the semester, whenever Christopher artfully tried to trip me up, I parried his thrusts with all the aplomb of a dashing musketeer. Take that, you rogue! And that! Slash and slash again, until the lad's white shirt was in shreds and my épée at his throat. But he knew, and I knew, that this was a battle to the bitter end. I won, of course; teachers almost always do in such situations. But I had come to the conclusion by semester's end that the kid hated me almost as much as I hated him. Thus I was completely taken aback when, at term break, he insisted on introducing me to his famous mother. Dean McIntosh was a handsome woman in her early forties, dressed in a no-nonsense black knee-length skirt and a dark cardigan over a starched white blouse, her sturdy low-heeled shoes those of an English schoolmarm, her dark hair close-cropped. Yet her eyes, dark blue behind her horn-rimmed glasses, revealed a woman not only of substance but of great good humor. And her self-imposed austerity was relieved by the generous, Elizabethan ruffle at the neck of her white blouse. Her son looked nothing like her, and I assumed from the kid's alabastrine skin that the father had to be an albino, until I saw Dad's picture on young McIntosh's dormitory desk: as dark as his mother.

"Christopher tells me this is your first year here." The dean smiled sweetly. "How are you enjoying teaching?"

Aside from your smart-ass, contemptible, malicious little offspring, just fine and dandy.

"Challenging," I said. "The boys here are in the main very bright. And the curriculum is far more demanding than where I went to high school."

"And where was that?"

"Northeastern Pennsylvania. Near Wilkes-Barre," I said. "Coal-mining country. Tough people. Tough area." I think I was trying not to impress her but to tell her that I grew up anthracitic. Much heat and little smoke. Not like the soft-coal mines. I sensed she was not impressed.

"I'm sure you'll do fine." She smiled graciously and, I felt in my paranoiac mood, a trifle condescendingly. I wondered for a moment whether young Pasty Face had let her in on his little game of Torturing Teacher? I suspected not. I was pretty sure Her Deanship would not have approved.

It was stifling hot in this refectory where tea and scones were being served, and Dean McIntosh suddenly unbuttoned her cardigan and slipped it off, revealing beneath that pristine blouse a bosom of amazing form and beauty.

"You have," I stammered, "a son of amazing form and beauty!"

"I beg your pardon?"

"I said, you have a son whose mind is beautifully formed."

"Thank you," she said, still eyeing me strangely.

And may his dainty shoes be cast in concrete.

That winter I persuaded Dexter and Manny Mansfield, the football coach with whom I had become good friends, to let me start a wrestling team at Pomfret. Much to our collective surprise, in December after the last football game, a dozen and a half young men from thirteen to eighteen showed up for tryouts. "Tryouts" was hardly the proper term, for with eleven weight classes to fill, virtually everyone was assured a spot on the team.

Their number was the good news; their physical attributes gave me pause. Why had I argued for such a folly? I warned my new charges that wrestling was as demanding physically as any sport. "It takes guts and stamina," I told them. "I'm going to punish you guys till you wish you'd never met me. Because if I don't," I said, "the first time you get out on that mat in competition you'll find yourself flat on your back so fast you won't know what happened. And that, if you have any pride, will humiliate you like nothing you've ever experienced. Unlike team sports, in wrestling you're on your own: nobody to blame but yourself if you lose. So, anybody want to bail out, now's the time." I gave them ample time to back out, gazing from one lump of pasty white to the other. They stared back at me, unblinking. I was impressed, but thought: I'll bet in a week or two, half of them will be back in their dorms, licking their mat burns. Wrong. Of the eighteen who showed up that first day, sixteen stuck it out. None had any experience wrestling. I had less than four weeks to teach them the rudiments of the grand old Greek sport, at least the variety practiced in America. I worked them hard. First a half hour of tough conditioning, for wrestling is nine minutes of grueling, unforgiving exercise, in which every muscle is stretched to the breaking point, and victory often goes to the best prepared. Then the basic moves: taking down the opponent, keeping on top, escaping from underneath, riding, riding, always aggressive, wearing him down, always thinking and moving toward the goal, a pin. My charges kept at it; they learned. Clumsily, but they did improve. They practiced on each other, even though we did not have a full lineup of equal weights, and they practiced on me.

This experience—coaching wrestling—also taught me a quick lesson, which I retained for life: beware of initial judgments. I had clearly misjudged these youngsters. I, who had always gone to public schools, had arrived at Pomfret impressed by its teaching staff and methods, its gracious leafy grounds, its ivy-covered brick walls, but with a built-in prejudice about my charges, about the student body in general. Virtually all came from money; many also came from broken homes, and sending them to boarding school was their parents' way both of assuaging their own guilt and of paying others to bring up their kids. Parents' day in the fall was often painful: in most cases only one parent would show up, usually dressed to the nines, sometimes chauffeured, looking awkward as they walked or talked with their sons, nervously glancing at their watches to see how long this semblance of intimacy had to run. In those instances, the pain in the kids' eyes was also palpable. In the small towns where I grew up, divorce was rare, so this landscape of children from broken homes was a new phenomenon for me. While from the start I pitied these kids, at the same time I also categorized them as the spoiled rich and assumed they were incapable of toughing it out, whatever "it" might be. Within four weeks, the "it" of wrestling had proved me wrong.

While the school had allowed me to start the wrestling program, it had no money for us to buy wrestling togs. I worried about the psychological effect when we arrived for our first match wearing presumably clean but mismatched sweats versus our opponents' slick jackets and tights, all identical, bearing the name and logo of the school. For a moment I considered buying the tights myself but scotched that when I heard the price: more than two weeks' worth of my lordly eight-thousand-dollar annual salary. Wendell, to whom I took my case, was sympathetic but said there was nothing he could do. Maybe next year.

Our first formal match wasn't till late January, but Manny had arranged with a prep school, which we'll call C——, to meet us in a preseason informal scrimmage a week or so after the Christmas break. Real rules, a referee, normal scoring, but not to count on C——'s record. At the last workout I called the boys together and gave them a short speech about image.

"Tomorrow, when we arrive at C——," I said, "you're going to find your opponents all dolled up in old-school jackets and smart-looking wrestling tights. You may look at yourselves and feel embarrassed. Don't. Think of yourselves as ragtags and bobtails; think of yourselves as revolutionaries going up against the British in '76. And you remember how those New England battles turned out."

A couple of snickers, three or four guffaws, and several smiles.

"The point is, clothes may make the man, but not here. If you're the better wrestler, or are in better shape, chances are you'll take your opponent, no matter what he's wearing. They're not considering this a regular match, since when I called, their season was all booked, but I talked them into wrestling us 'unofficially.' In their minds this is a tune-up. But in yours this is a real match."

As predicted, the C—— kids were dressed fit to kill: smart blue jackets with the school name emblazoned on the front and, on the back, each wrestler's name in bold white letters. When they saw us saunter in, no two Pomfret wrestlers looking alike, there was an audible and predictable undertow of disdain. Some frowned at their coach, as if to say, "Why don't you get us a *real* match?" A few muffled and deprecatory murmurs. "Jerks" was one of the words I picked up. "Hicks" was another. For a moment my heart sank, not because of how we looked, but because, glancing at the C—— lineup, their kids looked so goddamn fit and ready. Eyes steely, muscles bulging. Suddenly I feared a wipeout.

We lost the first two matches by decisions, 6–4 and 5–3, both close enough to bring a frown to the local coach's face. Then in the next two weights—112 and 121—both our kids not only won but pinned their opponents. Our 112 was a pure stroke of luck: the C—— kid, ahead on points 11–2, tripped and fell backward, at which point our kid leaped on him like a leopard closing on his prey. But at 121, Jay Long, a deadly serious ninth grader who worked harder at conditioning than anyone on the squad and was both swift and smart, took charge from the start and first harried his opponent across the mat as if he were driving a sled, then jerked up his legs, turned him 180 degrees, caught him in a neat cradle, and pinned him on the spot, giving us a momentary but exhilarating 10–6 lead. (In American wrestling, a pin scores five points, a decision three.)

Across the gym, the C—— coach was sitting chin in hand, clearly not happy. Here we were down to the last match with lowly Pomfret still in contention! We won, 23–22! I shook my head in disbelief, hugging each of my drenched youngsters in turn. They were whooping and hollering as if we had won an Olympic gold medal, which in a way we—no, they—had.

I walked across the gym to the C—— coach, who, though in shock, had the good grace to smile and say, "Some tune-up! How long ago did you say you started your program?" I laughed and swore that it was less than six weeks old. He shook his head. "Well, you've got some gifted youngsters there—or should I say a gifted coach?"

"Beginner's luck," I said, watching as the respective teams paraded past each other.

"Coach?" Jay asked.

Of all the epithets with which I've been saddled in the course of my life, I must confess that "Coach" is perhaps my favorite.

The bus trip home was boisterous. General elation had taken over the team. And I too was sharing the joy. I was even beginning to wonder whether I shouldn't stay a bit longer as coach of this fledging team. As we were approaching Pomfret, I felt it important to remind the boys that the fact that they had won today didn't ensure their success in future matches.

"I'd like to tell you and the team that conditioning is all-important in any sport, especially in wrestling. I've heard you guys griping at all the tough training I put you through before the Christmas holidays, and I'm sure you told your parents how this new coach named Seaver tortured you unmercifully—"

"My dad said, 'More power to you,'" Billy piped up. I took grateful note.

"Today you saw it pay off. You think: a wrestling match is only nine minutes, compared with, say, a two- or three-hour football game. True. But in those nine minutes you put your body to its toughest test. Every muscle and fiber of your being is stretched to the core. Take Jimmy, for example: your opponent is a better wrestler than you—sorry—but last week he must have cheated; he goofed off, thinking we were a bunch of patsies. And in that third period he ran out of gas, whereas Jimmy's hard work paid off."

The bus swung into the school grounds, past the stone pillars heading down to the refectory just in time for dinner. The Six Stalwarts, who had been oddly silent in the back, unfurled a hastily made banner that said:

Pomfret 23
C—— 22!

What pleased me most was that the Pomfret squad, over a period of three short months, had coalesced into a tough-minded, high-spirited, unified team, each caring about the other. After the last meet, I called them together in the gym and told them how proud I was to be their coach and that I was convinced wrestling had made them stronger and more prepared for whatever they would end up doing in life.

I had applied for an American Field Service fellowship to France, a long shot.

The letter finally arrived, bearing the return address of the American

Field Service Foundation, in glowing red. The AFS had been set up during World War I, before America entered the war, to recruit and send overseas young men to drive ambulances and serve as noncombatant medics, officially part of the French army. Ernest Hemingway was one of the recruits, as was the poet e. e. cummings, as was my father. After the war, a group of French and American veterans established the American Field Service Foundation, whose goal was to further cement relations between the two countries. Each year it awarded four fellowships, two Americans to France, two Frenchmen to America. I had applied, and though I was not holding my breath, I had continued to hope, and ratcheted up my crash course in spoken French throughout the school year.

I opened the envelope with hands that actually trembled. Yes, the answer was, goddamn it, yes! I was going to France, a year's study guaranteed. I felt a surge of pure pleasure, followed quickly by a feeling of guilt. All these boys I had come to know, many of whom I considered friends (more so, I must confess, than my fellow teachers, all of whom were at least ten or fifteen years my senior), I would now be forsaking. And there was Manny. He truly saw me as his replacement. And then the wrestling team I had started: What would become of it? "Don't ever start things you can't finish"—my father's dictum, one of many. Maybe I should give this fellowship a second thought. I decided to sleep on it.

Hell, yes. By mid-afternoon I had decided: there was no way I was going to pass up that year in France. If I didn't like it, if it didn't work out, I could always come back. Or could I?

Dexter was magnanimous. "I knew you'd go if accepted," he said. "My only hope was you wouldn't win. But you should know that if after a year you'd like to come back, there's a place here for you."

Manny was another matter. He knew where to hit all the right buttons. "What'll happen to your wrestling team?" he probed. "Probably down the tube without you."

"Hire a teacher who's been a college wrestler," I said. "There have to be dozens out there."

"Not as easy as you think," he said, "though I can plant that idea in Dexter's mind."

And then it was commencement, a grand ceremony in the handsome stone church, whose stained-glass windows were the envy of the region. Senior boys, resplendent in their black robes and caps, the latter of which, when the ceremony was over and the boys outdoors in the (at last) golden spring, spiraled skyward, five-and-twenty blackbirds settling swiftly back to earth. A couple dozen parents thanked me for teaching their boys well, with a special thanks from several fathers who had seen their sons flourish through wrestling. Even the dean of Hunter complimented me on the strides her lad had made not only in math but in Latin.

"My son is upset you'll not be returning next fall." She smiled, taking my hand in her firm grip.

When I had started the wrestling team and was in dire need of a ninety-five-pounder, I had suggested he give it a try. He smiled and said wrestling was not for him. "If you had lived in ancient Greece or Rome," I tried (for he was my best Latin student and flourished in the course), "I'll bet you would have been flattered even to be asked."

"Ah, but I don't," he responded, "do I?"

Most of his responses, I had noted through the year, ended in questions, in effect forcing the ball back into my court. Still, he finally agreed (the Latin allusion apparently having worked) to come to the gym at least to be weighed. But when he stripped to the waist and stepped on the scales, I knew mine was a lost cause. Eighty-two and a half pounds, and not a muscle, not a hint of a muscle, anywhere in sight. I thanked him for coming, suggested he might make an effort to put a bit more meat on his bones, and excused him. "I told you," he said primly, "didn't I?" The kid was a royal pain in the ass, and yet somehow I had a soft spot for him. I had always thought, despite his tender years, he sat in judgment on me, saw me as an unsophisticated boor uninterested in the finer things of life such as music and poetry (both of which did indeed interest me), but now, from what his mother had just said, I was apparently wrong.

"It will only be a year," I noted.

"Paris is very seductive," she said quietly, but as if she knew well whereof she murmured. "Once you've tasted it, I fear Pomfret will seem very pale and rustic.

"Good luck in France," she said, finally (to my regret) releasing my hand, and headed over toward the headmaster, around whom a dozen parents were clustered.

I pictured Paris, whose sites and sounds I had explored vicariously untold times over the last few weeks, and all doubt was erased.

Besides, I reminded myself, you can go home again.

10 ✌

To Paris, by *Tiger*, by Foot, by Bus, by Bicycle

TO MAKE IT TO FRANCE, I had agreed to join the summer work program in Le Chambon-sur-Lignon and was ostensibly to monitor and oversee three work campers, whom I met for the first time at the Collège Cévenol American headquarters on East Twenty-ninth Street. One student was a senior at Harvard, the other, Princeton, and the third, a girl, a junior at Smith.

Our ship was a three-year-old, ten-thousand-ton, broad-beamed product of the Kaiser Shipyards in Vancouver, Washington, the USS *Tiger*, one of several hundred such vessels, labeled C-50s and C-60s, built starting in 1942 for cargo and troop transport and rushed into service. The *Tiger*, one of the last of the breed, was commissioned in 1945 and saw only limited wartime service transporting some nine hundred men to the Pacific and then, after Japan surrendered, carrying the forces of occupation from San Francisco to the Far East. Now, as Europe was once again open to travel, it had joined the youth movement, bearing American students eastbound and displaced persons to the States on the way back. A worthy endeavor both ways, for most of the students were part of one group or another—SPAN (the Student Project for Amity Among Nations), American Friends Service Committee, American Youth Hostels, Experiment in International Living, Institute of International Education—whose goal was to help rebuild the still-ravaged Europe, foster international relations, take part in conferences, or broaden horizons. A quick check indicated that roughly three-quarters of those on board were affiliated with some organization. We were six hundred in all, which made the ship seem incredibly crowded, and I could only imagine what it must have been like with another three hundred during wartime. We had been warned ahead of time that as berths we would have hammocks, not beds, which was fine with me but a cause for grumbling among some. There were two below-deck sections, one for women, one for men, and the heads—naval parlance for toilets—were in both instances military latrines. I had to laugh wondering how the women would deal with the urinals, but cope they surely would, to judge by Tish, who, even on shipboard, dressed in halter and shorts and stout hiking shoes as if she were ready to scale the nearest mountain as soon as we landed.

Built more like a tortoise than a hare, the *Tiger* could make seventeen knots on smooth seas but was far more comfortable at twelve or thirteen, so that we averaged barely three hundred nautical miles per day. We were scheduled to make Cherbourg in eleven days, calling at Plymouth just before. Our progress was steady when the seas were glass, which, thank God, they mostly were. But when on two occasions the winds were up enough to raise and churn the waves, our gallant *Tiger* groaned, wallowed, pitched, and rolled. Some of the passengers were seasick some of the time, many were sick most of the time, and a few seemed affected not at all. Tish took everything in stride, packing in breakfast, lunch, and dinner without missing a beat. I was queasy two or three times but never sick. But Harvard and Princeton were miserable day and night. The problem was the ship's motion was far worse topside than in the ship's bowels, where the hammocks were stretched. But down below, the stench was virtually unbearable, no matter how hard the sturdy crew tried to mop and clean.

After the first difficult day—day four, as I recall—when hammocks turned into stretchers and the youthful above-deck exuberance that had marked our first three days out suddenly disappeared, I had, after a brief trip below to make sure my male charges were still alive, decided to abandon those foul depths for the rest of the voyage.

I had done my senior English thesis at UNC on Hemingway, and like Robert Jordan in *For Whom the Bell Tolls* I kept waiting for the earth to move. But how could it, when beneath us the sea was constantly stirring, if not roiling? Perhaps in the instance I should have looked for the earth to stand still.

Also on board was another Hemingway, Patrick by name, a gangly youngster of about nineteen with whom I struck up a conversation our second day out. An art history major, he was on his way to visit French and Italian museums and to hook up with his brother, who was in Rome. He was interested to hear about the Chambon work camp, and I saw his eyes light up when I told him after Le Chambon I'd be in Paris on an American Field Service fellowship. "My father was in the AFS during World War I," he said, "on the Italian front," and suddenly I realized that this pleasant, unassuming young man was Ernest's son. If the heavy legacy of his famous father affected him in any way, it was nowhere apparent. Did he have literary aspirations of his own? I asked, and he laughed, almost wickedly, and said, with an emphatic shake of his head: "Absolutely none." Math was a favorite subject, and when I told him about my mathematics mano a mano with young McIntosh, he roared. "I probably would have throttled him," he offered, but the gentle look in his eyes suggested he was incapable of throttling anyone. I had always pictured bigger-than-life Papa with a constant swagger, but with Patrick there was none. Shy, diffident, he seemed to want the world to know he was not using Papa's name to clear him a patch in life. Only when he talked about painting and art did he become passionate, and I wondered aloud whether he might end up the curator of a major museum. He pooh-poohed the idea. Something far more exciting than that, he said, though exactly what he wasn't sure. Maybe Africa, a possibility he owed to his father.

I finally had to confess that I had done my senior thesis on his father. "Do you have a copy with you?" he asked. "I'd love to read it."

I did, though I cautioned him that this was an undergraduate work with few pretensions. "It did, however, force me to reread all of his work, from the Nick Adams stories onward."

"They're great, aren't they?" Patrick said.

"The best," I agreed. "But you'll see from my essay that I'm a pretty big fan."

After reading the piece, which I had called "Ernest Hemingway: The Good Inner Feeling"—the subtitle taken from his definition "what is moral is what you feel good after"—Pat handed it back to me and said he thought it a damn good job, though he disagreed with my assessment of *For Whom the Bell Tolls*, my least favorite of the opus. "You should send it to my father," he said. "I'm sure he'd like it."

Pat gave me Papa's address in Cuba, with the request I not give it out in turn. I promised I wouldn't. Back in Paris in the fall, I reread what I'd written, found I liked it far less than I remembered, and never sent it on. I probably should have, for at one-and-twenty I had a boundless, probably excessive, admiration for the man and his razor-lean prose, but I have always found communication with famous people difficult. My problem. Oddly, several years later, when my new Paris friend George Plimpton, another Papa fan, read a shortened version of the piece in Sindbad Vail's *Points*, his first reaction was "You should send this to Papa." Later, George interviewed Hemingway for *The Paris Review,* and the two became friends. In another life, I'll put such reluctance behind me and steam boldly forward, as George did instinctively, as if it were his birthright—which it doubtless was.

At dawn on the eleventh day, virtually all of us were topside as we approached the shores of France. Gentle hills of green rose up to touch the lowering clouds, inviting undulations were speckled with black-and-white dots that, as we drew nearer, became herds of cattle. Onshore, despite the early hour, there were already hundreds of blue-clad longshoremen loading and unloading the dozen ships tied up there. A tug eased us into the dock, and we quickly disembarked and headed for the customs shed.

My plan was to walk. Wherever I went, through field and forest, village and town, vestiges of the war remained. Burned trees stood stark and lonely in farmers' fields, in which burgeoning stalks of wheat and corn now rose, peaceful and uncaring. Whole apple orchards, of which there were many, were scorched, and yet on the far side of the road others might stand unscathed. Stone walls were pocked in places, totally decimated in others, the debris scattered for hundreds of yards. I could almost hear the sharp rattle of the machine guns, the howitzer's roar, the scream of the bullets back and forth, one side inching forward, the other retreating, slowly but surely. I had read and seen newsreels of those first chaotic days and weeks, units dispersed or lost, paratroopers landing in the flooded marshes, tanks creaking forward without clear knowledge of their destined goal.

What had made me take this lonely trek? To atone for my absence here on D-day? I had been twelve when the war started, fourteen at Pearl Harbor, eighteen when it ended. More than once I overheard my mother say to Father how deeply happy she was that I was too young to be caught up in this new war.

At seventeen, I announced I was joining the navy. Mother protested that I was too young, that I should wait at least until I was eighteen. Father said, "Let the boy do what he wants," which ended that conversation, and on April 22 of my senior year I went down to the local navy recruiting station and filled out the enlistment forms. I graduated on June 10 and three weeks later, on July 1, was inducted in Philadelphia, one of seventy or eighty youngsters swelling the navy's ranks that Pennsylvania day, and immediately dispatched to boot camp. Apparently on the basis of my score on the navy exams I had taken in April, I was sent into an officers' training program called V-12 (I never learned what either the *V* or the 12 stood for) in the South, first to the University of South Carolina in Columbia, an institution that clearly had seen better days, with its crumbling walls and peeling paint, offset by the Southern welcome the townspeople offered the thousand young sailors stationed there. Then, six months later, for no apparent reason, orders arrived sending me and a couple dozen others to the even deeper South: Howard College, a tiny Baptist institution in Birmingham, Alabama, so desperate to survive in these lean wartime years, when most of its former student population was now in uniform, that it had accepted the navy's takeover of its premises without even inquiring whether any of these blue-suited young men who now roamed the campus were Baptists. Two semesters later I was shipped off again, this time to what, upon arrival, struck me as paradise: the University of North Carolina at Chapel Hill. The piney woods, the congenial surroundings, the first-rate teachers, the lofty oaks that lined the streets of the prim, neat town, whose every store and business was focused on serving the campus population— all combined to make me feel immediately at home. The war was winding down, but UNC was still very much dominated by the military. Even at war's end, in the summer of 1945, thousands of cadets still filled the dormitories and classrooms as the powers that be in Washington pondered how many of these rising officers would be needed to keep the peace and police the brave new world. But with the fall semester, a group of men and women who had fought the war began returning, under the auspices of a brilliant program that enabled young veterans to avail themselves of a college education, the GI Bill.

Finally, in the spring of 1946, the military decided most of us could be released, and I was discharged in July. Though I was only two years out of high school, I had been on the accelerated navy program and, again a civilian, was in my college senior year. In short, though I had worn the uniform for two years, I had really missed the war.

Now, in Normandy, embarking on this voluntary hike, was I trying to make amends for being a year or two too young? None of my high school classmates had died, though some had seen battle, but two classes above me, in my sister Joan's class, there had been several wounded and one dead. Did I owe a debt to those who were not so lucky, who simply by their birth date, a grain of sand in time more than mine, paid the ultimate price, whereas here I was, walking sublimely in the gentle sunlight through the fields and farms where they had fought and died only cosmic seconds before?

That evening, my fourth in Normandy, clouds began to gather, growling on the western horizon, and I knew I was in for a wet night. Should I find an inn? Ask a peasant for shelter in his barn? Lightning, followed by thunder no more than thirty seconds away, convinced me that refuge was the better part of valor. I strode to the nearest farmhouse, a neat dwelling with a storybook thatched roof, and rapped on the door. Shuffle, shuffle from within. The latch came unbolted, the door squeaked open, and a wizened old man appraised me up and down.

"*Soldat?*" he said. A soldier? I was wearing khaki army-surplus clothes. I shook my head. "*Étudiant.*" A student. I thought I saw a look of disdain flit across his face, but in fact he was inscrutable. "*Il semble vouloir pleuvoir,*" I ventured, poetic without intent, for I later learned that what I had said was, in essence: "It seems rain would like to come." And for good measure, glancing backward at the fast-darkening sky, "*Tonnerre,*" I said. "*Éclair.*" Thunder. Lightning.

He laughed. "*Anglais?*"

"*Non, Américain.*"

"Ah!" his head arched back, and his mouth opened wide to reveal an almost toothless interior: only two upper teeth, one left, one right, premolars, I believe they're called. I had no idea whether this was a good sign or bad. "*Entrez,*" he said. "*Entrez!*" And, half turning, he shouted over his shoulder, "*Marie, viens, on a un visiteur.*" Marie, do come, we have a visitor. Thus it was, by a roll of the dice, I spent my fourth night in France, my first as a guest, at the home of the Massans, Marie and Jean-Luc.

I asked for use of the barn; they insisted I sleep in the big double bed in the room next to theirs. I said that I had my rations for food; they insisted I share their frugal dinner. That night I learned the French definition of "frugal." We began with a hearty French vegetable soup, followed by a rabbit stew and small potatoes cooked crisp, then a green salad such as I— in America used to a thing called iceberg lettuce—had never tasted. The dressing, a subtle mixture of oil and vinegar spiced with finely cut garlic, was also a revelation. And for dessert an apple tart—for this, I learned, was a region of apples, which were transformed into hundreds of dishes and liqueurs. All this washed down by a bottle of local red wine. By my later standards, it was doubtless *ordinaire, un gros rouge,* but for me then, for whom the taste of wine had been limited to the chalice at Communion, and that years ago, it was a giddy experience. Later, my host insisted I taste some Calvados, the local apple brandy.

During dinner, most of the talk was of the war, in which Jean-Luc and Marie had lost their younger son Pierre, a few scant months before the end of the occupation. He had been in the Maquis, the Resistance movement, not here in Normandy, no, but down in the Cévennes in central France, where he and several of his comrades had gone to join the Resistance. Seven boys, all friends. Caught by the *Boches.* Shot by the *Boches.* Cold-blooded bastards! They knew the war was lost. Why did these boys have to go gallivanting so far from home? War is terrible, terrible, nothing good has ever come of it, and nothing ever will. Death. Death and destruction, that's all. And in a few years nobody will remember what it was all about. Just you wait and see.

On the far side of the table, Marie was knitting fiercely, but I could see that she was both angry and fighting back tears. Angry at her husband for talking so much to this unknown American, tearful at the resurgent memory of their irretrievably lost son.

He was only eighteen when he died, Jean-Luc was going on.

"*Père,*" Marie said softly, not looking up, "you go on too long. These are things our visitor can't know about or understand."

It was true that I was getting only part of the thread, the monologue provoked by my presence, my army fatigues, this American who reminded them of the countless others who had pushed on through these parts only four years before, but I did get the gist, and understood about their son.

"Yes," I said, "war *is* terrible. But weren't we all—French and Americans and British—fighting because we had to, because Hitler was a madman who had to be crushed, *écrasé, éliminé.*" I knew my grammar was far from perfect, but hoped the point I was trying to make got through.

Jean-Luc shook his head. "War," he insisted, "has no justification. None! Only people who have never gone through it can think otherwise!"

Over our glass of Calvados—that the Massans had made themselves— I asked naively if the manufacture of alcohol in France was government controlled. Jean-Luc gave me a look halfway between disgust and disdain. "In principle, yes," he responded, "but we do not too often follow what the government tells us to do. Especially in such matters. We make our own not for sale to others but for our own use. No one can argue that."

It was no tiny tasting glass he offered but a good eight ounces in a thick water glass filled to the brim. It was slightly harsh to my untutored palate but immediately warming when it hit the belly. The problem was, fifteen minutes later, with barely half the glass downed, the weathered wooden beams, the already-uneven stones of the tall kitchen fireplace, the windows themselves began slowly to revolve in a clockwise direction. Or was it counterclockwise? Try as I might, I couldn't get the damn room to stop. By dint of will I forced it to slow, but then it would speed up again at every sip. For God's sake, Seaver, don't get sick. Please, dignity before all. The pride of a nation is riding on your formerly teetotaler shoulders. How would Hemingway have handled it? I wondered. Tossed the first glass off, doubtless asked for another, then donned a pair of gloves and gone six rounds with the farmer's six-foot son.

Somehow I made it upstairs, knapsack and all, having thanked my hosts with a profusion of French I did not know I possessed, some of which they seemed to understand, and slept so soundly that Marie had to tap discreetly on my door at eight o'clock—late for them—and announce that coffee was ready.

I said I would be taking a bus to Caen, and they offered to take me to the nearest stop, a couple of kilometers away, but I knew that under normal circumstances Jean-Luc would already have been in the fields a good two hours before, so I politely declined. Although we had known each other less than twelve hours, they insisted on sending me on my way with more ham and cheese, a fresh baguette, and a half liter of Calvados, which, they said, they were delighted to learn I had enjoyed. They also insisted on kissing me on both cheeks, Jean-Luc's two- or three-day bristles grating me like Gallic sandpaper. They carefully noted down my name, my address in the Cévennes, where I had promised to go see the family who had sequestered their son in 1944, and made me promise to return in the fall when I was back in Paris.

At the road, I turned and waved goodbye. My last image was of them standing there stock-still, looking for all the world like a version of *The Gleaners*. Only the pitchfork was missing.

Just before eleven the bus swayed into sight, packed to the gills both inside and out, for the roof was filled with a disarray of crates and baggage, none too stoutly tied, that shifted and jostled with every bump in the road, of which there were many. The heavy rains of the night before had created dangerous patches of the road, so this top-heavy monstrosity bearing down upon me looked far more drunken than Rimbaud's boat. Surely it would be better to walk than risk death aboard this rattletrap farting its way toward me. Even in my blissful ignorance of French vehicles, it had to date from World War I.

I half turned to walk away, but the driver, who had caught sight of me standing on the roadside, would have none of it. He bent low over the wheel—the better to pull on the emergency brake, I presumed, which, if logic prevailed, led me to deduce that the foot brake was inoperative—and the bus ground to a halt barely a foot in front of me. The door creaked open, and the driver motioned me aboard. I shook my head. "*Merci! Marcher. Préfère marcher!*" Thanks, but I think I'll walk.

"Ah," the driver turned back to his packed house and roared: "*Un Américain! Nous avons un Américain!*" We have an American! How could he tell? At worst, I'd been told, I might be taken for a Burgundian. Standing there hopelessly, I felt like a fish that had just been hooked, with the driver irresistibly reeling me in. "Reeling" was doubtless the operative word, given the previous night's alcoholic intake, and my resistance was low, very low. So in I went, slinging my knapsack off my shoulder. Not only was there no empty seat, but the aisle was filled as well, with men, women, children, and several crates of clucking chickens.

"*Pas de place,*" I said with a shrug. No room. But the driver only smiled, motioned me toward the rear, slammed the thing in gear, and rocketed away, sending me sprawling into the arms of a well-endowed young lady, who reacted to the incident not with horror or distress—which one might expect back home—but with great good humor. I excused myself and struggled to my feet. She shook her head, as if to say she hadn't minded a bit, straightened her slightly rumpled blouse, and lowered her eyes. I was upright again but hanging on for dear life as the driver, who seemed to revel in the contest between him and the road, barreled forward into the blinding sun.

Somewhere in the middle of the bus a strapping lad stood up and motioned for me to take his place. I shook my head. He insisted. "*Pour l'Américain,*" he said. "*Pour vous.*" Both palms thrust outward, I shrugged and, hopefully, for my Calvados-influenced fluency had suddenly vanished into the far recesses of my brain, reiterated my polite refusal. Suddenly the whole bus chorused, "*Pour l'Américain, pour l'Américain!*" leaving me little choice but to make my way cautiously down the crowded aisle and take the seat, bowing to the young man as I did. The whole bus applauded. I felt the fish was now in the net. Where next? The frying pan?

They—I refer to the bus collectively, for several took turns asking questions—wanted to know, first, why was I wearing this army uniform, was I a soldier left over from the war? What was I doing on this local bus, on which no American had, to the best of their knowledge, ever set foot? Did I like Normandy? Had I tasted the local Calvados? I nodded vigorously, pointing to my temples and turning both forefingers in quick circles. Good for a collective laugh. They wanted to let me know, again collectively, how much they loved Americans, how grateful they were for the Normandy landing, how sad they were to know how many had died in these fields and marshes (for the Germans, shortly before D-day, had flooded many of the fields so that the parachute troops, primed to land on terra firma, had often landed in treacherous waters, with little chance to escape). I, who had contributed nothing to their salvation, was nonetheless basking in the glow of their praise for what my older compatriots had done.

"Only in the air did we have a problem with the Americans," growled one grizzled farmer, a crate of chickens athwart his knees. "The British were far braver than the Americans. I speak not of the infantry, for I saw many instances of extreme bravery with your fighting soldiers, but of the air force. The British pilots flew in daytime and always came in low, much more dangerous to them, but they focused on their targets and rarely missed. The Americans came at night, they flew high, well beyond the Germans' antiaircraft range, and when they dropped their bombs, sometimes they hit their targets and sometimes not. On more than one occasion they hit schools, even hospitals. There was no need for that."

"You can't blame them for playing it safe!" another male voice from the rear objected.

"You can when it costs the lives of women and children," someone else countered.

"That doesn't mean we're not grateful," the chicken-laden farmer added. "We are, and always will be. God knows how long the Germans would have been here if you Americans hadn't joined the war."

"*Les Allemands sont tous des salauds! Des connards!*" an adolescent voice piped up from somewhere up front. All Germans are bastards: that I could get. But *connards*? "Jerks" was my immediate guess, but later I learned the condemnation was tougher, something like, "Germans are assholes."

"May they all burn in hell!"

"If I ever see another German, I swear I'll shoot him on the spot."

"Well, thank God, Germany's finished for the next hundred years."

"That's what we thought thirty years ago, and look what happened."

"No, this time they finally got what they deserved."

Back home, there was certainly a feeling that, thank God, Germany was defeated, now we could get on with our lives, but little of this personal animosity, this deep-rooted, visceral hatred. And suddenly I understood, if I had not before, the difference between a people who had been at war, a distant war, and those who had suffered physical occupation, who had had to deal day in and day out for four endless years with the reality of an enemy who could knock on your door at any hour, order you out of your home, and cart you away, or shoot you on sight, maybe your children too. One hell of a difference!

At the Caen train station, where the bus made a special stop for me before proceeding to its final destination in the center of town, it took me a good five minutes to make my way down the chaotic aisle to the open door, as I was obliged to shake hands with virtually everyone. As the bus pulled out, still wheezing, a dozen undulating hands and arms poked through the open windows, waving goodbye and wishing me a *bon séjour* in France. I was moved. Before I left America, many people had warned me that the French were a very private people, generally wary of foreigners, and might strike one as cold. Cold? During these first days I had found more immediate warmth than I had ever known. This raucous busload, Jean-Luc and Marie, even the baker and the grocer had gone out of their way to welcome me. Less than a week? I had a feeling I had already been here for months!

High on the Cévennes plateau sat the Collège Cévenol, a school of three hundred students, many from Protestant families throughout France, but with more than a symbolic number of foreigners of varying religions or none at all. "Ecumenical," a term with which I was till then only vaguely familiar, applied. In those early postwar days similar work camps abounded in Europe, as low-cost, high-principled means to rebuild the shattered core of that continent. Our main task that summer was to build, from the foundation up, Le Luquet, the future administration building.

My closest female friend that summer at Chambon was the head of the Collège Cévenol, Pastor Theis's eldest daughter, Jeanne, who did as hard a day's work as any of the men. Completely bilingual and bicultural, Jeanne was a graduate of Swarthmore and in the fall was heading back to the

States to teach French at Bryn Mawr, with the hope of becoming head of the French House there the following year. Her knowledge of contemporary French literature was impressive, and knowing my plans for the Sorbonne, she drew up a personal curriculum of what she thought should be my required reading: some sixty-five works in all—more if you counted Proust as multivolume, which it is. Looking at her list, drawn up in careful columns of blue ink, her handwriting tight and neat like her, I was already tired: Proust (all eighteen Gallimard volumes), Martin du Gard, Camus, Denis de Rougemont, Romain Rolland, Saint-Exupéry, Gide, Giraudoux (all fifteen plays!), Cocteau, Claudel, Valéry Larbaud, Bernanos, Mauriac, Duhamel . . . I'd read Proust in English, in what struck me then as the elegant Scott-Moncrieff translation (which later I came to distrust, for his liberties are too free and frequent, his self-imposed post-Victorian restrictions unacceptable), but I was not sure my French was up to reading him in the original. Jeanne assured me it was, adding that even if I didn't get it all—and many French didn't either—it would be well worth the effort. When I chided her for providing a list that would take me years to plow through and urged her to prioritize it for me, she chided me back for sounding like a lazy American. When I retorted that perhaps she would like me to draw up an essential list of English-language writers she should concentrate on in her new American teaching post, she assured me that even without knowing the particulars, she'd bet me a thousand francs she had read most. At which point I threw in the towel.

I kept her list, carefully folded, in my French-English dictionary, and over the following years in Paris I checked off those I had read, grading them from one to ten. As time went on, I marveled at the perspicacity and thoughtfulness of Jeanne's list, the number of eights and nines it scored, its only deficiency being that in drawing it up, she had doubtless relied too heavily on her Protestant background and failed to include the more radical, more revolutionary writers that, as time went on, I increasingly related to, like Sartre and Jean Genet.

And so it was, on a brilliantly clear day in late August—the twenty-third to be exact—after one last icy plunge in the rushing, crystal-liquid waters of the Lignon, the campers said goodbye to our hosts, Jean-Pierre and Claire, and all the Theises big and small, and boarded the narrow-gauge railway that was to take them down the mountain to St. Étienne and our connecting train to the City of Light. From Paris, most of the Americans were heading off to Cherbourg to catch the ship home. Apart from my friend George Booth and his fiancée, Joanne, I was the only one staying on, and the other campers' good-natured banter about our year abroad and the many dangers it entailed, especially in Paris (George and Joanne were headed to Geneva), scarcely concealed the smidgen of jealousy they felt.

So, on that sad day—sad because we had all bonded so deeply—the camp was suddenly empty, shorn of the energy and electricity that had infused it for weeks. Since I wasn't pressured to be back in Paris until late September, and Jeanne's ship to the States was more than three weeks away, I had suggested to her, almost offhandedly one day, that after the work camp we take a bike trip together. I fully expected her to decline on whatever pretext or say she'd have to check with her parents (as any proper American girl would have done), but she simply smiled and nodded. "Lovely idea. Where to?" "How about Italy?" I said. "If our legs hold out." "Mine will," she assured me, and giving them a fair perusal, I was sure they would. Very feminine but lithe and strong. "Don't forget," I countered, "I was a college wrestler. Strong legs an absolute necessity."

Three days post-camp, off we set, knapsacks and sleeping bags snugly strapped fore and aft. Down the Cévennes was a cinch, the only danger being that if the brakes of our 1930s Citroëns failed to hold up, one or the other (both?) might hurtle into the abyss. But we made it down in record time. In flat country now, we headed south, always opting for the small provincial roads, flanked by fields of wheat and corn, of truck gardens galore, of ripening vines and soaring sunflowers whose already-darkening faces drifted with the changing daylight. In villages we bought bread and cheese and ham and a pâté Jeanne informed me was called rillettes, made of pork and utterly delicious. There were virtually no cars on the road, but I knew this was but a brief respite: within a few short years, if not months, even these narrow, tree-lined bucolic roads would be chock-full of gleaming new Renaults and Citroëns hell-bent on heralding this new era called "postwar."

Our overly ambitious goal was Rome, but it was already the seventh day when we crossed over into Italy, and I realized we still had a good two-thirds of the trip ahead of us. I decided that I should remind my Protestant companion that even God had rested on this day, but Jeanne had a smile that always started slowly, then opened to full glorious measure. She shook her head. "We must press on. We're at least a day behind schedule."

It was then I learned we had a schedule. "Sixty kilometers," she said. "That shouldn't be too hard." And onto her bike she leaped, beckoning me to follow.

In Italy, we hugged the western coast, pedaling up mountains that seemed Alpine to me, though Jeanne assured me they were little more than hills. "Steep hills," I said. "The Cévennes are *steep* hills," she said. "These are *hills*." At night we camped out on rock-strewn shores, cooking over a makeshift fire, bedding down in our trusty sleeping bags, which had the soothing effect of cushioning us from the stones beneath, but only slightly: throughout the night one had the feeling of a never-ending, not-so-gentle massage.

On day eleven I was ready to give up: at rest, my legs were doing a version of Saint Vitus's dance, unless it was some lesser saint. Jeanne saw me massaging my calves and could not refrain. "How are those wrestler's legs?" she asked, strictly deadpan. "Oh, fine," I lied. "And yours? They must be hurting. I'm sorry I suggested such a long trip." That gentle smile again. "I'm ready to head for Rome if you are." She was serious. I politely declined. We settled for Florence and on day fourteen bicycled triumphantly into its outskirts, two exhausted but conquering heroes. For the next two days we touristed from morn till night, taking in the art and beauty of this incomparable city on the Arno, which neither of us had seen before.

Originally, I had thought we should bicycle back, but that was when I had first consulted the map, where distances seemed blessedly small. Mere inches apart. So the train it was, with Jeanne descending at St. Étienne to catch the narrow-gauge up the mountains to Le Chambon, while I continued on to Paris, where I had shipped my gear to Frank's family, the Manchons, three weeks before.

Looking across the quay, I glimpsed Jeanne's right hand holding the handlebars of her bike, her left waving gently, with that *Mona Lisa* smile once again gracing her lips. "That," I remember thinking, "is one hell of a young lady!" And then, from deep within my subconscious, I assume, came this afterthought: If ever I marry, I know it will be to a girl like her. A French girl. They have some extra dimension, a worldview, an attitude I've never seen before. And they're also damn cute.

11 ～

A Room with a View

IN PARIS my first task was to find a place to live. Anything but student quarters. I had come to Paris far more for the city than the university. Sure, I would check out the courses, but I had no intention of spending my days in the gloomy classrooms and auditoriums of that storied institution. Despite the fellowship, my budget was tight, because I was already entertaining the thought that I would stretch my stay to two years if, as I suspected, I loved it here. Frank, my closest friend in Paris, and later the best man at our wedding, was a member of the Collège Cévenol family and was in charge of welcoming and guiding the new students. From Frank, I had the addresses of three or four people who rented rooms in their apartments to students, but having visited two, I made up my mind for privacy. So I began to make the rounds of the Latin Quarter hotels, only to hear invariably, "Sorry, monsieur, we are fully booked." I had almost given up hope when I trudged up the dimly lit steps of the Hôtel de l'Ancienne Comédie, on the street of the same name hard behind the bustling carrefour de Buci, to be told, yes, we have a room available, but we rent it only for a minimum of six months. Could I see it? Of course, monsieur. The *patron*, tall and stern but impeccably polite, unfastened from a display case behind his desk a formidable-looking key, to which was attached a wooden triangle bearing the number 16. Room 16, it turned out, was a converted bathroom: in place of the tub was a narrow bed, with room for a table and chair and a battered small armoire, nothing more. Its major virtue was a broad, sunny window that looked out onto the neighboring roofs. René Clair, he who loved Paris's chimneys and roof-tops, would have snapped it up. Its inconvenience, I pointed out to the *patron*, was that to get to number 16, you had to pass through number 15. My visions of privacy flew out the sun-filled window. "I'm afraid," I said, "this will not do." He looked pained. "How," I managed, trembling for lack of proper French with which to vent my outrage, "how can you conceive of offering a room attainable only by passing through that of another tenant?" The thought seemed not to have occurred to him, or so I in my naïveté thought. He rubbed his chin. Knowing I was playing a losing game of this mad chess, that most certainly the *patron* had played it many times before and always won, I decided at least to attack with a knight. "What if I took both numbers 15 *and* 16?" I asked. "How much would that be?" "You mean you'd take *both* rooms. Ah, then you would be comfortably off, very com-fortably." He quoted me a price. I shook my head. "Far too much," I said. "I'm afraid with great reluctance I'll have to book the room down the street I saw earlier," I lied. "Which hotel?" he asked. I knew that if I gave him the name, he'd know I was lying. I moved my knight once again, its aim unclear, to me at least, and hopefully to him. "I can't remember the name," I said, frowning. "You know, two blocks toward the Seine, then one block left, toward the Institut." He looked flummoxed. "Lovely *patron* there, very friendly. *Loves* Americans." Even more perplexed. "I'll tell you what," he said, and I'm sure this was not his final offer, "I'll let you have both rooms for fifteen thousand francs per month." "Twelve thousand," I countered, "and I'll give you the money *tout de suite*—immediately." Knowing the French now as I did not then, I suspect the temptation of cash on the bar-relhead swayed him more than the counteroffer itself. He extended his hand, I thought to shake mine, but actually to receive the twelve thousand francs without further ado. Thus it was that having clearly turned my back on New England and its conscience-filled customs, in which bargaining was looked upon with disdain, I became the proud possessor, a stone's throw from St. Germain and the Latin Quarter, of what amounted to a two-room suite, all 140 square feet of it, overlooking the rooftops of Gay Paree. The world was my oyster. The only drawback was that my brilliant bargaining had eaten a mammoth hole in my budget. Let's see now, twelve thousand francs: How much is that in dollars? Okay, divide by four hundred: yes, thirty dollars a month. What the hell, you only live once.

My roommate in the navy's V-12 program at North Carolina had been Jack Youngerman, who hailed from Louisville, Kentucky. Blond and blue eyed, he had straw-colored hair, very fine and straight, which the wind combed willy-nilly as it passed from west to east and, indeed, from north to south or vice versa, whenever that happened, however rarely. Jack was slight of build and completely nonathletic and possessed a rare combination of nonchalance and intensity. Less than a year older than I, he had been at the University of Missouri, majoring in journalism, when the navy had snapped him up and shipped him off to North Carolina. Fate, in the form of the navy, had cast our lots together, and we also shared many classes, from calculus to navigation to military history. Though bright as hell, Jack seemed completely uninterested in whatever class, focusing most of his energies on sketching his fellow cadets, the professor, or the classroom itself. Even on those evenings when we were presumably hitting the books, in preparation for some impending test of our worthiness to be included in this officers' training program, Jack would sit with an open book before him while his right hand, in clear command, sketched and doodled endlessly. On one such night I paused in my own brown study and asked him point-blank: "Why were you majoring in journalism?" "Why not?" he said. "A chance to travel, maybe, meet interesting people. Far better than a stodgy nine-to-five job." "At Missouri," I said, "did you also spend most of your time sketching?" "You've noticed. I guess so. Why?" "Have you ever thought of studying art?" He looked at me strangely, then shook his head. "Not really," he said. "You should," I said, "because you're damn good."

After the war, which we saw through to its bitter end in these same classrooms, Jack went back to Missouri and got his degree in journalism. We exchanged letters, and in each succeeding missive it became clearer that his heart was no longer in journalism, though where it had gone he wasn't sure. One thing he did know was that following graduation he was going to France, probably to—now, listen to this—"study art"! I'm not sure he even remembered my advice of the year before, for he wrote as though he had come to that conclusion on his own. (Neither of us could anticipate or predict he would become one of America's foremost artists.) During my year at Pomfret, he had applied for and got accepted into the École des Beaux-Arts, no easy feat for a foreigner. He would write enticing postcards, some depicting alluring views of the City of Light, others depicting buxom, half-clothed lascivious lasses with poetic texts such as "Get your ass over here," or "You have no idea what you're missing, Richard." I needed no urging, only the means, and when the AFS came through, fate landed me a scant two blocks from where Jack was living, in an equally tiny but wonderfully cheap hotel on the rue de Seine, where he shared a room with a charming young Italian lady, Yolanda by name. We took up where we had left off. Jack's idle sketching had turned into a serious commitment, and his innate intensity, once scattered, was now firmly fixed. He drew incessantly, both in class and out, and like many before him increasingly repaired to the Louvre, where he spent days learning by copying old masters. On several occasions we went to the Louvre together, I to look and absorb, he to muse and comment. He had become a student not only of art but of artists, reading their lives and scrutinizing their work in detail. As we walked the halls, we would pause before a work he especially liked, and he would free-associate about it, talking more to himself than to me. It was during those mostly afternoon strolls that I came to see art in a new way and admire the seriousness of purpose, and knowledge, with which Jack had embraced his new calling. Then one day perhaps a year later I climbed the steps to Jack's room to see, sitting on the paint-spattered table, a view of Florence, from which I had recently returned. But it was an abstract view of Florence, seen from the hill above it, the rotunda of the Duomo and the campanile clearly visible among the squares and triangles, mostly in green and blue, that made up the rest of the city. "A breakthrough, no? I mean, is that the first abstract painting you've done?" "No," he said, "but it's the first one I felt good enough about to stand face out." "I love it," I said. "I think that's maybe the best thing you've done." "It's okay," he said, "a little derivative, but I think I've captured something of the city." Jack had gone to Florence a few months before I had. In that painting, he had—to my untutored mind, but having roamed and loved the city—in a work no more than eighteen by twenty-four inches, painted not on canvas but on wood, beautifully caught the essence of that very special place. I offered to buy it on the spot, not having the vaguest idea what price Jack might put on it, or whether I had in my dwindling budget the wherewithal to pay for it. "It's not for sale," he announced firmly. Would it ever be? I asked. He shrugged. "Who knows if I'll ever sell *any* painting," he murmured. Yolanda was listening intently, and though her command of English was limited, she understood enough to know I was offering to buy the work. "Why don't you let him buy it?" she asked in French. "We could use the money." "It's not for sale," Jack repeated, closing the discussion.

Jack never returned to realism, except when he was sketching, seeing something in his mind's eye he wanted to seize and record immediately: a person, a place, an expression, a chance encounter, a flower, a mere leaf. I followed his artistic evolution with growing admiration, but I learned to limit my compliments, for they elicited only rebuttal. "I admit I'm a fan, but we're not talking about blind faith here. You're just damn good. Period." That was generally where we ended, an unsatisfactory draw, but as time went on, and after his first show at the highly regarded Paris gallery of Denise René, his painterly self-esteem rose a notch or two. It was Jack who turned me on to the writings of Louise Labé, a poet of astounding depth and beauty, and in turn I would talk to him of Joyce, my hero, whose works, especially *Ulysses*, I studied with the same reverence and intensity as Jack did his favorite painters. I could quote whole passages of *Ulysses*, and after hearing a recording by the master himself of the Anna Livia Plurabelle section of *Finnegans Wake*, I would recite it with a broad Irish accent and in the same high tinny voice—the "tinny" doubtless from the ancient recording rather than from Joyce himself, who I knew had a lovely tenor voice. What I especially liked about Joyce was not only the quality of his work but his exemplary focus as an artist. No problem of self-esteem there. "Imperious" was the term that usually came to mind. Imperium. Emperor. Arrogant and self-assured. He knew he was changing the face of literature, and if that meant taking advantage of friends and family, so be it. Jack, I thought, equally dedicated to his art, could have used a little of that Joycean quality. But either you have it or you don't. As for myself, I was very much in Jack's camp.

I attended half a dozen classes at the Sorbonne, only one of whose professors seemed enamored of his subject or even vaguely interested. Most were held in large, stuffy amphitheaters where the professor read from notes that, I guessed, had not changed much from the end of World War I. Not the slightest effort to inflect or inform. Further, despite my summer in the Cévennes, I realized that I grasped only half, at best two-thirds, of what the old boys were saying. I had overestimated my fluency. I could speak quite well by now, with only a trace of an accent, but that had the inevitable drawback of making people think I understood more than I did, and their rapid-fire responses soon found me floundering or, worse, pretending. The only exception to the doddering-professor generalization was a youngish professor by the name of Charles Dédéyan. Comparative literature was his domain, and he was clearly in love with his wide-ranging subject. His hour vanished in a trice, and he invariably, having kept us on the edges of our seats, finished with a flourish that, like the last scene of the serial movies, announced the exciting subject of next week's episode. He also had the virtue of enunciating each sentence, each word and syllable, with such clarity that I understood virtually all. But aside from him, I quickly decided to move my education out of the classroom and into the streets and cafés. Where the action was. Where life was.

Back in Paris, in late fall, Walter, one of my fellow campers I liked very much who was born in Belgium and whose family had been killed in the war, noted almost in passing that he was moving out of his room. Had he found a place? He shrugged. Not yet, for his budget was ridiculous. Half joking, I mentioned my two-room suite on the rue de l'Ancienne Comédie. If you don't mind sharing, I said. Truth was, my own budget was getting tight, and relief of half the month's rent would be welcome. He accepted on the spot.

Over the months, when we had gotten to know each other well enough to be totally comfortable with whatever subject, I tried on several occasions to sound Walter out about his family, about the war, but after half a dozen of what I thought were discreet questions I gave up, because I could immediately see his jaw tighten. Though he was still in his mid-twenties, I knew he had experienced and suffered more than enough for a man twice his age.

Frank Manchon and Louis DeJuge were another (for me) fascinating pair. Inseparables, they formed an almost comical duo, Frank, tall, aristocratic looking, Louis, short, dark. They both had joined the underground soon after the German occupation.

It was in the early Resistance movement that Frank met Louis, a working-class kid from the near suburbs. Initially, their job was as courier, passing coded documents from one cell member to another, or from cell to cell. Most of the time—and apparently this was de rigueur throughout the underground—most members of a given cell did not know the rest, let alone the members of another cell. As in the case of Frank and Louis, people sometimes worked in pairs, but that was the extent of the collusion, for if one did not know the cell's other members, under torture one could not crack and betray. Further, once the Germans knew how tightly compartmentalized the system was and how little each cell member knew, they would be less inclined to torture.

Later, both Frank and Louis moved south, on the initiative of Pastor Theis, whom they helped seek out, sequester, and wherever possible move to safety the Jewish children.

After the war, both young men found themselves pretty much at loose ends, as were many in France. By birth, Louis had been destined to manual labor of some sort—carpentry, masonry, plumbing—the French school system being relentless in its triage process between the haves and the have-nots, those who will go to university and those who will not, those who will rule and those who will serve. Frank had a degree in law. He opted to take a position in an architectural firm. Louis for his part did odd jobs, carting and carpentry, often servicing worthy clients such as the Chambonnais for little or nothing. Careerism was a concept that seemed not to exist in these two men, and indeed in many of the French I met in those years. Being fulfilled meant focusing on matters you most cared about, whether or not they were lucrative. In fact, in all my years in France, I don't recall anyone inquiring about another's earnings, which would have been considered crass and uncouth. Both men, but especially Frank, were passionate about world politics, and one of the first things that astonished me—less a patriot than an expatriate, but one who had come here not with the basic intent of attacking my own country from the safety of foreign shores, as many Americans seemed eager to do in those postwar Left Bank days— was the relatively common view, to which both Frank and Louis subscribed, of looking equally askance at America and the Soviet Union, of viewing both giants with a wary eye. Again, in all our discussions I had a strong and growing feeling of how different our optics were, mine and my French friends', that those back home who had witnessed the war from afar and generally via the evening news, whose lives had never been physically threatened and whose deprivations consisted mainly of gas rationing, could never understand the actions and opinions of those who had known not only the physical but the psychic trauma of living in daily dread under the occupation.

Since I had arrived in Paris, it had become a sort of unwritten new tradition for me to spend Christmas Eve with the Manchons, who seemed to have adopted me. In addition to Frank's friend Louis, and upon occasion his sister, Souris, and her Englishman husband, Jeanne and Frank usually invited a handful of close friends. I say "Jeanne and Frank" because they looked and in many ways acted like a couple, sharing the apartment on the square Port Royal, often going to the theater and concerts together, not to mention entertaining with Frank acting as the host. In fact,

Jeanne had a beau, a dashing Austrian count, a composer of some note. He divided his time between Paris and Vienna and often missed Jeanne and Frank's lively dinners. As gray November melted into darker December that year, 1951, Frank reminded me that I was expected once again for Christmas Eve. Time to polish my shoes and fetch from the closet my better suit, for I had but two, the good one of pepper-and-salt wool, which the mothballs frequented far more than I.

Before I had left for France, my father inquired about my wardrobe, a term generally absent from my vocabulary if one excepted the obligatory blazer that came with my year at Pomfret. When I responded that I doubted I would need more than one suit, and I already had one I had bought off the rack at a thrift shop in North Carolina three or four years before, he asked me to produce it. He took one look and snorted.

"Get in the car," he ordered. "We're going to New London to have you fitted."

"Fitted?" I said. "I'm a forty regular. What's wrong with Bugbee's?" That was our local department store.

"You're getting a real suit," he said. "Made to order by Hans's father. From the finest wool available." Hans was my father's factory foreman, a gangly man in his early forties who looked, acted, and talked like Ray Bolger.

I was twenty-one at the time, and although from my mid-teens on my father and I had had monumental political arguments, I decided in this instance not to argue. Father was making me a gift, based less on his generosity than on his conviction that if I were to arrive in France without a proper suit, I would be making a damn fool of myself (one of his favorite expressions not only about me but about anyone he considered stupid or unworthy, of which, in his inner landscape, there were many, mostly Democrats). He had made it plain years before that once out of high school—or college if I were lucky enough to get there—I should never expect another penny from him. From that point, I was on my own. So I was touched, though a trifle irritated, by my forced trip to New London, just days before my departure, when I had places to go and people to see, specifically Maureen three houses down the road. I made a quick call to the pretty lady, explained my quandary, groveled in mortification, and pushed our rendezvous back till that evening.

So it was, and now, three years later, I pulled it from the armoire, dusted it off, and gave it an approving look. As good as the day it was bought.

When I arrived at the Manchons' punctually at seven, Louis and Frank were in the kitchen busily opening oysters. Of all my talents, of which there are few, shucking oysters with that damn knife was not one. "Here," Louis said with a grin, "give it a shot." I demurred, but they would not let me off. My main concern was not losing a finger. I grasped the damn beast with my right hand, probed the delicate spot with the knife point, thrust, and turned. Nothing. On the fourth try, both Frank and Louis doing their best to keep from laughing, I succeeded, to loud applause. "Bravo, *mon vieux!*" Frank said. "A couple more years and you'll be working at the seafood counter of the Dôme."

Jeanne's count was there, and another couple, the Medinas, with their young, dark-haired, striking-looking daughter, a budding violinist who was a student at the Paris Conservatory. Paul, the father, a man of medium height whose high forehead was framed by a shock of carefully combed graying hair, was dressed impeccably in a dark suit, a white shirt, and a red tie that matched his lapel's decoration, the Croix de Guerre. Though soft-spoken, he had about him an aura of intensity and intelligence that made him seem twice his size. Behind his rimless glasses, his gentle blue eyes could, when the subject interested him—and most things did—catch fire and blaze. A highly regarded journalist, he was Paris correspondent for the *Frankfurter Allgemeine Zeitung*, Germany's leading postwar newspaper. Roszi, the mother, one of Jeanne's oldest and closest friends, was also a violinist, classically trained like her daughter, not in Paris, but at the Budapest Conservatory, and later in Berlin, where, I had been told, she roomed in the 1920s with an up-and-coming actress named Marlene Dietrich. Between the wars she had, to earn a living, turned her talents to popular music and made a name for herself as a Gypsy violinist, whose nightclub on the Champs-Élysées had become famous throughout Europe. I had seen the Medinas, also at Jeanne's, two or three times the year before, but this was the first time I had met the daughter, Jeannette. Before dinner, Jeanne and her almost namesake had given an hour-long recital in the Manchons' elegant living room, furnished with embroidered Louis XVI chairs and couches but dominated by an imposing grand piano, a run-through for a program the young lady was to give a week or two hence. I was overwhelmed by both the beauty of the program and that of the young performer and complimented both musicians after the performance. "The young lady's very talented," I said to Jeanne during dinner. "Very," she said. "She'll go a long way."

As usual, dinner that night was a mixture of politics, literature, exquisite food, and fine wine. The increasingly bitter dispute—indeed rift—between Sartre and Camus was very much the topic of the day: discussed,

analyzed, criticized, justified, as sides were taken and the battlefield prepared. Frank was adamant that Camus was forsaking his past, retreating
into conservatism; Paul, acknowledging Sartre's enormous mind and talents, saw him nonetheless edging toward leftist dogmatism, but felt of the
two he was with Sartre. I too sided with Sartre, a man I admired, for among
other things he seemed to defy the normal bell curve of life, growing
younger and more politically vigorous by the day. "No question," Paul murmured, "he's a *grand bonhomme*." But he questioned the existentialist's
increasingly blind commitment to Communism, especially his Maoist leanings, which struck Paul as naive at best, dangerous at worst. "I'm not comparing Communism to fascism," he said, "but the abuses of dictatorship are
inherent in any such system, and under Stalin millions of lives have been
broken, untold others sent to gulags to die. Because of his role in the recent
war, many view him as a demigod, but if you reread an objective history of
Russian Communism, you'll get quite a different picture. Ruthless and
paranoid. A dangerous combination. You must understand that for decades
the French Communist Party, much more than the Socialist, fought for the
rights of the workers and peasants. Deep down, the French are conserva-
tives, and the majority detest and fear the Communists. To give you but one
example, Léon Blum, who had between the wars headed the so-called
Popular Front, on March 11, 1938, when Hitler annexed Austria in the *An-
schluss*, convoked the members of all parties, left and right, in the Salle
Colbert of the Palais Bourbon the next day and gave a stirring plea for
national unity, asking that the French of all persuasions come together
and form a 'unity government,' to show Hitler France was not weak and
divided—which, alas, it was—and hopefully to deter him from any further expansionist plans."

I listened, mesmerized, as Paul described the background of postwar
French Communism, of which I was still woefully ignorant.

"For Blum to constitute a unity government, however, he had of course
to include the Communists, and there was the rub. Many—maybe most—
Frenchmen thought of Communists as potential traitors who took their
orders from Moscow, and to some degree they did. But they were also proud
Frenchmen, and as Blum pointed out, doubtless echoing Shylock's famous
speech: 'If worst came to worst, and were we forced into war once again,
would we exclude the 1.5 million Communist workers, peasants, and small
shopkeepers and the various worker organizations throughout this land?
Of course not, for at the same time, if war comes, these men will bleed for

France, die for France, just as will the rest of our countrymen.' I paraphrase of course.

"And when war came, these workers and peasants did rally to the flag, without hesitation. Of course, you know the rest. After the year of phony war, in June 1940 the Germans overran the country in a matter of weeks, the French army in disarray. But during the occupation—and this is key—many former Communist soldiers, and indeed civilians, joined the Resistance movement early on, and their efforts were generally heroic, as opposed to many of their rightist fellow citizens, who collaborated with the Germans, not because they too were evil, but because their fear of Communism was so deep-rooted they saw Hitler as their bulwark against the Bolsheviks. So to answer your question: today the Communist Party here is still strong both because the workers still look to it as their protector and because their conduct under the occupation was generally exemplary." He glanced around at his captive audience. "Please excuse me for monopolizing the conversation," he said. "That was inexcusable, but I'm afraid our American friend inadvertently set me off."

"On the contrary," our hostess said with a laugh, "I must say you clarified it for me as well. Now, who will have coffee?"

I spotted Jeannette and Jeanne in deep conversation at the far end of the table, and I asked Frank, as casually as possible, how old Jeannette was. He looked at me strangely, as if the question were gauche or out of place. I know, one doesn't ask a woman's age, but I could not tell for the life of me whether this young lady, of a rare beauty, was fifteen or twenty-five. Physically, she looked closer to the latter, but there was something about her that made me think she might still be a teenager. "I honestly don't know," Frank said. "Seventeen or eighteen, I think." Then, as if to turn the world back on its proper, even keel, he asked suddenly: "By the way, what do you hear from Patsy? When shall we see Patsy back in Paris?"

"Soon," I said, "soon. Probably by early summer." But in truth I did not believe it, not for one moment. "Don't ever forget," she had warned me more than once, "I'm a leaf in the wind. A wanderer. One day you'll look up and I'll be gone."

12 ❧

Patsy of My Youthful Heart

VIENNA, late summer of 1950. I had in my infinite spirit of adventure decided in early spring that I wanted to experience firsthand the daily workings of the four-power occupation. It was already eminently clear that a seismic political shift was taking place, that our former Soviet allies, whom we had so recently embraced and toasted, were fast becoming enemies, as Communism became the West's, or at least America's, new bugbear.

Berlin was the obvious choice to experience that four-power cauldron firsthand, but after several efforts to obtain credentials, including the fact that I was freelancing for two New York newspapers, I settled for Vienna, a city that had long intrigued me.

Money as usual was a factor—perhaps *the* factor—but life in Europe was still cheap, and, I was sure, my infallible nose for finding inexpensive food and lodging would stand me in good stead there, despite my relative lack of language. Frank and I had been studying German the past winter, but we both seemed to have a slight but distinct *Deutsche*-block about these guttural sentences filled with nouns, adverbs, adjectives, now and then a preposition, climaxing with a stentorian verb.

At the Vienna train station, as I looked at the hotel listings posted there, my unerring eye fell immediately upon one: a former air raid shelter now converted to a hostel, not for youth especially, but for anyone with shallow pockets and mole-like proclivities. A tram ride away, and, voilà, there was the answer to my prayer: the reception, one floor below ground and therefore Stygian, announced single rooms for the equivalent of thirty-five cents a night, doubles for sixty. My initial thought was to look for a room-mate to take advantage of the bargain double, but I quickly put that thought, mean even for me, out of mind. Running water, mind you, though not in the room, actually pretty far down the hall, about a football field away, but that no deterrent, given my room on the rue Jacob, a real character builder. Gazing down the corridor, painted all in black, lit every few yards by a single bulb, ensconced in a mesh of metal, hanging from the ceiling, I wondered, mentally dismantling the walls, how many Viennese this vast underground might have held in those worst of times. Thousands, surely. I could see them sitting there, on hard benches that lined both walls, silent and stoic, listening to the dull thuds above as bombs rained down, as they had for more than a year, the biggest of which, I knew, had been on the night of March 12, 1945, roughly five years before. Did they, in their inner musings, blame and condemn the evil little man their soil had spawned, they who had welcomed him with flowers and adulation only seven years before?

My room, a flight down from the reception, was cell-like: a single metal bed, a wooden chair, a rickety table that no manner of leveling with folded paper, cardboard, or wood would render stable. A washstand with a porcelain bowl and a pitcher half-full of water, with which presumably to shave and brush one's teeth, perhaps to wash up if one were into that. But where to empty said water? A hundred yards down the hall, I had to presume. And, needless to say, no closet for my clothes, which mattered little, since I traveled light. (Not till years later, almost twenty in fact, did I find a man who traveled even more lightly: the poet and playwright Jean Genet, Chicago 1968. But that, as they say, is a whole other story, in a country far away.)

Emerging from my lair, I took several minutes to adjust to the light of day, although between my arrival at the station, where bright sunlight had greeted me, and my reappearance aboveground, dark rain clouds had scudded eastward, burying the sun. My first impression was that the city looked like an ornate tomb. Past grandeur everywhere, but the streets were virtually empty even at this hour, mid-afternoon, and the few trams in operation seemed to move at a crawl. To remind me of my mission, half a dozen jeeps bounded by, filled with GIs sitting stiffly and looking grim. None of the few pedestrians paid them any heed. I headed for the American Express building, to signal my presence at the mail section and cash some dollars. On my way I passed the American embassy, the entrance to which was guarded by two blue-coated marines, rifles poised outward at exactly the same angle. I marveled at their rigor. Then it happened.

Heading toward the entrance, not walking, but bounding, her blond hair cut fairly short, her bright green skirt cut radically high, her suede jacket, once beige but darkening with use, snugly hugging her waist and hips, her legs athletic but totally feminine, her feet shod in penny loafers scuffed beyond redemption, was a young lady, obviously American, who, for reasons I cannot fathom to this day, caught not only my eye but my being. Perhaps it was the guitar case slung blithely over her shoulder. She approached one of the marines, smiled, and uttered a few words, which melted his military bearing: not only did he smile back, but he allowed his rifle to dip a good five degrees, heaven forfend! He asked her a question, she responded, again with a smile, and he waved her in.

Suddenly I had urgent business in the embassy. I approached the same marine and flashed him my passport. He glanced at the picture and waved me through as well. "Check in at the desk," he said. Inside, I looked for the girl, who was nowhere to be seen. I asked to see the consul. Did I have an appointment? No, but I was here as a journalist, to do a story on the four-power occupation and the dynamics of same, and wanted to ask the consul some questions before I began. The clerk looked at me dubiously, in my garb of half GI, half bohemian, half-broke, if that is not too many halves. "Just a moment," he said, and dialed a number. "Yes." "Yes." "No." "I don't think so." Much to my surprise, and doubtless to his, he looked up and said: "The vice-consul will see you now. Second floor, fourth door on the left."

Inching my way down the corridor, looking left and right into each office, I spied, in the third office on the right, her. The sign on the door said PASSPORTS. The line was long, twenty or more, with only one clerk. I had a choice: go see the vice-consul and take my chances he would not be long-winded, or stand him up and join the passport line behind the apparition. It would be a good twenty minutes, maybe half an hour, before she reached the window, I judged. Surely, the busy vice-consul would not indulge me that long.

Her name was Patsy, I learned from one of their questions. Feeling completely left out, I contemplated retreat to the waiting vice-consul, who by now was probably fuming. Then I had a brilliant idea. These, I was finding, usually led straight to catastrophe, but maybe this would be an exception. "Excuse me," I said, tapping Patsy on the shoulder. She turned around and eyed me squarely, if quizzically. "Would you mind holding my place"—for now there were half a dozen behind me—"while I nip down and pay my respects to the vice-consul? He's waiting for me." Yes, I actually said "nip down," probably a leftover from a recent trip to London. I had a habit of picking up expressions in whatever country I visited and regurgitating them until eventually they fell away. "Of course," she said, smiling, "I'd be happy to . . ." "Dick," I said, in answer to her hesitation. Her full face was everything I had imagined, for at the embassy gate I had only seen her angled from behind, at most one-third, a flash of chin and cheek. It was an open face, no hidden nooks and crannies, its features nigh perfect, at least to my already-smitten eyes—pert little nose, full lips, saucy, opinionated chin, and deep brown eyes that locked into yours, probing: So tell me who you are and what you're about?

I gave the vice-consul short shrift. "I wanted to touch base with you first," I went on, "to see if there are any restrictions or political sensitivities." "What exactly are you looking for?" "My impression on how the four-power occupation is working. Or not working." "Wherever you have Russkies," he said, "you have problems." "So there's no objection to my talking to the Russians?" His right eyebrow raised a good inch. "If they'll talk to you"—he shook his head—"which frankly I doubt." I thanked him and started for the door. "If you do get the Russkies to talk, I'd be interested to know what they have to say." Ah, I thought, from semi-prevaricator to semi-spy.

I spent the next couple weeks hanging around the headquarters of three of the four powers. The vice-consul, whom I had visited again, had given me a letter of introduction to the Brits and the French. As for the Russians, I was on my own. I talked to dozens of soldiers and civilians, most of whom were open and friendly, about the inner workings of occupation, about how the locals treated them, what they thought of one another, how they parceled out the city and their rotating duties. There was a fair amount of backbiting and bickering, but, as the vice-consul had forewarned, Berlin was where the action was, the real tension, especially between the Russians and the Americans. The Brits were above the fray, following but not quite buying the increasingly vocal American anti-Soviet line. The French, on the contrary, were closer perhaps to the Russians than they were to the Anglophones, again for political reasons, for although de Gaulle and his center-right coalition were firmly in power, there was a strong leftist opposition, both socialist and Communist. I was, in my underground lair, steadily writing my piece. But I knew I could never finish it till I had pierced the Russian armor. Increasingly depressed in my bleak quarters, I decided one night to splurge and have a proper meal at the Hotel Sacher with a French journalist I had met a few days before, who said he might help me contact a Russian or two. Barely had I sat down—I was the first to arrive—when I heard her voice. Her laugh. I turned, and there she was. This time, I decided, I would not screw up. I approached her table and started to remind her of our chance meeting at the embassy when she interrupted and said: "Dick, this is Monique, my friend from Paris." She had remembered my name! "I held your place as long as I could," she said. "Then I had to run." "All straight with the embassy?" I asked, the better to ascertain the reason for her visit to Passports.

"Not quite"—she laughed that wonderful silver laugh—"but I should be in a day or two. After which I'm off to Italy. Please," she said, "do sit down. You make me nervous standing there."

"I really can't," I said, kicking myself mentally, for unmitigated strategic stupidity. "I'm waiting for someone."

"Ah," she murmured, turning to her friend. "*Il attend quelqu'un. Une jolie fille viennoise, sans doute.*"

"*Non, un journaliste français.*"

"So, you speak French," she said.

"I live in Paris."

Her embassy visit had been occasioned by a stolen passport. Theft of foreign passports, especially American, was rife in those early postwar days, and the embassy was backlogged with demands for replacements. Since the American authorities also suspected that certain of their younger, more impecunious citizens might be colluding—that is, selling their passports, for they brought a pretty penny on the black market—there was a wait of sometimes several weeks while the State Department checked the bona fides of its aggrieved citizens before issuing a new document. "Have to check with Washington" was the daily explanation, always with a smile of commiseration. Anyway, Patsy's passport had been promised her—for the fifth time, she added—probably tomorrow, but surely, without fail, absolutely, on Wednesday. Which meant that time was running out for me, if indeed that initial explosion ten days earlier somewhere in my lower depths meant anything.

"Why don't we all have dinner together," Patsy offered. I immediately pulled a chair for Jean-François and me. Jean-François was a connoisseur of fine food, I learned as we pored over the surprisingly ample menu. "The wine is on me," I said grandly, despicably insinuating that the meal would be on Jean-François. I picked a Grüner Veltliner. It was pricey—five dol-

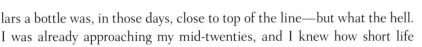

lars a bottle was, in those days, close to top of the line—but what the hell. I was already approaching my mid-twenties, and I knew how short life could be.

After dinner, I offered to drop Patsy off at her hotel, but she politely declined. "Where are you staying?" she asked. I started to lie, groping from my vague memory of the guidebook for the name of some respectable hotel, but in vain. Then I blurted out the name of my miserable underground lair. She burst out laughing. "But that's where *I'm* staying," she said. "Isn't it great?"

After breakfast, she said, "I'll introduce you to some of my Russian friends if you like."

We hopped on a tram, so crowded at that hour we had to hang on for dear life on the rickety, unstable running board, if that was the proper term. We scrambled off, crossed the Ring, and headed up the street. A massive sign, in the center of which sat an imposing hammer and sickle, announced that we were arriving at the Soviet sector. Two tanks sat toadlike on either side of the sign, in front of which were parked half a dozen Russian jeeps, just a few feet behind the red-painted barrier that, as we approached, was raised to let a sleek black limousine through. Two wooden guardhouses, also red, stood on either side of the barrier, each manned by two guards.

"Not exactly welcoming," I muttered as we approached the first guardhouse.

"Wait," she said. Leading the way, she headed directly for one of the soldiers, who looked pretty grim to me, and waved gaily. "Sergei," she called, "Patsy. *Kak vy pozhivaete?*"

"Patricia!" He grinned. *"Ochen khorosho!"* Then, in a heavily accented English, he said, "Where haf you bin? We had singing at soldiers' club last night. We missed you."

"I was going to come," she said, giving me a knowing glance, "but I got, uh, how shall I say, waylaid."

"What is . . . waylaid?" he asked, his brow furrowing. His pale blue eyes were set in a slightly rounded face so youthful it looked as though it had never known a razor. And yet Patsy had assured me on the ride over that most of the Russians she had met were battle hardened. Surely not this one, who five years earlier could not have been more than fourteen or fifteen.

"Kidnapped," she ventured. And when that didn't work, "Ambushed."

"Ah, ambushed. That word I know from war. Bad. Are you all right from ambush?"

"Fine," she said. "It was a friendly ambush."

"Friendly ambush? No, that I do not understand."

"I met a friend from Paris," she said, nodding toward me, "and we had dinner together."

"Ah. Then that is not ambush, really."

She laughed. "You're right," she said. "Now you're correcting my English, Sergei. Bravo!"

"Who you want to see, Patricia? Where is your guitar?"

By this time the three other guards, wooden stiff, were following, if only with their wary eyes, the conversation between Sergei and this pretty Westerner and her nondescript male friend. Sergei, sensing their interest, launched at rocket speed a series of Russian phrases that brought grins to all three faces.

Patsy explained my mission, assuring Sergei I was a "good guy" and to be trusted not to twist the truth. He heard her out, stared at me for a long moment, then nodded. "You must see Comrade Timofeyev," he said. "Or perhaps Comrade Smirnov." He muttered something to his colleague, then walked us over to the compound door, hard beneath the broad banner, and explained our presence to the guard there, who escorted us inside. The silent corridor seemed endless, all doors on either side shut tight. No sign of anyone working; in fact, no sign of anyone, period. "Pretty lugubrious," I whispered to Patsy, who did not react. At the next-to-last door on the left, our guard knocked and announced himself, and a moment or two later the door swung open to reveal a short, bulky man with a Stalinesque mustache, whose epaulets proclaimed him an officer of middle rank, who listened impassively as the guard explained our mission. The name Patsy was dropped two or three times, which was almost all I could glean despite my valiant year at the Institute of Oriental Languages in Paris learning—no, wrestling with—the Russian language. I picked up a *khorosho*, or two, plus an *Amerikanka*, but not much more.

"I'm not sure I'm needed here," she whispered. "Maybe I should wait outside."

"No, no, for God's sake, stay."

Comrade Timofeyev stepped aside and said, in almost unaccented English, "Do please come in."

The room was spare: an antique wooden desk that doubtless dated from Franz Josef's time, in front of it two random wooden chairs, and beneath the solitary window a long wooden bench. Timofeyev gestured us to the chairs, then circled the desk and took his seat, garnished with a generous pillow, the better to elevate his stubby person, I presumed. The only light was a green-shaded desk lamp, which cast a weary, unconvincing glow. After a few perfunctory but probing questions—What paper do you work for? Are you here in any official capacity? Do you have any ties to OSS or another government agency?—he seemed satisfied enough to launch into a long monologue about the efforts of the Western powers to undermine the peace. We Soviets fail to understand this growing schism between us former allies, especially on the part of the Americans. The notion of rearming Germany strikes us as not only dangerous but absurd. Haven't we learned from history? Twice in this century Germany has led the world into war, to unprecedented death and destruction. What makes us think, if they are rearmed, they will not strike again? You Americans were great: you supplied us with important matériel, you sent us through Al-Sib, more than eight thousand aircraft from your factories. We still wonder why it took you so long to mount the second front, we expected it to happen a year earlier, which would have saved us Russians maybe two million lives. Still, we were grateful when you came, you forced the Germans to divert troops from us to the western front. Without you we would still have won the war, but it would have taken much longer, cost many more lives. Your casualties were fewer than half a million dead. We lost at least twenty million. Neither you nor the English knew the utter devastation, the untold numbers not just of our brave soldiers but of innocent civilians who died at the hands of the Nazis. We should be friends, not enemies. Brothers! I was at the Elbe in April 1945. We embraced, we drank toasts to the future, we sang American songs, you sang ours. What has happened?

I said that I agreed, adding that many Americans were against rearming Germany, that we were indeed aware of the immense losses, both military and civilian, the Russians had suffered.

"Soviets," he corrected.

"And here in Vienna, but even more in Berlin, how is the four-power occupation working? How—"

"It's not," he cut in. "We used to meet and discuss. Now no longer. 'Suspicion'—that is the word. Everyone is suspicious of us. Even France, with whom we had close ties. But we realize France is beholden to America for aid, so it cannot express its own views. The British, too. But then, the Americans and the British always make common cause."

I started to demur but thought better of it, and asked about the mechanics of the four-power occupation.

"Mechanics," he blurted. "No mechanics. It is dead."

He went on to explain that earlier the occupying forces had met regularly, but no more. "Once in a while, when there is a major issue," he said. "Sporadically, is that the right term?"

I told him it was indeed, and beneath his mustache he smiled, clearly pleased.

"Tell the American people they should not fear us," he concluded. "Tell them to extend a hand and we will grasp it."

I thanked him for his time and his thoughts. I got up and extended my hand. Across the desk he reached over and grasped it.

"You see," he said, "we do as we say."

Outside the office, the guard who had escorted us in was still waiting, and walked us back down the endless corridor into welcome daylight. Sergei was still at his post, and before leaving, Patsy promised to bring her guitar to their next get-together. When will that be? Sergei said with a grin. "Tonight," she said. "This time," he said, "careful not be waylaid."

"How would it be if I bring my waylayer?" she asked, pointing to me.

"He welcome," Sergei said. "Tonight, then. Same place."

That evening we returned to the Soviet sector, armed with the pass Sergei had given us, and headed toward a building again decorated with a Soviet banner, beneath which floated a smaller banner announcing it as the Red Army Club. After a time, the soldiers egged Patsy up onto the stage, where she shook hands with each of the accordionists. Someone brought out a mike, while a self-appointed emcee announced that "Miss Hartley from America" was going to play. Without hesitation, Patsy immediately broke into "Kalinka," which elicited a roaring round of applause, as the entire audience belted out the words. I stood beside the stage, hedged round by a gently swaying horde in pale khaki—arms locked as they hummed or sang the familiar lyrics, totally ignoring this Western-clad outsider, mesmerized as they were by the *Amerikanka* onstage. When she climbed down, slightly flushed and with faint beads of moisture dotting her forehead, she was mobbed.

"Where did you learn all those Russian songs?" I managed amid the chaos.

"Mostly Paul Robeson," she said. "Also some Russians I know in California."

"Well," I said, "you have a career in Moscow if you want to pursue it."

"I might," she said. Then, after a pause, she looked me dead in the eye and added: "If I did, would you come with me?"

I knew just enough Russian so that I was able to get by for the rest of the evening, which went on till almost midnight. Mine was a stiff, textbook Russian, and I saw more than one indulgent smile as I misused a word, but when they corrected me, always gently, I never felt put down. Unremarkably, my Russian got better and better as the evening wore on, doubtless due to the increasing intake of vodka. As for Patsy, she babbled on, never having cracked a Russian textbook, with what looked like consummate ease. The average age of those to whom I talked that night was roughly my own, perhaps a year or two younger. Some had seen war, many had not, and I could tell the difference, for in the eyes of those who had, there was a hint of darkness, with the dim candles of fear lit behind their eyeballs. Without exception, they wanted to know why America had turned so suddenly and so virulently against them, why the term "Communism" had suddenly become anathema over there. From where did this strange man Senator McCarthy derive his power? Was it true he was running America? Is it true America is looking under people's beds hunting for Communists? If anything, one said, we should be terrified of you, with your atom bomb. At least now, another put in, we have the bomb, too. Virtually every family in the country had suffered at least one dead or wounded, often more. No one there wanted war, just the opposite.

Though the questions were pointed and often emotional, I did not feel in the least under attack. "Not all Americans believe in Senator McCarthy," I said. "In fact, I'll warrant that most do not." It was too difficult to try to explain the politics of anti-Communism in America just now, but I did get across that many politicians use fear as a weapon for advancement. Since elections, and the notion of political parties, were beyond their ken, when I tried to explain how often cynical politicians adopted positions without regard to personal convictions, eyes glazed, not in disbelief, but in incomprehension. Back in our bunker, weary but inspired, over a glass of white wine Patsy and I ruminated on the evening's events. Half of the young Soviets, I observed, had fallen in love with her that night. How could they not have?

"No question you changed their opinion of American womanhood," I said. "You don't have a very high opinion of American womanhood, do you?" Patsy said.

From the depths of recent memory, the image of Jeanne Theis suddenly appeared on my mindscreen. "Let's just say that after living in Europe for the past two years, I find American women—how can I put it?—one-dimensional."

"You speak from vast experience, of course."

"Very limited, I admit. But still . . ."

"Am I one-dimensional?"

"You! With the full knowledge of less than two days, I can state un-equivocally that you are the most multidimensional woman I've ever met."

"Yet I'm true-blue American, I swear."

"So, Patsy, you are clearly the exception that proves the rule."

Next morning, I still abed slowly working the vodka cobwebs from my brain, Patsy burst in waving a fuzzy green something that slowly turned into a passport.

"Finally made it," she said. "I told you I was true-blue American, and now I can prove it.

"As I told you the night before last, I'm off to Italy in a few hours."

I said nothing, but apparently my expression betrayed me.

"There you go," she said, "that puppy-dog look again."

"Where in Italy?"

"First Genoa, then Rome. I have friends in both places. And my girl-friend Ruth Roman is making a movie at Cinecittà. I promised her I'd take some still shots of her on the set."

It took me all of three minutes to pack: my one change of clothes, my dirty laundry stashed in a paper bag, my copiously covered notebooks, my copies of Dante and Dostoyevsky, of Eliot and Pound, of Hemingway's disappointing latest, plus my two dictionaries, English-German and English-Russian, secured by a sturdy rubber band.

In the taxi to the station—a rare indulgence for me, an accepted prac-tice for Patsy apparently—she reached over, took my hand, and squeezed it tight. "For God's sake, don't fall in love with me. Remember, I'm the world's worst wanderer. One day you'll look up and I'll be gone."

In Genoa, while Patsy caught up with her friends, I managed to finish my article on four-power Vienna and post it airmail to New York. At night, we dined in tiny, intimate trattorias Patsy's friends had discovered, each more delicious than the other. By day, I explored the city, redolent of history, its narrow streets and bustling thoroughfares, its churches and palaces. The only writing that came of those brief hours was a parody of Pound, a canto of my own, that seemed to come almost automatically, without variation, and whose merits were probably commensurate with its ease of birth.

In Rome, we stayed at a small, exceedingly modest hotel near the Tiber, which proved a major disappointment. The history of Rome had filled me with the belief that this storied river was as consequential as its magnificent city, yet its muddied banks and the thin rivulets trickling through its bed made me pine for the fast-flowing Seine, along whose stony quays I had so often wandered. But having minored in Latin and taught it at Pomfret, I marveled at the imposing Roman ruins, reconstructing them daily in my mind's eye, roaming all seven of the city's hills for hours on end, while Patsy spent most of her time on the set of her friend's movie.

Mid-September found us back in Paris. Before leaving, Patsy had given up her hotel room and stored her belongings with a friend. I was sure that my top-floor room at the rue Jacob, with its roller-coaster floor, inclined roof, and restricted square footage, would never suffice for two, but Patsy insisted she at least have a look. "If it doesn't work, we'll find something bigger," she said, which seemed to settle the issue of our staying together once back in Paris, something we had never discussed.

When she reached the top floor, with its skylight overlooking the St. Germain des Prés church, still enshrouded in its eternal scaffolding, she laughed out loud. "How in the world did you find such a place?" she said. "Don't you need roller skates to navigate?"

"It's pretty rudimentary," I agreed. In fact, until that minute I had never realized how unlivable the damn room was, even for one. Like most of the top-floor rooms in Paris, this had once been a maid's room. One look at the size and placement of these maid's quarters said more about class distinctions at the time than all the weighty tomes written on the subject over the years.

"Ridiculous," she added, opening the doors of the one generous piece of furniture, the armoire. Gazing inside at its near-empty state, she gave a quiet "hmmm" and nodded in approval.

"We'll have to get a larger bed," she said. "There's plenty of room if we put it under the skylight."

The only problem was, I pointed out, how the hell did you get a double bed up those *colimaçon* stairs?

"How did you get the single bed up here?" she wanted to know.

"It was here when I arrived."

That afternoon, I and my friend and next-door neighbor Jean Toulet wrestled a single bedspring and mattress up to my aerie. We arrived at my door only to find, twist and turn as we might, the damn bed would not go through.

"Unscrew the hinges," Patsy said. "Once the door's removed, you'll be fine."

A tad irritated that she, not I, or Toulet for that matter, had come up with the thought, we lowly workers nonetheless did as she had bid, and—of course—the bed slid through. We placed as she had suggested the now double bed beneath the skylight, snug against the wall, moved the table and chair to bottom center, just to the left of the door, found at the Salle Drouot an easy chair and lamp, ridiculously inexpensive, which miraculously fit neatly in the corner to the right of the door, added a red-and-white-checkered tablecloth to the table, hung a couple of paintings on the bare walls—one Ellsworth Kelly, one Youngerman—and, voilà, my miserable *garçonnière* was suddenly transformed into a welcoming studio, most, if not all, of its inadequacies concealed, within days hardly remembered.

There was of course Madame Germaine still to be reckoned with.

In mounting or descending the stairs, one had to pass the frosted glass of the first—not ground, but first—floor, where Madame Germaine held sway, which contained her own quarters and also the ample but antiquated kitchen and the dining room, where the boarders met daily in sullen convergence. Most days I could enter and leave the house without being perceived from beyond the frosted glass, but there were times in summer or when the fancy struck her when she would leave the door ajar, even fully open. At these times, from her perch deep in an ancient, flower-embroidered chair that, she claimed, was descended from her grandfather, therefore dearly beloved, she would acknowledge my presence, or rather my passing, with a desultory wave, which meant all was well, the rent had been paid, the auditory effects of my ambulatory, amatory guests had been judged to be at an acceptable level. Once in a while, however, a vigorous gesture of her right arm, the good one, signaled that my immediate presence was required.

Eight days after Jean and I had wrestled my new bed up the unforgiving stairs, as I was returning from my prebreakfast foray to the carrefour de Buci, laden with fresh warm croissants, a pound of butter, and a copy of both *Combat*, which offered me the world from the French viewpoint, and the *Herald Tribune*, which connected me to what was happening at home, feeling a tad more than on top of the world, happy to be back in Paris, breathing in the special odors of the town, a mixture of bread baking and coffee brewing, spiced with a hint, emanating from the well-polished zinc café counters, of early-morning *rouge* as blue-clad workers steeled themselves for the workday to come, I arrived to find Madame Germaine's door wide open and she gesticulating as if the world, or at least the rue Jacob, were coming to an end.

I gave her my broadest smile, waved in return, and prepared to ascend to my aerie as if I had misunderstood the frantic movements of her arm as simply a friendly greeting.

"Monsieur Richard!" she thundered, in an amazingly low, almost baritone voice. And, as if I were deaf, a second time: "*Monsieur Richard!*"

I turned, bowed, and entered her lair. Without preamble, she demanded to know if my new friend was transient or permanent. I was tempted to say only time would tell, but caught myself. With that question, I knew I was in jeopardy. Please, not expelled, I thought, not after all that stalwart stairway effort and magic domestication.

"I suspect the latter." I nodded. "We met late this summer, under truly idyllic circumstances. A lovely young lady."

"Ah," she said, and I thought I saw her melting. But of course I was mistaken. "You understand then, there will have to be an adjustment in the rent."

I decided argument would be futile, perhaps even counterproductive. The thought of having to pull up stakes—worse, bring the bed back down those stairs—made me receptive to any reasonable offer.

"Of course." The words slid out almost of their own accord, despite my mind's resolve. "What do you think would be a fair adjustment."

"Well," she said, and I could almost picture the grasping cogs of her miserly mind whirling, calculating: How much, how much? "Bearing in mind that you are a good client," she said, "I was thinking"—one final gyration—"1,500 francs a month."

I looked disappointed. "I was hoping for 1,000."

"Let us settle on 1,250," she said.

I nodded. Agreed. That is the kind of negotiation—civilized, swift— that makes the French such a pleasure. Both sides parted feeling they had won a victory, minor, to be sure, but a victory nonetheless.

"Retroactive to last week," she added, obviously knowing the precise date of Patsy's arrival.

"But of course."

Upstairs, Patsy was fully dressed, the bed made, coffee boiling. "Did you get lost?" she said.

I related, in full detail, my downstairs encounter. "You are now legal. At a cost, I might add, of two dollars and fifty cents."

She laughed. "I now know what I'm worth on the open market," she said.

"Laugh all you want," I said, "but that represents a 23 percent increase in my rent."

"No," she countered. "A decrease, actually. I'm paying half."

Patsy resumed her singing stint at L'Abbaye, increased now to four nights a week. I spent my days writing the great American novel and, when inspiration flagged, would read, mostly in French, the authors on Jeanne Theis's list, various classics I had missed, and increasingly the new crop of younger writers. That winter I also reenrolled in the Russian courses at the Institute of Foreign Languages, partly as a result of my Vienna experience, partly because I wanted to catch up linguistically with Patsy. As had happened before the war, there were a number of fledgling writers and painters who had landed here, because Paris was still magical for those who cared or dared to probe beneath its soot-streaked surface. I saw a lot of Jack Youngerman, whose friendship would last for the rest of our lives.

Paris in the 1950s. Artist vied with artist, writer with writer, philosopher with philosopher, sprinkled freely with the spice of politics. For young Americans such as Youngerman and me, these intellectual jousts were odd, for we had known no local equivalent, certainly not to the passionate extent of these European quarrels. Foremost among them, though the fires were by now banked by the intervening years, was the feud between Braque and Picasso. Though Jack admired Picasso greatly, he found Braque the more profound, the more painterly of the two. Painfully close before World War I, they had become increasingly estranged during and after—Braque had not only volunteered for active duty as soon as war broke out but been wounded almost unto death in 1915, while Picasso, invoking his Spanish nationality, had remained aloof, untouchable because of his neutrality and, of course, his growing fame. Then there were Sartre and Camus, also once close but now embattled. What fascinated me was the passion these debates could engender, not merely in the press, but in the common Frenchmen. On café terraces, at dinner parties left and right, at street-corner encounters, and in exchanges over *rouge* at the zinc counters of one's local café, both men's positions were debated and dissected as if the future of the nation depended on it. My friend Armand, a plumber by trade, who had heeded a desperate call to unblock my sink after Madame Germaine had shrugged her ample shoulders and had (no pun intended) washed her hands of the problem, called up from his supine position beneath the contumacious receptacle, his begrimed hand holding a major monkey wrench, and said, "Quite a battle between those two, *hein*?" "Who?" I wondered, my mind grasping for the latest pitched soccer war, only to hear "*Mais*, Camus and Sartre of course!" Only in France, I thought, would there be a plumber sophisticated enough to be not only aware of but fascinated by his country's two leading intellectuals battling it out!

Later I would write an article on the Sartre-Camus debate for *Merlin*, which concluded: "Undoubtedly both men are sincere. There are certain elements of truth in both their arguments. Indeed, practically all of the contemporary truth makes its appearance in one form or another in their bitter contest; that, in a word, is its significance."

Mentally, I dedicated the piece to Armand the Plumber.

In this winter of my content, life took on a reasonably normal routine. Twice a week I would catch the end of Patsy's act at L'Abbaye, which was seldom before eleven, often later, and she and I would head off, alone or with friends or other performers, for a late-night dinner at Les Halles. I enjoyed the mixed population of muscled truck drivers delivering their wares—great sides of beef, hams, and lamb, not to mention horsemeat, a discovery for me that, overcoming my American prejudice, I had forced myself not only to eat but to like; fresh-plucked fowl tethered by the dozens and tossed in gentle waves from one man to another, like the classic fire brigades, till they came to rest in the vast warehouse from which, in the next hours, they would be disseminated throughout the city; canvas-covered prewar Citroën trucks from whose sides hung a rainbow of produce from the provinces, all picked fresh that day; vegetables from the south, apples and pears from Normandy, and, in season, peaches both white and yellow, juicy, and succulent. Less frequently, but increasing monthly, came the trucks that lumbered from farther south, bearing mountains of oranges and grapefruits, probably transshipped from Spain and North Africa. From midnight till dawn the place was a cauldron of activity. Mingling with the truck drivers were roving bands of elegant women in their Right Bank plumed and sequined gowns, with their black-tie escorts who tended to nonchalantly flip white silk scarves long over one shoulder, smoking in their silver holders not the local Gauloises or Gitanes but the milder

American cigarettes that were just beginning to make their appearance on the French social scene. And amid all the shouting, the banter and clamor of the deliveries, slipped in the bevy of prostitutes, most too heavy for their jobs, or too old, their faces made up grotesquely as if for some vaudeville show. Perhaps they were left over from the war, as the new crop had not yet arrived. And, I wondered, what kind of society would turn these women out onto the cruel streets, expel them from their former well-ordered bordellos, where they had had a sense of camaraderie and a caring madam to look after them? I had seen these outcasts standing in the cold and rain in Pigalle and Montparnasse, sad and disheveled, huddled in narrow doorways, and felt venom for the hounds of decency who had willed them there.

Yet here, in the bustling predawn hours at Les Halles, the ladies of the night seemed transformed, either by the friendly presence of the truckers, most of whom they knew, by the glitter of the swells, by the enchanting odor of *steak frites* sizzling and the lava-like onion soup overspilling its porcelain bounds, or by the accordion music that drifted from the cafés and restaurants and gave them a feeling that life still had its moments. Here no longer the submissive and passive pawns of darkened doorways, they felt part of the cast, and their faces and postures showed it. What entranced and seduced was the sheer energy of the place and the night. If, as the pundits continued to proclaim, this Paris of the 1950s was nothing, a pale reflection of the "real Paris" that Hemingway and Fitzgerald, later Henry Miller and Elliot Paul, had espoused and made their own, still, I had long concluded, Les Halles was as authentic and seductive as it had ever been. But then, maybe Hemingway and Fitzgerald had never spent time at Les Halles, or only as part of the swells, slumming, soaking up the atmosphere, slyly taking notes for an anecdote or two to be inserted as local color. It was a long, long way from the Ritz to Les Halles. Out of curiosity, I had visited the Ritz once a year or two earlier. But I had fled as if from enemy territory after one awkward drink. If this, Ernest's nest, was Paris to him, then I feared he'd missed most of the fun.

13 ✺

Enter Enrico (Stage Left)

"W HY don't you start your own magazine?" Patsy asked me one
morning.

"Money," I said. "It takes money. Not mountains, but
even with the dollar as it is, a hundred times more than I have. Or could
raise."

"Suppose you *had* the money. Would you find running your own literary review fulfilling?"

"In fact, yes, I'd love to have a magazine as good as some of those prewar
guys. As, say, *Transition*. Sinbad's is the best of the bunch, but . . ."

"Well," said Patsy, "I *may* have the answer to your prayers. *May*."

Things had been too peaceful these past few weeks. Almost orderly—
that is, in the context of a basically untidy existence. Besides, last night I
had not picked her up at L'Abbaye, and she had slithered into bed in the
wee hours. I didn't have to wait long. Patsy, the total extrovert, had barely
taken her next sip of coffee on the terrace of the Deux Magots when she
began to tell me about this guy who had come to the club the night before.
His name was Enrico, and he had invited her out for a drink, showering
her with compliments and champagne. "Not much champagne," she assured me.

"Let me finish," she said, "and stop acting like a husband."

This was the first time she had ever used that term in all our countless conversations, and suddenly I wondered what it would be like to be just that. For the first time since that smitten moment outside the American embassy in Vienna, I had what I presume is called a pang of doubt.

An Israeli scientist, Enrico had invented a process for turning yellow diamonds into white! Could you believe it? A high-intensity furnace in which one subjected yellow diamonds to such pressure and temperature that in a matter of days, or weeks, she couldn't remember which, but anyway a blink of the cosmic eye, that furnace accomplished what nature takes millions of years to bring about: turning ordinary carbon into a colorless crystalline allotrope.

A shadow of doubt crossed my face, and she was quick to see it. "It seems too simple," I said. "If it's that easy, why didn't someone think of it sooner?"

"Why didn't somebody cross the Atlantic before Columbus?" she responded.

"Somebody did. The Vikings, if memory serves."

"Do you want to hear the rest or not?"

I ordered two more coffees. Clearly this was going to take some time. "Of course," I said.

"Enrico buys yellow diamonds in Switzerland, transports them, either directly or via France, to Israel, where he does his thing and, voilà, he makes a fortune each trip." Looking me straight in the eyes, she said, "This is where your magazine might fit in. I want you to meet him."

Wednesday night, at the stroke of midnight, I strolled as nonchalantly as I could into L'Abbaye and, from the doorway, cased the joint, looking (in my own mind) like Jean Gabin in *Pépé le Moko*, trying to spot Enrico. "Ah, there you are," she said, seeing me slowly rise to my feet. "I didn't see you come in." Liar. "Have you had dinner?" I had. "Well, why don't you join us anyway? I'd like to show Enrico around Les Halles."

We shook hands. Mine was icy cold. His was warm and firm. Fifteen–love, Enrico.

"Patsy has told me a great deal about you," Enrico said. "Your literary plans and aspirations. Admirable. To write, to paint, to create—what is more important than that? I gather you're something of a journalist, too."

"Freelance," I said. "I send articles to various New York newspapers, mostly on the theater and movie scene here. More to the point, Patsy has told me that you're an incredible engineer—"

"Inventor, I'd like to think." He smiled. "Engineering was required, but I had a vision. Without a vision one is nothing. My experiments," he said, "had to do with constructing ovens so strong and powerful that we could subject objects to temperatures and pressures such as the world had never seen. As I'm sure you know, it takes millions of years for nature to produce nearly pure carbon in crystalline form. The less pure yellow diamonds take forever, too, but far less than the pure white—the world wants diamonds both for jewelry and for industry. Why, I said to myself, can't we speed up that process by subjecting the yellow diamonds to such conditions that, presto, we make them white? It took me years and years, and many millions of dollars, to perfect such an oven, but I have finally succeeded." He reached inside his suit jacket and pulled out a velvet pouch more or less the size of a glasses case, from which he extracted several yellowish stones of various sizes. "I buy these in Switzerland," he said. "I'm taking them back to my ovens in Israel day after tomorrow." I was delighted to hear about his impending departure. "Two weeks from now, having sold some, if not all, of these same stones, but now as white diamonds, I'll be back." I was sorry to hear that.

Where was the flaw? "Aren't you worried about competition?" I wondered aloud. Enrico shook his head. "Of course, others could do the same," he said, "but it would take them years. Besides, if some major corporation went into the business, it would throw the diamond market into a tailspin. My small-scale operation will not affect it in the least."

If he had indeed made this discovery, which was like having a key to the mint, why the hell was he telling us, virtual strangers? Wasn't it paramount to keep such information completely secret? The row of girls sitting at the bar like so many sparrows perched on a wire had not failed to note the contents of the pouch and must have been thinking that anyone openly carrying those impressive stones around had to be crazy, a perfect target.

Either the man was a genius, an Edison of diamonds, or he was a con artist, a mountebank. If the former, he was, or soon would be, so rich that indeed funding a small magazine would be like pocket change to him. "Of course, Dick, what do you need to get it going and to assure, say, the first year's issues? Here"—taking out his checkbook, flattening it carefully on the café table where this transaction was taking place, and writing a check for, say, five million francs (okay, say, half that: more than enough for a dozen issues)—"are you sure that'll be enough?" But in that same scene, what was Patsy doing wearing an inch-wide collar of diamonds, for Chrissake?

A couple years before, Colette's novel *Gigi* had been turned into a movie starring a charming young actress, Danièle Delorme. A huge success in France, the movie had arrived in the States at the Paris theater, and I had been assigned to write a piece about the film and the new young star, which had appeared in *The New York Times* in February to coincide with the American opening. Now America wanted to know more about this fresh French face, who was shooting a new film, *Agnès de rien*. The PR person I called was delighted to hear the New York press was interested and invited me to go out to the set in the suburb of Billancourt. I spent most of the afternoon listening to this pretty actress go through half a dozen scenes. She was not Hollywood beautiful, but there was about her an ineffable grace, a vulnerability that both belied the character she was playing and added to her complexity. And her eyes, dark and soulful, enveloped one in their embrace. For several hours I forgot Patsy completely. Well, almost completely.

In her dressing room, Danièle greeted me warmly, thanking me for the article on *Gigi*, which, she said, had been a great success. Do you not think it is too French for Americans to understand? Not at all. I think they will—I paused, then lapsed into English—I think they will eat it up. I beg your pardon? Ah, it's an old American term, I told her: *Ils vont se régaler*. Ah, good. Where did you learn your French? You have almost no accent. You must have learned as a child. All Americans and English have very thick accents, even when they speak the language well. No, I learned it here. I still make many mistakes. And the French r may be my Waterloo. But I have worked hard *not* to have an American accent. She shook her head. I wish I knew English half as well. For this film I may be going to America for the premiere, and I fear I won't be able to open my mouth. Don't worry, I said, you'll do fine. First of all, Americans love the French. The GIs all came home from the war with amazing stories of Paris and French girls: over there you're almost mythical. And besides, switching to English, if you look at New Yorkers the way you're looking at me right now, you won't need to talk. What did you say? I said that you have very pretty eyes, and they'll do the talking for you. "Ah," she said, "still, I'd feel much more comfortable if I had more English. I thought of going to Berlitz, but that is too slow." I admitted I had once taught there, and wholly concurred with her assessment. She hesitated.

"I know you have no time from your other work, but would it be possible to give me some private lessons? I'd be immensely grateful. We finish shooting in two weeks, after which I'm quite free."

I thought of Berlitz; I thought of Air France: Had I not been a disgrace to the profession? Then suddenly I thought of Enrico.

"Of course," I said. "I'd be delighted."

Two weeks later, Enrico was back in town. Patsy moved out and again took up lodgings in the same little hotel a couple of blocks away. I promised this time to maintain my cool, to eschew all jealousy. "I don't have to see him again. Remember, I am doing this for you," she assured me. "If you want this to stop right now, just say so."

"We've gone this far," I said lamely, "we may as well see how it plays out." I didn't feel proud of that statement, which struck me as a sad combination of cowardice and avarice.

It was agreed we would communicate via the night clerk, to whom I had slipped five thousand francs. He must have felt he was playing in *Casablanca*, for whenever I arrived to deliver or pick up a message, he immediately turned up the collar of his greatcoat, which he wore indoors and out, and looked furtively left and right before slipping me the folded piece of paper.

Enrico was back at the Ritz. I was sitting on the terrace of the Rhumerie Martiniquaise on the boulevard St. Germain, a place I patronized but rarely—one has one's little habits, what can I say?—when who should come walking past but my friend Ellsworth Kelly. "Join me for a drink?" I called out to him. Why not? He climbed the two steps to the terrace and pulled up a chair. "I'm on my way to an exhibit at the Museum of Modern Art," he said. "Want to come along?" "Sure. This morning I just sent off my article on Danièle Delorme's new movie, so I'm free as a bird." A few nights before, I had filled him in on the movie assignment and the teaching job that had emanated therefrom.

"You're teaching Danièle Delorme English!" he salivated. "And *other* things?"

"Ellsworth, you have an evil mind."

"You're not going to drag that along," he said, pointing to the Royal Standard at my feet.

"No," I said, "this is Patsy's. She asked me to drop it off after I'd finished my piece."

Ellsworth looked at me oddly. He knew we were living together. "Drop it off where?"

"Right up the street, at the little hotel on the rue de l'Échaudé . . . I know, I know," I said in response to Ellsworth's slightly malicious grin. "She's there for just a few days." He waited for more. He was not above a good tidbit of juicy gossip. "It's a long story," I said, gesturing to the waiter. "I'll be right back," I said, picking up the typewriter.

"No, I'll go with you," he said.

Magnanimously, I folded an extra hundred francs into the bill, and we headed up the narrow street—more an alley, really. Inside, the hotel lobby was in semidarkness, as opposed to the darker darkness once the sun, if it happened to be out, had set, offset only by a lone twenty-five-watt bulb dangling on a meter-long cord above the reception. One thing I could say about all these Left Bank hotels: they wasted not an extra franc on illumination. I hoisted the typewriter onto the counter, where the day clerk was a mousy fellow I had seen a few times and whose salient feature was an ill-fitting toupee that he changed three or four times a month: the short version, worn just after the ritual non-haircut; the middle version, donned for week two; and the third, and sometimes fourth, when lengthening curls and unruly sideburns made it evident it was time for the non-haircut. "Bland" was too exciting a word for him, but today, as I entered with Ellsworth trailing close behind, he looked almost apoplectic. I debated asking him if he was all right, for his eyes were bulging and his brow bathed in sweat, but thought better of it and said simply, "Would you kindly make sure Mademoiselle Hartley gets this typewriter." Barely had Patsy's surname escaped my lips when out of the shadows behind the reception stepped two rather large men who said without ado, "You're under arrest," and snapped a pair of handcuffs not only on me, who was clearly the object of something judicial, if not criminal—though in rapidly scanning my recent past, as I am told a drowning man does, I could find nothing to warrant this—but on poor Ellsworth as well.

"What—what's this—what's this all about?" Ellsworth stammered. "Tell them I'm a teacher," he insisted, "at the American School. They can call and verify right now. Go ahead, tell them this is a big mistake." Meanwhile, in his panic, the desk clerk had removed his middle-of-the-month toupee and was furiously mopping his brows. The clever cover was blown. Would the poor man ever be able to face us again?

"Sir," I said to burly and, to put it kindly, rather jowly Plainclothesman Number 1, assuming for the nonce a rather pronounced American accent, "this gentleman was with me purely by chance. He is a respected art teacher at the American School in Paris. I vouch for him totally."

"Get a move on" was his growled response, prodding us out the door onto the street, then across the southern segment of the carrefour de Buci, thankfully shuttered and virtually empty at that hour, now that the normally bustling food markets were over. The few people who loitered there looked at us inquisitively but not inquisitorially. The police were not much beloved in Paris these days, the memory of their often too close collaboration with the Germans still fresh in most minds. Still, our grim-faced guardians were marching us briskly, as if to the gallows. Ellsworth, with each step, was increasingly upset, protesting his innocence, which he kept pressing me to convey. When I told him I already had, his brow furrowed even more deeply. "Try again," he suggested.

When we reached the English Bookshop on the rue de Seine, with the proprietor, Gaït Frogé, standing in the doorway, her eyes widening as she saw us thus manacled, I drew the line, even though I figured it might cost me. I stopped in my tracks. "Whatever's going on," I said in my most impeccable French, casting aside all efforts to shroud myself falsely in my American identity, "I can tell you, you have the wrong men. We are both American citizens and demand our rights. I have lived in this *quartier* quite some time. I'm well-known here, and yet you are parading us through the streets as though we're common criminals. I repeat: this gentleman with me is an esteemed painter and a teacher at the American School, and has nothing to do with whatever the problem is." At least my mini-peroration had resulted in our guardian angels' pausing in the street, apparently wondering whether, indeed, an error might have been made. "I also demand to know where you are taking us," I added, feeling slightly more sure of myself, despite the inescapable suspicion that all this was somehow linked to Patsy. Clearly they had staked out her hotel. So this fucking Enrico . . .

"To the prefecture," they said as one.

"Then either remove these handcuffs or take us in a car."

"Anything I can do?" Gaït whispered, for we were stationed directly in front of her store.

I shook my head. "Big mistake," I said. "But thanks."

The two plainclothesmen conferred, keeping a careful eye on their quarry, muttered a few words, then hailed a cab, which fortunately happened by. I was only glad that Madame Germaine, who sometimes did her shopping at Buci, had not witnessed my arrest. Immediate expulsion from her domain, I suspected, without appeal. I could hear her telling the other

boarders in hushed tones, "*Je ne savais pas que j'hébergeais un* criminel!"
I didn't know I was housing a *criminal!*

At the prefecture, the drabbest of buildings, whose corridors were endless and whose soulless paint was both flaking and peeling, we were hustled up to the second floor, where we were unhandcuffed and our shoelaces
removed.

"Why are they taking our *shoelaces?*" Ellsworth wanted to know.

"Suicide," I muttered. I'd read my share of police procedurals. "So you
don't use them to commit suicide."

"Suicide with *those!*" Ellsworth said, with utter disdain. "There must
be some other reason."

Just then a well-dressed man—white shirt, coat, and tie—arrived, legendary *mégot* hanging from his lips. How the French could smoke and talk
at the same time, without using their fingers, I had never fathomed. Probably a Gallic gene.

"*Monsieur,*" Ellsworth cried out, deciding that it was time to bring out
the major artillery, namely, his full command of French, only half a dozen
words of which I had ever heard. "*Monsieur, je suis une peinture,*" he declaimed. And as if to make his case even more convincing, he added:
"*Une peinture au quatrième!*" The new arrival's head turned smartly, as if
he were trying to adjust his hearing to a new language, for literally what
Ellsworth had reported was: "Sir, I'm a painting on the fourth floor!" Perhaps, the man must have thought, this is a case for St. Anne, the local asylum, not the prefecture. I knew what Ellsworth was trying to say: he was a
painter, which indeed he very much was, and he was living on the fourth
floor of a building on the Île St. Louis. But those basic facts had been
slightly mangled in the telling. I urged the chief of detectives—for that is
who he turned out to be—to verify my friend's story by calling the director
of the American School, which he promised to do. I explained that Ellsworth, an old friend, had happened by that afternoon on his way to an exhi-
bition at the Museum of Modern Art and invited me along. I even named
the artist whose show we had planned to attend there. Within the hour
word came back that Mr. Kelly's bona fides had been verified, and he was
released forthwith.

"I'm sorry to have ruined your afternoon," I said.

"Hey, it was kind of exciting." He smiled, feeling much better now that
his shoelaces had been restored. "When you get out, *if* you get out"—
Ellsworth's sly sense of humor was usually accompanied by a slightly ma-
levolent leer—"I assume you'll tell me what this is all about."

Just as he was leaving, two other plainclothesmen who could have been cloned from our own escorts entered the room, bearing between them a lovely young lady, smiling broadly: Patsy! Ellsworth looked even more astonished. If till now he had figured that this afternoon's shenanigans were imputable to some misdemeanor or indiscretion on my part, seeing Patsy thickened the plot. He shuffled out, shaking his head.

"Hi, Dick!" Patsy said, pecking me on both cheeks, perfidious child. "I see they got you first."

"What an unexpected pleasure!" I said.

"A big mistake," she said as they hustled her toward the far door. "It's all a big mistake, I assure you," she managed over her shoulder. "A couple of phone calls and we'll be out of here. I promise!"

"Enrico?" I called after her. "Enrico?"

But she was hustled out the door before she could reply.

They installed me in a small, poorly lit room, its only window overlooking the prefecture courtyard, and left me there for two hours. The only torture was that I had nothing to read. I suddenly imagined hell as a place consciously devoid of reading matter. Finally, as I was beginning to obsess on the shoelaces, two men arrived and began to question me about my relationship with Enrico. I barely knew the man, I said, had spent one evening with him a couple weeks ago. Did I know he was a big-time diamond thief? No. That he dealt in diamonds? Vaguely. He made some claim about being able to change yellow diamonds into white. And you believed him? It seemed possible. He could be very convincing. Have you ever traveled with him? Traveled? Exactly: to Switzerland, for example, or Israel? Absolutely not: I told you I barely know the man.

No? Were you involved with him financially? Suddenly I wondered what Patsy might have said to them about our mad plan of using him for high literary purposes. It would only add to the confusion. No, never. They left the room, presumably to confer, then returned a couple minutes later.

"You can go," the lead interrogator said.

"What about Mademoiselle?" I said, tying my shoes.

"We're keeping her a bit longer," one of them said.

I went down and bought the two biggest tabloids, figuring the story would be in one or the other, if anywhere. And there it was, on page 3: "Gendarmes

Nab Major Diamond Thief," with a two-inch-wide picture of Enrico look-ing somber and depressed. As well he should. A diamond thief, no less. And to think I half swallowed his exotic story. The French and Swiss police had been tracking him for months. His thefts amounted to mil-lions. He was currently incarcerated in the Santé, Paris's most notorious prison.

Five months passed. One day, Patsy got word from her friend at the old hotel on the rue de l'Échaudé that she'd received a *pneumatique*—Paris's antiquated but highly efficient method of rapid communication in those days—from Enrico. He would be freed next week and wanted to see her before he left France (read: expelled). We suggested he meet us at the Bras-serie Lipp, and promptly at one in came (for me) the ghost of Enrico, his once elegant clothes hanging on him limply. He could have applied for the role of scarecrow in any peasant field. He had lost, he announced, some forty kilos, ninety pounds.

A choucroute garnie and glass or two of wine cheered him up, but I could tell that he really wanted to see Patsy, not me, so before coffee I excused myself on the pretext I had a three o'clock appointment and hur-ried off. Later, Patsy told me he had roundly rejected the charge of jewel thief, claimed again that his story was absolutely true, that his mistake had been not in changing the yellow diamonds to white but in transport-ing them across the border. He would head back to Israel that night, re-sume his production, and make sure in the future to handle his finished goods more carefully and discreetly. How, after rotting in the Santé for all those months, had he finally been sprung? He remained vague but implied that someone "important" in the Israeli government had contacted some-one in the French government who had intervened. He was considering instituting a suit against the police for false arrest. He promised Patsy she would hear from him again "soon."

Three months later, on the eve of our departure for the States, we still had no news of Enrico. Or if Patsy had heard from him, she didn't share the message.

14 ~

Name-Dropping; or, An Evening with Orson

ONCE PATSY WAS GONE—and after I finally came to the realization that she wasn't coming back—I consoled or distracted myself by dating a few ladies. I ended up going out with an American girl who turned out to be Orson Welles's secretary, Catherine, a buxom young lady from Middle America who, when the Great Man had decided to pull up stakes and leave America, whether for good or temporarily only time would tell, had accepted the job of Paris secretary. One of his secretaries, she hastened to add. How many does he have? I wondered aloud. Wasn't one enough? She laughed and shook her head. "Have you ever heard of the human dynamo? The concept of perpetual motion? Orson incarnate. He never has only one project going. Generally half a dozen. Writing scripts, directing, casting actors for projects not off the ground, accepting roles major and minor, usually to raise money . . ." "After *Kane*," I said, "I assumed he was never short of money." She shook her head. "He's *always* short of money. When he has it, he spends it like crazy, mainly because he has this theory that if you don't live high on the hog, people will think your career is slipping." Sounds like a monster, I said. No, no, she reassured me. Arrogant, yes; certain of his own genius, yes. But also plagued by doubts, which I guarantee are sincere and, for me, make him human. Why did he leave Hollywood? I wondered. I would have thought he could take his pick of projects. He's had his share of commercial flops, she said. Besides, he's convinced that Hollywood has it in for him, resents him, and that if he had stayed there and played by the rules—*their* rules—he'd never make another original movie. In Hollywood he felt straitjacketed, whereas in Europe he feels free, able to move in any of a dozen directions, both geographically and creatively. Plus, of course, he's espoused a lot of liberal causes, and this current American witch-hunt mentality drives him insane. People less liberal than he have been targeted, blacklisted, called before congressional committees, all of which he views as outrageous, ridiculous, time-consuming, and way beneath his dignity. Here he feels free from all that. He's the most peripatetic man on the planet. He flits from country to country on a whim, so I see him only sporadically. He'll announce one morning he's off to Rome for a "couple of days," and he'll be gone for a month. Dublin, London, Morocco. Much of his nerve-racking travel has to do with Shakespeare, with whom he's enamored. That was not news to me, but Catherine let it slip one day that he not only revered the Bard but felt he and he alone was capable of translating him—or at least certain of his works—to the screen. Pretty strong words when actors such as Gielgud and Olivier were still in their Shakespearean prime. Still . . . The project he was obsessed with these days, she reported, was *Othello*. He had a dozen other projects in various stages of development, including a play in French he was directing—she'd seen it and thought it "awful," but she'd never dare tell him that. "So you're scared of him," I ventured. "No," she said, "simply there are times, and situations, when discretion is advised." "So you *are* scared of him," I concluded, as if I had just taken one of her pawns.

I admired the man no end, but even after Catherine's intriguing nuggets I had no desire to meet him. Legends and their flesh and blood are best kept separate, I felt. Nonetheless, when one evening in late winter Catherine asked me if I would care to meet her boss, I of course said yes, especially after she mentioned in passing that he had read in the *Trib* not only the article I had written on *Gigi*—apparently, he was a fan of Colette's— but one I had written a few weeks later on Jean Gabin, the French actor he also greatly admired. At least I had a tiny credit or two to level the playing field, I told myself, then quickly put things back into perspective: this was God I was going to see, and I was sure I'd be suitably tongue-tied, making a fool of myself, with morning-after self-loathing.

Welles, Catherine told me, usually stayed at a posh Right Bank hotel, the Lancaster or the Ritz, but because of a French play he was directing, he had rented an apartment off the Champs-Élysées. At precisely seven o'clock Catherine opened the door to me. Would there be a dozen other guests? A hundred? But no, it was only the three of us, at least for the moment. The apartment was as expected: sumptuous and gilded, with massive doors, its generous windows framed by heavy drapes of some brocaded material in immaculate taste. But what did surprise and take me aback was the imposing size of Mr. Welles. I remembered him as the dashing demented incarnation of William Randolph Hearst, not as slim as Joseph Cotten but, let's say, normal. And here was Citizen Kane offering me a drink. Whiskey? he suggested. I hadn't had a Scotch in all my years in Paris. "That would be fine," I said, and he poured me a major, under-the-table tumblerful. "Ice?" he asked. "No, neat," I said, remembering the term from some Cary Grant, or maybe Gary Cooper, movie, uttered through tight lips so the words barely squeezed out. I think he was impressed. "Catherine tells me you're a writer," he said. *Jesus, in trouble already.* I had never told her that. "I write," I said. "Not quite the same thing." He told me he had been intrigued by my piece on *Gigi*—not the Danièle Delorme, but a later interview with Colette. She must be a hundred by now, he said. How did you ever get to her? I thought she didn't give interviews anymore. It's a long story, I said, if you really want to hear it. He did. So I had to thumbnail back into my wrestling, my fortuitous encounter with Maurice Goudeket, Colette's husband, our bonding through the classic sport of wrestling, my assignment to write about *Gigi*, and Goudeket's immediate and generous response that I could interview the author anytime. As I ended, I feared the two-, maybe three-minute roundup must have bored the man to death, but apparently not. Well, said Welles, you really caught her flavor—when I read your piece, I felt I'd met her. Is she actually bedridden, surrounded by all those cats? On the bed, in the bed, around the bed, I said: there were easily a dozen. One thing I especially liked, Welles said, was when she asked you where you lived and you said rue Jacob, she thought a second and said—his accent thick, his delivery impeccable, sounding like Colette's specific intonation from Burgundy—"*Je n'ai rien contre la rue Jacob.*" I don't have anything against the rue Jacob. Yes, that's it. A rather strange way of putting it, no? I'd never heard that expression before, but I think I know what Colette meant. She probably has positive feelings about some places, negative about others. About the rue Jacob I assume she's neutral. It was not only the words that came tumbling across the room; it was the sonority, that voice one would have recognized anywhere.

By this point in the conversation I was relaxed, feeling almost at home, certainly not in the state of tongue-tied awe I had feared. And the rest of the evening—which went on until almost midnight, dinner having been brought in at 8:30—was the same. In five minutes the man had put me at ease, ministered a small dose of flattery, and set the tone as only a true director can do. Catherine clearly had his confidence, and she, unlike some of his other secretaries, who, she had told me, were often treated abominably, seemed to be immune to his broadsides. Contrary to my fears, the Scotch had simply put me in a state of momentary grace, and the food, unlike any I had eaten for months, was as superb as the wine (when I discreetly checked the label, it was a Château Latour).

Most of the evening was spent listening to the master, who, with his otherworldly proportions, seemed more like Jove than a mere mortal. He had plans, great plans. Most immediately, getting the damn *Othello* finished. Then more Shakespeare and Don Quixote. I still kept looking at the door, expecting others, hordes no doubt, but it remained obstinately closed.

Next evening, over dinner at Raffy's, Catherine asked me what I thought.

"Is he always that friendly and forthcoming?" I asked.

"More often than you'd think. But he'll also fly into rages. He does not suffer fools gladly, and he thinks a great many people—especially in the world of movies—are damn fools."

"He and my father should meet." I saw that I had lost her. "Dad's favorite expression is 'damn fools.' He thinks the whole world, not just the movies, is peopled with them. In any event, I found your boss as brilliant as he was gracious."

"He liked you," she said. "It's that simple."

Catherine and I kept seeing each other for the next couple of months, at least two or three times a week. Neither of us was in love, but we enjoyed each other's company and felt no pressure to move beyond that. Of all my Left Bank friends she had met—for on the days when we did not see each other, I knew she was part of another life on the Right Bank, a life of diplomats and bankers and businessmen, of actors and writers and directors, and though from time to time she invited me to one of these soirees, I did not feel comfortable there and generally declined—the one who attracted and intrigued her the most was Ellsworth Kelly, with whom we had dinner once or twice at the rue du Sabot. Ellsworth also liked Catherine, whom he found intelligent and uncommonly knowledgeable about modern art. He invited her to view his work on the famous fourth-floor room on the Île St. Louis. She loved his work—the strong colors, the clean lines, the self-assurance—and was charmed by the man. "I'd like to sleep with him," she declared one day. She didn't feel the need to ask whether that might bother me, but later, when I posed myself the question, I realized it wouldn't in the least. She shared her strategies with me, hoping for advice. "I've seen him often enough; it's not that he's lacked the opportunity. So what is he waiting for?" she wondered aloud. "For me to ask him?" When, gently one day, I felt compelled to tell her that Ellsworth was—how did I put it? the term "gay" had not yet been invented—not really attracted to women, she was crushed. "How do you know?" she asked. I shrugged. "I just do." "Frankly, I don't believe it for one minute. He's really so . . . so masculine!" I agreed, but added some imbecilic remark about looks sometimes being deceiving. When later we went to bed, I felt she was not really with me. Suddenly she sat up, her pert breasts staring me in the face. "Want to bet," she said, "that I can make it with him?" "I don't want to take your hard-earned money." "Chicken!" "All right: to make it meaningful, five thousand francs." We shook. "When will the test take place?" I asked. "I'll keep you informed," she said. "And how will I know that a conquest truly occurred?" She looked hurt. "If you won't take my word," she said, "just check out the flush on Ellsworth's cheeks next time you see him. His only problem is, he hasn't yet met the right woman." With that, she settled back and fell into a deep, self-satisfied sleep.

Roughly a week later we met for dinner. She was wearing a superb new burgundy gown—at least I had never seen it before—and a flower in her hair, all heralds of victory, I assumed. Our eyes met, I probed the depths of hers: nothing. She was making me sweat it. So what if Ellsworth had yielded to her charms for one night; it did not change the basics. But if he had, then I had lost.

Suddenly her tightly clasped hand slid across the table, met mine, uncurled my fingers, and slipped a note into my palm. A note describing her conquest in intimate detail, blow by blow? I couldn't wait to read it. I opened my fingers to see in my palm not a folded billet-doux but a fresh five-thousand-franc note.

"I failed," she said, "miserably. I could have sworn . . ."

I slid my hand across the table and returned her money. "I can't take this," I said, "it would be like cheating."

She slid it back. "A bet's a bet," she said. "I tell you what: Can we use it to have a bottle of champagne? Waiter," I called, "a bottle of Veuve Clicquot, *bien frappé*!" It wasn't Château Latour '29, but hey, it was pretty damn good!

15 ⤫

Brendan Incoming

THE NOISE WAS DEAFENING: first a loud knock, then a voice, unless the voice was first and the knock following. Sequences, when one is deep asleep, are not readily discernible, but the result is the same: supine, one bolts upward, suddenly awake but still lost in dreams, so that for the moment one has no idea where one is. Or, sometimes, even who.

"SEAVER! I'm looking for RICHARD SEAVER. HIMSELF! I know you're in there, SO OPEN UP!"

The dim bed light, now on, showed barely half past twelve, so it could have been anyone of the male species. The voice at the door was deep baritone, more toward bass. And had I detected, in the words still ringing, still roaring, more than a touch of the Irish? Drunken Irish? Or was that a redundancy?

"Who is it?" I ventured, suddenly ashamed at being caught asleep so early by one of my night-owl friends, of whom there were many. A dozen flashed through my mind, sitting in all the old familiar places, the evening just getting into high gear, red wine flowing, pot boiling, dried hemp hallucinating, with weary me, long prostrate, more recently supine, now on the vertical frantically stuffing legs into trousers.

"WHO IS IT?" I shouted, trying hard to match the door-side decibels.

"BRENDAN," the voice said. "BRENDAN BEHAN'S THE NAME. SO OPEN THE FUCK UP! WE NEED TO TALK."

Wary, I unlatched the door to see a hulk virtually filling the frame. Full, round faced, body rotund but still young, eyes glowing, with life or drink. Doubtless both, for the undeniable odor of whiskey, perhaps Scotch but on second thought more likely Irish, the difference for me is virtually indiscernible but for those two peoples—I refer to the Scots and the Irish—as distinctive as race, followed him in. (I trust you have unraveled the syntax.)

"What took you so long?" he said. "I was out there in the cold for a fucking fifteen minutes."

"Cold?" I said. "It's fucking August." I've mentioned I tend to lapse into the vernacular of those around me, a failure, I know. I was now fully awake.

"I go by the mercury, not the month," he said, taking a seat. "I tell you, it's fucking cold outside . . . And you know why you didn't answer right away? You were fucking fast *asleep!*"

"I was fucking reading!" I lied.

"Show me the book!" he roared.

I'd only known the guy for a scant minute, and already I felt his prisoner, under deep interrogation, sure to screw up and be led directly to the nearest jail. Still, I pulled the book from the hastily shoved-together covers and handed it to him. He looked at the front, disdainfully at the back, and tossed it to me.

"French!" he said. "I don't read fucking Frog language."

It was time to turn the tables. "I was just getting ready to go out," I proclaimed. "I tend to sleep by day and operate by night. You might say my nights are white . . ."

"Can't you fucking speak English?" he countered, and suddenly I felt that, though not even actually acquainted, we were moving quickly toward the endgame, my king in severe jeopardy, my queen cowering, despite her wealth of twenty-seven possible moves. Who was this Gaelic monster who had just invaded my den, my world? "Anyway," he added, struggling to his feet and almost falling in the effort, so that I realized he had been drinking most of the day, "since you're going out, fetch your wallet and let's go."

We repaired to the Royal. My fear we might run into the gang was offset by the thought that this well-lit place would close in under two hours, and I could easily lose this Behan by pretending I had a romantic rendezvous at which he was unwelcome. A surefire strategy. *Sursum corda,*

Seaver, you've dealt with stranger types before. Or had I? For his visit was not random, as I had first assumed.

"Read your piece in *Merlin*," he was saying, "about this man Beckett. I'd never heard of him. If he's half as good as you make him out, I have to meet him."

I must confess, despite my early-morning antipathy, the endearing brogue was eroding my ire, especially after Mr. Behan had ordered us a second round of whiskey, his neat, mine tempered with a touch of soda.

"You mean, on the basis of that piece you came all the way from Ireland just to meet Beckett?"

"Absolutely," he said. "I missed Joyce. I hated that fucking Yeats. Flann O'Brien leaves me cold. He's so fucking *Irish*. The same goes for John Millington, who stuck his fucking ear to the fucking wall to overhear how the peasants really talk, then put it into his fucking plays as though he'd made it up himself! Damned thief! Anyway, from what you wrote about Beckett, he sounds like the real thing. So tell me how I find him."

I shook my head. "Actually, I've never met him—"

"What? And I'm supposed to believe that?"

"Believe it or not, it's true. I've read everything he's written, but he's a very private person. Very hard to get to."

"But I assume he's read your fuckin' piece about him."

"I don't know. I sent it to him, but I've never heard back. He may have hated it."

"Hated it? How could he, when you make him out a fuckin' genius? Better than Joyce, didn't you say? When I first read that, I thought you were fuckin' crazy. Then I thought: What if he's fuckin' right?"

Mr. Behan, I noticed, had begun to drop the *g* from his favorite term. Did this linguistic progress mean we had moved to a newer, higher plane in our budding relationship? Or was it a downward, merely more familiar move? In any event, he was continuing, assuming he had ever paused.

"So you sent it to him. That means you *know* his address." His right index finger pointed skyward, in Gaelic triumph.

I shook my head, feeling suddenly very protective of this mythic creature I had never met. I knew I was procrastinating at best, lying at worst, for I did know exactly where the man lived. But revealing that arcane knowledge would somehow be a betrayal. "No, I sent it to him via his French publisher," I said. "Now that I think of it, I have no way of knowing if the publisher even forwarded it. He may have thought it not worthy of his favorite author."

"So you know his publisher!" Behan went on, looking more and more like the bulldog he was, on a newly hot scent. "Just give me his name and I'll go see him, since *you* won't help me—"

"Damn it, Behan," I said, "it's not that I *won't* help you. It's simply that I *can't*." But I knew that, too, was a lie.

"To tell the truth," Behan was saying, "I didn't actually come here of me own free will. Me fuckin' countree expelled me from its hallowed shores. You see, I've spent most of me life in jail. I was a Borstal boy at sixteen, then spent the next seven years in one penal institution or another . . ."

Suddenly I pictured the young man beside me wielding a butcher knife or an ax—guns were forbidden—as he committed one heinous crime after another. And I had opened my door to him without so much as asking who sent him?

"Politics," he said. "I was part of the IRA, starting when I was a fuckin' kid. They let me out six years ago, but I knew they were watching me every move. I managed to keep them guessing all that time, but they simply kicked me out and deported me to France."

"So it wasn't my Beckett piece that brought you . . ."

"Yes and no. I'd read the essay and decided I must meet the man— only the Irish can understand the Irish, you know—but the timing wasn't me choice. You see, I'm a playwright in me own right—pretty funny, that, no? 'playwright' . . . 'right'?—and I gather this Beckett fellow is, too. So we have a lot to talk about."

The waiters had already begun stacking chairs on tables, a none too subtle sign. Time for me to look at my watch and talk of my romantic rendezvous, but again he took me by surprise.

"Listen, Seaver, you look tired, so I don't want to keep you up any longer. By the way, you didn't fool me with this white-night shit. You were asleep when I knocked, and you're ready to return to the arms of Morpheus"—I couldn't believe he had actually used the term, but checking, there it fucking was—"so, let us pay and go." I took note of the word "us" and glanced to see if he was reaching for his wallet, as I was. No, not the slightest movement. I paid, rose to my full height, and extended my hand, my not very subtle indication that the night was over. Taking it, he looked almost boyish—bad-boyish, but nonetheless—and for a very brief moment, I felt that under other circumstances, I might have found a new friend, whom I would like to see again in a year or two, perhaps three, when with a sly grin he said: "Good God, man, it's going on three, and I haven't a place to stay. Would it be all right if I bunked with you tonight? I saw you had an extra bed. Just till I find a place tomorrow first thing."

What could a man do? If loving one's enemies was part of the Christian creed—a dubious part, but still—could I, even agnostically, if not atheistically, turn this mad Irishman away at such hour? I nodded, and side by side we made our way unsteadily back to the rue du Sabot. As we passed 7, rue Bernard Palissy, I started to say, "That's Beckett's publisher," but caught myself just in time. Safely home, I pulled from the cupboard a pillow, blanket, and sheets, quickly made up the spare bed, and turned toward my own, when a suddenly seductive voice behind me said: "Sure and I wouldn't mind a nightcap before I turn in. I do hope you'll join me." If I'd had a gun, I might well have shot him. I did have a hammer, but would that have made any impression on his thick skull? Instead, I pulled an almost full bottle of Scotch from its hiding place and poured us each a final drink, his neat, mine laced with an ounce or two of water.

"You wouldn't by chance have anything to eat handy?" he inquired as the hands moved past three into four.

I rummaged and found some *saucisson*, which I carefully—*very* carefully—sliced, and some Camembert cheese, well over the hill, ready to run.

"Food," he said between munches, "is the great enabler."

I thought that profound, but asked what it meant.

"To get on with the drinking," he slurred. "Without food you pass out much too quickly."

"Ah," I said, "of course . . . What did you do with the bottle?"

"Last time I looked, you fuckin' had it," he murmured. "I t'ink it rolled under the fuckin' bed." He got down on all fours and peered. "There it is! You see, I never yet have lost sight of a bottle . . . Ah"—his voice was tinged with sadness—"it's fuckin' almost empty. How could that be?" He shook it, as if to restore life. At best there was a faint swish.

He suggested the hour was perhaps appropriate for song. "Song?" I inquired. "At quarter to four?" "When better?" he asked, clearing his throat. "No, no!" I said with a vigorous shake of the head. "There are people living upstairs. Lots of people. Working people. They anger quickly when their sleep is disturbed. Call *flics*. *Flics* drag Irishman and American friend to station across from St. Germain. Not good." He seemed to get the message. "Maybe just one," he said, "a simple Irish ballad. One of my favorites," and the first line came out before I forced a halt by offering "one last snort."

Rosy-fingered dawn found us both in a state of deep slumber, not in our respective beds, but in the selfsame chairs wherein we had downed the last dregs of the trusty bottle, now supine, if not prostrate—it was hard to tell—on the harsh cement floor of my humble abode.

Awake, I vaguely recalled that I had a mission. Ah, yes, to forewarn one Samuel Beckett that his life was in danger. Behan was, if sonority was any clue, still fast asleep. First thought: bicycle over to rue des Favorites and leave a message. No, Christopher had borrowed my bike and never returned it. Take the metro? A possibility. But wait! Minuit was right around the corner. Forewarn Lindon, who could then forewarn Beckett. Brilliant: the greatest reward for the least effort. I put one foot on the floor, a Herculean effort—or was it *an* Herculean? I must check—my head, though crystal clear, beset with pain as never before—well, seldom—as I brought the second foot to the floor. Quietly, I pulled on trousers, only to find a pair was already there, more than enough. Shirt too, wrinkled but serviceable. Shoes, socks, the works. I edged toward the door, unlatched it, cracked it open, nary a sound. I was in luck, till the morning light struck me full force and I staggered back. Looking around—stealth my motto—still no movement on the Irish front. I tiptoed out, literally, down along my familiar corridor, still cobblestoned as before, my own little universe, the inner button found and pushed, the solid street door clicked open, out into the rue du Sabot, swarming with life.

At Minuit, up the endlessly winding stairs to the landing, then left and up again to the reception. I smiled. She smiled back. She knew me by now. Was Monsieur Lindon in? Yes, but *occupé*. Was it important? Very. She looked worried, reached for the phone, checked it in midair. The hand that held it, I mean. Could she ask me a question? Of course.

Was I feeling all right? Fine, just fine. Thank you for asking, very kind of you. Because, Monsieur Seaver, you look a bit pale. I nodded, I assumed the proper gesture, and finally blurted out that I had an important message for Monsieur Beckett. Urgent. Could I leave a note for Monsieur Lindon? Would she make sure it reached him at the earliest possible moment?

With as steady a hand as I could muster, I related in writing the previous night's story, that young Mr. Behan of Dublin was intent on seeing him, come hell or high water. I tried to encapsulate his curriculum vitae, as much as I had gleaned or could recall, starting with his Borstal youth, but remembering suddenly that he had also claimed in the wee hours to be, like Mr. Beckett, a budding playwright, a nugget that had escaped me till then. Therefore with much to discuss. But beware: he seemed to have a slight propensity to drink. For the moment, I added, he was lodged at the rue du Sabot, though my intent was to end that situation in the immediate future, if not sooner. (Mother's expression; credit where credit is due.) He had tried to worm Mr. Beckett's address from me, I underlined, and though I had drunk far too much last night, I believed that sacred information inviolate . . .

Rereading my note, I thought it seemed gibberish, so, apologizing to the motherly receptionist, I tore it up and wrote another, shorter and surely more cogent. Folding it, I marked it URGENT, thanked her, and repaired to the Royal, where I had a double café crème. Then another. At which point, almost human, I gathered my wits, girded my loins, and headed home to rid myself of the Gaelic invader.

Even as I turned the corner from the rue Bernard Palissy into the rue du Sabot, I knew I was in trouble. Deep trouble. I could hear the voice as loud and clear as if it were right next to me, singing, in what I took to be perfect pitch, an Irish song of some renown. The sound swelled with every step I took until, the door open, it almost swept me off my feet. As peaked as I must have looked, Behan looked the picture of health, his cheeks ruddy, his eyes clear, his hands steady. The smell of coffee filled the room.

"Where have you been, Seaver?" he boomed. "Coffee's brewing. Have yourself a seat. And make yourself perfectly at home."

Make *myself* at home? From gate-crasher to king of the roost in a mere half day. This was not going to be as easy as I had hoped. Over coffee, Behan pressed his case. He would be going by to see Beckett's publisher, who, he was sure, would provide him with the desired address. I could only hope my message had been passed in time.

I told him I'd be needing his bed tonight, for a friend passing through. "That's all right," he said, "I can sleep in the chair, as I did last night." "No, no," I responded, "the bed is for a *lady* friend." "Then you won't be needing two beds at all, will you?" He winked, and again I thought of the gun I didn't have. "You know I haven't a penny to me name," he went on. "Deported from me own country without so much as a farthing or thank-you. You wouldn't want me sleeping on park benches, would you? Anyway, I rarely get to bed before three or four in the morning, so I won't be any bother. Just leave the door unlatched when you turn in . . . So I'll be off."

He was back in half an hour, unenlightened but also undeterred. Lindon had refused to see him, but he swore he'd go back the next day, and the day after that, until he wormed the information out of him. Much as I loathed him at this point, I had to admire his persistence.

"It's not as though Beckett wouldn't *want* to see me," he reasoned. "He'll receive me the same way Joyce received him."

For a moment I thought I might have been dead wrong: Who was I to judge whom Beckett would see and whom not? But Behan had already formulated his next obsessive step.

"I know he hangs out at Montparnasse," he said, "so I'll spend me day there, asking around till I find him." And he was out the door as spry and serene as if a drop had never touched his lips the night before.

As for me, I flopped on the bed and slept a good three hours before, awake once again, I felt human. Well, almost human.

True to his word, Brendan spent all day—and night—roaming Montparnasse, asking hither and yon if anyone had seen Samuel Beckett, his old friend. Given his obvious Irishness, both of word and of drink, more than one local imparted information willingly. No, he hasn't been around, at least not recently, but have you tried the Closerie des Lilas, he's often there? Also the Dôme or the Coupole. At each of these spots Behan would pause to refresh, so by late afternoon, early evening at most, he would be roaring drunk, singing at the top of his lusty lungs until he would either fall asleep or be ungraciously ushered out onto the unwelcoming sidewalk.

The second night, in stark defiance, I had bolted the rue du Sabot door. I'd not come home myself until after two, warily checking to see if my boarder had somehow snuck in. Great! A good night's sleep in the offing. Wrong! At what turned out to be four a.m., first the Voice and then the insistent pounding. "OPEN UP, SEAVER! I'M HOME!"

"Home indeed!" But unlatch the door I did, however reluctantly. This time no bottle was unearthed, yet I was obliged to hear how he was still waiting for Beckett, despite several promising leads. The Rotonde and, especially, a pub called the Falstaff were places to which Beckett now repaired, Behan had learned, and on the morrow he would reconnoiter both. Would I mind if we had just one song before turning in? Just one? Fine, but not too loud . . . "I know, I know, the working people upstairs. I've no use for working people. You know the old Irish saying: 'Work is the curse

of the drinking classes'!" and he roared with laughter, as though he had
made it up.

Next day, in much better shape, I hied myself around the corner and
scaled the now-familiar stairs two at a jaunty time, only to meet head-on,
on the first-floor landing, Sindbad Vail. "Nice piece about Samuel Beckett
in *Merlin*," he said, either smiling or scowling, I wasn't sure which. "I
thought you promised *Points* your next offering." It's true, I had, but it was
Trocchi who'd suggested the Beckett, so I had no choice. "I have something for your next issue," I said, "I think you'll like." "Fiction or nonfiction?" he asked. "I'll give you one of each, and you pick," I offered, and
he seemed happy.

At reception, the motherly lady looked pleased at my improved appearance. She confirmed that my note to Monsieur Lindon had reached him.
He was grateful, and she was quite sure he had alerted Monsieur Beckett
to the problem. As I took my leave, she said, "I'm glad you're feeling better
today." I nodded, gracefully, I hoped, and scooted downstairs and back
around the corner to prepare for the next episode in my Irish saga. Gingerly, I opened the door, so as not to awake my honored guest, only to find
the room empty. A note, penned in large and generally readable script, informed me that he was off to seek his prey, but assured me he would return sometime early morning. "DON'T FORGET TO LEAVE THE DOOR
UNLATCHED!"

Three days' further sleuthing were, as Behan put it, "a washout." He had to
conclude that Beckett was not around, for surely he would have heard in
these past few days that Brendan Behan, a fellow Irishman, a fellow playwright, a friend-waiting-to-happen, was in Paris and eager to meet. "I actually got his street address," he said. "Rue des Favorites, though nobody
could give me the number. I stopped in several pubs in the neighborhood,
but no luck. But I can tell you, most of the pubs in the area have decent
whiskey. A good sign, no?" He paused. "Or rather, they did. I fear I may have
forced most of them to replenish their supply . . .

"Anyway, on the fourth day—I sound like the fuckin' Bible, don't I?—
one pub finally did have the street number—15, by the way—so I went up
and pounded on the door till himself answered. Had a lovely conversation.
Three hours at least. At nine or so, however, he said he had to leave for a

rehearsal of his play *Waiting for Godot*, which is apparently going on the boards shortly—do you know anything about it?—but he was most grateful for me visit. Most grateful. Not sure his wife agreed. Suzanne. She scarcely said a word . . ."

"Nine o'clock?" I said. "You left him at *nine* o'clock after three hours? Which means you went there at *6:00 a.m.*?"

He frowned, all cogs working, then nodded. "Must have been," he said. "I don't watch the clock the way most people do. Anyway, I didn't *leave* him of me own accord. At one point he said he had to go to a rehearsal of his play and escorted me out. He asked where I was stayin'. 'Rue du Sabot,' I told him, at which point he hailed me a cab and paid for it. God bless! I told you we Irish always stick together!"

Shit! Behan's revelation of my address as his Paris hospice meant Beckett would quickly put two and two together and think I had sicced Behan upon him. This only weeks after I had sought his collaboration for the magazine. Now I was sure I would never hear from him, about *Watt* or any other matter.

So all my efforts had been in vain. Months later, one afternoon at the Dôme when I was having a drink with Beckett, I brought up the subject, recounting my side of the Behan saga. He shook his head. "Don't worry," he said. "Lindon told me the efforts you made on my behalf. Poor lad," he said, shaking his head, "at the rate he's drinking, he won't last another decade."

Beckett was almost right. Behan died twelve years after that initial 1952 encounter, at age forty-one. Beckett was to see him only once thereafter. When he was in London in the fall of 1961 attending rehearsals of *Happy Days*, his cousin John Beckett, one of his uncle Gerald's three children, who was a longtime friend of Behan's, persuaded Sam to go along with him to visit Brendan, then confined to a nursing home in a vain attempt to cure his alcoholism. Though he had predicted this end, Beckett was profoundly shocked at what he found: "a hulking carcass lumped under the wrinkled bedsheets" which "signified a terrible waste of spirit and talent."[*]

I, on the other hand, was to meet my uninvited boarder several times later, in my role as his editor at Grove Press in the 1960s. But that is a whole other story, on a continent far away.[†]

---

[*]Quote from Ulick O'Connor, *Brendan Behan* (London: Coronet Books, 1972), p. 292.
[†]In her earnest but badly flawed 1978 biography of Beckett, Deirdre Bair places Christopher Logue at the rue du Sabot when Brendan stumbled in that morning, but, alas, it was only me holding the fort.

16 ～

Thief, Pederast . . . and Genius

BACK TO OUR STORY, with number 3 of *Merlin* hot off the press. We had delivered two copies to Sartre, courtesy again of the ubiquitous and always-accommodating Jean Cau. Two days later, Cau called and asked if Trocchi and I could meet with Monsieur Sartre the following afternoon. "He is impressed with what you are doing," he said. "I think he has an idea or two for you."

My immediate reaction was "Oh, shit!" because in that issue I had written a piece on Sartre, summing up the long-running political feud between him and Camus. Still, since I had given the clear nod to Sartre, I thought there was little with which he could take exception.

What's more, I reasoned, even if he saw the piece, he wouldn't bother to read it, for one thing I had learned is that the French in general have a penchant to ignore any foreigners' attempts to understand, much less explain, the finer details of their history, culture, and politics.

As Cau ushered us again, promptly at four, into the sanctum sanctorum, Sartre rose to greet us. Copies of the magazine were on his desk.

"I am glad you did the Nyiszli," he said. "It is such an important document, and now at least English readers will have an insight into that death camp. Too little is still known." Then he turned his oblique gaze on me. "Your piece 'Revolt and Revolution,'" he said. "You doubtless sense how painful my rupture with Camus has been. During the war he was exemplary. *Combat* was the most important clandestine newspaper, and as the editor he showed rare courage and great intelligence. And Meursault is one of the major characters of contemporary fiction. But I always suspected that Camus was more interested in heaven than in our mere earthly matters. The Germans actually brought us together in a common cause. But when that pressure was removed, we went different ways, which is perfectly acceptable and normal. My suspicion, though, is that Camus looked upon the German occupation years as an unwanted intrusion, which forced him into a daily servitude he was all too happy to end so that he could turn to matters more transcendental, more—" He broke off, saying he had gone on too long, though I demurred. I wanted to hear more, for Sartre spoke with an intensity and intelligence that, despite the obvious emotional involvement, did not become bellicose.

"I would like to suggest another French writer for your consideration," he said. "You may find you're veering too much from your basic mission as an English-language magazine, but I wonder, do you know the work of Jean Genet?"

I nodded, for though it was carefully not in Jeanne Theis's canon, I had read not only his *Journal du voleur* but the even more daring *Notre-Dame-des-Fleurs*.

"He is very important," Sartre went on. "Unlike any other writer in France today. Or maybe ever. In fact, he has so fascinated me that I have written a book on him." He reached down and pulled out an enormous tome with the intriguing title *Saint Genet*. "I meant only to write an introduction to one of his books, but the more I learned, the fatter this became." He sounded almost apologetic. "Here," he thrust the tome across the desk, "use whatever you want from it, if indeed you publish something by Genet himself. There is, by the way, an English translation under way, perhaps done, of at least one work, I'm not sure which."

"*Journal du voleur*," Jean Cau said.

"How do we get in touch with Monsieur Genet?" Alex asked.

"He is very reclusive," Sartre said, "and will be difficult to contact, though I will have a word with him and see if you can meet."

We thanked him and prepared to leave.

"One more thing," he said, standing. "I notice you have published"—

I think he looked in my direction, but his walleye made that uncertain; at least he turned in my direction—"a piece in your second issue on Samuel Beckett. I did not read it all, but I gather you think very highly of him . . ."

"Of his work," I interjected. "I don't know the man."

"And in your current issue I gather you have an extract of one of his novels, *Watt*, the last work he wrote in English. Now he writes in French. Some years ago, we published a story of his in *Les temps modernes*. I don't remember the title—I think it was called 'Suite'—but I recall he became very upset, claiming we had published only half the work, whereas what appeared was the entire manuscript his agent Tony Clerx* had sent Simone. It turns out it was indeed but half the story, but that we learned only later, and Beckett became quite incensed with us when we told him we did not publish sequels. 'It is not a sequel,' he said. 'It is the second half of the story. The crucial half, for without it you allow me to speak only to cut me off before my voice has had time to become meaningful.' Or words to that effect. He wrote Simone a stinging letter, using, if I recall, such terms as 'nightmare' and 'mutilation.' 'Then why did you not send us the entire piece?' Simone asked. 'Because,' responded Beckett, 'when it was first submitted we were told it was too long to be published as such. But we were assured by Madame Allard† that the second part would be published in the autumn issue.'" Sartre shook his head, doubtless wondering if any editor could ever satisfy any author. "Still," he went on, "he has since published two novels with Minuit, *Molloy* and *Malone*, both of which are fine, and a year ago we published a long extract—some fifteen thousand words, I believe—of the latter in the magazine, under the title 'Quel malheur.' So while I wouldn't say that fences are fully mended, I think it proves we hold no grudge against him. On the contrary. But I suspect he still does against us. Certainly against Simone. So I thought you should know that, however talented, he can be difficult. *Very* difficult."

*"Tony Clerx" was the pseudonym of Jacoba van Velde, the sister of Beckett's friend Bram van Velde, a Dutch painter Beckett greatly admired. In dealing with editors, be they magazine or book, Beckett preferred not to negotiate directly but to use an intermediary such as Clerx or George Reavey, or even his beloved Suzanne, who had personally traipsed around Paris for years with copies of *Molloy* and *Malone* under her arm, looking in vain for a publisher. Beckett's own self-doubt, plus the plethora of painful rejections he had suffered over the years at the hands of publishers, made him editor-shy, until at long last not Suzanne but the Becketts' mutual friend Robert Carlier finally had the good fortune of dropping off his work at Les Éditions de Minuit in 1950.
†Paule Allard, one of the magazine's editors.

We thanked him for the warning, shook hands, and were again escorted to the door by Jean Cau.

"I'll make sure to put you in contact with Genet," Cau said. "Sartre is right. To publish him would be a real coup for your magazine."

Early in the new year I received a *pneumatique* from a man named Bernard Frechtman, who announced himself Jean Genet's friend, agent, and translator. Once again Jean Cau had been as good as his word. Frechtman had heard we were interested in publishing Genet's work in the magazine. Could we meet? Possibly next Friday at three? We suggested the Old Navy, a popular bar on the boulevard St. Germain that, along with the Royal and later the Café Tournon, was a place where one could spend the better part of the afternoon reading, writing, or just talking without the management batting an eye, even if all we had ordered over the hours was a couple of coffees or, if suddenly felled by hunger, a sandwich and a glass of wine. Promptly at three, Frechtman arrived, tall and bespectacled, shrouded against the cold in an army jacket that had clearly seen better days, perhaps even battle. His were no ordinary glasses, the lenses so thick he had to peer at everyone and everything that met his gaze, his head thrust slightly forward as if to help the magnification. I wondered how, with that eyesight, he had ever been accepted in the army. Looking past him, I was hoping to see the saint himself, but there was no one. Frechtman was an American GI who had stayed on after the war and was firmly ensconced here. He was carrying a package, wrapped in brown paper. There were five of us at that first meeting: Alex, Jane, Austryn, Patrick, and I. We were all drinking coffee, but Frechtman, good Frenchman that he had become, ordered a glass of red wine. We had three or four copies of *Merlin*'s latest issue on the table, one of which we pushed toward him, but he shook his head. "Thanks, but I've already read it," he said. "And I've talked to Jean about you and the magazine. He'd be pleased if you published an extract from *The Thief's Journal*. I've brought the manuscript with me. Have any of you read him in French by the way?" Both Austryn and I had. "He's a genius," Frechtman said, "pure and simple. If you haven't, you should read Sartre's *Saint Genet*. That says it all." I wasn't sure about "genius," but it was true I had never read anything quite like Genet, a mixture of lyricism and lower depths, of grit and soaring imagination, all in a prose so personal and complex it defied a simple reading. Damn hard to translate. I was intrigued to see how well Frechtman had done. "Read it and pick a passage," he said, sliding the manuscript across the table. "When you've decided, I'd like to see it." We chatted for half an hour or so, about Genet, about *Merlin* and the other little magazines in Paris—all of which, Frechtman confessed, had turned down Genet as "too daring," "too dangerous," "too obscure." "Maybe you will, too," he added, "but I don't think so." I mentioned to Frechtman that Sartre had asked to meet him.

To date, the only publisher in France courageous enough to publish Genet, whose books dealt with theft, murder, pimping, and above all homosexuality, vividly if poetically depicted, was L'Arbalète, a small and relatively impecunious house in the south of France. Perhaps geography had something to do with it: with Paris the center of everything in the country, the periphery could get away with things impossible even to envisage in the capital. Daring was in direct proportion to the distance from the Île de la Cité.

That night again, in our rue du Sabot refuge, our world headquarters, we sat around reading *The Thief's Journal*. We knew we were reading an important work. Studded with stunning images, of language almost liturgical and yet of the gutter. Thief and saint at once. Abject and proud. And, in its introspection, as deeply honest as man can be about himself and the netherworld around, a world of pimps and crooks, of racketeers and escaped convicts. For me it did not have the multileveled beauty of Beckett, but, no question, Genet was opening doors into hidden rooms, dark landscapes that had never before been depicted with such candor and candescence. As with *Watt*, however, very difficult to extract. Finally we picked a section in which the narrator, enamored of the criminal, the "splendid beast" Stilitano, roams the lower depths of Barcelona, thieving, whoring, lying, self-castigating.

From Sartre, who had written hundreds of thousands of words on Genet, with whom he was obviously fascinated, we picked a scant two pages, which Austryn and I translated:

> Not all who would be are Narcissus. Many who lean over the water see only a vague human figure. Genet sees himself everywhere; the dullest surfaces reflect his image; even in others he perceives himself, thereby bringing to light their deepest secrets. The disturbing theme of the double, the image, the counterpart, the enemy brother, is found in all his works.
>
> Each of them has the strange property of being both itself and the reflection of itself. Genet brings before us a dense and teeming throng which intrigues us, transports us and changes into Genet beneath Genet's

gaze. Hitler appears, talks, lives; he removes his mask: it was Genet. But the little servant girl with the swollen feet who meanwhile was burying her child—that was Genet too. In *The Thief's Journal* the myth of the double has assumed its most reassuring, most common, most *natural* form. Here Genet speaks of Genet without intermediary. He talks of his life, of his wretchedness and glory, of his loves; he tells the story of his thoughts. One might think that, like Montaigne, he is going to draw a good-humored and familiar self-portrait. But Genet is never familiar, even with himself. He does, to be sure, tell us everything. The whole truth, nothing but the truth, but is it the sacred truth . . . He reassures us only to disturb us further . . . Genet the novelist, speaking of Genet the thief, is more of a thief than the thief; the thief and his double are alike sacred. Thus there comes into being that new object: a mythology of the myth (like the blues song that was called *The Birth of the Blues*); behind the first-degree myths— The Thief, Murder, the Beggar, the Homosexual—we discover the reflective myths: the Poet, the Saint, the Double, Art. Nothing but myths, then; a Genet with a Genet stuffing, like the prunes of Tours. If, however, you are able to see at the seam the thin line separating the enveloping myth from the enveloped myth, you will discover the truth, which is terrifying. That is why I do not fear to call this book, the most beautiful that Genet has written, the *Dichtung und Wahrheit* of homosexuality.

17 ~

Big Decisions, Taken Hesitantly

So here we had come around to another Christmas Eve at the Manchons'. Replay of the previous Christmas. Again I arrived to find Frank and Louis in the kitchen opening oysters. Again I shed my jacket, donned an apron, and joined in. I had made enough progress not to seem like an oyster dunce, but still my non-knife hand was encased in a heavy mitt, the better to save the fingers from unwilling amputation. In the living room the other guests—a dozen or so in all—were sipping champagne around a handsome Christmas tree that was adorned not with the ornaments I had grown up with but with golden garlands and real candles, as yet unlit.

We oyster openers joined the others and shook hands all around, or double bussed the ladies if that degree of intimacy had been reached. For me it had not, except for Jeanne, who a year before had proclaimed me a family member, therefore free to brush my puckered lips across both her cheeks. Her paramour, the count, limited himself to kissing her hand, a practice I knew I would never achieve no matter how many years I lived here: one was born to it, I decided. Hand kissing was a dying custom, but when in its presence, I always felt I was being given a privileged glimpse of an earlier, gentler period.

Among the guests were Paul, Roszi again, along with young Jeannette in a stunning pale green dress. I had thought about her often. She was even more beautiful than before. I made a point of sitting beside her.

While I had little memory of the evening's no doubt scintillating conversation the next day, I remembered virtually every word Jeannette had said. Even by European standards, she was surprisingly mature for her years, which I ascribed in large part to the fact that her adored father was a font of information on all subjects: political, economic, cultural, artistic. At home he was just as likely to ruminate aloud on subjects as he would with his colleagues at the Chambre des Députés or the Quai d'Orsay. He was unquestionably one of Paris's most respected journalists. What's more, he was passionate about his work and could never delve doggedly or deeply enough into a given subject in his search for the hidden meaning, the deeper truth. I had been present at enough dinners with him to share that general esteem. He was never pompous, never overbearing: he listened as intently as he spoke, and if he contradicted, he did so with an elegance that made it seem as if he were agreeing, not contending. On more than one night I went home and, even though it was the wee hours and my mind not the clearest, recorded in my journal his thoughts and opinions about European politics and literature.

Near the end of the evening, Jeannette turned to Frank and said: "I've been invited to a dancing party New Year's Eve. If you're by chance free, would you be my escort?"

Frank, the epitome of courtliness, smiled and raised his hands palm out in a gesture of self-deprecating hopelessness. "My dear Jeannette," he said, "I'd be honored. But the problem is, I don't dance."

"Ah," she said.

"I do," said a voice to her left. Mine. "I'd be happy to escort you."

She looked at me as if for the first time. "You would? Thank you. That would be lovely."

Then I suddenly had an attack of very cold feet at the idea. "Bear in mind," I said, "I'm no Fred Astaire." I was waiting for her to say, "That's fine. I'm no Ginger Rogers," but all she said was "I think you'll have a good time."

New Year's Eve. I almost didn't recognize Jeannette. She slipped off her fur coat to reveal a sleek silver dress that even to my untrained eye was clearly haute couture, her feet shod in Cinderella slippers, also of silver. All of a sudden I felt awkward and rustic in my too-shiny dark blue suit. I also knew the collar of my white shirt was slightly frayed, and as I shook her hand, I hoisted my suit coat a smidgen higher.

After dinner Jeannette's parents drove us to the dance, a good half-hour drive across a Paris more brightly lit than I had ever seen it, as the City of Light struggled mightily to regain its prewar glory. The "dance" was in Neuilly. We crossed the Pont Alexandre III, passed the Grand Palais, circled the Rond Point, and headed up the Champs-Élysées toward the Arc de Triomphe. Despite my Left Bank prejudice, I marveled and had to admit this was one of the great avenues of the world. Tonight its pavements were packed with milling throngs, its restaurants and cafés were crowded to overflowing, and the relatively few cars, mostly prewar, passing up and down in slow succession, noisily honked their welcome to the New Year, sounding for all the world like a flock of oversized geese.

Marie-Claire greeted us at the door and introduced us to the hosts, her sister and brother-in-law, who responded with smiles so perfunctory and artificial I wanted to flee. But a look at Jeannette, all innocence and smiles, quickly reassured me. I spied several of the men appraising Jeannette with lupine eyes. My suit, and especially my frayed collar, I felt, were becoming more and more conspicuous by the minute. Fortunately, the also tuxedoed orchestra—how can you tell the guests from the hired help?—that had been warming up on a platform in the far corner broke into its first number. Taking the Cinderella child in my arms for the first time, I prayed that my wooden feet would not betray me. "Where are you, Miss Cassidy, now that I need you?"

Jeannette was a natural dancer, and we flowed across the room—yes, yes, at least in the mind of the beholder—like Fred and Ginger. This was the first time I had danced in years. And this beautiful girl in my arms was making it a total pleasure. So Miss Cassidy's Dancing School of my tender Connecticut youth was not a total waste, after all.

I was eleven or maybe twelve when my mother broke the news. "This fall, you'll be attending Miss Cassidy's Dancing School"—and my world suddenly darkened. None of the boys my age knew how to dance nor had any desire to learn. Sports was my life: football in the fall, wrestling in the winter, baseball in the spring and summer. Saturday afternoons from September on, I would sit glued to the radio broadcasts of Cornell's Big Red football powerhouse, to the exploits of Brud Holland, Cornell's black running back.

"Why do I have to go to dancing school?" "Because it's part of growing up. A social grace you're going to need. One day you'll thank me for sending you." Whenever my mother made me do something I knew was wrong, or useless—like forcing me to take Latin just because she had been a Latin teacher years before—I was sure I would hate it. And Miss Cassidy's was the pits. Twenty-five or thirty boys and girls all dressed up—they in dark velvet usually, we in white shirt and tie—standing on opposite sides of the room until the piano began and we had to move to the center and take a girl around the waist with one hand, which was bad enough, then grasp her right hand and start to move our feet. Half the time I would walk on her toes and have to say "Sorry," and she would say, "Oh, that's all right," which it wasn't, so why did she say it? Things got a little better when two of my boy classmates showed up. By the end of the year I had actually mastered the two-step and the waltz, though I could only do that one-two-three so many times before I lost it and had to start counting again.

Jeannette and I felt good in each other's arms, and my awkwardness, which had returned as the champagne wore off, receded with every new song. Most songs were American and familiar, the French having taken to American music after the war as though they owned it, so much so that many American jazz musicians had pulled up stakes, taken the first available transatlantic, and begun to play in nightclubs throughout Paris. Besides, in France black musicians were not only truly welcomed but celebrated as musical heroes. Here one could mingle freely with whites, marry a white woman. France had its own objects of prejudice, but blacks were not among them.

We danced, we held hands, we sat, we drank more champagne, we danced again. We were both falling hopelessly in love.

At midnight we heralded the New Year—1953! Almost timidly, I kissed Jeannette. We danced again. I couldn't let go of her.

At dawn, we emerged into the nearly empty streets. It was time to send Cinderella home, but instead of hailing a cab to take her home, I spotted an all-night café on the near corner. We had to greet the gray new day together with warm croissants and steaming coffee. It was after seven when I kissed her good morning and put her in a cab. My head may have been light, but so were my feet. Spurning the idea of taking a taxi myself, I decided to hoof it home—a good hour's walk. Occasionally, when walking simply wouldn't do, I'd twist and twirl to some inner rhythm, a silent song on my lips. That morning, Maurice Chevalier had nothing on me. I was in love. My tour back home, first to the Arc de Triomphe, down the Champs-Élysées to the Place de la Concorde, across the now-silent bridge, its pale yellow lights like a necklace to dawn, and onto St. Germain, made me feel that morning as if I owned this city I loved. At least for a couple hours.

A few weeks before that magic night, when I had danced not in the rain but, ebullient if unappreciated and oh so in love, across all of Paris, modest posters on the Left Bank announced that a play by Samuel Beckett, *En attendant Godot*, the same work of which I had heard intriguing fragments at the French radio almost a year before, was scheduled to open in early January at the Théâtre de Babylone, a stone's throw from my abode.

At long last! Ever since that partial performance at the French radio, I had been obsessed with seeing the whole. Or even with reading it. My efforts to cajole a manuscript copy from Monsieur Lindon, by now a fledgling friend, were in vain. He was adamant. Had he read it? Of course! And? *Extraordinaire!* he would say. As good as the novels? He frowned. As good, but different . . . His words intrigued but didn't satisfy. We will publish as soon as the play is on and Monsieur Beckett has approved all changes. Will Blin play Lucky? No, Beckett wrote the play with him in mind for Pozzo. So the intriguing tidbits fell thick and fast, whetting but not satisfying.

When it was confirmed the play would open on January 5, I suggested to the *Merlin* group that we all go, but only Patrick spoke French well enough, and he was busy that weekend at his teaching post in the provinces. So I went alone, and when I say alone, I am close to literal, for there could not have been more than a dozen souls in the audience. As the play progressed, I realized I was in the presence of something special, the likes of which I had never read or witnessed. And that included the plays by two other new playwrights fresh on the scene of the Paris theater, the Romanian Eugène Ionesco and a Russian, Arthur Adamov, both of whom, like Beckett, were writing in French. (From my Paris notebook, spring 1953: "Note to self: Why are so many foreigners not only writing in French but, possibly, doing the most interesting work in their adopted language? Investigate.")

I came out of the theater that night with one goal: to see the play again, and to read the text, just out from Minuit. I had read the review by Robert Kemp in *Le monde*, which was generally positive, though in no wise enlightening. He found the Pozzo-Lucky duo, the master-to-slave relationship, "a rather heavy banality," then redeemed himself slightly by calling it "ultimately poignant." But he warned potential theatergoers: "This is probably a play devoid of genius . . . Still, *Godot* is *sympathique*." *Sympathique*? Devoid of genius? Had Mr. Kemp and I seen the same play? The most damning review merely said: "This is a play where nothing happens. Twice."

Two or three weeks later I invited Jeannette to see the play with me. That night the audience had more than doubled, a good sign, but scarcely enough, I figured, to pay the actors, director, and theater, much less the author. Thirty-some, if memory serves. At the curtain, the applause was scattered, hesitant at best. When the lights went up, half the audience had already left, and several of the remaining heads were shaking, either in disbelief or in disappointment.

Outside, we wandered silently toward the Luxembourg Gardens. It was a damp night, with a biting wind, but both of us apparently felt the need to walk and talk. How did she like it? She was stunned, fascinated. But she professed not to understand much of the play's deeper meaning. How did she know it had a deeper meaning? Oh, of that she was sure. "Aren't we all waiting for Godot," she said, "whoever or whatever that might be? I found it funny and sad at the same time. Isn't it maybe about how often useless it is to hope? And yet they come back night after night, which means they haven't entirely given up hope?" I looked at her with admiring eyes. "Didn't you have the feeling that Vladimir and Estragon had been waiting not just those two days but *forever*?" she went on.

Here I had come out of my second viewing armed with all sorts of literary theories and enlightened precisions—for since that first performance I had given the play much thought—with which to answer her questions, which I assumed would be plentiful, and in a handful of sentences she had left me at the gate. "You didn't live through the war here," she went on, "but you tell me Mr. Beckett did. I doubt he could have written this play if he had not suffered the German occupation." Why? I asked. "Well, one reading might be—and I'm obviously wrong—that Pozzo is the Germans and Lucky is us French, don't you think? They too had a leash around our neck, they beat us and killed us for no reason at all, they made us sing and dance to their tune, were as cruel and senseless as Pozzo is. Then, in the second act, Pozzo is laid low, blinded, just as the Germans were in 1945 and later. Just a thought. I'm being far too literal, I know, for this play's universal. I'd like to know what *you* think."

I looked at this budding musician, this lass who had read perhaps a tenth of the books I had, and said: "I think we should go have dinner."

18 ~

Bigger Decision, No Hesitation

I HAD MENTIONED to Alex the two Beckett stories I had uncovered from *Les temps modernes* and *Fontaine*, namely "Suite" and "L'expulsé," extolling their virtues and saying we must publish one or the other, perhaps in due course both.

"Sure," Trocchi said, "but we need them in English."

"Only Beckett can do them," I said. "I'm sure he'll oblige."

I was wrong. "No, no." Beckett shook his head emphatically, over a drink one afternoon at the Coupole in Montparnasse. "I couldn't face those old chestnuts again. All I see is their shortcomings."

I must have looked disappointed—I had told him we ardently desired one of the stories for our next issue—for he suddenly brightened and said, "Why don't you try your hand at them, Seaver? I'd be happy to look over your translations once they're done."

I knew both stories well, having read them three or four times at least, and nodded. Why not? "If it would save you time for your own work," I said. "It would that," he said. "It would that . . . I have an indigestion from old work."

Now, two weeks later, back in my rue du Sabot emporium, I was having second thoughts. I had reread "La fin"—the title of the second part of the work called "Suite"—slowly and quietly. Better even than the first reading. In fact, one of the most moving stories I had ever read. Some references obscure, the prose daunting but not impossible, I concluded. Such is the cockiness of youth. The seeming obscurities Beckett would elucidate, I was sure. I figured at worst I could come up with a draft of the story's twenty-five pages in two to three weeks. That schedule was set back a trifle when, after the three weeks were up and I had indeed done a full draft, I read it through the next day and decided it needed to marinate, if that's the term, so I set it aside and went back to my own writing. The only problem was, the words I managed to put on a page were constantly haunted by my memory of "La fin." My own sentences so mundane and one-dimensional next to Beckett's. As I came to realize just how dense, how simple yet fraught with meaning his story was, I found myself writing less each day until I came to a complete halt. Frozen. Blocked. Hopeless. Finally, feeling very near the end myself, I went back to my Beckettus interruptus. Four hours later, I had fashioned two full paragraphs of what I considered "ready-to-show" material. A triumph or a disaster? At least something, which I had learned was generally—not always—better than nothing. I went to bed at some wee hour feeling utterly depressed, convinced I was letting Alex down, and Beckett too, for he had told me more than once how relieved he was, not having to face that "old muck" again. I awoke with a major hangover and realized, too late, where the time had gone: a bottle and a half of *gros rouge* followed by several cognacs. I quickly dressed and hurried off to St. Germain des Prés. "Coffee," I said, "black. Double. No, triple."

"So," the silhouette of Alex boomed when he found me at my corner table at the Royal, "you look as though you've just been interrogated by the CI of A."

"CIA," I corrected mechanically. "It's simply that . . ." I started to explain, then thought better of it. "Nothing. Chalk it up to a bad night."

"And the Beckett story," he said, "will it make the next issue?"

"No," I said. "I misjudged the damn thing. I've done a first draft, but it's not easy. I mean, for Chrissake, you've read the man's prose. And the stories are even more complex and difficult than *Watt*. I reread my draft the other night and kept thinking Beckett was looking over my shoulder."

"You're too harsh on yourself. He's grateful you're doing the job. Can't you just polish it up and give it in?"

"No," I said. "I'll work on it for the next couple of weeks and send it off to him."

"He has to see it *beforehand*? I thought he gave you carte blanche."

"He did. Still, I can't imagine him not seeing it before we go to press."

"Then we'll run the Genet," he said. "And I have a couple of poems to fill out the pages we'd reserved for Beckett."

Over the next two or three weeks, I heavily edited the draft and again set it aside. Finally, a month to the day after I had translated the opening lines—

> They dressed me and gave me money. I knew what the money was for, it was for my traveling expenses. When it was gone, they said, I would have to get some more, if I wanted to go on traveling. The same for my shoes, when they were worn out I would have to have them repaired, or get myself another pair, or go on my way barefoot, if I wanted to go on . . .

—I produced a fair copy I thought worthy of submitting to the author. Meanwhile, though, Trocchi begged me one last time, just before the printing deadline, to give it one more shot to make the issue for which it had been intended, Spring–Summer 1953. I still felt guilty, because I knew "La fin" was to open the magazine. But I also felt strongly that I had been right to spend as much time translating it as I had, for when I sent it off, at least it read smoothly and struck me as faithful to the original as I could make it.

Ah! The cockiness of youth.

I paid largely for the fourth number of *Merlin* out of my earnings as the official translator-interpreter for an American construction company under contract with the U.S. Air Force to build a base in eastern France, just outside the village of Chaumont.

Let me explain. One breathtaking icy morning in January, having biked to the embassy on the Place de la Concorde to have my passport stamped, I had seen on the bulletin board an announcement seeking applications for the job and indicating a salary that struck me as astronomical, compared with my then-current income, derived mainly from the occasional article in a New York paper on French theater and cinema. The job would last from three to six months; payment was in dollars. On a whim, I filled out the form and left it with the embassy clerk.

I had almost forgotten, when two or three weeks later a letter arrived at the rue du Sabot summoning me to the embassy for an interview. Did I really want to leave Paris? The city had become not only home but a cherished place, where each day when I woke up I felt good, challenged but comfortable. And what about my budding relationship with Jeannette, whom I had not seen nearly enough since New Year's Eve? And would my absence mean lessening my involvement with the magazine, just as it was finding its stride? On the other hand, there was the lure of much-needed money: even three or four months at Chaumont would pay for one issue and leave me enough to live on for another six months, maybe longer, without worry.

That night I mentioned casually to Jeannette that I might be leaving Paris—not permanently, I assured her, but for a few months. I would be back in Paris every weekend. She understood, she said, and even encouraged me to take the job. For a moment I felt panic. Her cavalier reaction was a clear, and obviously negative, comment on our new relationship. Oh, well, easy come, easy go—next! But I was dead wrong. "Work, the coming two or three months will be so intense for me at the conservatory," she explained, "I won't have much free time anyway. So we—that is, if you want to—can see each other every other weekend." I now felt a sudden stone settle in my stomach. Every *other* weekend! I realized that if indeed I were to commit this folly of leaving Paris, I had hoped and planned to see the young lady *every* weekend. "And maybe," she continued, "at Easter break I could come out and see you." Easter! That was fucking months away! For several days I argued ardently with myself, until I was so confused I decided to toss a coin: heads I go, tails I stay. It was heads.

Before the interview, I borrowed a French technical dictionary and brushed up on engineering terms. At the embassy I was greeted by a trim, blue-clad air force colonel, who was shortly joined by a short, squinty, mustachioed French employee of the Ponts et Chaussées—the French government department in charge of building and maintaining roads and bridges and, I assumed in the instance, airstrips—who fired questions at me thick and fast, in a Burgundian accent that at first threw me off but to which I adapted sufficiently to see him finally nodding in approval as I responded. After fifteen minutes or so, the two men withdrew to confer. I sat there wondering what the hell I was doing there, dreading a positive result. When the colonel reentered, thanked me, and said I'd be hearing from him, I was almost relieved. I figured it was a polite kiss-off.

Safely back on the Left Bank, I told Alex and Jane that if I took the job, I could pay for a good part of the next issue. They exchanged glances that betrayed relief, if not delight. As for Austryn: "paranoid" was the word that came to mind.

"Mark my words, Dick, this is not *defense*: America's preparing for World War III. Do you really want to be part of that?"

I was beginning to be allergic to him.

"It *will* pay for the magazine, Austryn, which means a great deal to us," Alex said. Jane nodded her pretty bangs in agreement.

"Turn it down," Austryn said.

"They haven't offered it to me yet."

In any case, four or five months wasn't long, I told myself. Still, it was with a very heavy heart that I boarded the train one Sunday morning in early February at the Gare de l'Est, battered suitcase containing engineering dictionary in tow, for this unromantic town in the Haute-Marne called Chaumont, population 18,452. Exactly 265 kilometers from Paris. Infinity. What in the world was I doing?

I had spent the evening before with Jeannette, both of us trying to make light of the "adventure," as she called it. Only when, late in the evening, a silent tear rolled down her pretty cheek did I know how she truly felt. I was hopelessly in love with this young lady, and the first thing I was doing was pulling up stakes and moving away. Smart fellow, Richard: straight to the head of the class!

19 ✌

A Bigger Decision

CHAUMONT was a nothing place, one of those bleak French towns that either had seen better days or, more likely, had never known any, but had played its dismal role in World War I, battered by both sides, occupied by the advancing Germans, retaken by the stalwart French, as if its possession were key to victory, whereas if the successive occupiers had taken a closer look upon arrival, they would probably have skedaddled without a backward glance. Which was more or less how I felt after a cursory stroll through town, replete with its echoes of that earlier war: avenue du Maréchal Foch, rue de Verdun, rue Victoire de la Marne . . .

The only half-decent hotel in town was L'Étoile d'Or, whose rooms were pseudo-sumptuously furnished in faded velvet and imitation Louis XV furniture. The baldachin bed was so tall you had to high-jump into it, and so soft you sank into its generous center as if enveloped in Leda's Spartan arms.

The deal, air force arranged, was that you took your breakfast and dinner there, lunch at the base itself, where there was an American canteen. The raw terrain, soon to be an air base, was several kilometers out of town, on a slight plateau with magnificent views in all directions. At present, the only man-made edifice among the fields and trees was a wooden prefab that served as the engineering office. My first day on the job was a shock, both culture and work. After four and a half years in Paris, it was as though I had been suddenly transported back to the States without passing Go, despite the presence of the French engineers, one of whom was the Burgundian who had interviewed me rapid-fire at the embassy. The room was filled with long tables, on which were unrolled vast blueprints. After introductions—in addition to the colonel, who was in charge, there were half a dozen American engineers from the civilian construction company under contract with the government, and two French civil service employees of Ponts et Chaussées—and before I had even finished my first morning coffee, I was urgently pressed into service, for none of the Americans spoke a word of French, and vice versa. I wouldn't say I won the immediate respect of both sides, but given that they were equally cross-language-crippled, the fact I was fluent, even though technically challenged, gave me an advantage, and I scored extra points with the French by having little or no accent—certainly not the heavy American accent they especially mocked and detested, for reasons known only to them, for other countries' citizens, notably the Spanish, massacred their beloved French without incurring a trace of reproach from the Gauls.

The day started frostily and ended warily, as both sides, like two boxers feeling each other out in the first round, were clearly sizing each other up. One must remember that although the Americans, just eight years before, had been received gratefully and warmly, indeed unreservedly, as liberators by the French, political schisms had quickly intruded as America's growing obsession with the dangers presumably posed by the Soviet Union collided with France's—and indeed most of Europe's—more subtle and complex views wherein the Soviet Union posed not nearly the threat that Germany did, even a Germany on its knees. The French had seen it all before: defeated and humiliated in 1918—"never to rise again," many political pundits had predicted at the time—Germany in less than a generation had not only been resurrected but set out once again to conquer France, if not the world. In 1939, France was still war weary and blood thin, its potential military ranks depleted by the devastating human toll of World War I, its politicians' attitudes tempered by their firsthand knowledge of the horrors of war, not pacifists per se but, in their own eyes, realists who would do their damnedest to avoid armed conflict.

The American building of military bases on French soil, a ring to act as a second tier of defense, was looked upon dubiously in many quarters, fed and nurtured by the influential French Communist press. If Americans simply did not understand how the Europeans, and especially the French, could be blind to the clear and present danger posed by the Soviets, the

French simply did not understand what they termed American paranoia on the subject. So my job, I quickly realized, was not only to translate but, wherever possible, to interpret and explain, hopefully without bias. So when Monsieur Ponts et Chaussées would corner me and ask, "What did *le colonel* mean when he said this or that?" or, from the Americans, "Why does Monsieur Grenouille have a hair up his ass this morning?" I would placate or smooth ruffled feathers as best I could. Each side had a job to do, but suspicion was rife, and I had to show, especially to the French, that I not only was impartial but understood and respected their reservations and concerns.

By the end of the second week the frost was thawing, and a month into the job the early wan smiles had evolved into guttural laughter, and even a jovial slap or two on transatlantic backs, as both sides became aware that they were dealing with fellow professionals with no hidden agenda.

The colonel, a gruff man of few words, hovered, responding only when a technical question was posed or a decision had to be made. To his credit, for this was an American project, bought and paid for by Washington, the colonel by now most often conferred with his French counterpart before lowering the gavel. Much of that early time was spent discussing the orientation of the runways and the placement of the buildings, centering on the control tower. If I understood, this was to be a fairly large base, accommodating the largest heavy bombers. In spite of the various cultural bumps, a camaraderie set in, and we all, ultimately and improbably, worked well together for four months, building the base. Soon after my stint in Chaumont, American fliers arrived and encamped at the airbase as if it had been there for years. Little did I know or could possibly foresee, one of those flyers would be James Salter. Our paths did not cross until years later in Paris and New York, when we became close friends. In fact, I always regretted not being his publisher, but his work was spoken for elsewhere.

Those first days passed inchingly for me. My colleagues, both American and French, were housed together at the other end of town, in private houses rented by the government, and though they were perfectly affable at work, none made any move to integrate me into their evenings. Nor, in all fairness, did I exert any visible effort to ingratiate myself, quite content to spend my evenings reading and, with the resources remaining, writing. Billy Mack, a man from upstate New York who had graduated from Cornell only three or four years before, offered, "But, fuck, man! I spent a week in Paris before coming out here, and as far as I could tell, all they do is sit on the goddamn café terraces and drink wine from breakfast on. How can you call them *industrious?*"

"They do drink coffee in the morning," I assured him.

"Hell, man, maybe some do," he conceded, "but I saw a bunch of them at eight in the morning, right there on the Champs-Élysées"—he pronounced the first word as if it were what a horse does to its bit, and mangled the second beyond recognition, but no matter—"at the counter downing a glass of red wine! And not just one. Anyway, maybe it's because their goddamn coffee is so bitter. I tried it one day and couldn't get the first sip down."

"It's strong," I admitted, "but you know what the French call American coffee? *Jus de chaussette*—'sock juice.' They think our coffee's so weak *they* can't drink it."

"Do *you* drink it?" he challenged. I nodded. "Well, damn," he said, "takes all kinds, I guess." However I had till then been ranked in his mind, which could not have been very high given all my wasted years in France, clearly I had dropped another full notch.

Friday afternoons I was on the train to Paris, still wondering what I had got myself into. I had signed on for six months, a month longer than I had bargained for, but long enough, I figured, to fund at least one, and perhaps even two, issues of the magazine.

I spent the weekends with Jeannette, walking hand in hand, both enamored of the city and each other. And I talked more about this transplanted Irishman Samuel Beckett, whose play we had seen together and one of whose stories I was now translating. Translating? Why in the world would you be translating an Irishman's writing into English? Like Joseph Conrad before him, I explained, Beckett had recently chosen to write in his adopted language. My suspicion is, he felt comfortable in French, France had become home for him, and possibly, after writing for fifteen years in English with almost no recognition, he thinks he might find a more perceptive audience here. And besides, France is his home now, and like Joyce he has no intention of returning to Ireland. French is the language he wakes up to, the language he thinks in, the one he speaks all or most of the time every day, the one that now courses through his Irish brain. So in a way it's natural for him to write in French. Jeannette remained pensive.

As winter had moved into spring, Jeannette's parents could not help but notice their daughter's growing infatuation, which she made scant effort to conceal.

At Easter, Jeannette announced to her parents that I had invited her to Chaumont for the long weekend. Hers was not a request, it was an announcement; theirs was not to give permission but to bless. This they did wholeheartedly, which both pleased and surprised me, for in these 1950s I had trouble imagining American parents assenting to a similar situation. But they apparently reasoned she was of age and had had a mind of her own since she was four. Besides, her father told her, I like the American. Of all the young men you have brought home, this one strikes me as by far the most interesting, the most attractive, the most solid. He is different: I like the fact that he's both an athlete and an intellectual. How many young men play tennis with Charles Lapicque, wrestle with the French Olympic team, and can also talk about Stendhal, Proust, and Sartre?

If there had been any doubt about our relationship, those four Easter weekend days dispelled it. They were magical. As I took her to the Chaumont station Monday night, I felt as if the world were coming to an end. My world. This was the girl of my life. Sorry, the woman of my life. On the station platform, with the lights of the train still in the distance but bearing down hard, I turned to her and told her how I felt. Would she marry me? Would she share her life with me? In all candor, I said, I had no idea in which direction it would be heading over the next few years. Her arms tightening around my neck and the long kiss that followed gave me my answer.

We decided on a July date, July 18, to allow recovery from the Bastille Day festivities. Moving forward, I learned that in France, one had to post banns, a published proclamation of your intent to marry, to forewarn one and all in the event there was reason to oppose said ceremony. Hear ye, hear ye! It all seemed medieval to me. I was still learning the ways of the Old World. Anyway, the banns had been duly posted: to date no irate ex-suitors, creditors, or other potential objectors had appeared to give cause why I was unworthy to bind my life to this young woman. I was on tenterhooks for several weeks, but now figured that if anyone in officialdom cared, he would have appeared long ago. Ours was to be a civil wedding, at the Courbevoie town hall, followed by a reception at Jeannette's parents' house. We both wanted a simple, intimate affair. My parents were alerted but not formally invited, a major social blunder on my part. Patsy was the reason or pretext, I wasn't sure which. Mother had made it clear, when after three years in France I had brought Patsy home, that she did not approve of my blond girlfriend. It wasn't merely Patsy's bleached-blond hair that had made my dear mother raise an eyebrow; Patsy was a few years order than me, and horror of horror, to top it off, she was a divorcée! But the final straw came when Mother realized we were sleeping together under *her* roof. Though we were allotted separate rooms upon arrival, they were fortunately connecting, so we would repair to our assigned lairs, then conjoin in all senses almost immediately, till dawn sped us back to our respective cells. Mother wondered aloud at breakfast one morning the third or fourth day of Patsy's stay, would a single person of sound mind and body have to sleep first in one bed, then in the other?

In short, with those memories rushing back, and not wanting to be judged again for getting involved inappropriately—with one so young, of such different background and culture, whose English was virtually non-existent, what else?—I informed the Dear Ones by telegram, only a week or so before the blessed event, that I was hitching my life to a rising star, but not issuing therein a formal invitation to come.

It was an unfortunate miscalculation—for which I still, to this day, feel guilty. Not to mention Jeannette, who was perplexed and disappointed. Perhaps one should, in winding down, make a full and candid account of all one's egregious mistakes in life, no holds barred, and the one with the fewest misjudgments wins. Mine, I fear, would place me near the bottom of Dante's circles.

The joyous day dawned bright and clear, not a given in Paris even in midsummer. I donned my best suit (correction: my better, for I had but two), the pepper and salt from Dahlgren and Son, a starched white shirt, and an impeccable (for never having been worn) pale blue tie. I looked at myself in the mirror and thought that in the main, I was suitable for the occasion. A closer look: I could have done with a haircut.

Paul greeted me at the door, a boutonniere peeking coyly from the lapel of his dark blue suit, which made me realize I should doubtless have had one, too. His spectacled glance showed his full approval of my sartorial effort.

"The ladies are still dressing," he said. "We'll go on ahead and have a *pot** before the ceremony, if that's all right with you."

Anything he proposed that morning would have been all right with me, for not only was I on automatic but Jeannette's father was still, for me, an Olympian figure, a man so quietly erudite and many-sided that I generally listened in awe and without comment when he held forth on the state of the world, personal or professional. If de Gaulle, Adenauer, and other postwar leaders read him daily for information and enlightenment, how could I but bow to this early-morning suggestion? We descended the three flights of outdoor stairs to where his car was parked and drove the three or four minutes to the Courbevoie Hôtel de Ville, across the street from which was a sidewalk café. We sat on the terrace, he relaxed, I just short of stone, desperately searching for words to break the sudden silence when, blessedly, he said: "So what will you have to drink?"

"What are you having?" I deferred, not wanting to blunder.

"A Fernet Branca," he said.

"Make it two," I said, having no idea what it was, even after all those bar-worn years.

The waiter arrived with two small aperitif glasses containing a thick-ish dark brown liquid.

Paul raised his glass. "To your health," he said. "And happiness."

I raised mine and bid him the same. If I had tasted the drink before doing so, I might have toasted differently. It was the vilest concoction I had ever tasted: bitter, foul, all but undrinkable. I sipped, glancing desperately around to see if there was a nearby plant I could douse.

"It's better if you gulp it down," Paul said, matching his words by emptying his glass.

Seeing no saving plant in sight, I braced myself and did the same.

"Good, isn't it?" Paul said approvingly. "Excellent for the digestion. And one's health in general."

I nodded and managed a thin smile.

"Want another?" he said. "Good for the nerves, too."

"Maybe later," I said. "My nerves are fine, thank you."

Just then, two cars pulled up, one bearing Jeannette and her mother, the other with Frank and Jeanne, Michel and Francine Holley. Frank was my best man, Francine Jeannette's matron of honor. In this civil ceremony,

---

*French slang for "drink."

they were dubbed simply "witnesses," there to sign our marriage papers to prove we had not made the whole thing up. Jeannette was stunning in a white silk suit with thin gray stripes, the skirt not full-length but well below the knee, with matching hat and gloves, and a modest bouquet of baby's breath and roses clutched to her waist. We sat in stiff-backed chairs before a long desk of plain wood, behind which stood the assistant mayor, who could not have been more than twenty-five or so but looked solemn enough to appear twice that, his marriage book open. Behind him was a French flag—*bleu, blanc, rouge*—at rest on its silver pole.

The ceremony was of a rare and welcome simplicity: the banns having been duly posted and no objector forthcoming, you both having declared your desire to become man and wife, the State so declares and wishes you long life and happiness. Sign here. We signed. Now change seats and sign the second set of papers. We rose and I passed behind her, whispering as I moved, *"Bonjour, madame,"* for at a stroke her status as mademoiselle had been erased forever. We signed again, stood, kissed, and were embraced by our six attendants, to emerge minutes later into the blinding sun. Outside, photographs were taken, after which we were whisked back to rue Charcot to await our guests.

We were thirty in all, only our closest friends, among them the photographer Brassaï, a lifelong friend of Paul's, and his much younger wife, Gilberte, a birdlike, dark-haired beauty, who hid, or tried to hide, her insecurity by chirping a constant string of inanities. Paul and Brassaï had been buddies in Montparnasse since the 1920s, spending untold hours together at the Coupole exchanging lofty ideas that, had they been put into effect, would doubtless have changed the world for the better. Brassaï, a talented artist, had not yet found a meaningful outlet for his work and was often on the verge of starvation, as was another of his buddies, the American writer Henry Miller. Miller and Brassaï would often get together at the beginning of the week, at the Select or the Coupole, to map out their culinary plans for the coming days—that is, who among their respective admirers would be likely candidates for a free lunch or dinner. When asked what his job was, Brassaï often responded that he was a "telephone salesman," neglecting to mention that what he was selling was himself and his friend. In any event, one day in the late 1920s when Paul and Brassaï were chatting on the terrace of the Coupole, Brassaï complaining that no one, but no one, was buying his paintings or sketches, Paul suggested he consider photography. "You have a great eye." Brassaï shook his head. "A lesser art," he said. "For lesser artists. Not for me."

The next time they met, Paul hauled a package, which his German shepherd had been guarding jealously beneath his chair, up onto the table. "Here," he said, "try playing with this." It was a fairly expensive camera that Paul had picked up in a nearby pawnshop. Brassaï turned it over and over, as if examining a totally foreign object, with increasing disdain. "I wouldn't even know how to use this—" he began, but Paul cut him off. "I had the fellow I bought it from show me," he said. "It's really very simple." Within weeks, Brassaï, intrigued, became increasingly seduced and could be found prowling the streets of the city, night and day, taking pictures that, fifty-odd years later, became legendary. He still sketched, but in his heart of hearts he knew he had, with Paul's help, found his true calling. Still, his wedding present this day was not a photograph but a wonderful pen sketch of a reclining nude. He was a small, increasingly rotund man, the salient feature of his pixie face being froglike, protruding eyes, which he used to great advantage in telling brilliant stories or jokes, of which he had an endless supply.

Champagne was flowing on the balcony, before we sat down to a Rabelaisian lunch, accompanied by rare wines that Paul had carefully chosen for the occasion. A limo was scheduled to take us back to the rue du Sabot at five o'clock, but Jeannette signaled she was having too good a time to leave, so I canceled and ordered another for six, which also proved to be too early. "Seven?" I ventured. She shook her head. "Eight?" She nodded, so on we went for another three hours, I drinking too much, she not at all, until after a full fifteen minutes of double-cheek au revoir kissing, we finally made our way down to the more modest Renault of my new father-in-law, who, at Jeannette's request, had been designated to drive us back to the rue du Sabot.

"Honeymoon" was a word we had not even discussed, for I was due back at Chaumont on Monday morning bright and early. Emerging at two in the afternoon the next day, and after a celebratory lunch at St. Germain, we both took the train to Chaumont.

In Chaumont, the closest I had been able to come in finding an apartment was the top floor of a rooming house in the center of town. Not exactly the Ritz, but within days Jeannette had spruced it up with lace curtains on the windows—something that became one of her lifelong signatures—flowers blooming in two of our water glasses (we had four), and candles on the table for dinner, along with wineglasses that had appeared from somewhere, as had two porcelain dinner plates and four smaller matching plates, two for salad and two for dessert. Not only that, I came home those first nights to find fragrant odors wafting down the hall. Apparently, I had married a seasoned chef, an attribute of which I had no inkling. And on a two-burner stove!

An army PX on the air base, to which I introduced Jeannette, provided new and exotic goods generally unavailable in French stores. She entered the PX as Alice into Wonderland. Frozen goods were a novelty to her, and she was fascinated by these new American products. One day, unbeknownst to me, Jeannette brought home half a dozen cans of frozen orange juice, not knowing that one would have sufficed for several breakfasts. That night, some time past midnight, we were jolted awake by what sounded like a major bombardment. Had the Russians finally come? Had some Nazis hunkered down, hidden for a decade in the nearby forest, to finally emerge in retaliation for the ill-gotten Allied victory? And not a defensive weapon anywhere in sight! "Those shots," Jeannette said, clutching the blankets to her throat, "I think they're coming from across the hall," which was where our "kitchen" was. I tiptoed to the door, cracked it open, and peered into the dimly lit corridor. My three neighbors were as wide-eyed and pale as I. Chalk one up for the American frontiersman! Just then another explosion rocked the premises, and all four doors slammed shut as one. Ah, these brave French! It was the smell that brought me to my senses, for the entire area was suddenly permeated with the fragrant odor of oranges. Like the Light Brigade itself, I charged across the hall, thrust open the door to our kitchen, and snapped on the light, just in time to see—and hear—the last can of juice explode in all its orange splendor, sending gobs of soft, not frozen now but almost sultry, OJ onto the ceiling, the walls, the floor. Not to mention the furniture. I didn't know whether to laugh or cry, so settled for sitting down in the gooey mess and bursting out laughing. Russians? Germans? Merely the American arctic troops, unfrozen at last, who had been assaulting us in the night. Four heads peeped around the door frame, one of them Jeannette's. Seeing what the problem was, three dissolved into the darkness, leaving my darling new wife to share this moment of nocturnal bliss with me.

"Shall we start cleaning up?" she said.

"I think we should have an early-morning drink," I countered.

"I think we should buy a refrigerator as soon as possible," she suggested.

"Or start buying fresh fruits and vegetables," I hinted. "You know, the way your countrymen do."

20 ❧

Enter Maurice

I HAD NEVER FELT SO HAPPY, so totally at peace, so secure, so sure that the person I had chosen, and who had chosen me, was right. I couldn't have cared less what the future might bring; the present was all that mattered, day by precious day, moment by blessed moment. The sun was in its heaven, and, oh, yes, all was right with the world.

Sometime in mid-August one of my colleagues at the base, an American two decades my senior married to a Frenchwoman of some station and considerable breadth, asked me where I would be living in Paris. How would you like to rent our apartment on the rue de Rennes for a few months? Two bedrooms, two baths, a large salon, formal dining room, kitchen, and pantry. Your wife's a musician? We have a grand piano in the living room. My interest piqued, I asked for how long. Four or five months at least, maybe longer. His asking price was more than reasonable. That evening I mentioned it to Jeannette, who brightened visibly. The next day we closed the deal. So in September we would begin our married Paris life in comfortable, bourgeois rather than bohemian style. After five years of self-imposed penury, I had no objection. And when I told Alex and Jane, they loved me anew, for it meant they could have the upstairs rue du Sabot quarters for several more months.

Reentering Paris that summer was like emerging from an overly long, troubling dream. That's really not fair, for during those months I had learned that I could cope with a steady job, that my fellow Americans were just fine. Paris had never seemed so bright, so cheerful and lively, so full of light and joy. Just to stroll the old familiar streets was stimulating. We were home again.

Merlin had entered a new phase. Trocchi was still the editor, Jane the putative publisher, but in the contents Austryn began appearing with his own strange, esoteric—though not untalented—work where Trocchi had center-staged himself before. The editorials, too, became less literary, more polemical and political, as Austryn's influence also made itself felt. All I could see was that Trocchi, despite his brave words, deep into drugs, was writing virtually nothing while paying scant attention to the magazine. In the year and a half just past, I had felt as close to him as I ever had to another man, a brother really, and, looking back, I feel remiss for not having been more forceful in my admonitions.

It was all well and good making these great literary discoveries, but money was always at the forefront of our minds. I don't know whether it was Beckett or Genet—perhaps both—who gave us the idea of starting to publish books. Our twisted logic: If you couldn't afford a magazine, why couldn't you not afford books as well? It kind of made sense, in a 1950s sort of way.

What books? Well, we had two to start, and possibly four. The first was Beckett's *Watt*, which, surprisingly, the author had agreed to let us publish, perhaps because for almost a decade now he had failed totally even to interest any British publisher. At first, Beckett had given the manuscript to the agent Richard Watt—he loved the idea of Watt handling *Watt*—and when his efforts failed, the project was taken on by his old friend from prewar Paris days George Reavey, who also struck out. Routledge, Beckett's publisher of *Murphy*, called it "too wild and unintelligible . . . to stand any chance of successful publication over here at this time . . . sorry indeed we cannot feel the same whole-hearted enthusiasm for *Watt* as we did for *Murphy*." Half a dozen others felt the same. One came close to taking it on, or was at least complimentary. Fredric Warburg of Secker and Warburg called the manuscript "too difficult" but added that it showed "immense mental vitality" and "a very fine talent for writing," concluding intriguingly, "It may be that in turning this book down we are turning down a potential James Joyce." Beckett, the most patient and unassuming of writers, was understandably bitter. Was this the same manuscript we had sat up all night reading, laughing and reading, crying and reading, with the growing feeling we had discovered a genius, the word is not too strong? Were we so perceptive, or were the others so blind? In any event, *Watt* was the catalyst, if not the cornerstone, of our mad new book-publishing enterprise, which appropriately we dubbed Collection Merlin. To boot, Frechtman had clearly implied that if we were to publish an excerpt in our magazine, Genet would surely approve our publishing the entire work if, as we had blithely let drop, we began to publish books as well. Not a bad beginning . . .

I worried about the money. Alex and Jane were reassuring. Could Papa Lougee, I asked, be counted on to help? For we were now talking real money, four or five times what an issue of the magazine cost. No, Daddy had anted up all he was going to. Remember, he had not been reimbursed, even in part, for his outlay for *Merlin* number 1, and never would be. His capitalist calculations that the ship, once launched, would return its investment in due course, sooner or later, if not in jig time, had been completely thwarted.

"Your convincing Beckett to forgo an advance is half the battle," Alex said.

"I didn't convince him at all," I said. "He knew we were short and suggested it on his own."

Enter Maurice. With my Beckett translation of "The End" lagging, the space in issue number 4 had been filled with the Genet and an extract from Henry Miller's *Plexus*, thanks to a new element in the magazine, a French gentleman by the name of Maurice Girodias, who came into our lives via Austryn. Girodias had an impressive publishing background, having founded at the start of the war, when he was only twenty-one, a publishing company, Les Éditions du Chêne, specializing in art books. By war's end, the then twenty-four-year-old decided to branch out into the broader, more challenging realm of literature, which he did with considerable success, rightly seizing on the Russian classics, then out of favor—and in most cases out of print—reissuing old translations and commissioning new. Girodias, a true chip off the old block, decided also to emulate his father, Jack Kahane, an Englishman from Manchester who had volunteered to give his life for his country in World War I. In the words of Maurice:

> The outbreak of the first World War coincided with a great emotional
> catastrophe in [my father's] life. He gave away everything and volunteered

to die; but instead of quickly dying he discovered through a telescope, from the gray-white cliffs surrounding Marseilles, a new facet of the life he was not yet to quit, a bubbly, charming, piquant young French bourgeoise, Marcelle Eugenie Girodias, who he was to marry in 1917, after having been through the hell of Ypres and a good bit of what followed.

After the war Jack Kahane settled in Paris, living in the lap of luxury in his in-laws' apartment on the avenue du Bois, later renamed avenue Foch in honor of the great French hero of that war to end all wars, named commander in chief of the Allied armies in 1918. In 1929, he and a partner started a company called the Obelisk Press, whose goal was to publish daring, some would say titillating, works in English intended for the tourist market—novels and memoirs the English-speaking world could not purchase in its native lands. One of the company's daring authors was a poverty-stricken American expatriate, Henry Miller, whose talent Kahane, to his immense credit, immediately recognized. In 1934 he published Miller's *Tropic of Cancer*, later in the decade his *Max and the White Phagocytes* and *Tropic of Capricorn*, thus bringing the unknown at least to the attention of the literary world, if not yet to the world at large. Kahane also published works by Anaïs Nin and Cyril Connolly, and two short works of another still barely recognized genius, James Joyce. But as the 1930s waned, it was becoming clearer every day that another war was brewing, and Kahane, who had been writing his autobiography, *Memoirs of a Booklegger*, quickly polished off the work and, virtually on the day war was declared, left this world, "stricken by the sheer horror of it all," his son wrote. At twenty, then, young Maurice suddenly found himself the head of the family. With no experience or training of any kind, and for working capital an impressive collection of his father's bar debts, he set out to carry on the family tradition and founded, as the world was literally exploding around him, the aforementioned Éditions du Chêne. The very notion, and the timing, seemed ludicrous, yet to its founder's great surprise, the company thrived. More surprising was the fact the half-Jewish Maurice made no attempt to hide or flee once the Nazis arrived; his own flair and youthful self-confidence, plus his mother's good Catholic name and background, apparently sufficed to keep the Nazi exterminators at bay, or at least in the dark. In any event, he survived the war not only intact but having learned a great deal about his father's old profession. After the war Maurice revived the Obelisk Press and began to republish his father's Henry Miller titles, plus a new version of that famous old erotic thriller *Memoirs of*

Fanny Hill, which sold almost a hundred thousand copies. Miller's works had sold only a few hundred copies before the war, but now, as thousands upon thousands of GIs descended on Paris or passed through on leave, they bought in droves books they knew were forbidden at home.

Further, thanks to Girodias's father, Miller had come to the attention of the French literary establishment just before the war. In 1940, the distinguished literary publisher Gallimard had acquired the French rights to Miller's *Black Spring,* and a smaller and even more daring colleague, Robert Denoël, the rights to *Tropic of Cancer.* Thus Miller, still unpublished in the United States, was about to appear in French translations in 1940, when the Germans' sudden arrival that June put a swift end to all such plans. But now, with the Germans finally gone and the memory of their brutal occupation still fresh in everyone's mind, one figured that the new government, whatever its political orientation, would take no measure that would remind people of the Nazi censors. Thus, toward the end of 1945, Gallimard and Denoël coordinated to issue the two volumes, already translated, simultaneously. Young Girodias, who through his father still owned the rights to *Tropic of Capricorn* and *Max and the White Phagocytes,* decided to join the game and, with Miller's approval, rushed through a translation of both. In December 1945 these four works by Miller appeared, but to the surprise of the publishers, bent on a *succès de scandale,* the literary critics chose largely to ignore the Miller onslaught, and those readers who happened to open any of the books, through chance or design, were sufficiently shocked to report their contents to priests or police. Hatred of the recent German censors did not seem to have carried over to the not-so-brave new world aborning: one must remember that the French are, despite the rhetoric and political ranting, an essentially conservative people. Already, fourteen years before, Céline's *Journey to the End of the Night* had shocked and upset France, and Miller was even sterner stuff. For several long months, virtual silence greeted the Miller. While silence may be golden for some, for purveyors of the written word it can mean slow death, for without controversy sales stagnate. Finally, in Camus's *Combat,* Maurice Nadeau, one of the braver and more perceptive members of the critical establishment, labeled the American a "genius," though warning the public of his "monstrous immorality." Still, sales of all four books remained slow. Girodias, convinced he had an easy winner, if only by the coattail effect, had printed fifteen thousand copies of *Capricorn,* most of which were gathering dust on, or more often beneath, the shelves. Given his fragile finances—which were stretched even thinner by his decision to launch, at almost the same time as he reopened Obelisk, a costly new magazine, *Critique*, edited by the highly regarded Georges Bataille, and a number of other equally entrepreneurial but cash-draining ventures—his substantial investment in Miller seemed a lost cause. Girodias, having survived the war, was almost sure his fledgling house was about to founder. What he needed was a miracle, and he did not believe in miracles. In late July 1946, however, a group calling itself the Cartel of Social and Moral Action sued all three publishers, who were summoned to appear before the public prosecutor. The last two French works to have been prosecuted for outraging public morals were Flaubert's *Madame Bovary* and Baudelaire's *Les fleurs du mal* almost a century before, which, as Nadeau later noted, "had left an uncomfortable impression in the memory of all French magistrates." Those precedents, plus the painful recollection of the Germans, played in the publishers' favor. Within a week of that suit, all fifteen thousand copies of *Tropic of Capricorn* were gone from the bookstores, and Girodias had gone back to press for another fifty thousand. By September, after the publishers met in an open radio debate with members of the cartel, *Capricorn* had sold more than a hundred thousand, *Cancer* even more, for the reaction to the attempted censorship, as the publishers had hoped, was virtually unanimous.

Despite the Obelisk victory over the voices of repression, and the ensuing sales success for Miller, Girodias, who confessed to having little real notion of money, was warring on another front: his estimable Éditions du Chêne, to which he had been paying scant attention in the flush of this exciting new venture and the attendant publicity, was deeply in debt, and to save it, Maurice came to an arrangement with his creditors whereby, as he noted,

> I slaved for three years on the tiniest salary in order to pay my debts, and I had nearly accomplished that noble aim when one of the creditors conspired to get control of my firm—and then sold his ill-acquired interest to a big publisher. I was expelled from my own company, unable to understand or resist that piece of capitalistic maneuvering . . . It was a cruel lesson. I tried to put up a fight to recover my property and wasted in the attempt one whole year, as well as money I did not possess, and what little energy I still had in me.

That "cruel lesson," however, led Girodias straight to the next stage of his life, namely, "the urge to attack the Universal Establishment with all the means at my disposal." In the spring of 1953, exactly a year after *Merlin*'s first issue, he had founded the Olympia Press, an English-language publishing venture whose stated purpose was to shock the establishment and publish, for the growing tourist (and military) market, works certain to be banned "back home."

When Austryn brought us word of his new acquaintance, he had the story only partly right. For the dandy Maurice, clothed in his impeccable black suit, white shirt, and tasteful tie, his dainty hands sheathed in leather gloves that fondled the wheel of his gleaming dark blue Citroën *traction avant*, had struck Austryn and Muffie as blessed with not only sound publishing credentials ("Les Éditions du Chêne? You founded *that*?") but the wherewithal to back them up. The truth was, in words that Girodias voiced only years later, Olympia was "a shoestring operation par excellence," whose office was a tiny room in the back of a bookstore at 13, rue Jacob, exactly five doors down from where I had earlier spent two deliciously happy years chez Madame Germaine. He had far more hope than money, and his past publishing experience had taught him to trust no one, for after he had lost Les Éditions du Chêne he had "led an uncertain, inactive life, trying to absorb the enormous blow I had suffered." But to us that early September day in 1953, when he drew up in his posh dark blue Citroën in front of Jeannette's and my door at 76, rue de Rennes to meet the Merlinites, of whom Austryn had talked so enthusiastically, he looked and played the part of the suave, knowledgeable man of the world, someone who with a snap of his well-manicured fingers could solve our mounting problems in a Paris minute—about triple a New York minute—if not in a trice.

For after issue number 4, *Merlin* had reached a critical point in its young life: our reputation as slow payers was extending further and further from the center of our universe, and I had wound up my stint at the Chaumont air base, having funded issue number 4 and part of number 5.

Maurice that day arrived as the messiah. As we sat drinking sherry in our sumptuous, elegant third-floor apartment on the rue de Rennes, Maurice was saying, in impeccable English: "You see, part of *Merlin*'s problem is that, like any company in this country, you must have a French *gérant*— 'manager.' That is the law, no matter if the company is wholly owned and operated by foreigners, as is your case. I have mentioned to Austryn that I could well fulfill that role for you, which would free you to pursue your literary goals."

We nodded as one. The will, nay, the *need* to believe clothed Maurice that day in a mantle of silk. Of gold. He could do no wrong. We were putty in his hands. "I hear that you would like to branch out into books. Here too we might be of help to each other, for I have just founded a company to publish books in English here in Paris. There may be some possible overlap, mutually beneficial. I have printers . . ."

Looks of relief and unrestrained joy crisscrossed the room in swift currents in response to the magic word "printers."

"I gather you have a name for your publishing venture: Collection Merlin. Most apt, most apt . . ."

"We have four books planned," Trocchi said. "And we have several more in mind, including Austryn's translation of Sade, of which I believe you're aware."

"I am indeed," Maurice said. "In fact, Austryn and I have already discussed his *Philosophy in the Bedroom*. A fine translation. I'm prepared to take that title on immediately. You see, I very much doubt you could publish it yourself without grave danger to your status here. You would all be expelled, alas. We are, when all is said and done, a conservative people, and that sad aspect of the French character, put largely on hold during the war, is, alas, reemerging." He paused and gazed around the not-so-crowded room, I will not say imperiously but with his chin, therefore his entire head, lifted in the manner of someone who knew that if this was a game, say of chess or even poker, he was certain to win.

"We will have to draw up some papers," he drawled, as if the very thought bored him. "I have a lawyer friend, a man I used in my efforts to win back my company. He knows all the ins and outs of the Code. We shall keep it simple. I shall be named *gérant*, relieving you of that responsibility"— he smiled—"which you foreigners cannot exercise in any event."

"We'll of course need to preserve the integrity of *Merlin*," I ventured.

"Both the magazine *and* Collection Merlin," Alex added.

"To be sure," Maurice said, "to be sure. You should understand," he added, "that I have had more than a few battles with those that would stand in the way of artistic integrity, or freedom to publish. More than a few. And I have won. So you need not worry. In fact, I intend to not rest until censorship here is a thing of the past."

As he left, he shook hands with all of us and made a point of bringing Jeannette's fingers delicately to his lips.

The two reasons Maurice had been summoned to the rue de Rennes rather than to the rue du Sabot were: first, to impress him; second, to convince him we were not the impecunious, cheap-to-hire down-and-outers his first impression from our initial meetings in the local cafés had undoubtedly led him to believe. If we had fooled him on any count, however, it was not for long. Alex, a bit of the con man himself and thus doubtless blinded to one of that ilk, was overjoyed. "You see," he said proudly, raising a glass to the assembled crew, "our worries are over. Not only will the magazine have a *gérant*, ergo legality, but Collection Merlin can now really take wing."

If Maurice was what he claimed to be, then he could fill our biggest need, namely, the ability to *sell* our books. It was one thing to print books, quite another to sell them. In the course of the afternoon Maurice had boasted that he already had a substantial mailing list, inherited in part from his father, plus his many contacts, through Les Éditions du Chêne, in the bookstore network.

Suddenly the pipe dream of Collection Merlin seemed, if not a reality, at least a distinct possibility.

21 ∿

High Finance and Misdemeanor

E SIGNED PAPERS, which Maurice assured us would simply free us from the financial worries that had plagued us to date. No, he would not fund the magazine, that was still ours to deal with, but he would help us find a printer who would not demand up-front payment, and he would assure the distribution of the books, of which four more in addition to *Wand and Quadrant* were already signed up: Beckett's *Watt*, Austryn's *Hedyphagetica*, Jean Genet's *Thief's Journal*, and, on the back burner, a translation of *Molloy*, though that we knew was pretty far down the pike, since Beckett had no interest in assuming the task of rendering it into English.

First on the agenda was *Watt*. Beckett had already given his approval before Girodias came into the picture. We "*Merlin* juveniles," as he had affectionately dubbed us, had passed the "*Watt* test" and published in *Merlin* the demanding excerpt he had stipulated. A contract would be required, together with an advance, however modest. Since the *Merlin* exchequer read "empty," even "modest" loomed disturbingly large. Finally it was Beckett who gently but firmly removed us from the horns of our dilemma. "There need be no advance," he said. I wondered if somehow he had access to our bank statement. "Use the money to make sure you print on a proper paper." He knew better than we the woeful quality of paper used by most French book publishers after the war, which yellowed and crumbled after only a few years. That evening I shared the good news to, literally, a round of applause. Time for celebration.

"But for *Molloy*," Alex said, "I'm sure Lindon will want a decent advance. No way around that."

"What would our first printing be?" Austryn rightly asked, then answered: "Probably a thousand copies, no?"

Trocchi nodded. "So at a 7.5 percent royalty . . ."

"What's the list price?" I ventured, and suddenly, looking around, I saw this entire bohemian group, for whom money had always been as elusive as water through fingers, metamorphosing into Rembrandt's burghers. Only the linen ruffs were lacking.

"Say fifteen hundred francs," Trocchi said. "Same as Austryn's novel."

"Anybody have a slide rule?" Charlie Hatcher asked, frowning to blank looks all around.

"That's roughly a hundred francs per copy," Trocchi calculated.

"That's a hundred thousand francs of royalties," Austryn said.

"If we sell every copy," Trocchi added.

"So, what if we offered fifty thousand francs?" Pat suggested.

"From whose bank account?" Trocchi asked.

The conversation came to a sudden halt. After all, we were talking about well under two hundred dollars. Somewhere, in this time and place, such a sum must be available.

"Maybe we abandon the project," Austryn suggested. "At least defer."

"How would you feel if someone else bought *Molloy*?" Trocchi said. "Like the *Paris Review* crowd? Beckett was Dick's discovery, but don't think they're not watching what we do and whom we publish."

As the night wore on, as was its wont, further suggestions flowed with the wine, one more absurd than the other. It must have been two or three in the morning when suddenly I leaped—no, staggered—to my feet. "Eureka!" I exulted.

"Speak, O Archimedes," Charlie said.

We knew, I said, that Lindon wanted to publish a translation of *Watt* in due course, and Beckett had unthinkingly granted us world rights. "What if we offered Lindon the French rights to *Watt* for, say, fifty thousand francs, a respectable sum, and offered to pay him the same advance for the English rights to *Molloy*?"

Trocchi looked at me with new respect. "Brilliant," he said. "In other words, we'll exchange checks." He paused. "But what if Lindon cashes the Merlin check before his has cleared our bank?"

"A chance we'll have to take."

Trocchi cast a questioning glance around the assembled throng. Murmurs of assent from all sides.

The following day I ventured around the corner to Les Éditions de Minuit, where I was now known, and asked to see the *patron*. He was busy, I was told, but could see me on the morrow at ten o'clock. A trifle early, went through my mind, but this was important. At 9:59 on the dot I was there. Ushered upstairs, I made my proposition to Monsieur Lindon. He gave me an owlish look.

"In other words, a wash," he said.

I shrugged. "Nonetheless, Monsieur Beckett will receive the benefits of both, will he not?"

Lindon nodded. I took that to be agreement. "We will draw up the contracts," he said. "They will be ready next week. Call ahead to confirm."

Two minutes later, back around the corner, I reported to the waiting troops.

"Get out the checkbook," I said. "We'll have the contracts next week."

With some trepidation, the following Tuesday, having called ahead, I appeared with a slightly rumpled Merlin check made out for fifty thousand francs, to the payee, one Éditions de Minuit, for the English-language rights, outside of the United States, Great Britain, and the British Commonwealth, to the novel *Molloy*. In other words, practically speaking, for publication of the work in English everywhere in the world where English is not spoken.

In exchange, I received in my outstretched hand the pristine Minuit check, looking very official, for the French rights to *Watt*. When I emerged, I rushed to our bank on the corner of the rue du Four and deposited the document no more than four minutes after it had been tendered. Then the wait began. Whose check would clear first, ours or theirs? Trocchi and I checked next day, and mirabile dictu, our account showed a positive balance of 57,653 francs.

We were now, legally and unquestionably, the proud owners of a novel called *Molloy*.*

---

*Years later, recalling the transaction to Lindon, I indelicately asked him over lunch if he knew how important it was that we deposit his check first. He nodded. "Of course," he said. "In fact, I held yours for three days."

Now, many months later, with Girodias's financial backing finally, however reluctantly, assured, *Watt* was poised to go to the printer. I read it again, to see if I could detect any errors, misspellings, confusion of syntax, problems with sequence of tenses, questions of punctuation. I found none. Impossible . . . Doubting myself, for surely there must be some, I wrote to Beckett at rue des Favorites informing him *Watt* was a week away from the printer, and asked if there were any last-minute changes or emendations he cared to make. He said there were none, assuming I had paid careful heed to the corrections he had made by hand in bright green ink on the manuscript. But of course he must see proofs. I assured him he would.

There was still one final, last-minute unanticipated obstacle to overcome. On page 247, the novel having presumably ended on page 246. Beckett, one may recall, had inserted addenda, the footnote to which stated in no uncertain terms: "The following precious and illuminating material should be carefully studied. Only fatigue and disgust prevented its incorporation." There followed eight pages of notes, most in English but some in Latin, others in German, and including a descant for four voices (soprano, alto, tenor, and bass) "heard by Watt on way to station" and a threne "heard by Watt in ditch on way from station." Among the addenda's jewels were three worthy of special note: "for all the good that frequent departures out of Ireland had done him, he might just as well have stayed there" (good for Joyce, better for Beckett); "change all the names"; and, finally, the true ending, "no symbols where none intended."

A day or two after Beckett had given his blessing for *Watt* to print, Maurice sent a *pneumatique* marked URGENT, summoning Alex, Christopher, and me to the rue Jacob office. Immediately. Why not Austryn I have no idea; I can only assume that because of Sade, Austryn held a privileged position, and this afternoon we sensed that reproaches were in the air. When we arrived, Maurice's expression was not cordial. "How are you today, Maurice?" Alex ventured, offering him a Gauloise, which he refused with a dismissive wave of his hand. That in itself was upsetting, for Maurice was a chain-smoker and, when offered, always responded automatically, extending his well-manicured fingers to the pack and withdrawing not one but generally two or three, "for later use," he would say with a smile. We sat before the trestle table that served Maurice as a desk, like three recalcitrant schoolboys about to be admonished by the teacher. The manuscript of *Watt* lay rather too conspicuously before him, open to the addenda section. "Not too well," he said. "Aside from the usual infirmities, there is the Beckett problem. I have now read. *Watt*. Closely. While it has some scatological moments, it can in no way pass for one of my 'normal' books. Think what it could do to my reputation. Imagine, a customer receives the flyer, responds with an order and advance payment, postpaid—for my clients are eager, nay, burning to read what they have purchased—receives the tome, and begins to read. Lost by page 15, perhaps sooner, he riffles through, desperately searching for the good parts—by which I mean the bad parts—finds none, or virtually none, throws the book across the room, goes to his desk, and writes me a stinging letter of rebuke, asking not only for his money back but—picture this!—for removal of his name from my mailing list!"

We listened in silence. "At least we can do some paring," he said. "Paring?" I cut in. "There will be no paring. Mr. Beckett, I can assure, will not suffer a word to be changed without his approval." Maurice raised his hand wearily. "The addenda," he said, "even the author invited it to be cut." He gestured to the pages on the table, donned his glasses, and read: "The following precious and illuminating material should be carefully studied. Only fatigue and disgust prevented its incorporation." He looked up, a thin smile of triumph on his lips.

"Maurice," I said, "you miss the point. That's Beckett's mind at work. Constantly intruding and commenting—usually negatively—on his work. Absolutely essential."

Maurice looked not defeated but outflanked. Outnumbered. Frowning, he glanced around as if seeking allies. "I shall sleep on it" was all he said.

"Maurice," Trocchi said, "this is a Collection Merlin book, so it will not be confused with the normal green Olympia Press offering. We will give it another color cover—blue perhaps, or off-white. Further, you need not include it in any catalog. We'll do a separate flyer for it, a subscription form . . ."

I suddenly wondered, as did we all, about the artistic integrity we'd been guaranteed by the Man. I could not, indeed would not, face Beckett with the proposal. And if Maurice persisted, then our fledgling arrangement was for naught. "I intend to publish books in English that will confront the censorious Western world" were still ringing in my ears.

Morning brought him to his senses. He agreed the addenda could stay.

"Nonetheless, we must do a smaller-than-normal print run. Much smaller." We had suggested half of Maurice's normal 5,000, conveniently forgetting that when he had figured Beckett's royalties we had calculated printing only 1,000. He lowered our figure to 750. Apparently aghast, Alex lowered his eyes. "All right, Maurice, you win: 1,500," he said resignedly. We settled on a printing of 1,100 copies for the ordinary edition, with 25 copies *hors commerce* lettered A to Y, each signed by the author. It had long been a custom in France, at least for those deemed worthy, to print a limited number of copies *hors commerce*, "not for sale," as an artist making lithographs would pull a number of APs, or artist's proofs, before the regular printing began. Even Girodias, who had initially balked at the added expense, for these copies were generally printed on vellum stock, capitulated without much of a fight. Beckett, though yet unknown, fully merited the honor. The regular edition of 1,100 copies would be priced at 850 francs, or roughly $2—10 shillings if you were paying in English coin—while the limited edition would nominally sell for 2,500 francs, or about $6 at the latest exchange rate. Each member of the Merlin inner sanctum would receive three copies of the limited edition, with seven going to the author.*

The print order having been settled, the hour having struck one, Maurice's color slowly returned. He managed a smile that, while thin, struck us as the still-veiled sun returning after a deadly storm. He rose, extended his hand first to Trocchi, then to Christopher and me, and suggested he take us to lunch.

---

*It turned out that Trocchi, by his own admission years later, had kept most of the *hors commerce* copies for himself, planning to sell them off as needed to feed his growing heroin habit. By a sad stroke of poetic justice, someone in Paris, probably a fellow junkie, stole them from Trocchi and sold them to Gaït, who in all innocence offered them to her customers for the stated rate of 2,500 francs. In a 1981 interview, Trocchi also acknowledged that he had kept the manuscript of *Watt*, which should have been returned to the author, and, again to feed his habit, sold it in the 1960s for £400. In today's market, Lord only knows what that precious manuscript would fetch, but it's safe to say it would be in six figures. More to the point, the manuscript should be in the Beckett archives, for when he thrust it through the door at the rue du Sabot that rain-sodden night in November 1952, he gave me to understand that it was his only corrected copy.

22 ∾

Questions of Conscience

DOZEN DAYS LATER, on a sparkling early fall morning that promised to be exceedingly warm, the leaves quivering, or giving the impression of doing so, and the grasses also, beneath drops, or beads, of gaily expiring dew, in short the day having made an excellent start, we toted, on a northbound bus—on the open back platform of the bus, to be precise—the manuscript of *Watt*, still bound in its slightly rain-spattered cover of black imitation leather that Beckett had handed us more than half a year before. Ceremoniously, *Watt* was given to the printer, L'Imprimerie Richard, 24, rue Stephenson, Paris XVIII, with the admonition to have the typesetters pay special attention, for this was English and there were anomalies, many anomalies, including verse and music. Spacing was also sometimes unusual, but very important. Monsieur Richard, the founder and owner, a man of both weight and sensibility, if one could judge—and one could, by his girth on the one hand and the ruddy complexion on the other, which bespoke both hearty repasts and a minimum consumption of red of at least 300, perhaps 350, liters per annum, substantial but not that much over the Gallic average in the time of which I speak—Monsieur Richard assured us not to worry, his typesetters were the best, excelling in English, of which they knew not a word. For once the question of money—that corrupter of all things large and small—did not arise: paid—or assured—by Maurice in advance, *Dieu merci*. For in seducing us, Maurice had, as all good con men do, deployed flattery, hoisting us onto the pedestal of art while reserving the mundane, tedious work of dealing with printers and distributors to himself. "As serious literary artists," he had said, "you intend to produce and, through Merlin, propagate new forms of writing. You must devote yourselves to the novel, to poetry, to drama." And, duly flattered, we believed him to a man. And woman.

We had specified an off-white cover. While the book was on press, Monsieur Richard called. From his mournful tone I knew there was a problem. He apologized and said the paper merchant had failed to deliver our cover stock, what should he do? Wait three weeks until the proper paper stock arrived or use what he had on hand. What was on hand? we asked. A lovely magenta, he said, really lovely. Alex and I bussed over to see it. Appalling. What would Beckett, who had been promised off-white, think? But what would he think if he were told the book would be a month late? Besides, we were already advertising its availability in the next issue of the magazine. We settled for magenta. Should I inform the author? Discretion, Trocchi advised, was always the wiser course.

Three weeks later, on September 30, to be precise, we were holding in our hands a copy of *Watt*, still redolent of ink, fresh from the press. We fondled it, as one fondles one's firstborn. The magenta looked glowing. Positively lovely, as Monsieur Richard had said. We sent copies of the ordinary edition, as well as seven alphabet letters of the limited edition, to Mr. Beckett. Silence. Perhaps it was the time of year. Perhaps he was away from Paris. Perhaps he was busy writing. Perhaps he had told the concierge to hold all mail, lest he be importuned.

"Perhaps," I ventured, when two weeks, then three, had passed and this most meticulous of men remained, like his creature Godot, eloquently invisible, "he dislikes the magenta."

As it turned out, as soon as he had received the copies, he wrote to George Reavey: "At long last, *Watt* is just out in an awful magenta cover."

So it *was* the magenta. But to us not a word of reproach. When word finally came down from on high, it was gratitude and kindness, both marks of the man: Thank you for the copies of *Watt*. They look splendid. I fear, however, a few errors crept in, despite all efforts. I enclose a list herewith. I trust if there is a second edition, these will be corrected. As it turned out, Beckett had found a number of errors and, worse, a dropped sentence on page 19, and apparently was furious with us. But, always the gentleman, he never let on, at least to us.

I wrote back thanking him, assuring him the errors would indeed be corrected, and reminding him that the same had happened to Joyce's *Ulysses*, that French printers, in both cases knowing no English, had, in making the first-round corrections, slipped in a few of their own. Inadvertently, but apparently inevitably. All this despite the robust assurances of Monsieur Richard.

Maurice was only mildly pleased with our first feature production, for while he had agreed as part of our arrangement to print and distribute the novel, it was not exactly what he had in mind for his main thrust. Certainly not for the public he intended. There were, he averred, a few "dirty" scenes in *Watt*, but not nearly enough for "his public," which he now laid out for us in some detail to avoid further confusion. The major imprint of his Olympia Press would be named Traveller's Companion and bear a pale green cover to distinguish it from the "more respectable items," as he put it. He trusted there would not be too many of the latter. While for the Traveller's Companion he planned to reprint, or translate, some of the "classics"—not only the aforementioned *Fanny Hill* but storied names such as Apollinaire, Beardsley, Sade—what he sorely needed to feed his greedy maw was new work, original tales, aimed at the Anglo-American readers who were being needlessly deprived of such tantalizing fare in their own retarded countries. The number of such potential "constituents"—his term—coming to France each year was increasing exponentially, as the world reverted to normalcy and the thousands, no, millions of tourists whose traveling had been thwarted for five long years by the war would return "in countless numbers." Again his expression. "Not to mention," he added, "the thousands of sailors from the Sixth Fleet, guarding the Mediterranean against all comers," whose long sojourns at sea made them achingly ready for the books he had in mind. Ah, and the soldiers, the untold soldiers occupying Germany; where was the first place they would head when they had a few days' leave? Paris, that he was certain. Thus greenclad Olympia would fill a crying need. He was inviting us Merlinites to join him!

Were we, by allying ourselves with an avowed purveyor of eroticism ("pornographer," Patrick said, calling a spade where it fell), sacrificing our artistic integrity—an expression we used quite frequently? Austryn, with his Sade and his vision of translating other French underground works ad infinitum, had no problem with the alliance. His only concern was being found out by the French authorities and expelled, for he saw France as his long-term haven, convinced that McCarthyism was here to stay. Christopher, whose left-wing leanings were profound, was not sure. Not that he minded a bit of the salacious; on the contrary. But would his poetry suffer? Pat was having trouble enough getting on with his overlong-gestating novel, so was maddeningly neutral. *Merlin* could not survive without help from an outside source—I had given all I could from my months at remote Chaumont—and besides, so far Maurice had been as good as his word, had he not? Jeannette found Maurice utterly charming. "Let's face it, mon," said Alex, "there are two virtues here: first, we can get our books published, and, second, we can eat." It was true, most of us were living on roughly two or three dollars a day, and had been for years. There was really no choice. And besides, having eked out the first four issues of *Merlin*, we were entering a new phase of the magazine's, and our own, existence, which could be fun. Challenging. Daring. Even dangerous . . .

Trocchi was first in with *Young Adam*, which for two years now had made the rounds of the established publishers, roughly a dozen in both England and America, without a taker but many polite turndowns, some full of praise but inevitably ending with "We regret, however, that we are unable to make you an offer for publication at this time," and the closing cliché "We wish you better luck with another house." "I'll let it sit, old man," he said. "Like a good Bordeaux. Maybe it will age well. Anyway, I'm not sending it out again!"

Now, more than a year later, he showed *Young Adam* to Girodias. It had a fair amount of strong sex in it, especially between the protagonist, Joe, and Ella the barge woman, but Maurice wanted more. "You'll have to dirty it up," he told Trocchi. That won't be a problem, Trocchi declared. Jane confessed he was disappointed that the novel, into which he had poured his heart and talent, was becoming a mere DB—Dirty Book. While Alex was reworking *Young Adam*, Austryn, having handed over Sade's *Philosophy in the Bedroom*, took on the task of translating Georges Bataille's *Histoire de l'oeil—A Tale of Satisfied Desire*—which the distinguished philosopher and novelist had written under the pseudonym of Lord Auch. My assignment was to translate Apollinaire's *Les exploits d'un jeune Don Juan*, which we freely retitled *Memoirs of a Young Rakehell*, a charming work on the eroticism of adolescence the great poet had written a quarter century before.

The first green-covered titles of the Traveller's Companion series appeared as though overnight. We marveled at the efficiency of Olympia's printers, for whereas we had waited weeks for each issue of *Merlin*, Maurice seemed to move from manuscript to finished book in a matter of days.

Trocchi, having sullied up *Young Adam*, turned to the other, more outrageous Apollinaire novel, *Les onze mille verges*—literally, *The Eleven Thousand Rods*—which Girodias rebaptized *The Debauched Hospodar*. How Alex, with his limited French, managed to "translate" Apollinaire remains a mystery. Did he get help from a native? I never knew. Whatever else he was, Girodias was a genius at both titles and pseudonyms. For the Apollinaire, he dubbed Alex "Oscar Mole," one of his less brilliant choices but one that, once again, stressed the underground nature of the operation he was launching. Having acquitted himself admirably, and in jig time, of both *Young Adam* and the Apollinaire, Alex next transmogrified himself into a lady of little virtue, Frances Lengel, and dashed off, in a matter of weeks, a novel entitled *Helen and Desire*, an updated version of *Fanny Hill* that served as a kind of model for the genre.

Our new connection with Girodias and Olympia did not come without its pound of flesh. None of us was on very solid ground when it came to our legal status with the French authorities. Some had student visas, others short-term papers that left us open to penalties or outright expulsion if the type of literature we were churning out was ever discovered.

As the weeks wore on, we turned in our manuscripts and received the coveted five hundred dollars, with promises of more to come if the book reprinted. As noted, Olympia's usual printing was five thousand copies, which meant in effect that Girodias was paying us a royalty of ten cents a book. To collect our money—so many pages, so many francs—we repaired to 13, rue Jacob. The front of the place was a bookshop, and Maurice had sublet the back, a tiny space mostly filled by a trestle table, behind which, enthroned on a slightly sagging mattress, sat Maurice, while off to one side, before a small desk littered with letters, invoices, and manuscripts of varying stripes and origins, sat his assistant, Lisa Rosenbaum, a green-eyed, dark-haired beauty. I mention the shop because it had revealed to us beyond the shadow of a doubt that the man who had become our *gérant*, the impeccably dressed, finely manicured owner of a Citroën *traction avant*, a person whom we had to a man, and indeed a woman, unquestionably accepted as our financial savior, was almost as poor as we. So poor, in fact, that when we turned in a manuscript, he would usually take out a thinning wad of franc notes and, instead of paying the total sum due, peel off a few to keep us going, he said, until we needed more. Often when we came for more, with further pages in hand of the promised work, he would evince surprise at the speed with which the earlier sum had disappeared, wondering out loud whether we had suddenly changed our *façon de vivre*, our "lifestyle," pondering too whether indeed he had not paid us already the entire sum due, he could not recall, and when we assured him he had not, he looked pained, a parent wondering where and how the child had gone wrong, had so disappointed him, until finally, with sincere reluctance, he would reach into his shallow pocket for the storied wad and peel off a few more notes. This happened so often that we decided we should, we really should, put something in writing, both at the time of initial agreement and when sums were doled out, for we too ultimately found it difficult to remember how much we had received and how much remained due.

When a book reprinted, we would receive an additional sum. If it was hard, indeed heroically difficult, to pry out of him the money due for our Olympian labors, eventually he did settle, though the additional sums due for a reprint somehow never materialized.

23

Meeting Barney Rosset

OW SAFELY BACK IN PARIS, I had to face up to our new challenges. The first of these was a decision to honor my fellowships and complete my Sorbonne doctorate. It was like my break with religion when I was fifteen or sixteen: though I no longer believed, not to break my mother's heart, I performed the ritual, stopping only at the sacrament, which to indulge I felt unacceptable, hypocritical. To his credit, Professor Dédéyan had finally yielded, admitted Joyce was sufficiently dead to allow for commentary. So upon my return to Paris, I began working to prepare for my *soutenance de thèse* the following June, pausing only when the urge of a poem or short story of my own, or an afternoon with Beckett, intruded.

Second on the new agenda: Jeannette was preparing for her conservatory final, which would determine whether she left with First Prize in Violin. The lovely apartment that had been a sort of honeymoon spot for us was soon a fond but fading memory.

Meanwhile, back in the States, Bernard DeBoer may not have sold many copies of *Merlin* into his Eastern Seaboard accounts, but proof that he had landed some came in the form of half a dozen letters to me, including one from Dexter Strong at Pomfret; another from Al Sussman, my classics professor at UNC; a third from my old roommate there Wyc Toole, a man of sharp wit and intelligence with whom I had written a humorous column for *The Daily Tar Heel* under the byline of Wyc and Dick and who, for reasons I had trouble understanding, had opted to remain in the navy after graduation and was currently a lieutenant commander stationed in Washington.

I paid some attention to a letter I received one day from a gentleman who said he was a New York publisher. His name was Barney Rosset, and he had recently bought a publishing house called Grove Press, after the street in Greenwich Village. He had read and liked my piece on Beckett in *Merlin* number 2 and the extract from *Watt* in the following issue, and both the extract and what I said about the Irishman intrigued him greatly. He would be coming to Paris in late summer or early fall and wondered if we could meet, perhaps have lunch. Could I possibly arrange a meeting with Mr. Beckett as well? I wrote back saying I would be pleased to meet him, warning him, however, that the Irishman was fiercely private and difficult to reach, so while I would try to set up an appointment, I could offer no guarantee. With regard to Beckett's work, I informed him that we—*Merlin*—would shortly be publishing *Watt*, and, probably in 1954, a later novel, *Molloy*, which had been written in French—for that was the language to which Mr. Beckett was now seemingly committed—and was shortly to be translated. I added that if he were interested in Beckett for America, he should get in touch with Monsieur Jérôme Lindon of Les Éditions de Minuit and gave him the address on the rue Bernard Palissy. I would, I added, have a word with Monsieur Lindon, saying he could expect to hear from Mr. Rosset.

Rosset wrote back a few weeks later, thanking me for making him read Beckett, saying he was now in contact with Minuit and had in fact made an offer for Beckett for America, which he hoped would be accepted. He noted that he would be coming with his wife, Loly, a German girl he had recently married. I found his letters lively and enthusiastic and looked forward to meeting the man behind them. I was to pick a restaurant. I chose a nice Chinese restaurant behind the Sorbonne.

Then arrived a few days later an unexpected, and frankly jarring, intrusion into my Parisian life. The intruder was a very official-looking package that lay against my rue du Sabot door one afternoon when I returned from the Bibliothèque Nationale, where I was spending most of my days. I picked up the prim white package, turned it over, pressed it to gauge its bulk under the mistaken notion that heft and importance were proportional, then took it inside. It read OFFICIAL BUSINESS on both front and back. I did not like the look of it, not one bit, and so decided not to open it immediately. Next day it looked slightly less menacing, so screwing my courage to the sticking place, I ripped it open.

Shit!

The U.S. Navy, to which I owed my education and into whose reserve ranks I had automatically signed my life away upon graduation, had decided I was essential to the national defense. Korea? Wasn't it winding down? Surely they would be mustering out personnel, not mustering them in? My orders were to report to Germany for a physical in the next thirty days. Now, I was as patriotic as the next expatriate—but still . . . I procrastinated for a week, then hied myself over to the Right Bank, made an appointment with the military attaché, showed him my orders, and asked if this wasn't all a big mistake. He scrutinized the papers, looked up over his rimless glasses, and assured me it was not. Further, since the thirty days mentioned would be up next Thursday, he suggested I get my ass on a train and head for Mannheim ASAP, or I might be considered AWOL. I was not yet into acronyms, but my RADAR sensed this situation spelled DANGER, and next day found me on a slow train to our former enemy's now fast-recovering country. No sense rushing. I had led such a wanton, dissolute life the past five years, I half convinced myself, there was a fair chance I might flunk the physical. Then I recalled with dismay all those grueling sessions with the French Olympic wrestlers, tennis matches two or three times a week with Lapicque *père et fils*, not to mention swimming spring, summer, and fall at the Deligny pool. In short, I was found not only fit but a fine physical specimen. Depressed, I re-entrained for Paris. I would have to tell Jeannette. She knew of the navy's intrusion but had no idea what it meant or what the timing might be. I had kept her intentionally in the dark because, after all, I wasn't sure myself. Maybe the admirals would have a change of heart. Maybe they would take a closer look at my noncredentials. It had been six or seven years since I had taken those V-12 navy courses—navigation, seamanship, engineering, whatever—and if any vestiges of that far-off book learning remained, they were embedded deep within my sub-subconscious. Maybe the war would end. Maybe, given my fluency, I would be assigned to the Paris embassy, replacing the jerk I had visited there a week ago, who confessed he had barely learned a phrase of French in his almost year as attaché.

A week later, follow-up orders ended all ambiguity: "On July 31, 1954 you will report to the Boston Naval Base, there to receive further orders and assignment to your ship." Your ship! You mean I would not be running things in Washington? I must have been a senior ensign by now, for God's sake!

I broke the news to Jeannette as gently as I could. Taking it in stride as usual, she said, "You know, the timing may be perfect. You'll have defended your thesis on June 24, and I'll have finished the conservatory the day before. Maybe it's time to test new waters. Besides, I'm told that if I do win First Prize, I'll qualify for a place in the Galician Master Class at the Juilliard School in New York, and I can study with the absolute best violin master in the world, Ivan Galamian."

I was beginning to discover new sides, new depths, to this young lady that I had not even suspected before. And learning how important positive reactions in life can be.

Rosset and his wife did appear on schedule and, I noted, on the dot of one o'clock. In my early Paris years, I had tended to arrive ten or fifteen minutes late to most appointments—knowing that most Parisians considered timeliness a show of weakness—until I made the grave mistake one day of being late for an appointment with Mr. Beckett. His only reproach was a raised eyebrow, but it stung me. From then on I arrived almost invariably two or three minutes early to every appointment.

Barney was a slight, intense, wired-up young man, whom I judged to be in his early thirties, although his receding hairline made him look older. He was wearing thick horn-rimmed glasses, and when he laughed— which he did often, though nervously, as if he weren't quite sure a laugh was appropriate to the remark—he looked strangely equine, baring both gums. His wife, Loly, was taller than he, a lovely, statuesque, blue-eyed blonde, German by birth but with almost perfect English after several years in the States. She was the sales manager of Grove, Barney informed us, and added with the now-familiar laugh that he had married her to keep her from leaving the company. I assumed he was joking, but he assured me he was perfectly serious and told the following tale: As part of her job, Loly had gone to the West Coast, where she happened to run into an old beau, who suddenly proposed marriage. She called Barney to inform him of this development. She was inclined to say yes and he had better look for a new sales manager. Not wasting a minute, Barney cajoled her into meeting him in his native habitat, Chicago, where on bended knee *he* proposed to her in turn. Thus he not only secured a new bride but kept a tried-and-true sales manager as well. Two birds, as they say . . .

Barney had recently bought the press for three thousand dollars—a sum he seemed to consider piffling but that struck me as a small fortune when I translated dollars into francs. He was looking for new voices, new talent, not the castoffs of the larger American houses. He thanked me for putting him onto Beckett and introducing him to Lindon. He had already contracted for some of Beckett's work in America—not directly with Lindon, whom he hadn't yet met, but through an American agent, Marian Saunders. He was in early correspondence with Beckett, who had warned him he'd not tolerate any changes in his work, though some aspects of it, he said, might be deemed censurable. No, Rosset had not yet met the man, but he and Loly were having a drink with him in a day or two, to which he was looking forward with some trepidation. In agreeing to meet, Beckett had warned he had only forty-five minutes to spare, which seemed a bit off-putting. What did I think of the man? Even better than his work, if that were possible, I responded.

Barney and his first wife, the artist Joan Mitchell, had lived in the south of France for a year. While Joan had profited greatly from the year on the Riviera, maturing in her art, Barney confessed he had spent most of the time staring out the window at the sea, trying to figure out what to do with his life. Then one day, a Chicago friend of Joan's, Francine Felsenthal, mentioned that two friends of hers had a small publishing house they wanted to sell. Only one of the two, a writer named Robert Phelps, wanted to throw in the towel. Phelps lived in Woodstock, New York, so Barney drove up and paid him fifteen hundred dollars for his half—which, by the way, included the inventory, which Barney piled into several suitcases and drove back to his apartment on Ninth Street in the Village, where he stored them till he could figure out what to do with them. All well and good, but he still owned only half the company. The other partner, a man named John Balcomb, had just one literary interest in life, Ezra Pound. "Any project I proposed he'd turn down. I bought his half as well. Anyway, since I had this publishing house, I figured I better learn something about the business, so I enrolled in some courses at Columbia and the New School. Not for credit, just to learn. At Columbia in the seat next to me was a man named Donald Allen, a freelance editor who struck me as very bright and in the know. So I hired him."

Who else were we publishing in *Merlin*? Barney asked.

"We've just published an extract from Jean Genet's *Thief's Journal*," I said, "with an introductory note by Jean-Paul Sartre, who thinks the man is a genius. It was he who turned us on to him. He's also a playwright—perhaps primarily a playwright—but I find his novels extraordinary. This said, if you're interested, you should know you may have a censorship problem with him." For years, I explained, no mainstream French publisher dared take him on. He was published almost privately by a small provincial publisher, L'Arbalète. But now Sartre had convinced Gaston Gallimard of Genet's importance, so they were bringing out the novels.

Any censorship problems here in France? Barney wanted to know. "None that I know," I said. "I think the authorities are afraid of taking on Sartre."

"And what is it about the novels that makes them censorable?" Barney asked.

"Sex," I said. "Pretty candid sex. Homosexual sex."

"Doesn't scare me," Barney said, as he took out a pen and began jotting down notes. "Who else are you doing in that issue?"

"A touching piece by Henry Miller, an extract from his novel *Plexus*," I replied. This clearly piqued Barney's interest. At Swarthmore, which Barney had attended briefly before the war, he'd written a paper on Henry Miller's *Tropic of Cancer*, much to his professor's chagrin. *Tropic of Cancer*? I wondered if I should mention that I knew a man here in Paris with a strong connection to Miller, especially the forbidden *Tropics*, but decided it was premature. Getting back to Genet, I said: "I can put you in touch with his translator if you like, an American GI who's been living here since the war, if you want to pursue."

No time this trip, Barney said. Was there anyone else on the Paris scene he should look out for? Ionesco, I said, Eugène Ionesco. He's Romanian, but has been living here for years and, like Beckett, now writes in French. Trocchi and I had met with him a few months earlier and would be publishing a play of his. No, he wasn't as good as Beckett—but then, Beckett was in a class by himself.

The next day Barney, Alex, and I met at the Old Navy to discuss how Grove and *Merlin* might work together, specifically whether Grove might distribute *Watt* in America, for of our original printing we still had well over four hundred copies unsold. A distinct possibility, Barney said. He had hoped to publish *Molloy* first, but now that had apparently been put on hold, he had heard, until the translation, which was slow going, was finished.

Later, when I asked Trocchi what he thought of Barney, "strange" was his one-word response. For the usually eloquent Alex, this struck me as both vague and ambiguous, so I pressed him. "The man squirms, didn't you notice?" Alex said. "He can't seem to sit still." Conversely, before he left

Paris, I asked Barney what he thought of Alex. "Impressive. But he scares me. I don't know why, but I find him intimidating." What did *I* think of Barney? True, as Alex had noted, the man seemed incapable of repose. I liked the way he acted on his impulses and made a mental note to look him up when we went to New York. Correction: *if* we went to New York.

24 ⌒

Beckett's Back in Town

BECKETT WAS NOW BACK IN PARIS, having gone in early September to Berlin to see the German production of *Godot*, which displeased him mightily. Although it was well received, he found it "badly directed," and when I saw him a few days later, he added with his usual wry humor: "I would have preferred the contrary." Shortly after his return he sent me a postcard: Could we pick up the translation of "La fin" where we had left off? Where we had left off, very simply: my draft sent to him before the summer, which had lain dormant, had been gathering dust but surely not quality for three months now. Beckett's initial response, which had cheered me momentarily, was that the translation was fine, though it perhaps needed "a little tinkering," a phrase that did not alert me as much as it doubtless should have. Meanwhile, Trocchi kept pressing me for it, and once again I reminded him that I needed Beckett's approval. A day or two later another postcard arrived, addressed as usual to "Dear Seaver." (First names were still far-off, for I addressed him, then and for many years thereafter, as "Mr. Beckett," until one night, dining at his favorite restaurant in Montparnasse, Aux Îles Marquises, he said, "Oh, for God's sake, call me Sam!" Even then, so imposing was he to me, my brain had constantly to send a special-delivery message to my tongue to avoid the habitual "Mr. Beckett.")

We met on the appointed day at the Dôme, at four in the afternoon, when the place was almost empty, at a table in the back, each with his copy of the English manuscript and the French text. Over the summer I had made a number of changes, which I first passed along, Beckett nodding approval of most, reserving judgment on others. Regarding the latter he would inevitably say: "You're doubtless right, Dick, but for the life of me I can't figure out what I was trying to say in the French." Then we went back to line one. In other words, instead of finding fault with the translation, he would gallantly blame the original—himself—for the problem. Such was the nature of the man.

After an hour or so we would pause, order another glass of red wine, and talk of anything but the text at hand. Beckett had just bought a plot of land, he told me, exactly one hectare square, in the tiny village of Ussy-sur-Marne, about fifty kilometers east of Paris, on which he had constructed a small, austere house consisting of two rooms. Why he had chosen Ussy, a nondescript hamlet, he never told me. But then, in all fairness, I never asked. Perhaps it was familiarity, for he and Suzanne had for several years, to get away from Paris, rented a house there for virtually nothing, and Beckett had done a fair amount of his early postwar writing there. The house's furnishings, as he described them with pride, as if he had just inherited a grandly furnished château or manor house, reminded me of the contents of the mandated passage from *Watt* that had graced issue number 3. Utterly spare and utilitarian: two single beds, a desk, some bookcases for his dictionaries, a round dining room table, a battered upright piano, and two cushioned wicker chairs. He had also indulged himself, he admitted almost sheepishly one afternoon between paragraphs, in a slightly used radio, apparently to keep himself company in that solitary setting but also, he further admitted, to follow crucial rugby matches involving Ireland, and important boxing matches as well. To me, for whom sports had always been an essential ingredient in my young life, it was reassuring to hear Beckett's quiet, almost matter-of-fact "confession" that for him, too, sports had always been important. In school he had played cricket and rugby, and later golf and tennis, at both of which he excelled.

With my *Merlin* friends, and my Parisian cohorts who were nonathletic, I rarely spoke of sports, for in their calcified minds "jocks" and intellectuals were incompatible. Even Lindon, who already revered his new author, apparently had no notion of his athletic leanings until one weekend he invited Beckett and Suzanne to join him in the country, warning them, however, that he planned to play a round or two of golf. Beckett said that would be no problem, in fact he wouldn't mind joining Lindon's group. Though a bit rusty, Beckett not only kept up with the foursome but, Lindon later reported, at least in one round came in with the lowest score.

Still on the subject of Ussy, he had bought the place, he said, with a small bequest from his mother, who had died three years before, plus the unanticipated earnings from *Godot*, which from its fragile, precarious opening in January had, by late spring, become the talk of Paris, which suddenly everyone—I assure you, my dear, you mustn't miss it, you simply mustn't!—was clamoring to see. What's more, the usually quiet, monastic office of Jérôme Lindon was suddenly deluged with phone calls from the four corners of the world requesting rights, both publication and dramatic. At age forty-seven, still largely unknown, Beckett had no inkling that the world was about to discover him and do him long overdue obeisance.

During this break from our line-by-line scrutiny of "La fin"—an inching progress—Beckett would always question the sense or validity of the original rather than that of the translation. He would sit back, push his glasses up into his thick shock of graying hair, take a sip of red wine, and say, "Now, what in the world did I mean by that?" Or: "That passage makes no sense. No sense at all." Then, having established that the shortcoming was his, not mine, we'd go back to work.

Ussy was a blessing, he said, an isle of tranquillity, especially now with the *Godot* nonsense. A place to work and rest. And, yes, listen to music, which was vital to him. The radio of course: it wasn't wholly for sports. So it was paradise, I suggested. He cocked his head. Not quite, he said. There was one problem he had not foreseen. The house was on a rise, roughly in the center of the property, which had the virtue of allowing him a lovely view of the Marne valley. But the other side of that coin was that passersby, who were becoming more frequent, could see him. An unwanted invasion of privacy. "There were even times," he said, repressing a smile because he could doubtless envision the absurdity of it, "when seeing people down at the perimeter staring up, I had to get down on all fours and crawl from one room to the other!" The imagined scene made me want to burst out laughing, but I refrained, for I knew it was a serious matter to him. Then he eased the air by laughing first. "But the sad fact is," he said, "I'll have no choice but to build a wall round the property. Those ugly cement building blocks, but nothing less will do the job. The pity is, they also cut off the lovely view I once had."

During another break about an hour later, I asked about the German production, and he lowered his head. "I wish I hadn't gone," he said. "It was a misery." I told him I heard the reviews were good and the public responsive. He nodded. "But the direction was wrong," he said, "all wrong." I asked, was there nothing he could have done to set it right? Again he shook his head. "First of all," he said, "I know nothing about the theater. And further, I did not go there to involve myself, simply to see." His response reminded me of the note he had sent to the French radio when the first fragment of *Godot* had been recorded a year and a half before, excusing himself for not appearing as promised—shades of his antihero?—and adding that his presence would have contributed nothing, since he was totally ignorant of what makes "good directing," or "good theater" for that matter. "If the Germans had listened to me," he said, "they'd have emptied the theater far faster, I assure you." This from a man who, a few short years later, would become deeply engaged in the details of each production, attend the rehearsals of virtually all his plays, often in essence becoming the director, and who in subsequently printed editions would indicate in minute detail the stage directions to be followed meticulously.

At the end of most sessions, Jeannette would join us, and for a moment Beckett seemed to put aside his anguish and derogatory feelings about his work, and we three would enjoy a wonderful, lively evening. Beckett would thank me profusely for my good work, which made me cringe, for all the afternoon had revealed, I felt, was my inadequacy. How had I ever let myself get roped into this? I kept asking, and I had constantly to remind myself that Beckett had professed his desire not to translate his own work, presumably to save his creative energies for original work. Indeed, over the five-year period following his return in 1945 to Paris from Dublin, where he had gone to see his mother at the end of the war, Beckett, having made the decision to write henceforth in French, threw himself into his work with renewed energy and purpose. After the relative paucity of writing and the constant rejections of the 1930s, followed by the war, when to focus on literature or writing itself was almost immoral, he engaged, as he put it to me one afternoon at the Coupole, "in a veritable frenzy of writing." He didn't know whether to ascribe this frenzy to his decision to shift languages or to the pent-up waters of his riotous imagination finally spilling over the dam of his own self-doubt. During that period he had produced no fewer than a dozen major works, including the masterpieces *Waiting for Godot* and the prose trilogy *Molloy*, *Malone Dies*, and *The Unnamable*, which had smitten me like three tons of bricks. He had in addition penned another novel, *Mercier and Camier*; the play *Eleuthéria*, which preceded *Godot*; five longish stories and a baker's dozen of short shorts; and a perceptive work of art criticism, *Three Dialogues with Georges Duthuit*. Few of these works—only a couple of short stories in Sartre's *Les temps moderne* and another in *Fontaine*—had seen the light of publication, and as for the plays, despite some "nibbles of interest" from three or four French directors, by the end of this extraordinarily productive period neither was even close to being staged. That relative lack of success on any front would doubtless have made any lesser man, especially one pushing fifty, give up and say, "I can't go on." But like so many of the misfits and downtrodden in his creations, Beckett knew that he had no choice: "I must go on," even if no one ever recognized the journey. Of the novels, only that "old chestnut" *Murphy*, which he and his friend Paul Léon had translated from the English, had been published in France, and that, as we know, to a disturbing lack of success.

But Beckett's luck was about to change, and change radically, with Suzanne's timely submission in 1951 of *Molloy* and *Malone Dies* to Jérôme Lindon's Éditions de Minuit. Beckett said later that if Minuit had turned him down, he would have given up, for there are only so many rejections a writer can bear.

Finally, after five or six sessions, Beckett pushed the English version of "La fin" across the table and said, "Well, that about does it. Thank you." 'Tis I should be thanking you, I thought, my mind filled with the wonderful Irish lilt. "I'm sorry I took so much of your time," he went on, making me feel worse, for it was to relieve him that I had accepted the task, to save *him* time. I said as much, but he shook his head. "I couldn't have done it, wouldn't have. So you've done me a service. You'll make sure I see proofs?" I assured him I would. "I'm sure this isn't the proper time to ask," he said, "but I hear *Merlin's* bought the English rights to *Molloy*." "We had indeed," I said, "though only for the Continent, not England or America," and was tempted to tell the story of the two checks, ours and Minuit's, but opted for discretion once again, for I wasn't sure what Lindon might have told him. "There's interest from England and America, too," he went on, "so the work will have to be translated." Could I take it on? Did I have time for it? He would help, be available for consultation, but, again, he simply did not have the time, or energy, or will, to face earlier works, much less translate them. He would be immensely grateful. I reread *Molloy*, my favorite of all his works to date, loved it as much as before, even gained a few new insights overlooked in the original readings, actually translated half a dozen pages, which came more easily than those of "La fin," for the work sessions with Beckett had taught me to some extent how his mind worked, his choice of words, his special turns of phrase, but still I was concerned, for Beckett had mentioned a deadline of six months. Still, by asking me, the Great Man had given me a vote of confidence for the translation of "La fin," slightly easing my guilt. On the other hand, having procrastinated for five years, I had finally decided, perhaps again out of guilt for having accepted two Fulbrights ostensibly for that purpose, to finish my Sorbonne thesis on Joyce, with the oral defense scheduled for the following June. He understood. Did I know of anyone who might take on the task? One of the Merlinites perhaps? The only one I could think of whose French was solid enough was Patrick. I mentioned the idea to Patrick, who warmed to it immediately. Had he read the novel? Only parts of it, but what he had read he found splendid. Read the rest, I cautioned, before you commit. It will be a challenge. And a privilege, Patrick stated. During that week he read *Molloy* and the following Friday greeted me at the rue du Sabot with a broad smile: he would love to do it. I told Beckett and suggested that he and Patrick meet. Beckett suggested I come along, as my experience with the story might help steer Patrick, "warn of the shoals," as he put it, which we did the following weekend at the Coupole. Now, months later, Patrick was valiantly struggling with the diabolically difficult text. Beckett, he said, had been a prince, responsive to every query, grateful for whatever progress, which he confessed was inching.

When, after their first month or two of working together, I asked Beckett how *Molloy* was progressing, he, the kindest of men, winced. "Patrick's very good," he said, "and I've become fond of him personally. But he has a very slow metabolism." It was less a reproach than a statement of a character trait. "Could you have a word with him, Dick"—he was now alternating between first name and last when we talked, a considerable breakthrough— "I'd be grateful." When I saw Patrick, I went straight to the point: How was *Molloy* going? "Well, I've done the first twenty or so pages, fully approved, and as you know they're appearing in the next issue of the magazine. But after that, piss poorly if you want to know. I'm not sure I'll ever finish. Beckett's been wonderful, but I feel he's becoming irritated with my snail's progress." He looked almost despondent. Publishers in America and England were champing at the bit. Not to mention *Merlin*. "Anyway, if there's anything I can do, let me know." He assured me he would.

As the weeks wore on, Patrick continued to struggle, as I had before him, and for much the same reason. However the pages came out, he would constantly ask himself: Is that the way Beckett would say it? Finally, in a desperate act of self-preservation, Patrick turned his back on the project and reimmersed himself in his own work, the long-planned novel he had, two years before, sketched out in his mind from start to finish, three volumes that, he announced, he would submit only to Jonathan Cape in London, whose list he found compatible with his taste. Now, with Pat gone silent, Beckett found himself obliged to reverse their roles: while it had been agreed that whenever Patrick had a dozen or so pages translated, he would contact Beckett either directly or via Lindon, now, when two or three of his *pneumatiques* had gone unanswered, Beckett became the stalker. More than once over the next several weeks he climbed unannounced the six steep flights to Patrick's garret room at the Cité Vaneau, knocked discreetly, never before eleven, to make sure his prey was up and about, and suggested they repair together downstairs to a nearby café to glance at whatever pages were ready. "It was as if I'd been thrust onstage before I'd even begun to learn my lines," Pat lamented to me after one of Beckett's visits. "True, I'd been avoiding him," he confessed, "because I was close to giving up. Yet after our session he made me feel so much better I will get on with it, I really will." I suggested again, having the experience of "La fin," that Pat force himself on a schedule of twelve to fifteen pages a week and show me them before they were sent to Beckett. For the next three weeks he did, and I found them strong and faithful, returning them with a few emendations and suggestions, which he said helped greatly. Again, I never told Beckett of my peripheral involvement. But Patrick, a true gentleman, admitted one day as, finally, fifteen months after it had begun, the translation was winding up, or down, to Patrick's great relief, and certainly Beckett's, that he had told the Master at one of their final sessions that at one low point in the endeavor "Seaver stuck a rocket up my arse and put a match to it, or this damn translation might never have been finished."

I had never realized till then what a fine, poetic, metaphoric soul Patrick possessed.

25 ⌖

The Sun Also Sets

IT WAS ONLY NATURAL that with my absence from Paris and from the daily confabulations that had been an integral part of my *Merlin* life for the better part of a year, my relationship both to the magazine and to Jane and Trocchi had changed. Alex too had greatly changed. Deeper into drugs, he became more and more remote, as if communing with other mortals and other worlds that were not mine. Further, he, who was much more a writer than an editor, had found a niche, perhaps a calling, with Maurice, and most of his time and energy was devoted to churning out manuscripts for Olympia. No question, he was the star workhorse of the green-garbed Girodias stable. Of all the Traveller's Companions, Trocchi's work was a clear cut above the simple DB. Still, it was hackwork, no literature there about which he had talked so much and himself written till then. Some of his early short stories were superb, and *Young Adam* was at least as good as most novels being published on either side of the Atlantic these days. One had only to read a paragraph or two of his latest work to see the talent. I had no quarrel with the dirt, you take it or leave it, but I did regret his abandoning the battle of quality. "You are wasting your time," Christopher deplored, "diverting your energies." Alex smiled, ever the charmer. "Nonsense. I can handle both. I have energy to spare, and the quality of my prose does not suffer. You'll see."

By the spring of 1954 the upcoming issue—volume 2, number 3 (we had long ago given up even any pretense of appearing quarterly)—in which at long last my (our) translation of "La fin" was to appear, still bore vestiges of my involvement, but the magazine had a whole new look, not to mention orientation. My contribution, in addition to the Beckett translation, was the appearance of the second writer I had mentioned to Trocchi the first day we met, Eugène Ionesco, two of whose plays I had seen and greatly admired that year. Daniel Mauroc was the intermediary, providing the playwright's address. Ionesco responded to my invitation immediately. We met at the café on the southwest corner of boulevards St. Germain and St. Michel. I invited Alex to go along. By the time Trocchi and I arrived, a small owlish man, already balding, with a cherubic face and slightly bulging, naive eyes—yes, the term is used advisedly, for we quickly learned he had an almost childlike view of the world, which seemed to make little or no sense to him, that carried over into his plays—was already there sipping a glass of wine. Mauroc, in describing his theater, had used the word "absurd," as far as I know for the first time, and it was an epithet that stuck in the years to come not only for Ionesco but also for a number of other dramatists who in the 1950s and 1960s labeled their work "anti-theater."

We had brought along earlier issues of the magazine, at which Ionesco only cast a glance, for he had no English and Mauroc's word was good enough for him. His two one-act plays *La leçon* and *La cantatrice chauve* were currently being performed at the Théâtre de la Huchette right around the corner—he gestured over his shoulder roughly toward the Seine—and like *Godot* had, after a mostly negative critical reception and correspondingly meager attendance, slowly gained both reputation and audience. "Mauroc thought *La cantatrice chauve* might be right for your magazine," he said. As he pushed the manuscript across the table, the noise in the street suddenly increased by ten or twenty decibels, and a number of police vans pulled up at the intersection. Blue-caped *flics*—riot police—poured forth with nightsticks twirling, almost balletic if they had not been so menacing. Barricades were quickly erected at all four corners—east, south, north, west, not necessarily in that order—blocking off the streets for no apparent reason. Ionesco was paying little heed to the growing hullabaloo outside, speaking of his play as if nothing were happening, nothing in any event to disturb his inner life. He talked, expounding its virtues and at the same time expressing doubts it would ever be published in France, saying how pleased he was it might come out in English. We were, however, distracted during our meeting by the growing clamor in the streets, where the *flics* had now been joined—or, more properly, confronted—by banner-carrying young men and women, their numbers in the thousands by the look of it, shoulder to shoulder, probably students from the nearby Sorbonne only a block or two away, marching down the boul' Mich singing the "Marseillaise" at the top of their lungs (Rouget de Lisle would have been proud), followed in close succession by the resounding "Internationale," protesting what, we couldn't tell. It took little these days to send the students from their classrooms down into the streets. Trocchi and I watched with growing alarm as the two sides girded for battle, the *flics* with their truncheons and, now, metal shields raised before them, an almost medieval scene, forming a seemingly impregnable wall of steel. Those customers who had been sipping or eating at the outdoor café tables had now sought refuge inside, and the waiters, casting worried glances at the vulnerable windows, which fronted on both boulevards, had barred the doors, fearing the worst. Meanwhile, Ionesco was saying that if *La cantatrice chauve* was too long for publication, he had a shorter play, *Le nouveau locataire*, or *The New Tenant*, that might just fill the bill.

"I think you'll find *Le nouveau locataire* to your liking," Ionesco was saying, taking another sip of the red wine before him, still apparently oblivious to the mayhem a few yards away.

"Excuse us, Monsieur Ionesco," I said, "but we're slightly distracted by what's happening outside."

He looked up, peered, and sighed. "Ah, yes, the students. They are always *mécontents*." Discontented. "They should learn to know how lucky they are."

Nonplussed by what had struck us as Ionesco's callous disregard of the violence outside, we nonetheless agreed that the shorter play would be a nice fit, asked if we could look at it, thanked him for his time, and took our leave.

On June 22 and 23, 1954, Jeannette and some thirty other finalist violinists of the Paris Conservatory performed and presented their final programs on the stage of the Salle Gaveau concert hall, all vying for a First Prize, of which only two would be awarded. Jeannette was scheduled for the afternoon of the second day. Dressed in a pretty, demure pale green gown, she sailed through her demanding program. The audience had been warned to hold its applause. When Jeannette finished her last piece with a flourish, however, the entire audience burst into applause, several rows rising to their feet. I looked over at her mother, who was stone-faced, and

Paul, who was wearing a broad smile. Our concern was, would the jury use this blatant violation of the no-applause rule against her? Jeannette quickly made her exit, as if to minimize the potential damage. Throughout the hall, the tension was palpable, both in the audience and among the young performers. At six the jury, which had retired shortly after five, reappeared to announce the results. The first First Prize is awarded to . . . Jeannette Medina, with highest honors. Now the applause was even louder, as the audience rose to its feet. Jeannette bowed, then blew a kiss, which I assumed was meant for me.

The next morning, it was my turn: I was to defend my long-delayed thesis entitled *The Interior Monologue* at the amphitheater of the Sorbonne in front of a jury and an audience. I was struck by the interesting confluence of our lives, as though these two consecutive days marked a turning point for both of us.

At precisely 9:56 on a gloriously sunny, though brisk, Paris morning, buoyed by the previous day's triumph, I entered the grand amphitheater of the Sorbonne, which can hold several hundred scholars, and took my place behind a table beneath the imposing stage above, where sat the eminent Charles Dédéyan and two other notable *sorbonnards*, professors all, to test my wits and determine whether my literary reasoning was sound or fragile.

I was nervous as I walked onto the big amphitheater stage, decked out in my dark blue wedding suit, worn for about the tenth time of my six-year stay, replete with tie, a copy of my three-hundred-page thesis before me, as well as the manuscript of my secondary thesis, an analysis of one of my favorite French works, Benjamin Constant's brief but remarkable novel, *Adolphe*. In contrast to the several hundred at the Salle Gaveau the previous two days, this morning there were roughly the number who had attended the early performances of *Godot*, perhaps twenty in all, if you count the three or four clochards in the rear who had sidled in and were there not to be edified, I was sure, but to seek refuge from the morning chill. Also present were several of our friends and both Jeannette's parents. I presented my case, only glancing now and then at my three-by-five cards on which salient points had been penned, and went on for about forty-five minutes. It seemed like hours. Then the questioning began. I had come well prepared and was surprisingly eloquent, having been grilled by Frank the week before. My thoughts on Joyce were honorably set forth, noting especially the importance of France for him and his work, and his debt to a now virtually forgotten French novelist, Édouard Dujardin, whose use of the interior monologue had inspired Joyce to use it to such great effect in

Ulysses, all of which was not meant to flatter or remind the august triumvirate above me that France had long been, and doubtless still was, the mecca for so many artists and writers from around the world, who found here in Paris the intellectual climate and freedom to hone their art. After my formal presentation, it was clear from the jury's tentative probes that Joyce was too recent an academic specimen for them to voice strong opinions, and though a fair amount of his work had been translated into French, including *Ulysses*, he was, though generally admired, still pretty much an enigma to these learned gentlemen. In any event, having acquitted myself reasonably well on the Irishman, I turned to Benjamin Constant, the jury curious that an American had chosen a subject so deeply French, and pleased to see that I knew both man and work, and that my admiration for both was sincere.

Virtually at the stroke of noon they declared the session over, my doctoral degree granted, with the mention *très honorable*—"with honors." I had not hoped for as much. What I felt as I rose from my chair to shake hands with the members of the jury was less a feeling of pleasure than of relief. For if I had completed this doctorate, it was largely out of a sense of obligation to those who had helped fund my stay in Paris, both Senator Fulbright and the AFS. No, I could not have lived with myself if I had jettisoned Joyce. And if I had not been so familiar with his work, would I have reacted so strongly to the Beckett volumes that had beckoned to me in the window of 7, rue Bernard Palissy? Such were my ambivalent thoughts as I turned to greet the faithful few who had endured the morning session. In the back, the rest of the patient crowd congratulated me on both my *fond* and my *forme*, not to mention my syntax. We emerged onto the rue St. Jacques, tranquil and unusually warm, yet in all fairness we were just two— or was it three?—days past the summer solstice, the thirteenth-century stones of the university gleaming in the midday light. Jeannette's parents had invited us that night to one of their favorite restaurants, Chez Allard, for a dual celebratory dinner. As I feasted on one of the best meals of my life, I kept wondering: Had these past six years been an interim or a fulfillment?

Exactly six days later, we were off to Cherbourg with Jeannette's parents, a good six or seven hours away. By noon we had reached Caen, definitely on the mend but still showing in all too many places the painful scars of the war. Suddenly recognizing the street along which we were walking, the rue de Geôle, Prison Street, hard by the château, I realized that this was one of the stops on my Normandy journey six years before. Memories of the *autobus ivre* flashed before me, and I could not refrain from laughing out loud at the memory, which I was quick to explain. Could it really have been six years?

Chitchatting, we were reliving our respective triumphs as we were enjoying our meal at La Bourride, in the Old Quarter. Each of us, however, was valiantly masking the emotions of the impending departure. For Paul and Roszi, I knew, despite their reassuring smiles and good humor, the thought of seeing their only child leave was wrenching. For Jeannette, only days after our arrival, I was headed into the navy, and she would be much on her own in an unknown land. As for me, I was devastated at the thought of leaving my beloved so soon after we had started life together. A situation fraught with danger. Would we survive it? It would have been one thing to confront New York, and America, together. Was it fair to leave her to face it alone? In addition to the real sadness I felt at leaving France, which now was home, I was invaded by a sense of guilt as great as I had ever experienced. I was tearing her away from her home, family, and the beginning of her French musical career. Still, anyone who had seen us that afternoon would have sworn we were the happiest foursome alive.

Suddenly I felt a presence behind me, turned, and saw a beaming Jeannette.

"This is going to be great fun," she said. And all my concerns vanished into the late-afternoon sunlight.

"Of course it is," I said, smiling back, and gave her a long kiss.

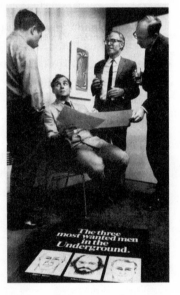

Part Two

New York, 1960s

Photographs on preceding pages, left to right: Richard Seaver; Nat Sobel, Richard Seaver, Barney Rosset, and Morrie Goldfischer; Richard Seaver and Samuel Beckett; Allen Ginsberg, Richard Seaver, Jeannette Seaver, Jean Genet, and William Burroughs

26 ~

America the Beautiful

FIVE DAYS LATER, at rosy-fingered dawn, our ship pulled within sight of New York harbor. Up early, my French bride rushed on deck, where I found her overwhelmed at the sight of the skyline. Her impressions of America were based largely on American movies, and now, the skyscrapers growing larger as we approached, the reality of that new American life ahead left her numb. Flanked by tiny tugboats, we edged our way up the Hudson, our slow passage offering glimpses of deteriorating and half-empty docks, for the days of the luxury liners were already numbered, and, below the elevated West Side Highway, a scattering of tawdry buildings that, I knew, would soon dispel Jeannette's Hollywood image of New York. But all she registered at that moment were the soaring peaks of the Empire State Building and the Chrysler Building thrusting their spires defiantly into the pale blue sky.

My parents had driven down from northern Connecticut to meet us. On the dock far below I saw them waving, eager to meet my new soul mate.

I had not seen either of my parents for almost three years. Father was unchanged, but Mother seemed older, her prim hair grayer, her face paler than I remembered. But they were all smiles, hugs, and kisses, and I could see from the glances they exchanged that they heartily approved of my life choice. Jeannette had been studying English, enough to make the formal greetings and to respond to their questions with brief but often poetic replies, delivered with a wonderful Gallic accent. Father was obviously smitten. Mother, innately warm but by nature reserved, was a trifle slower to accept her new daughter-in-law, but once she did, the two bonded deeply forever.

We loaded our baggage into Father's boatlike Cadillac, a 1953. *"Mon Dieu,"* Jeannette whispered as she climbed into the backseat, *"c'est aussi grand que notre studio à Paris!"* Good Lord, it's as big as our Paris studio!

We set off along the West Side Highway, the towers of New York to our right, the broad Hudson to our left, the lights of the George Washington Bridge before us, and headed toward Connecticut. Mesmerized, Jeannette was moving her head from left to right. Father, usually reticent, was babbling on, identifying each landmark, reminiscing about Paris, even lapsing into a few words and phrases of French. I sensed he was excited and pleased.

When her steak was served at the Red Coach Grill, Jeannette exclaimed: *"Mais c'est un rosbif entier!"* her eyes bulging—it's a whole roast beef! By her postwar European optic, that portion was more than enough to feed an entire French family. Father told her not to worry, the rest would be wrapped in tinfoil and taken along in what was called a doggie bag. I translated literally. "Lucky American dogs. You mean you feed such meat to them? *Mon Dieu!"* "No, no!" Father assured her, it was merely a term; the leftovers were meant for us, for next-day sandwiches usually.

Thompson, the picture-postcard bucolic village where my parents' home was, with its stately white wooden houses bordered by stone walls or white picket fences dating mostly from the mid- to late nineteenth century, ours an early Victorian proudly dated 1845 by the local historical society, fronting the Village Green, made a deep impression on Jeannette. In sharp contrast to our hectic Parisian life, Thompson was both beautiful and reassuring to her. The time had come for me to buy my navy outfits, khaki for general wear, white for summer, and dress blues for winter, their shoulder boards sporting their single gold stripe indicating ensign, the lowliest officer rank. I still had great trouble adjusting, both to the uniform and to the idea.

Next: New York, searching for an apartment. We were in luck; thanks to friends who lived in the Village on Jones Street, we found a studio apartment directly below theirs that had just gone on the market. By ten o'clock the next morning we had signed the lease.

27 ~

Join the Navy and See the World

I REPORTED TO BOSTON and learned my ship would be the USS *Columbus*, CA-74, a heavy cruiser newly refurbished, the shake-down cruise to take us to Guantánamo Bay, Cuba. After I had filled out the necessary papers, the executive officer, an Annapolis graduate, slight and humorless, called me in to his cabin.

"Seaver?" he said. "Yes, sir," saluting stiffly. "At ease. I gather you spent several years in France." "Yes, sir." "Military attaché?" "No, sir." "Ah, intelligence, I presume. I won't probe further." He looked down at his desk. "What are you doing with those ensign stripes? It says here you're lieutenant j.g." "I wasn't told, sir." "Well, get your goddamn stripes changed by tomorrow. You've had seven-plus years in the reserve. Don't you think that counts for something? Time served means promotion. Says here, too, that after six months on board you'll be promoted again, to lieutenant senior grade." I was fast learning the logic of military advancement, for the commander seated before me assumed that during those seven-plus years I had been serving my country, which maybe I had. In my own way. He went on: "Seaver, I have a rather delicate question to pose . . ." "Yes, sir." "Two officers to a stateroom," he said. "Yes, sir." "We have a slightly awkward situation . . . A new officer is reporting on board tomorrow, graduate of the Merchant Marine Academy. Would you mind rooming with him?"

"Of course not, sir." "But"—he hesitated, as if not quite knowing how to proceed—"you see, he's a . . . a *Negro*. Does that pose a problem for you?"

Suddenly the earnest, intense face of Jimmy Baldwin flashed before me, then in quick succession that of William Gardner Smith and the granite-handsome countenance of Richard Wright, all men I liked and deeply admired. "Would you *mind* . . ." Jesus! Would this stupid prejudice never end? I had a hard time not laughing, only wishing they could all witness this.

"If it does . . ." He left the words hanging in air, apparently taking my five-second remembrance as a hesitation.

"Not at all, sir," I said. I saw a look of relief pass over him, his frown dissolving with the good news.

"Thank you, Seaver. You're a good man." The next day I met Carl Burnett, my roommate for two years, who was to become my boon companion and closest friend in the U.S. Navy.

After four weeks at Guantánamo, in close maneuvers with other elements of the fleet, we steamed back to Boston, where, I was told, we would remain for roughly a month before joining the Sixth Fleet in the Mediterranean. Jeannette arranged to join me in Boston, where I found a well-situated one-room apartment on Commonwealth Avenue. In port, officers were off duty every third day and could spend it ashore, reporting back on deck at 7:00 a.m., an easy routine to live with. I adjusted to navy life better than I expected; my fellow junior officers, most younger than I, were an easygoing bunch, neither aggressively political nor overly serious, from an eclectic mixture of backgrounds and colleges, with whom it was possible to have discussions both profound and frivolous. Being separated for five months, for that was the length of our tour of duty in the Mediterranean, seemed endless. Not a wonderful way to begin a marriage.

Our long embrace on the Boston docks on the day of my departure reminded me of those photographs of World War II navy wives left behind. "Don't worry," Jeannette whispered, "I'll be fine."

After stopovers at Gibraltar and Barcelona, our third port of call was Marseilles, where I had arranged for a three-day pass to zip up to Paris. I had booked a room at the Hôtel Madison directly across from the St. Germain des Prés church, only a couple of blocks from my old rue du Sabot digs. You *can* go home again! I prowled the quarter, had a beer at the Royal, sauntered over to the Tournon, where Christopher and Jane were having a drink with George Plimpton, all charm and warm smiles beneath his tiny hat. *Merlin* was late again; *The Paris Review* was right on schedule. Earlier predictions that the latter would never survive were rapidly being revised. For while the masthead of *The Paris Review* listed half a dozen editors, it was George who was wholly dedicated and in charge as the others flitted in and out.

That evening, it seemed strange to be sitting at dinner in Paris with Jeannette's parents without her.

The second day, I met with several of the Merlinites. Patrick was still thrashing with *Molloy* but making progress. Christopher had never been in finer fettle: his poems were increasingly being published in London. Austryn was by now the editorial head of *Merlin*, though he shared the masthead title with Alex, who had clearly crossed some invisible river to another world.

Relationships had changed, too: Jane, to my utter surprise and shock, was no longer with Alex, who, while focusing on one Iris Owens, was spreading his sexual talents to as broad an array of local women as possible. Jane was consoling herself with Baird Bryant, whom she would later marry, but not before Baird had entered the lists, in competition with Alex for Iris's favors, while Baird's wife, Denny, had taken up with Austryn, who had left Muffie, or she him, either before or after Muffie embarked on an affair with Maurice, for whom she was now working, presumably by both day and night. The ballet, most of whose pas de deux or pas de trois were reported to me by Patrick, was dizzying.

I returned to Marseilles that Sunday night, delighted to have touched base with my beloved Paris, with Paul and Roszi, and a few friends, as well as with the Merlinites I could find. But I also felt purged of a part of my life now past, for which, I suspected, I would feel only the slightest nostalgia.

It was February when we touched American shores again at our Boston base, and I quickly entrained for New York on a two-week leave, to find Jeannette awaiting me with a sumptuous dinner next to a dangerously dry and brittle, but still-decorated, Christmas tree, which, sentimental as always, she had refused to dismantle till I got home. Jeannette's English had improved measurably, but I was concerned when she greeted me in a sumptuous fur coat, one far beyond our means. My mind having been perverted by my years in France, where gentlemen routinely lavish such gifts on their mistresses, I prepared myself for the worst. I refrained from questioning her for several days, until I could hold out no longer. She burst out laughing. "I have a distant 'relative' in Riverdale—who has loaned her coat to me. No, Monsieur Jaloux, eet is not a geeft from my lovaire!"

Then it was time to head back to Boston, where I had again rented a small apartment on Commonwealth Avenue to pick up the fragmented honeymoon we had left off. The *Columbus* was to remain in port for several weeks, for the installation of new equipment, general overhaul, and reassignment. Jeannette had taken a leave of absence from Juilliard. Again, officers had every third night ashore, and on the two days when we had duty on board, we were now allowed, in rotation, to bring our wives to dinner. For my French bride, climbing on board the *Columbus*, having dinner in the officers' dining room was very exciting. When she first appeared—looking like a cross between Sophia Loren and Gina Lollobrigida—she caused a major stir among the younger officers, bachelors all, who were instantly charmed by her smiling presence and her oh-so-French accent. Several of my fellow junior officers—though by now I was not so junior, time having once more worked in my favor, so that my shoulder boards now bore two full stripes—begged me to introduce them to Jeannette's sisters and didn't believe me when I insisted she was an only child.

Late spring found us ready to redeploy again, this time to the Pacific to join the Seventh Fleet. Citing the Sixth Fleet experience as precedent, I made formal application for Jeannette to come to the Far East and was turned down at the initial level. Jeannette decided to return home to France for a few months while we sailed off to the Far East.

The endless Pacific. I felt as though trapped in some bad dream. But we had arrived in Japan.

Yokosuka was only an hour from Tokyo by fast train, and they all seemed to be fast, crowded but efficient. The Ginza, with its myriad glittering lights, made Broadway look almost dull. People hurried everywhere, nobody paying us any attention, but we did not feel any antipathy there either. Because of the war, and the atrocity stories of Japanese cruelty that had been our daily fare for almost four years, I had arrived with a strong negative preconception, a chip on my shoulder, that vanished very quickly. The few Japanese we met were without exception polite, helpful, amiable. Visiting Japanese department stores, we were charmed by the pretty, kimono-clad elevator operators, who at each floor announced its wares, bowing with each mellifluous utterance. Officers and petty officers who had been here before warned me not to be fooled by the surface cordiality, below which, they claimed, was a thick layer of resentment. Still, as the days went by, I detected none, even when I explored the more remote reaches of the city.

Because my navy record contained the information that I had run a periodical of some sort in Paris, the executive officer called me in a few days later and asked if I would mind being detached from the ship for a couple of months and remain in Tokyo while the ship sailed on to Singapore, Saigon, and Bangkok, the purpose of the shore assignment being to edit a cruise book. I must have looked puzzled, for he quickly explained that each major ship in the fleet—cruiser, battleship, carrier—recorded its experiences in what amounted to a yearbook, given to each crew member at the end of the tour. I would be provided full details, shown earlier cruise books, put in contact with Japanese printers. I accepted, momentarily regretting the loss of other ports farther south but intrigued to explore Japan further. I was assigned to a small but clean hotel in the center of Tokyo. To whom should I report? To myself, I was on my own, though I was given the name and address of a local naval official in case of any problems. My per diem allowance for food seemed niggardly till I tried one or two local restaurants and found it was munificent. There was also a PX. So, armed with a stack of manuscripts—mostly cursory notes—from all departments of the ship, plus several hundred photographs, I set out to test the professional waters of this new Japanese-American relationship. The Japanese printers were highly professional. No one had more than a smidgen of pidgin, if you'll pardon the unpardonable juxtaposition, but somehow we managed to communicate over the next few weeks as the book took shape.

With ten days to go before the ship's return, I gave the entire work a final, careful read and pronounced it ready for press. In fact, I said, pride once again going before a fall, I found it rather handsome, a job well done, and at the compliment the men and women with whom I had been working daily all smiled and bowed, pleased by my praise. I visited the printer as, one by one, the forms rolled off and were collected and stacked, waiting to be bound. No hitch that I could see, though I felt the constant close reading, and rereading, was slowly driving me blind. When, two days later, I was delivered the first bound copy, I breathed a sigh of relief, for the *Columbus* was due back in Yokosuka in forty-eight hours. I leafed through page by page and saw, gratefully, that all the pictures were in place, resplendent in full color. I began to read, one final time, the text. No problems there, either. Thank God, for as with the Majorcan printer for *Merlin*, typesetting in Tokyo had been done by hand, each letter picked from a printer's tray and dropped into place, the page tightly bound by string and readied for the press. And then I reached page 136. Shit! An *e* missing—no, two—then an *l* and an *m* and two *t*'s! My God, a dozen others! The string doubtless had not been wound tightly enough about the plate. A disaster! The captain would have my head, and rightly so. What the hell were you doing all these weeks, Seaver? Can't you read! With heavy heart—I know, I know, but the expression is accurate—I carried the book over to the head honcho of the printer and showed him the page. My face must have betrayed my feelings. I expected a demurrer: Seaver-san, these things happen. Look at all the other pages where there is no problem, yes? In other words, tough titty. Instead, he smiled and said: "No problem, we fix." "Fix?" I said, "How you fix?" having learned by then not to bother with articles or complex verb forms. "Book is printed. All printed. Ship come two days. For me disaster. Captain kill me. Seaver-san dead. Executed." I ran my forefingers across my throat—no need for translation there . . . He listened patiently, and to my growing irritation the smile never left his face. "No problem," he repeated, "we fix." "How?" I said. "We show you. Go have lunch now. Come back in afternoon." He looked at his watch. "Come back two clock—uh, no, three clock, okay?"

I had no stomach for lunch, but had a sandwich and beer to kill time, then reappeared sharply at three. At two long tables, twenty-some women in brightly colored kimonos were sitting, our cruise books opened before them, each holding what looked to be a wooden match between thumb and forefinger, poised above the delinquent page, then dropped smartly onto it, at which point the book was passed to the next woman in line, who performed the same ritual. Top Dog–san strode back and forth behind them, his face still wreathed in a broad smile. "See," he said, "we fixing." And indeed they were. I found it difficult to believe, but the women, each armed with a single piece of type, which had been inserted into a notched wooden match, the better to aim, were filling in the missing letters one by one. I took one finished copy, checking to see if the missing letters were aligned or askew, and they were perfect. I shook my head. "Problem, Seaver-san?" the Head-san asked, his smile vanishing in a cloud of concern. "No problem," I said. "Seaver impressed." "Impressed?" he said. "Happy," I said. "Very good job, very good," and seizing him by the shoulders, I gave him a big hug, which doubtless destroyed several centuries of custom and protocol. Three thousand copies of the *Columbus* cruise book had been repaired in a matter of hours. I had a sudden thought: Given this sort of dedication, would Japan one day—soon?—become a major power again?

Precisely eight hours before the *Columbus* arrived back in Yokosuka, the repaired copies of the book were delivered on the dock in cartons of twenty, encased in rainproof crates. Hoisted on board, they were greedily seized by the crew and brought to their bunks for a closer look. "Good job, Seaver," the executive officer said to me, leafing through his. "You know, half the time these books arrive with a dozen or more pictures out of place or with the wrong captions. And believe it or not, with lots of letters dropped from the text. This looks nigh perfect." "Thank you, sir," I said, "I did my best," secretly wishing I hadn't sweated the previous forty-eight hours, but coming away from the experience with a deep new respect for Japanese ingenuity.

Before our ship's return to the States, the entire Seventh Fleet was ordered to practice high-speed night maneuvers without lights, without communication of any sort. We steamed out to the South China Sea, an impressive flotilla of thirty ships from destroyers to carriers and including one massive battleship. Shortly before midnight we set out on the maneuvers, the plans for which were in each captain's hands. Down in the engine room, I could feel the ship vibrate, doing over thirty knots, straining to its limits, racing through the dark seas. At four o'clock, my four-hour watch over, I went up and hit the sack. I must have fallen asleep immediately, for the next thing I remembered was a loud screech of metal on metal as I was thrown from my bunk and halfway across the stateroom. I struggled to my feet, checking arms and legs to make sure they were intact, crammed on my pants and shoes, and headed topside. It was still dark, but the lights of several of the other ships had snapped on, against orders, so the problem had to be serious. It was. In the course of the nighttime maneuvers, the orders had run that at a precise time the fleet would turn twenty degrees to starboard. One ship, either ours or a close destroyer escort, had turned to port, as a result of which we had sheared off the bow of our sister ship. It was in no danger of sinking, I was told, for the bulkhead had been immediately sealed off; the tragedy was, the missing bow contained the crew's sleeping quarters, so what was a harsh body blow to the thick-skinned *Columbus* was fatal to whatever number of sailors had been bunked down in the destroyer. It was still too dark for the fleet's helicopters to take off, but at dawn several did, to comb the waters for survivors. They found none. We circled funereally for the better part of the morning, all eyes scanning the waters, and when it was certain there was no hope, we were ordered to cut all engines as the fleet's chaplains—Catholic, Protestant, and Jewish in turn—performed the rites, commending the bodies of those lost to the deep. We and the wounded destroyer were ordered to head for Subic Bay in the Philippines, not too far off, for repairs, we under our own steam, the bowless destroyer towed. We limped into Subic, a sad, sober bunch, for word was filtering down that it was we, not the smaller ship, that had made the wrong turn. A court-martial was being convened to ascertain the truth. A dozen sailors were dead. It took five weeks for our ship to be declared seaworthy, two stout metal strips—which we immediately dubbed the Columbus Railroad Tracks—affixed awkwardly to our starboard bow, ugly and accusing, as we headed out of Subic toward the States. We arrived in Long Beach ten days later, sans captain, who had been detained for the court-martial in the Philippines. What should have been a purely joyous occasion, with families reunited after long months apart, was more than offset by the collision at sea, which still weighed heavily on all of us. We felt, too, for the captain, a career officer of twenty-five years, whose first major sea command the *Columbus* was, a decent man and dedicated sailor who, we knew, was up for admiral next year. His career was now over. Chief Petty Officer Brandon, a thirty-year veteran of a dozen ships, spoke for most of the career men when he said: "Problem with today's navy is, these Annapolis graduates spend most of their lives on shore duty, sometimes for decades, and by the time they get a command, the ship technology is so changed from what they had been taught they can't deal with it." In other words, too many senior officers for too few ships. I suppose the only solution to that dilemma would be to declare war on some rogue state, bring dozens of ships out of mothballs, and give all academy grads a fair chance . . .

Jeannette, after months back home in France while the *Columbus* was in the Far East, had returned to the States the week before and flown out to L.A. As the wounded CA-74 edged in—not proudly, for word of our collision had long ago reached the shore—I searched the throng of women and children crowding the dock, and then I spotted her, a bouquet of brilliant orange summer flowers imprinted on a dress of dazzling white. I waved wildly, she spotted me and waved back, all smiles, and suddenly the world was right again.

For the three weeks prior to my discharge, we lived in a small rented house in Long Beach, slowly catching up in a belated honeymoon spirit, then headed east, to start our new life.

28 ~

A New Life

I T WAS ALL WELL AND GOOD to start a new life. The question was: What life? For Jeannette, she had her career in music, no problem. For me, the sobering two years in the navy had broadened me in both mind and geography, taught me that Paris, while still "home" in my mind, was not the center of the universe. Still, it beckoned to both of us. I had dispatched letters to four or five people in Washington, in both the private and the public sectors, seeking gainful employment in France. Going back to Paris seemed the natural thing to do—not to my old life, not to *Merlin*, not to Olympia, but to something new. I had written to George Plimpton. Did George need a Paris editor? He did, but when he told me what it paid, that was quickly ruled out. Because now we had a child on the way.

Unable to locate a Parisian job, I ended up accepting a position in a totally new field. It seemed a lark, and we left for Venezuela shortly thereafter, me, most improbably, as management consultant for a pharmaceutical company. I spoke fluent Spanish and was told that all that was required was pure common sense to do what was needed. Our Venezuelan adventure turned out extremely positively for us both. As management consultant, I must have performed well because the CEO whose company I was helping reorganize begged me to stay on. As for Jeannette, she was able to pursue her music and give a few concerts there. But we were expecting our first child and were eager to return to the States for the birth. A few months later, when I reported to Scarsdale upon my return from Venezuela, at the world headquarters of Direct Energy—the management consultant firm—my boss was reassuring: of course I still had a job.

Within twenty-four hours Jeannette and I had found a place to live, a new building on Palmer Road in Bronxville, and paid an urgent visit to the doctor, who pronounced Jeannette in perfect health and predicted the baby's arrival in four weeks, maybe sooner. "Just don't go taking any airplanes," he warned.

Shortly after midnight on June 5, Jeannette woke me with a gentle jab in the ribs and announced quietly that her labor had begun. In fact, had begun some hours before, but she didn't want to disturb me. Disturb me? If not now, when? I jumped out of bed, thrust on my trousers, realized I had put both legs in one side, the left as I recall, stumbled across the room like a drunkard as I tried to pull them off. Jeannette, having turned on the light, started laughing so hard she couldn't stop, saying, *"Mon Dieu, j'ai épousé un unijambiste!"* Good God, I married a one-legged man! I stayed at the hospital through the night, holding her hand as the frequency of the contractions increased. At five, the doctor arrived and suggested I go home and get some rest. They'd call when birth was imminent. I crawled into bed, fell into a deep sleep, didn't hear the phone till the tenth ring. June 6. "Come down as soon as possible." When I arrived, Jeannette was fast asleep, having been given anesthesia an hour before the baby came. So I had missed the birth. It was a girl, I was told, would I like to see her? What kind of question was that?

I pressed my face against the glass of the nursery. A nurse's index finger pointed to my own, who was sleeping peacefully. I stared in disbelief, like every new father. After blowing my baby a kiss, I checked in on Jeannette, still asleep, and headed for the nearest florist, returning with a bountiful bouquet of red roses. When I reentered the room, Jeannette was just coming to. Minutes later I brought in the babe, so tiny, so small, to me, so beautiful, exactly seven pounds. Gently, I laid the child, still asleep, in her mother's arms. Mother and child. All those thousands of paintings over the centuries on the subject: it wasn't just the Christ Child that had inspired them; it was all the millions of moments exactly like this. We named her Nathalie Anne.

Meanwhile, a broken record kept playing in my head: Did I really want to be a management consultant? Of course not, was the answer.

Our friend Jerry Stone had the same idea. "You don't want to be a management consultant, for Chrissake. You should be writing. Or working in publishing—wait a minute, I have a thought. Call this man tomorrow—and mention my name. He's got a couple of book clubs, and his editor, George Brantl, who's been with him for years, is leaving. Or just left. Brantl's a friend of mine—I've been writing book reviews for their monthly newsletter—and if I knew anyone who might fit the bill, I should let him know . . ." He quickly scribbled a name and number on the corner of the paper tablecloth: George Braziller.

The following afternoon I called Braziller. Yes, Stone had told him about me. Several years in Paris, I understand, running a magazine and book-publishing company, no? I decided modesty was not in order, so failed to minimize or contradict the information received. From Braziller's rather high-pitched, slightly plaintive voice, I pictured a slight, effete man of late middle years, scarcely my type, so when the next morning—he had wasted no time making an appointment—I was ushered into his large, well-appointed, book-lined office overlooking Park Avenue South, I was surprised to see a muscular, athletic-looking man whom I judged to be in his late thirties. We had an hour-long chat, at the end of which he introduced me to his pretty secretary, Susan; his young lady in charge of publicity, Phyllis Bellows, all sweetness and light; his accountant, Herman Figatner, a small, owlish, unprepossessing man, born to the profession, I immediately decided, if looks have anything to do with choice; and last but certainly not least, my namesake Edwin Seaver, a short, curly-haired man in his late fifties, I judged, whose sly smile made me feel I would have an ally in more than name only. He then offered me the job of editor of his two book clubs, the Book Find Club and the Seven Arts Book Society, the former a politically liberal nonfiction club, the latter specializing in relatively high-priced art books. Could I let him know immediately? I'd like to discuss it with my wife. And I couldn't start for a couple weeks, because I would have to give notice. He agreed, handing me half a dozen newsletters for each club and suggesting I take a look at them, for I'd be writing them from now on. The term "writing" alone made me feel the move would be right, for I knew that what I'd done for the past year, however pleasant, had been a lark.

Next morning I told Barnum, my boss at the management consultancy firm, I'd be leaving. He seemed truly crestfallen. "I was grooming you to take over the business someday." I thanked him. "I'll bet you tell that to all the departing employees," I said to myself.

———

Two weeks later, I showed up at 215 Park Avenue South precisely at 8:51, a logistical triumph. Susan greeted me and showed me to my office, a nine-by-twelve cubbyhole next to hers, which was next to George's. Braziller was less expansive and welcoming than he had been at our initial encounter, his face all frowns with barely a "g'morning" as he strode past my nook, but I shook it off and settled in. We needed fourteen books a year for each club, twelve regular selections, a midsummer selection, and a Christmas selection. Twelve wouldn't do, Herman assured me, explaining the math: with that monthly-only number you might break even; the extra two accounted for the profit, assuming overhead remained intact and, of course, the main selections "performed."

At precisely 9:50, George called me in to his office. The core of my job was to comb every publisher's catalog for possible selections, he explained, then negotiate the deals, with his prior blessing of course. He would tell me how much I could pay, not a penny more. Business was tough, he said, because we were up against the two big guns, Book-of-the-Month Club and the Literary Guild. Survival depended on getting there first, before either of them, not picking at their leftovers. Didn't seem too daunting to me. You'll have to take people to lunch, George said, maybe as often as two or three times a week, charm them, especially the young sub-rights girls, so they think of Book Find first. No fancy restaurants, I'll give you a list.

Going back through the newsletters of both clubs, I was impressed. Next to the behemoths of the business, Book Find was small potatoes, but with roughly a hundred thousand members it still had an impact. Before I had been there a week, I was overwhelmed. It was one thing to lunch or call the publishers and request a book or two for consideration, quite another to deal with the flood of entries that flowed in, unasked for, at a rate of twenty to thirty a week, all of which I was expected to evaluate. I found myself reading as much as I could during the day, but mostly at night and on the weekends, to the gentle sound of Nathalie cooing or crying.

I was grateful to have at my disposal half a dozen freelance readers, themselves poets and writers and critics, to whom the most likely candidates for selection were given. They included an old friend of George's, a lovely man in his early sixties, Isidor Schneider, who had been blacklisted for his left-wing involvements, whose three or four readings a week were his sole source of income in these post-McCarthy but still semi-hysterical days, when the fear of the Communist menace was still rife. Another reader was Norman Rosten, a close friend of the playwright Arthur Miller's and himself a poet of note, whose constant smile and innate charm endeared him to everyone he met. Two younger readers were Dan Wakefield and Michael Harrington, the former an aspiring journalist and writer who would go on to publish several successful books, the latter the future head of the Democratic Socialists of America, a thankless task politically but one that put him throughout his life in frequent contact with the great socialist leaders of the Western world, from Willy Brandt to François Mitterrand. And of course the man who had steered me here, Jerry Stone. Still, despite this invaluable, nay, essential, help, I was reading as never before. Looking back, *Merlin* had been a cinch. Maybe I was simply entering the real world, or at least the real America, where work—intense work—apparently was the center, if not the goal, of life.

The reading pressure, which I was learning to cope with despite the growing flood of submissions, was compounded by George's daily, and to me irascible, demands. Nothing I did, wrote, or said seemed to elicit a positive response. Some weeks I would write him brief reports on a dozen books I had read, plus half a dozen more from the freelance readers, none of which passed the acid test. I heard him mutter "Brantl" under his breath at least two or three times a week, which made even my untutored mind understand that my predecessor would never have taxed his patience thus.

One day when I, though clean shaven, was likewise muttering in my figurative beard, wondering why the fuck I had taken this job, Susan loped around the corner and perched herself on the edge of my desk, her handsome, unsheathed legs swinging like two seductive pendulums, her ready cleavage adding to the unsettling scene as she leaned forward. Obviously, one or more of my mutterings had penetrated the thin wall between us. "Don't let him get you down," she said in a near whisper. "He's not as tough as he seems." Susan had been working here for two or three years, and my sense was that she and George were an item, though I understood from Herman that George's wife, Marsha, was a rare gem, a woman as beautiful as she was talented, who, when George was drafted and went to war, had run the clubs with a sure hand and clear vision, so that when George returned and took over again, they were thriving as never before. "He's a worrywart," Susan went on. "George sees the big clubs gobbling up all the best books. Which puts the pressure on you." I mentioned the repeated, under-the-breath "Brantl" references. She laughed. "He was just as tough on Brantl as he is on you. Except Brantl didn't seem to care. Wait'll you have a breakthrough," she added. "It will all change, you'll see."

"A breakthrough?" I asked.

"A main selection that sells 30 or 35 percent," she said.

The norm, I knew, was 18 to 20 percent; that is, about one out of every five members accepted the selection. So far, none of mine—ours, for George was the final arbiter, though when they fell below the norm, they automatically became Seaver's—had broken through. Still, a book Isidor and I had both just read and highly recommended to George, John Kenneth Galbraith's *Affluent Society*, struck me as a remarkable candidate. George concurred, urging me to make an offer immediately. That day. That hour. Our offer accepted, it became that month's main selection and, mirabile dictu, not only scooped the Book-of-the-Month Club, which belatedly added it to its Alternate Selection roster a couple months later, but became one of the Book Find Club's all-time bestsellers, with upwards of 40 percent of the membership taking it. Herman was ecstatic, Susan all smiles on the now-familiar corner of my desk. Phyllis made a point of kissing me on the cheek and offering her hearty congratulations, at the same time telling me she was leaving to take another job. I looked surprised, for in my months there I had found her a steady friend, like Susan telling me to weather whatever storm was brewing or unleashed by our BFM—Book Find Master. I did a double take when she said she was going to "Grove Press. As director of publicity. It's a young house, but they're doing some very interesting things . . ." Hmmm.

Predictably, George never acknowledged I had anything to do with that month's success. Waiting outside his office one day to see him about the next month's selection, I heard him on the phone saying: "Thanks, yes, it's a great success. One of our best in years. I sensed the minute I read it we had a winner." Still, as Susan had predicted, that mini-triumph made me less vulnerable, and George not only became immediately more affable but paid closer attention to my readers' reports. Further, at lunch one day the saintly Isidor offhandedly mentioned that George thought I was doing a great job. "Could've fooled me," I said. "Must be the Galbraith." "No," Isidor replied, "he's told me that almost from the start." All that reminded me suddenly of my father, who for most of my youth had carefully refrained from ever paying me a compliment, whether forehand or backhand. A problem of his makeup perhaps? Only Mother's frequent assurances that Father did in fact love and even admire me kept me from total self-doubt. "He simply has trouble expressing himself," Mother would say. "But I know he loves *you*," I would counter. "Of course," she would reply, but by her hesitation, and the slight downward tilt of her head, I knew that much the same doubt applied to her. And to sister Joan as well. Funny man, *mon père* . . .

Despite the general climatic improvement at the clubs, George still continued to worry day in and day out, with me the main target. I tried to leave the problem at work, let it simmer down on the twenty-nine-minute train ride home, but there were days when I couldn't, and at some point in the evening I would blurt out my frustration to Jeannette. "If you let him rant and rave without fighting back, he'll never stop." Of course she was right; I had till now avoided confrontation, out of insecurity—this was my first real job—and a sense that I still had a lot to learn. But in one of the nether reaches of my mind, I tucked that advice away.

One day a couple weeks later, George called me in and took me to task over two of the three alternate selections I had suggested for the upcoming newsletter, to which he normally paid scant heed. Calling them "terrible choices," in fact "disgraceful," he added that they would garner few readers, if any. A total waste of good space, he said, referring to the newsletter. I had cleared these choices with him a week earlier, I reminded him, before writing the copy, and besides, the full material was due at the printer tomorrow. Never mind, he said, find two new alternates. Today. Turning bright red, I'm sure, I slammed down the packet I was holding, the entire contents of the issue, on the corner of the desk and told him what I thought of him, no holds barred. He sat there stunned, hardly blinking, and let me go on till I could think of nothing else to add, at which point I turned and left the office, repaired to my cubbyhole, sat down, and wondered what to do next. Gather my belongings, I guessed. Susan, privy to the scene, sidled in and winked approval. Was I wrong about her relationship with George? I opened my desk drawer and started pulling out personal papers. What are you doing? she wanted to know. Packing to leave, I said. Did he fire you? He didn't have time, I said. So you're still employed, right? Why don't you put the newsletter to bed and then decide? I can't, I said, all the material's in George's office. Let me go fetch it, she said, pivoting and heading for the tiger's den, then reappearing moments later with the contents in hand. How was His Majesty? I asked. Staring out the window, she said. Not boiling mad? I asked. No way of telling, she said—maybe contrite, who knows? That I doubt, I said. A pause. What, I wondered aloud, shall I do with these "disgraceful" alternates? Is that what he called them? I nodded. She shrugged. I know what I'd do—tear them up. Eliminate them. Go with only one alternate? Another shrug. He can't blame you for eliminating what he said are terrible. I fingered the two "worst" culprits, extracted them from the pile, and ceremoniously tore them to shreds. Here, I said, handing her the truncated contents, would you be so good as to messenger this to the printer?

What is moral, Ernest had said, is what you feel good after. Simplistic maybe, but tonight I wholly concurred. Next morning, before I left for the train, I said: "You may see me home a bit earlier today." But, no: instead of passing my office on his way to his own with barely a word, the normal custom, this morning George popped his head in, smiled broadly, and said, "Susan told me you cut two alternates. Good! And I have a strong feeling about this month's main selection." That was a meaty book by Max Lerner, *America as a Civilization*, which not only Dan Wakefield and I but George as well had read and loved. When the results were in three weeks later, Lerner's book was almost as successful as the Galbraith. More important, from that "blowup" day on, my relations with George improved to such a degree that I can honestly say we never had another major confrontation. Disagreements, yes, but basically civil. As Susan had said, George was a born worrywart; while it wasn't always darkness at noon, by three o'clock most days the black clouds had gathered on the horizon and permeated the whole office. The difference was that now, generally, if not always, I was able to ignore them.

I had been at Braziller for several months when Barney called. In the evening, at home. Could we have lunch? Sure—lunches were now an integral part of my life, whether I liked it or not. Again to One Fifth Avenue. Again, for Barney, two martinis and little food, while I downed a hearty hamburger, much missed during my Paris years, I am forced to admit, and a beer. Halfway through the second martini he came to the point: Would I like to come and work for Grove? As managing editor of the publishing house and of his fledgling magazine, *Evergreen Review*. I'd been reading the magazine, a quarterly and damn good, an eclectic mixture of American and European writing, mostly avant-garde and solidly grounded, a rare mixture. Really impressive. "With your *Merlin* background," he said, "it's a natural fit. Beckett of course, in almost every issue. Artaud, whom we also talked about in Paris. And your friend Ionesco, too. We've signed him up for several plays. You'd feel right at home."

I was flattered, and I knew that Grove was where I should be. But I had a problem. Though we had spoken on the phone three or four times since our last lunch, I had never mentioned to Barney I had taken a new job, and it was high time I did. Barney looked puzzled. "I thought you were still with that management consultant guy," he said. "That world wasn't for me," I said. "Anyway, shortly after our last lunch, Braziller offered me a job as editor of his two book clubs, and I took it. There's no way I could switch now. It wouldn't be fair to George, leaving just as I've learned the ropes." He nodded, said he understood, and ordered another martini. This said, I told him I'd been reading *Evergreen Review* and thought it first-rate. He looked pleased. It's also a great way to get authors, he said. You'd be amazed. And there's so much going on, both here and abroad, that the big houses are completely ignoring.

We agreed to stay in touch, and if ever I changed my mind, I'd let him know. It sounded like an open invitation, as Jeannette put it that night at dinner, a nice backup when Braziller drives you over the edge. I duly noted that she had said "when," not "if."

To his credit, George, despite his lack of formal education, for he had never gone beyond high school, had a passion for books and aspired one day to be a real publisher, Alfred Knopf his idol. To his debit, he could not for the life of him make up his mind, I suspect for fear of making a mistake— something publishers do, I was learning, with alarming regularity. Went with the territory. Just because you loved a book, and your editors did too, didn't mean the world would. Chez George, month after month, deadlines arrived and passed, then passed again. Susan, I said, one day early in my second year there, how do we get the man to unstraddle the goddamn fence? Brantl knew how, she informed me. If Braziller hadn't agreed on a selection by deadline, Brantl picked it for him. The implication was clear. How long, I asked the disturbingly pulchritudinous young lady perched once again on the corner of my desk, her legs scissoring slowly back and forth a scant three feet from my face in time to some private rhythm, does it take to gain George's confidence? She shrugged. "Brantl was here nine or ten years," she said. "Maybe more. And he was very intelligent." I was beginning to love her more and more. She loosed her darts even as her flesh dangled invitingly. Was this a game played daily in offices throughout the country? It sure as hell wasn't for me.

Speaking of games, I had learned early that book clubs had a brilliant if diabolical modus operandi called a "negative option," under which members were obliged to respond to a main selection not if they *did* want it but if they *didn't*. Thus a certain percentage of acceptances came under the dubious rubric "sloth," or "Where the hell is the goddamn Book Find newsletter? I forgot to write and say I didn't want this month's selection."

Normally, I began writing George notes a good week before each month's deadline reminding him time was running out. Another reminder two days later, then a third with the notes now marked URGENT. In most cases, we finally came up with the selections with no more than two or three days' delay. But there came a month in the dark of winter when he not only ignored my notes but refused to talk to me when we passed in the hallway. No idea why. He had faulted me, ergo I was hated. I was beginning to learn how things worked in the world of business. Or maybe George was an exception. In any case, with the deadline more than a week behind us, George ordered me into his office one afternoon and demanded to know how on earth I expected to get this month's newsletter out without a selection? I mentally considered getting him in a half nelson and pinning him to his desk before he knew what was happening, but wisely refrained. In summer, when George had exchanged long-sleeved shirts for short, I had seen the rippling biceps as he strode past my cubicle and knew that despite my wrestling prowess he might wriggle out of my hold and toss me out the fourth-floor window onto Park Avenue South without so much as an au revoir. Susan had intimated Atlas had nothing on George in the build department; how she knew I did not inquire.

There was a sliding library ladder behind his desk that soared impressively from floor to ceiling and covered the full length of his voluminous bookcase. I saw George suddenly rise from his seat, clamber up the ladder, mutter to himself, reach forward and pull out a book, toss it in my general direction, then inch the ladder farther along, pull out another, toss it over his shoulder, repeating the process until the floor, his desk, my arms, were laden with a dozen books. "One of these," he said, "will be this month's selection. Narrow it down to two by tomorrow and I'll decide"—he must have seen my face, for he temporized—"*we'll* decide," and he turned his back to let me know the "meeting" was over.

Jeannette first burst out laughing when I told her the story that night, for she adored slapstick, then suddenly she turned serious. "You should get out of there," she said. "First of all, he's driving you crazy. And second, you're not spending enough time with the four of us." I paused to make sure I had heard right. "The *four* of us!" "Afraid so," she said. "Dr. Berenberg confirmed it today." "And when might this happen?" "On or about April Fools' Day. And that's no joke." Fifteen minutes later I was uncorking a bottle of Laurent-Perrier, vintage 1954, toasting our new son, for this time it would surely be a boy, while at the same time looking warily around our one-bedroom apartment and wondering where in God's name we'd welcome the lad.

Nineteen fifty-eight faded into 1959, and the overall climate at 215 had improved measurably: more often than not, after that Chaplinesque over-the-shoulder book tossing, deadlines were being met, most of our selections were exceeding the dread minimum, and Susan had stopped swinging her now-sheer-stockinged legs at my desk corner. In late January, plump, gentle Herman Figatner—Mr. Purse Strings—who rarely left his desk from dawn till dusk, called me in and announced that George had approved a raise for me. Five hundred dollars. Starting next week. I could hardly contain my joy. Should I kiss Herman or strangle him? I settled by thanking him, perfunctorily, I trusted, and rushed home to tell Jeannette the good news. "I haven't checked it out," I offered, "but it might just buy the new baby a pair of shoes." I patted her increasingly rotund belly and bent down to hear the infant's nightly thrashing. From the earnest kicking, I knew the little guy, more than six months old according to the Nepalese method of counting, was going to be a world-class soccer player, just as I was sure Nathalie would be a writer, teacher, or at least bookworm, for her favorite sport, now that she could walk, was to speed to the bookcase and take therefrom, in no special order but with obvious relish, the entire bottom shelf of books, one by one, and cast them onto the floor. Need one have better proof? Or was it her way of telling me to throw out book publishing and spend more time with her?

George admired Alfred Knopf more than any man in publishing and called him frequently for advice before making up his mind on a selection. He had learned to do so over the years because Mr. K., doubtless sensing his power, never failed to phone and berate George if he learned of a main selection of which he disapproved. For the moment at least, the club was doing fine, making reasonable money, but George was clearly tired of hawking other people's wares; it was high time he published on his own. He rightly understood that American agents would send him only leftovers, books already turned down by the major houses, and when someone suggested he look abroad, a light went on. But it quickly went out when submissions arrived from France, Germany, and Spain, with no one he trusted able to read them. He knew I read French; the question was: Did he really trust me? Still, one morning, instead of calling me imperiously into his office, he dropped by my cubicle waving a book with a familiar cover: Les Éditions de Minuit. It was a thin book by a certain Henri Alleg entitled *La question*, graphically detailing the tortures by the French military in Algeria of North African nationals. A most unlikely candidate for a country supremely uninterested in France's colonial wars, I thought. Nonetheless, I was delighted simply to have a Minuit book in my hands, and I read it that night, sharing its contents and my thoughts with Jeannette. It made harrowing reading: How could a country I loved so dearly, which had suffered firsthand the horrors of World War II, the mindless murders, the physical and mental agonies, allow itself to become the *bourreau*—the "torturer"—in turn? Next morning I wrote George a report attesting to the book's importance but cautioning that if he expected meaningful sales, he should desist. He came back and asked me to translate a few pages, which I did that night. He read them, peered back into my office, and announced he was going to publish the book, which was already a major bestseller not only in France but in several other European countries as well. George had the brilliant idea of asking Jean-Paul Sartre, who was at the height of his fame here, to write the introduction. A rushed translation, which I edited almost as quickly, and the book came out to major reviews. And it went onto the *New York Times* bestseller list! I was confounded. George was ecstatic. And now that it was a bestseller, he said, his eye always on the club, it should become a main selection of the Book Find Club, no? I nodded: a main selection, but of course!

29 ~

To the Budding Grove

IN JANUARY 1959, Barney called again and wondered whether we could have lunch the next day. I canceled a lunch I'd scheduled and said yes. Again to One Fifth Avenue. Lunch the usual euphemism: two martinis and, for Barney, food a toy to push about the patient plate. That day Barney was in especially fine fettle, barely able to contain himself. For years he had been itching to bring out *Lady Chatterley's Lover*, not the "acceptable" version published earlier by Knopf, which had licensed a paperback edition to New American Library, but the final, integral text D. H. Lawrence had written, a whole other kettle of unadulterated sex, bound to raise hackles. In the late 1920s, Lawrence had written three versions, the last of which was published unexpurgated in 1928 in Florence and known as the Orioli edition, long banned in both Britain and America. One of the work's champions was the distinguished professor of English at UC Berkeley Mark Schorer, who in 1954 had gone to Taos, New Mexico, to meet with Lawrence's widow, Frieda Lawrence Ravagli, and examine all three manuscripts. Barney had contacted Schorer that same year and indicated his interest in publishing the integral version. He also had sought advice from Grove's lawyer, Ephraim London, who warned that "chances are better than even that efforts to ban the book will be made if the third version is published." Undeterred, Barney had written to Lawrence's widow, explaining he wanted to publish the final version, and she had agreed. But before any action could be taken, Frieda died and Lawrence's British agent, Laurence Pollinger, refused to move forward. Still, Barney wrote to dozens of luminaries eliciting their support for the project: Edmund Wilson, whose *Memoirs of Hecate County* had recently suffered the censors' wrath; F. R. Leavis; Henry Steele Commager; Bennett Cerf, the head of Random House; James Thurber; Edward R. Murrow, the brave journalist who had dared take on Senator McCarthy, to name but a few. The responses were mixed, some counseling caution, others deeming the cause lost in advance. To complicate matters, Barney said, while Lawrence's American agent backed the plan, Pollinger still adamantly opposed it. Barney wrote to Pollinger, trying to sway him, to no avail. After a year of effort, Ephraim London advised Barney to "shelve the project for the time being." Reluctantly, Barney did. But the project was not dead, only dormant, waiting for a spark to reignite. That spark came two years later, when in 1956 the British publisher Heinemann, sensing an opportunity or perhaps taking a page from Girodias's book(s), published the third version in the Netherlands "for distribution except in the British Empire and the U.S.A." When the following year Grove began publishing *Evergreen Review*, Mark Schorer was commissioned to write an article that appeared in issue number 1, a defiant defense of the long-banned work. Almost simultaneously, a film version of *Lady Chatterley* was released and immediately banned in New York. Ephraim, who had successfully defended a film banned earlier in the decade on the grounds of blasphemy, *The Miracle*, assumed defense of the *Chatterley* film. The case worked its way up through the courts until, in December of the previous year, Barney said, the Supreme Court had agreed to hear it later that month. At which point London, confident he was going to win, told Barney he now felt the time was right to bring out the novel.

When was all this to take place? I asked. "In March we're informing *The New York Times* of our intent to publish in May," Barney said. "Sounds exciting," I said, wondering whether Barney and Maurice had actually met. I was sure they had been in sporadic correspondence from as far back as the *Merlin* years, and Barney had mentioned his belated attempt to buy the rights to *Lolita* roughly a year ago—too little and too late, he admitted, for by the time he did, Putnam's Walter Minton had flown to Paris and sealed the deal.

"Why don't you join the excitement?" Barney said, with a gesticulation so wild the contents of his martini glass went flying halfway across the room, barely missing several sedate patrons, while the glass itself clattered to the floor and splintered into a thousand little pieces, and he ordered another, which arrived promptly. "You're wasting your time at those book clubs." I reminded him that Braziller had now started publishing, and in fact already had a major bestseller. "But look at our list," he urged. "You'd fit right in," repeating his mantra of a few months before. "Beckett, Ionesco, Artaud, Genet, Sartre . . . And by the way, Brendan Behan, too. If I remember correctly, he was a friend of yours in Paris, no? What's more, I'd want you to co-edit the *Evergreen Review* with me. By the way, our Evergreen paperback line is doing better every year." I did know: a year or so after we met in Paris, Barney had—following the example of young Jason Epstein, who in 1952 had intuited that a ready market existed in that fertile but fallow realm between the standard hardcover titles and the inexpensive mass-market paperbacks, namely paperbacks of quality works—started a Grove paperback line, a mixture of Grove's own titles and reprints of out-of-print or neglected classics, which now numbered almost 150 titles.

What would I be doing? I asked. Managing editor of Grove itself, he said, defining that role in some detail—not just the shepherding of works from manuscript to finished book, the normal definition of the job at larger houses, but in essence the senior editor, finding and editing new works of fiction and nonfiction. What about Don Allen, the present co-editor of *Evergreen*? I asked. He had moved to the West Coast, Barney said, still involved with Grove but not on a day-to-day basis. In fact, except for *Evergreen*, Don was now working for Grove essentially on a freelance basis. And what, I dared ask, might my salary be? Barney mentioned a figure, better than my present income but not enough to be persuasive if money was the issue. "Let me talk to Jeannette," I said. "I'll let you know tomorrow."

Jeannette as usual was clear and precise: of course I should go to Grove. Would Barney be hard to work for? I wondered aloud. Probably, she said, but any harder than Braziller?

From my office at 215, shortly after nine o'clock, my voice hushed, my back to the corridor, I called Barney, who wasn't yet in, his secretary, Judith Schmidt, told me. Any idea when? Not really, she said. Try again in a couple hours. I reflected as I hung up that I was probably dealing with a rich dilettante, for whom working hours were governed largely by whiskey and whimsy, for I had heard stories that he loved to prowl the city deep into the night. But when I reached him, he apologized and said he'd had an eight o'clock meeting with the lawyers over the Lawrence book. Another facile cliché shattered . . . Anyway, he was pleased I was coming, very pleased in fact. When could I start? "I haven't told George yet, and in all fairness I have to put the next newsletter to bed." So, four weeks okay? How about three? Agreed.

The last weeks at Book Find were not pleasant. George did not take my departure kindly. "But I've just got you trained," he protested, "and you're already leaving! What about the new publishing program—doesn't that tempt you?" Then the eternal ploy: he was grooming me to be his successor! It was the second time in two jobs I had heard that tossed out. Maybe a decade or so older than I, George was not only in fine physical shape, his ego was such that he never, I suspected, planned to groom any successor, even if he lived to be a hundred.* Further, he felt that three weeks' notice was not enough, so I consented to four after consulting with Barney. "But for God's sake, no longer," Barney said. "Things are heating up down here."

And so it was, on Groundhog Day in 1959, I showed up bright and early at 795 Broadway, checked the downstairs landmarks—Nat's Clothing Store and the Hot Dog Emporium—and hastened up the rickety stairs, loaded for bear. Or was it woodchuck? In any event, the day was cloudy, a welcome omen. In contrast to Braziller's pin-dropping environment at 215 Park Avenue South, where sometimes days passed with barely an exchange among employees, circulating memos in a name-routing envelope, memos being the preferred means of communication, 795 Broadway, only a few blocks south, was a beehive of scuffle and scurry. Barney spent a good hour reintroducing me to the staff: his secretary, Judith Schmidt, a young woman of indeterminate age who, simply by the way she looked at him and listened to his every word, seemed to be in Barney's thrall; Fred Jordan, a man roughly my age in whom I detected a slight accent, which turned out to be the vestiges of his native Vienna, who had started at Grove in sales and was introduced as the head of publicity; to my delight Phyllis Bellows, who had been all too briefly a colleague at Braziller and who greeted me with a warm smile and hearty hug that made me feel immediately at home; a pink-cheeked young Englishman, the sales manager John Pizey, who punctuated every sentence with a hearty chuckle; Richard Brodney, the hirsute, purposeful production manager, whose ashtray was already half filled with cigarette butts and here it was only ten o'clock; and tall, thin, slightly stooped Donald Allen. Allen had been Grove's first editor, then left to work for New Directions, which he hated, then moved to another new house, Criterion, which

---

*In 1959, George was forty-three. In 2006, Jeannette and I attended his ninetieth. His hundredth? We've already entered the commitment in our calendar.

he found even more frustrating, after which Barney invited him back to Grove. He agreed, but only after working out an arrangement whereby he could work from home, for he had finally understood that he and office life were incompatible. Scholarly, aloof, diffident, Allen gazed at me with half-closed eyes as he shook my hand with such lack of vim, or was it vigor, that I suddenly wondered whether my arrival was the reason for his departure rather than, as Barney had put it, the contrary. So cold was his reception, in fact, that I thought I had better clear the air before it turned rancid. Pulling Barney aside, I asked him about Don. "I get the distinct feeling he wishes I weren't here," I said. "No, no," Barney said, "it's not you. I owe him a lot—he's the one who turned me on to the Beats, for one— but he's so glum. In all the time he was here, he hardly ever spoke. To me or anyone. And God forbid you should pay him a compliment. He'd look at you as if you're the most stupid person alive, and then make sure not to talk to you for weeks. But anyway, he no longer works in the office, in fact hasn't for some time now. He's moved to San Francisco. He just happens to be in town for a few days." Later, when I saw some of the work he had accomplished at Grove during his tenure, including his masterful *New American Poetry, 1945–1960*, which would influence, if not form, the poetic taste of an entire generation, I came to admire Don greatly. But always from afar. I saw, too, that he had translated four of Ionesco's plays, and looking at them more closely, I found the translations first-rate. Socially, however, Don was his own worst enemy. Currently, he was still on the Grove payroll, his official title being West Coast salesman, a pure sinecure, but his was an editorial mind, and in fact it was he who had planted in Barney the seed of *Evergreen Review*, whose first six issues he had co-edited. He was the man I was to replace in that role, and a careful look at the first two years' offerings made the Allen shoes look large indeed. The only other editorial person visible was a thin, intense, bespectacled young lady who, from our first meeting, seemed frightened of her shadow (although, as noted, there was none that day), Marilynn Meeker. Barney remarked that he thought of her as his utility infielder, capable of filling in at virtually any position. Despite her shyness, we made immediate eye contact, an important element in any incipient relationship, I have found. I liked her on the spot, an instinct borne out a thousand times over the next twelve years.

Rounding out the hearty crew were Frieda Slappy at the switchboard, a diminutive lady of uncertain age who artfully maneuvered the complex wires in and out of the console with the grace of a ballet mistress; and

Laura Martin, a tall, willowy black woman whose task was to receive and record orders, then transmit them to the warehouse. She kept track of the number of orders by means of—*Gott im Himmel!*—an abacus. When I queried Barney about what struck me as a sorely antiquated method, he said he'd spent most of the war in China and, impressed by the simplicity and accuracy of the ancient tool, brought it back to the States, where it was working like a charm, thank you! Or maybe the daily influx of orders warranted no more than this contraption.

There couldn't have been more than ten or twelve employees in all, but they all seemed to be moving simultaneously, without colliding, at roughly the speed of light. Richard Brodney was in and out of Barney's office a dozen times a day, a half-consumed cigarette inevitably hanging from his lips, bearing designs and cover or jacket mechanicals to be approved, further tinkered with, sent back to the drawing board, or trashed. Most of the covers and jackets were the work of a young freelance designer, Roy Kuhlman, whom Barney had discovered a year or so before and who by now had a virtual monopoly on the Grove list. I asked Barney how he had found Kuhlman. "I didn't," he said, "he found me. Literally walked in off the street armed with a portfolio of abstract paintings, which I loved. Remember, I'd been married to Joan Mitchell, and when we lived in the south of France for a year in the late 1940s, I watched her evolve from a realist to an abstractionist, a miraculous evolution. That doubtless affected my reaction to Kuhlman. When I'd finished looking at his portfolio, I said, 'Okay, Roy, you do our jackets.' 'All of them?' he said. 'Yes, all of them!'" Barney was not a man of half measures.

In Paris, I'd been as close to painters as I had to writers, and most, including Kelly and Youngerman but also a number of young French artists, were evolving into abstract if they were not already there. So Kuhlman's work made an immediate positive impression on me as well. Unlike the jackets of the big, uptown houses, where realism reigned, Grove covers and book jackets announced from the outset, to bookstores and customers alike, that here was a house with a difference: if you like the outside, check the contents. When Barney asked for my opinion of a Kuhlman cover, I could respond with more than a gut reaction. Kuhlman, I soon learned, did not take suggestions for change kindly, and criticisms or rejections set him spinning with rage. Barney, I also quickly saw, was almost as pigheaded as Roy, and before long he delegated me to deal with Kuhlman on a daily basis, to avoid a fatal break. I instinctively liked and admired Roy, and before long we became friends, so much so that he often showed his upcoming cover designs to me before they were shown to Barney. Upon occasion he even went so far as to listen to my opinion about possible design changes, if I thought it wouldn't pass muster.

During my first couple of weeks I had a pleasant surprise, a short letter from Beckett welcoming me to Grove and saying how pleased he was that we'd be working together again. The news of my arrival there, he added, had reminded him that he had not yet returned my translation of his short story "La fin," first published many years before in *Merlin* but now intended for *Evergreen Review*. I recalled his indignation—he a man very slow to anger—when Trocchi had not shown him galleys before publishing the 1954 version, so I had carefully gone through that earlier incarnation, made a few emendations, and sent it on to him. I had also, at his behest, translated "L'expulsé"—"The Expelled"—the second of the three stories, but was still tinkering, awaiting the master's judgment, before I, with considerable trepidation, sent it to him. What for me had started off in Paris as an altruistic act had become a mighty challenge. The more I read the man, the more I was certain that my youthful, dithyrambic 1952 judgment was, if anything, far shy of the mark: Beckett *was* a genius. Till then, Joyce had been my literary god, but in the last seven years my man Beckett was fast coming up on the outside, ready to forge ahead. The prose, seemingly so simple, was fraught with hidden meanings, allusions, intimations of works known or (to me) unknown—classical, biblical, you name it. He had not frequented Joyce and his circle for years for nothing.

On March 6, he returned the revised story, with a fair number of emendations, but fewer than I had anticipated.

> *Dear Seaver:*
>
> *Herewith* La fin *with my corrections. Your translation is excellent and they are for the most part just fussiness and contrariness and author's license. If there are any you disagree with let me have a note of them and we'll find something else or revert to your text. I can't remember if we worked on the other two together, perhaps only one,* L'Expulsé *it seems to me. I have just finished [translating] the first* Texte pour Rien . . . *"Esquire" wants it, of all improbable ducks.*
>
> *I saw Pat Bowles the other day, he seemed in excellent form.*

I wrote back with perhaps half a dozen minor suggestions, all of which he graciously accepted, and acknowledged that I had indeed done a first draft of "L'expulsé," which I said was to my mind one of the great short stories of the century. Was I exaggerating or simply smitten? Neither, really, for not long ago, to test myself and my memory, I reread all three stories, and if I were in academe, at least one, perhaps all, would be required reading.

I read, too, the first "Text for Nothing" he had sent: stunning! Of a piece with the stories, though even briefer, tauter, the prose sheer poetry from first line to last. I noted that when he consciously sat down to write poetry, it tended to be formal, even stiff, but when he wrote what was called prose, for want of a better name, it came out pure poetry. Wry poetry, bent and twisted by age (even, perhaps especially, when he was young); dark poetry (but shot through with lines that rend the soul, if one there is, at least the heart): "To think in the valley the sun is blazing all down the rav-elled sky"; or, "I hear the curlews, that means close of day, fall of night, for that's the way with curlews, silent all day, then crying when the darkness gathers, that's the way with these wild creatures and so short-lived, com-pared with me." I could go on . . .

My first weeks at Grove were both exciting and edifying, convincing me this was a job and a half, if not two. Given which, I was far from sure I could do a proper job within the time frame Beckett was proposing for the third story, "Le calmant"—"The Calmative." Yes, I would pursue "The Ex-pelled," go back to it, polish, rework, try to imagine, among the several choices, how Beckett would render it. A dangerous game, for one could guess wrong. But simplicity, always opt for simplicity. Maybe Pat could do the third story, I thought, since he'd already done *Molloy* and was on the spot, so they could work together. Later that day I mentioned my suggestion to Barney, who burst out laughing. I wasn't sure where the humor lay, but he got up, crossed the room, opened a file drawer, pulled out a manila file, and read from a Beckett letter from late 1954: "Bowles is hopeless. No ac-knowledgement of my last corrections and no sign of the concluding pages. I do not even know where he is."

"Jesus," I said, "I knew Pat had been slow, but I never knew Beckett was that down on him. I'm afraid I'm the culprit. I suggested Pat translate *Molloy.*"

"I always felt Beckett had to be his own translator," Barney said, "but he resisted for a long time."

"That's the only reason I volunteered to take on the stories," I said. "In my wild imagination, I thought I was saving him time to create. I gathered only later the well had apparently gone dry. Still, when we first met, he shuddered at the idea of translating his French into English. 'I couldn't face those old chestnuts again,' he said. 'All I see is their shortcomings.'

"Anyway," I said, "I had a letter from Beckett this morning, returning 'La fin,' which we can now include in the next issue if you like. In his last sentence he mentions having seen Patrick recently and found him in excellent form. So whatever problem there was between them seems to be over."

That same day I wrote Beckett back, thanking him for his kind words and saying that if he truly felt I was doing him a service that would save him time, I'd be happy to give "Le calmant" a shot. Would we call it "The Sedative"? I wondered. How about "The Calmative," he wrote back. Closer to the French, and more poetic, no? More poetic, yes . . . That night I sat down with the French text, which I knew almost by heart, and tried the first lines:

> I don't remember when I died. It always seemed to me I was old when I died, about ninety years old, and what years, and that my body showed it, from head to foot. But tonight, in my icy bed, I feel I'm going to be older than the day, the night, when the sky with all its lights fell down on me, the same sky I had so often gazed upon since I first drifted on the distant earth.

The first page took me only three or four evenings. A second round a week later produced:

> I forget when I died. It always seemed to me that I died old, about ninety years old, and what years, and that my body bore it out, from head to toe. But this evening, alone in my icy bed, I have the feeling that I'll be older than the day, the night, when the sky with all its lights fell on me, the same sky I had so often gazed on since I took my first awkward steps on the distant earth.

Better? Worse? Translating Beckett was clearly not like translating anyone else. Except Joyce, of course. During my Paris days, I had translated half a dozen books from the French, both fiction and nonfiction, and felt the results were competent and relatively faithful and read largely, if not wholly, as if the work had been written in English. But to try to translate with the Man looking over your shoulder, even an ocean away, was the way to madness.

Two months later I had a full translation, the fourth or fifth version, and was still dissatisfied. Further procrastination, or one more revision, would lead nowhere, I decided, so I gently slid the pages, some thirty in all, into an envelope, addressed it to 6, rue des Favorites, Paris 15ème, a site still vivid in my mind, and consigned it to the sea. Or, rather, to the air.

From the stroke of nine, it seemed, the phone rang incessantly at Grove, stretching Frieda to her four feet something. Barney grabbed his black instrument as though it were a lifeline, listening and nodding incessantly before barking a response. He had suggested I spend most of my time in his office the first few days, "to get the hang of things." Despite all the other frenetic activity relating to the upcoming list of books, most of the focus and energy was on *Chatterley*. In the course of that first week, Brodney had brought in the design for the jacket, pristine white, with simple black lettering. Barney asked me what I thought of the jacket. I thought it perfect. Whether it would deter the would-be censors I had no idea, but it certainly could not be construed as provocative or appealing to "prurient interests," an expression being bandied about the office those days. Any suggestions for change? "Only one: I note the price is five dollars. I think you could ask more." Barney said that five was already at the higher end of the price for a hardcover novel that length. But this isn't a normal book, is it? He's right. Let's ask a dollar more. Done. My only contribution to the enterprise, but one that eventually helped pay for the lawsuits, which we knew were almost certainly waiting in the wings. Though Grove was now publishing as many as sixty or seventy books a year, its volume of business, and its profile among publishers, were still fairly modest. If the uptown publishers were even aware of its existence, their attitude was either dismissal or disdain. If that fazed Barney in any way, I never discerned it in our early meetings. I had initially been unsure of his commitment to book publishing, because over that first lunch in Paris in 1953 he had spent far more time discussing the film he had produced, *Strange Victory*, than he had talking about Grove's books and authors. But after a few weeks there, I was convinced he had found, however obliquely, his chosen profession.

If it did nothing else, *Lady Chatterley* would put Grove squarely, and very visibly, on the publishing map. Viewed as an upstart by some of the older publishers, a maverick by others, Grove and its growing stable of younger Americans—Frank O'Hara, Allen Ginsberg, Jack Kerouac, Lawrence Ferlinghetti, John Rechy—were catching the attention of other young writers, who urged their agent, if they had one, to send material our way. So what had been a trickle of new material when I arrived swelled to a near flood only months later, when we decamped from the overcrowded 795 Broadway to a spanking-new four-story building a few blocks away at 64 University Place. There was a Daitch Shopwell supermarket on the ground floor, and on the upper floors two other small publishers had just moved in: Fred Praeger, with a list of political books, on three; and Sheed and Ward, a Catholic publisher, on four. As we carted in our boxes of books and manuscripts, Barney gazed at the lobby board and remarked, since we were now labeled, as a result of advance word of *Lady Chatterley*, sex fiends, that this building had the world covered: food on one, sex on two, politics on three, and religion on four. A comforting thought . . .

Everyone knew that Barney was rich, but one never knew to what degree, for his banker father had carefully—Barney would say unforgivably, others would say foresightedly—tied his son's trust fund in so many knots that much of the endowment was not available. In fact, at one point Barney had been so frustrated by his father's restriction of money that was, as he put it, "rightfully mine" that he threatened his father with a lawsuit. "Go ahead, sue me," Father said with a shrug. So Barney did, and to the consternation of all, he won. Still, the trust fund thus freed did not make him a millionaire.

Now, in the dawn of the 1960s, with Grove nearing ten, it was still losing money. Ignoring the *Chatterley* revenues of 1959 and 1960, our volume was just over a quarter of a million dollars, which in today's dollars would be between 1.5 and 2 million. At lunch one day not long after we had moved to University Place, Barney, on a slightly used envelope, made some quick penciled calculations until, after one more sip of the ubiquitous martini, he looked up and pronounced: "All we need to break even is to bill $350,000 a year. That will do it!" And he nodded and smiled happily, as though our future had just been assured. Only $100,000, he must have been thinking, not a helluva lot. But even by my calculation, that worked out to an increase of 40 percent over our current volume, no easy task with the normal hardcover book selling at roughly $4.00, sometimes creeping up to $5.00, and the paperbacks between $1.00 and $1.95. *Evergreen Review*, which was not included in his calculations, made no money and probably never would. Barney had rightly seen it as a vehicle for finding new writers, with the bottom line a secondary, if not inconsequential, consideration.

Still, the young Grove was decidedly aided by the widespread belief that Barney came from great wealth. Only son of a Chicago banker. Daddy Rosset, who was Jewish, had married Mary Tansey, who was Irish, during the Roaring Twenties, when Chicago was the home to such disparate luminaries as Al Capone and Jake Arvey, a politician who ran much of the city. Arvey was a friend of Barney's father, who was very much a self-made man. Though he had only a high school education, Barnet senior had taken night courses at Northwestern and become a certified public accountant. By the time he was twenty-five, he was the head of one bank. In those days there were no bank branches in Chicago, so the city was peppered with dozens of small banks, with limited capital. Working for several of these in his capacity of CPA, he knew where the vulnerabilities lay, and when one got into trouble, he knew how and when to bail it out. By 1929, Barnet senior was the head of no fewer than three different banks. During the 1920s, essentially an entrepreneur, he went down to Texas, where he got involved in the oil business, returning to Chicago far wealthier than when he had departed. "My father," Barney told me at one of our early meetings, "had the unique ability to make money hand over fist during the Depression, when the rest of the country was going broke." What he didn't say, or bruit about, was that the Rossets had suffered considerable losses in the early 1930s, to the point that the posh apartment they owned at 2920 Commonwealth Avenue was taken from them, though they were allowed to stay on as renters as long as they paid the new owners. During the following two decades, however, Father Rosset regained much of his former fortune. Then, suddenly, he died of a heart attack in 1952, leaving his fortune to his wife and son. Thus printers and paper suppliers vied for the Grove business, never asking for bank references or fiduciary proof, offering generous terms as they sensed here was a growing business, run, like Jay Laughlin's New Directions, by a cushy millionaire. As further proof of Barney's untold wealth, he had bought a large tract of land in East Hampton, Long Island, where he already owned a strange and unique house, originally owned by the artist Robert Motherwell, a Quonset hut cleverly converted by the French architect Pierre Chareau into a two-story main house, complete with two guesthouses, a tennis court, and a swimming pool, rare luxuries then, to which Barney repaired most weekends. On the choice tract at almost pristine Three Mile Harbor he was building attractive houses on spec for sale or rental, keeping architects, builders, and designers—most of whom were friends—busy year-round.

Meanwhile, on April 2, 1960, after kissing little Nathalie and Jeannette a fond goodbye, I entrained for the office, arriving just at nine in a drizzling rain. As soon as I opened the door, Frieda, hoisting herself three inches from her seat so that she became almost visible, said, "Report to St. Vincent's. Jeannette is on her way." Apparently, minutes after I left, her first contractions had occurred and she had ordered a cab. Our office was only minutes from St. Vincent's, and I ran rather than walked, arriving soaked and excited to see Jeannette's cab just pulling up to the entrance. The poor driver looked as though he needed a stiff drink, immediately. When he had picked up his passenger, he had no idea of the ordeal in store. According to Jeannette, he spent most of the forty-minute drive looking in the rearview mirror, trying to remember what one had to do when a passenger gave birth in a cab, while Jeannette, between spasms, pleaded with him to please, for God's sake, look ahead, not behind, for he was apparently missing whizzing cars and trucks by mere inches. It was hard to know which of the two had suffered more from the experience, but only Jeannette was smiling. As for me, I must have looked to the hospital staff grandly Beckettian, a sodden object of sartorial neglect.

I paid the cabbie handsomely and helped milady into the lobby, whence she was quickly whisked to a room on the delivery floor. With Nathalie we had had classic, old-fashioned childbirth, the father unwelcome and the mother anesthetized. Both exiled from the miracle of birth. In all fairness, with so short a time between Venezuela and the girl child's birth, we had not had the luxury of exploring other methods. This time we had opted for the method propounded by Dr. Grantly Dick-Read, the English author of *Childbirth Without Fear*, whose principles had quickly crossed the Atlantic and gained the adherence of a number of American doctors. So there I was, sitting by Jeannette's bedside, holding her hand with each contraction, breathing deeply as she breathed, suffering as she suffered (no, not quite!), coaching her as I had been coached, until at long last (in reality, only thirty-five or forty minutes, an eternity) I heard her say: "It's coming!" I corrected: *"He's coming!"* And indeed, peeking under the covers, I saw the lad's head, the crown of his lovely head, pushing its way through. I rang for the doctor, who appeared within endless seconds. One look and he ordered Jeannette wheeled into the delivery room.

I paced the lonely room, staring out at the gray drizzle, cursing those other parents who unthinkingly had opted to have their babies that same day, when my selfish thoughts were suddenly interrupted by Jeannette's return, smiling and holding in her arms . . . a baby boy! She had been awake the whole time, seen him arrive in all his waxy splendor, heard his first sound, a healthy wail, and held him seconds after the umbilical cord was severed. Jeannette had never looked more beautiful. This time we had decided on a name weeks before: Alexander—which again, we figured, worked in both countries—and, as middle name, Medina, after Jeannette's father. A moniker to live up to. I held the babe in my arms now, that little one so longed for.

30 ~

Lady Chatterley's Lawyers

MY NEXT SEVERAL DAYS were spent to-ing and fro-ing between Grove and St. Vincent's, my mind split between Lady Chatterley and Lady Jeannette, for on the former front things were heating up. Everyone at Grove was focused on the book, knowing that it could move us into the big(ger) time, give Grove a new, higher profile. But there was also the distinct possibility it could bring the still-fragile company down. The novel had been living underground for almost three decades, tolerated—only in its native English—in a country or two, but judged obscene in most. In the United States, both the Customs Service and the Post Office Department had banned it, the former from our ports, the latter from the mails. But Grove had carefully assessed the risks and decided the Chatterley War was worth waging. Curiously, although Barney relished the censorship battle and the notoriety that was bound to ensue, he did not really like the book. He found it weighty and often boring. In fact, despite its reputation, he had never read it until he was at Grove. The book he really loved, however, and was intent on publishing come hell or high water, was Henry Miller's *Tropic of Cancer*, with *Capricorn* soon to follow, if indeed the two were not published simultaneously.

At Swarthmore, in 1940, he wrote his freshman English paper on Miller's *Tropic of Cancer*. So his real goal, he confessed, was to publish Miller's banned works in America. But wiser heads had counseled that if he did,

Grove was sure to lose. There had to be a prior test case, one that he had at least a fighting chance to win, and whatever he might think of *Lady Chatterley*, it was an ideal choice in many ways. First and foremost, Lawrence was an acknowledged master of English literature, widely read and increasingly included in the curricula of major universities. So one knew a goodly number of respected academics would attest to the novel's worth.

The only crack in Barney's wall of stoic calm came when he announced, not long before the novel's scheduled release, that Ephraim London, on whom he had relied to handle the *Chatterley* case—or cases—had been fired. Barney had some strong ideas on how the case should be handled, but Ephraim, whom Barney described as imperious—"he thought he was Abraham Lincoln; he wasn't"—had said it was his way or no way. Period. Replaced by whom? both Fred Jordan and I asked aloud. A man named Charles Rembar, Barney said. I had never heard of him. How had Barney chosen him? Did he have experience, as Ephraim had, fighting censorship? Was he a well-regarded First Amendment lawyer? Barney shrugged and admitted that he had been out in East Hampton for the weekend when the decision to fire London had been taken. He knew two lawyers out there, one reasonably well, the other only from having played tennis with him a number of times. He called the first, and there was no answer. He called the second, his tennis friend Charles Rembar, who had the great good fortune to be home. Barney explained that he had just had to fire his lawyer and asked Rembar if he'd like to take on the case for him. What case? *"Lady Chatterley."* Not much time to prepare, but . . . "Sure, I'd be happy to."

I met Rembar the first day he came to the office, and his relative youth— relative to London's—and seeming self-assurance suddenly made us feel as if this case were already won, whereas this man, who was later to become an expert in censorship, was probably not at all self-assured, having little or no experience in the realm. A crash course was in order, and Rembar began studying in detail all the English and American obscenity cases, starting with the *Hicklin* case in England in 1868, in which the test of obscenity was defined as "the tendency . . . to deprave and corrupt those whose minds are open to such immoral influences," a decision, one could claim, that strengthened the already disturbingly rigid class system, for one could only assume the lord chief justice—in the instance Lord Cockburn—firmly believed that minds open to immoral influences perforce belonged to the poor and uneducated; on to the famous, or infamous, Anthony Comstock in the 1870s and his New York Society for the Suppression of Vice; and, more important, the more recent cases that would be precedents, either helpful or harmful: the *Ulysses* decision in 1934 (helpful), those on Lillian Smith's *Strange Fruit* in the 1940s and Edmund Wilson's *Memoirs of Hecate County* (harmful). Despite Rembar's infectious upbeat attitude, he knew he had a formidable task ahead of him. In fact, in arguing the *Chatterley* case, he would be creating new law if he won, and new law, especially in areas as sensitive as these, never comes easy.*

A first printing of twenty-five thousand copies had been decided on—huge for Grove—and the first copies were due off the press in a matter of days. What did Rembar expect would happen once the books hit the mails and, hopefully, the stores? He shrugged but suspected the Post Office would be the first to move. Was he prepared? Not as much as he would have liked, he admitted. Having spent the last several weeks studying in great detail the recent history of censorship in both the U.K. and this country, he could safely say none of those books presented anything like the problem of *Lady Chatterley*, with its blatant scenes of sexual activity and unparalleled use of "four-letter" Anglo-Saxon words. In short, Rembar felt he was embarking upon uncharted waters. As I talked with some of my fellow editors at other houses in the days before the book's release, I was upset to learn that many felt this was an act of madness on our part, that publishing Lawrence could well result in further censorship, for harsh anti-obscenity laws were already very much in force in most states, with the backing of the Supreme Court as recently as two years earlier, when Samuel Roth and David Alberts, both book publishers, were sentenced to jail for publishing obscene works. So the stakes were high, the dangers real. Nonetheless, not once did I detect among the members of the Grove staff the slightest qualm about being involved. On the contrary, a feeling of rare camaraderie and excitement prevailed as C-day approached.

Then, finally, the first copies arrived at the office, pristine and beautiful, historic and . . . and, oh my God! so terribly flawed! I don't remember who in the office, Brodney, I believe, discovered and pointed out the error: Mark Schorer's name had been misspelled! So the celebration had to be deferred while the correction was made. Fortunately, the error appeared

---

*For a detailed history of both *Lady Chatterley* trials, those of Henry Miller, and the problem of literary censorship in general, see Rembar's *End of Obscenity*, originally published by Random House in 1968 and reprinted in 1986 by Harper Perennial. Highly informative, it also demonstrates that lawyers can write in lucid, understandable prose.

only on the jacket, so the repair was swift, and books began shipping to the stores in early April. First reactions were favorable: a number of reviews cited the importance of the novel and praised it as a major contribution to contemporary literature, long overdue in the form the author intended. A phone check by Nat Sobel—who had replaced Pizey as sales manager—of several dozen stores verified that the book had indeed gone through the mails unobstructed, and sales at stores that had received copies were reported as "brisk," as a result both of the reviews and of word of mouth. But word of mouth can be a double-edged sword. The third week in April, a deputy police chief in Washington, D.C., hearing a rumor the book was available, called Brentano's, which verified it was indeed, at which point he seized its copies. The newspapers, sensing a hot story, began to feature it, fanning the fires. On April 28, Grove sued the deputy chief, but before that case could proceed, the postmaster of New York, Robert Christenberry, jumped into the fray and ordered several cartons of *Chatterley* that were in the mails to be seized, then asked Washington for instructions. At Grove we didn't learn of the seizure for several days, and by the time we did, a trial date had already been set by Washington: May 14. The case was to be heard at the New York Post Office. It was the first time I knew that postal authorities could act as judiciary, but Rembar explained that while its decisions could be reviewed by the courts, it did have such powers where the mails were concerned. Since *Chatterley* had already been judged obscene, therefore unmailable, thirty years before, it would remain banned until that ruling was overturned.

Fortunately, Grove was not alone in its suit. A small but highly regarded literary book club, the Readers' Subscription, had pointedly chosen the book as a main selection, knowing full well that if Grove got into trouble, so would they. Thus when the Post Office hearing got under way, Rembar, who had never tried a case before, had at his side two lawyers from the large and very prestigious New York law firm Paul, Weiss, Rifkind, Wharton and Garrison. But it was evident from the first day that the neophyte Rembar would carry most of the legal burden. At the outset, he and Grove had decided that it was not the Post Office's ambiguous powers of seizure that we wanted to contest but the freedom to publish under the First Amendment, which, if we won, would immediately, in Rembar's words, "shrink the scope of the anti-obscenity laws."

On the day of the trial, most of the morning was spent setting the ground rules, with Rembar and the Post Office's lead counsel, Saul Mindel—like two boxers—sizing each other up. Rembar and the Readers' Subscription lawyer, Jay Topkis, began by asking that the ban on the book be lifted temporarily until a decision had been reached, citing the severe financial strains the ban was imposing on both publisher and book club. That motion was not denied but deferred, the judicial officer, Charles Ablard, saying in essence he would sleep on it, but not decide until the trial was well under way.

In his opening statement, Mindel admitted that Lawrence was a writer "of standing" but that "to the community at large"—not to specialized critics or academics—the dominant effect of *Lady Chatterley*, taken as a whole, was one that appealed to "prurient interests," an expression that, strangely, derives from the Latin word for "itching" but has been transformed in English to "lustful." Over the next several years, I heard the same term in case after case, and whenever I did, I had an irrepressible desire to scratch. In any case, Mindel's strategy was to undercut Grove's effort to demonstrate Lawrence's importance by acknowledging it from the start and then to minimize the importance of the weighty witnesses he knew Grove would call, by stating they represented an "elite," not the community at large. It was a strong and effective argument. Even though this was the Post Office and not an important court of law, all of us there that day were impressed by the level of the statements and testimony on both sides and the evenhandedness of the Judicial Office.

Barney was Rembar's first witness, and he handled himself well, looking and acting like the serious publisher he was. The point to establish here was threefold: that Grove was highly reputable, that it had published in its first decade a number of important writers; that its presentation of the novel itself, and the advertising that accompanied it, was in impeccably good taste; that a number of newspapers and magazines had accepted our advertising without question—until the chilling effect of the Post Office suit had induced one to back down—proving that by current community standards the book was not viewed as objectionable. At lunch around the corner, the lawyers' assessment was that, whatever the outcome, both Ablard and Mindel were worthy opponents, and we were getting a fair shake.

The afternoon session was marked by the appearance of two impressive witnesses, Malcolm Cowley and Alfred Kazin. The former, a white-haired, rosy-cheeked, cherubic gentleman of sixty was, in looks and demeanor, a perfect witness. He defined himself as a literary critic and historian, specifying that he had worked in those fields for more than three decades. During his more than hour-long testimony and the cross-examination that followed, he established quite convincingly two key points: the unquestioned position of Lawrence in modern English literature, and the evolving tastes, the change in the range of tolerance in the reading public over the past thirty years.

Cowley was followed by the younger but no less impressive Alfred Kazin. Rembar led Kazin to focus on the changing literary tastes and trends, "the increasing tolerance and increasing acceptance of wider and wider areas of human experience discussed in literature," the point being that what one generation may refuse, a new one may accept or embrace.

Barney's testimony had been interrupted so that Cowley and Kazin would not have to sit and wait. Once their testimony ended, Barney came back to the stand, gave further background on how and why Grove had decided to publish the work, and ended with: "It occurred to me that it would be incomprehensible if this book were published today that the public would be shocked, offended or would raise any outcry against it; but rather that they would welcome it as the republishing, the bringing back to life, of one of our great masterpieces."

It was getting late, and the parties involved looked weary, but to me it had been a fascinating and enlightening day. For a man who had never tried a case before, Rembar, I thought, had done a masterful job. If I had been a betting man, I would have given heavy odds to anyone who thought Grove wouldn't win hands down. Well, I was dead wrong. When Ablard indicated that temporarily lifting the ban was beyond his authority, Grove applied the next day for a decision from Postmaster General Arthur Summerfield, who after a week of reflection refused to lift the ban. Two further applications were sent, the first on May 29, the second on June 5, to no avail. At which point, more than a month having passed, Grove together with Readers' Subscription decided to go to court, suing New York's Mr. Christenberry, the man still holding the bag (of books), in the federal district court of New York. The judge in the case bore the imposing name Frederick van Pelt Bryan, a man known for his intelligence and no-nonsense courtroom manner. The testimony of the Post Office trial was available to both parties, of course, though persuading courts to reverse Post Office rulings was an uphill battle, apparently. But it was clear that Judge Bryan not only had come with an open mind but was well prepared. Rembar's opening gambit to the court was, I thought, both dangerous and brilliant. He argued that Bryan should ignore the Post Office material and conduct a trial de novo, that is, from scratch. "It is up to you," Rembar told the court, "to decide whether D. H. Lawrence was an author or a pornographer." It was a daring challenge, but one sensed that Rembar, and perhaps the

Readers' Subscription lawyers, felt instinctively that they had before them a rare, independent-minded judge who just might make new law, if they conducted themselves with total probity. Which they did. After all the arguments were heard, the court adjourned, and on July 21 the decision was announced: Grove's request for summary judgment was approved, and Christenberry was admonished not to deny the mails either to the book or to the Readers' Subscription newsletter. Rejoicing all around? Not quite, for, predictably, the government appealed, but since the court of appeals was on vacation till fall, the government asked that the mailing ban remain in effect till the appeal could be heard. A three-judge panel denied that request. At long last, *Lady Chatterley's Lover* could safely be sent through the U.S. mails.

It was not until March 25, 1960—roughly a year after the book first appeared—that the court of appeals affirmed Judge Bryan's decision. It had been a long year of concern and worry on the one hand, but of triumph on the other, for over those twelve months the book had been approved and applauded, not only by Messrs. Cowley and Kazin, but by most critics coast-to-coast, as a result of which a Grove book, for the first time in its short history, headed to the top of the bestseller lists.

But euphoria, we soon learned, is a sometime thing. Let me explain. Because of *Chatterley*'s itinerant history, the copyright status, at least in the United States, was ambiguous at best. This was common knowledge. On the sidelines, various publishers, not to mention drooling pirates, watched the legal proceedings with increasing relish. To their credit, before the appeals court decision Simon and Schuster's co-owners Max Schuster and Leon Shimkin sent an envoy, Larry Hughes, to buy the paperback rights from Grove for Pocket Books. The offer, in our view, was far from sufficient. Besides, our six-dollar hardcover edition was doing just fine, thank you. Our unrequited suitor took revenge by suddenly publishing a thirty-five-cent paperback, and our hardcover edition dropped precipitously from the bestseller lists. Semi-panic in the office. Have you no honor, book buyers of the world? (Of course not—who would pay six dollars if he could buy the same novel for thirty-five cents?) In self-defense, Barney contacted a friend at Dell, Bud Baker, suggesting they distribute *our* paperback edition. Bud took the idea to Dell's fearless president, Helen Meyer, and virtually overnight our paperback appeared, with the challenging statement that this and only this was the original Grove Press edition, an admonition meant to appeal to all those with a modicum of decency, to cast doubt on the authenticity of the Pocket Books edition, and to justify our higher price of fifty cents.

Pocket Books did not take our statement lying down. They cajoled some guy in Brooklyn who had a bookmobile—not even a bona fide bookseller!—to sue us for unfair competition. How could little he compete against Big Bad Grove, which was casting aspersions on his wares and claiming his purveyor was a downright dirty pirate? To make the farce even more absurd, Simon and Schuster hired Thomas E. Dewey to represent the bookmobile fellow. Thomas Dewey, no less! Counterpunching, Rembar hired the head of the Brooklyn Bar Association, who probably had more clout than Dewey in his native habitat. The suit ended up in magistrate's court, a level of the judiciary that, Barney lamented, was generally reserved for cases such as urinating in the subway. So the magistrate took one look at the case, so far above his head he could not even contemplate handling it, and threw it out.

But for every victory there were many defeats. To further complicate matters, two other publishers entered the lists, New American Library, whose virtue stemmed from its having published the expurgated version all these years, and Pyramid, a small and in our view loathsome Johnny-come-lately. In all, well over six million copies were sold of the various paperbacks. Had they all been ours, the financial crises of later years would never have occurred.

Roughly a month after the birth of Alexander, Barney had thrown a party at his house on Eleventh Street in the Village to celebrate the publication of *Lady Chatterley*. Grove was still in litigation, but why wait, when the book was already high on the *New York Times* bestseller list? It was a glittering affair, with dozens of writers and critics, fellow publishers, and a smattering of painters, including Larry Rivers, Howie Kanowitz, Jasper Johns, and Roy Lichtenstein, most of whom Barney knew from East Hampton. Post-Loly, Barney's new girlfriend was Linc Bonnell, herself a sculptress, a striking, lissome blonde who looked—and was—the epitome of American aristocracy: cool, a trifle remote, the perfect hostess. I had urged Jeannette not to attend so soon after giving birth, and she had reluctantly agreed. So, great was my surprise when the door opened half an hour into the party and there she stood, resplendent and regal in a new dress, her old trim self, her dark, cascading hair framing her face, her smile warming the room. Barney welcomed her with an enveloping hug, steered her to me. As I kissed her, I asked her nervously who was taking care of the kids. "The Howards," she said. "As soon as she heard about the party, Mrs. Howard volunteered immediately to babysit." The Howards were a couple, old enough to be our parents, who lived across the hall from us at Palmer House and with whom we had become close friends. Fine, but how in the world had she, Jeannette, gotten here? She stepped back and said, "I drove, of course!" Barney, who had met her only once before, at that Beckett lunch in Paris, went out of his way to introduce her to as many of the assembled guests as he could. He clearly liked the lady, and over the coming years, when work frustrations surfaced, she always carefully considered Barney's side before pronouncing herself. True, he was opinionated. True, he sought and savored the limelight. True, he could be irascible, shoot from the hip, court trouble unnecessarily. But, boy, did he have guts! He also had brains. And what other publishing house was even remotely as exciting as Grove? As always, I listened to her with a mixture of wonder and admiration, for I knew she possessed, and always had, an innate wisdom far beyond her years.

31 ❧

Back with Beckett

ROM THE TIME Barney read my essay on Beckett in *Merlin*, and our lunch in Paris where he asked me to help set up his meeting with Beckett, Grove had published several of Beckett's key works, starting with *Waiting for Godot* in 1954, which had a slow and decidedly checkered reception in the United States (as indeed it had had the year before in Paris), the American public obviously not ready for its pessimistic, eternally questioning—"Where now? Who now? When now?"—view of the world, as told by a couple of down-and-out clowns. Two years after its publication, it had sold only a few hundred copies. For any of the major, uptown houses, that initial "disaster" would doubtless have deterred them from going on with this strange duck Beckett, whose works of fiction were, if anything, more complex and daunting than the plays. But it had not stopped Grove, which over the next four years published the grand trilogy, *Molloy*, *Malone Dies*, and *The Unnamable*, in 1955, 1956, and 1958 and the plays *Endgame* and *Act Without Words I* also in 1958.

High on the agenda of the not-yet-published works in America was *Watt*, to which Grove had acquired the rights from Collection Merlin in 1954 in a series of complex and comic negotiations that would have made Chaplin proud. We—*Merlin*—had bought world rights directly from Beckett, in retrospect an act of folly on his part, but one must remember that the author had all but given up hope of ever seeing that novel in print after so many rejections from England over the years. Determined as we were to make Beckett the linchpin of our *Merlin* book program, we had also acquired the "European English-language rights" of *Molloy, Malone Dies,* and *The Unnamable* from Minuit. Since Barney was also negotiating to buy the American rights to these and other Beckett works, we had been in contact with him since April 1953 about working together, on translations, production, and distribution. In the middle of all these weighty transactions on both sides of the Atlantic sat Jérôme Lindon, whom both we and Grove were besieging with proposals for Beckett's work and clarification of the rights situation. Having told Barney we held world rights to *Watt,* which we firmly believed, for Beckett had granted them to us, we learned the author had written to Grove that *he* owned the rights, the news of which Barney imparted to Alex on June 18. Alex, Austryn, and I were all involved in these comic, if not cosmic, negotiations, the former two more than I that spring because of my absence from Paris. But on the weekends we had endless strategy discussions late into the night.

As if matters were not complicated enough, I went to see Lindon on August 10, for I could not believe, knowing his devotion to Beckett, that he would not want to publish *Watt.* But since he spoke no English, and had no intention at that point of involving himself in the early works written in that language—*More Pricks Than Kicks, Murphy,* and now *Watt*—we decided we should approach another publisher. George Plimpton, whom we had invited on the board of Collection Merlin, suggested we sell the French rights to the old-line house of Plon, with whom *The Paris Review* was allied. He put us in touch with a Monsieur Bourel, the director of Plon, who seemed interested but turned out to be a tough negotiator. Over several weeks we thrashed out terms, only to find that Lindon, for whom I had nothing but admiration, suddenly awoke to the fact that, *au contraire,* he *should* concern himself with Beckett's English-language works. Through us, he insisted on certain contractual restrictions that, ultimately, Monsieur Bourel found untenable. "In which case," wrote Lindon on October 30, "we are prepared to commit to the project ourselves and arrange for the French edition of *Watt* as soon as possible [*dans les plus brefs délais*]."

At our first lunch meeting in Paris back in September 1953, Barney had brought up the subject of *Watt,* for in signing Beckett earlier that year, he knew that much of the work would have to await translation, Beckett having informed all and sundry unequivocally that he had no interest in undertaking that task himself. *Watt,* on the contrary, was already available. Back then, the original idea—*Merlin's*—was that Grove should distribute four hundred copies of our edition in the States, first as a way of helping get Beckett published in America, second as a rather transparent ruse to lighten our inventory, for of the eleven hundred copies printed, we had orders for only about four hundred. At first Barney had agreed, but later he changed his mind and said Grove would need to print its own edition. Perhaps the notion of having to bring our magenta-covered *Watt* through customs, with all its bureaucratic red tape and surly censorious habits, determined his decision. In any event, shortly after I had arrived at Grove five years later, *Watt* had still not been published in the States.

One summer morning in 1959, Barney asked me if by chance I had a copy of the Merlin edition. I did, but it was copy letter *L* of the limited, signed, *hors commerce* edition, and something in the very back of my mind, which was filled with the detritus of my almost thirty-three years, therefore clogged as the most laden of ancient arteries, warned me that this precious relic was in serious jeopardy. Still, newly hired and intent on making a good impression, I admitted I did, wondering out loud why it mattered. Barney cleared the air by asking if I might bring it in, if not on the morrow, then within the next day or two. I said I would, made a note not to forget, and stuck the tiny reminder in my breast pocket, unless it was the left trouser pocket, the one with the hole, which I must remember to ask Jeannette to sew. Searching two days later, I could not find the note, and penciled another—WATT: SEARCH AND FIND. BRING TO OFFICE—this time making sure to add it to the bulging contents of my wallet, carried loosely, all too loosely, in my back trouser pocket, an invitation to theft, where I promptly forgot it again. When a week later Barney reminded me, I called home, had Jeannette fetch it from our Bronxville bookshelf, and duly brought it to the office next morning, offering it as if on a platter soaked in blood, for I feared for its fate. Next day Barney called me in, where I found him fondling the off-white relic.* He thought we might use it to print the Grove edition, which he wanted to bring out as soon as possible, for the contract was about to expire. "Offset" was the term he used, as I recall, a word with which I was scarcely familiar. "But you would return it after use," I said. Of course. It would have to be dismantled, to be sure, but would be carefully glued back together when no longer needed. And some corrections would have to be made, at the request of the author. Would it not be easier, I asked, in my innocence or ignorance, to simply reset using the

---

*Only the regular edition was the "awful magenta." The *hors commerce* copies were a lovely off-white.

Merlin text? It would save Grove several hundred dollars if we offset, was the response. Since I knew my new company was far from well-heeled, despite the stories of Barney's untold Chicago wealth, I was ready to consent. But then I remembered that Barney some years before had described, to Trocchi or perhaps even to me, the Merlin typesetting as "scrubby and ugly." I ventured as much, perhaps in kinder terms. He leafed through the volume, shaking his head from time to time, and concluded: "It seems fine to me."

In the six years since my lunch with Barney in Paris, Beckett had become, or was fast becoming, one of the stars of the house. For the moment *Lady Chatterley* was the North Star, shining brightly in the Grove firmament, and Henry Miller, just over the horizon, was poised to be the house's aurora borealis, electric and electrifying, but Beckett would soon outshine them all. New works no longer poured from him as they had in that magic postwar period of the early 1950s, and in response to queries about new works in the offing, the reply was most often that the well was dry, or new efforts so painful they had to be abandoned. Nonetheless, shorter plays and prose works filtered in, always accompanied by comments of self-deprecation—not sure, not sure these should be published, let me know what you think. Curiously, for having in the late 1940s switched to writing in French and seemingly having found his true voice there, suddenly some of the newer works arrived in English, starting with *Krapp's Last Tape*. Perhaps, I suggested one morning to Barney, he was simply weary of translating his French into English. To which Barney replied that the problem still remained, for with *Krapp* and the other prose and plays in English, only he could turn them into French.

32 ~

Reenter Trocchi

ONE MORNING only a few short months after I had joined Grove, I arrived at the office to find a scrawled note from Barney on my desk bearing two words: SEE ME! I asked Judith if he was in, and her reply of "Oh, yes!" raised both my curiosity and my pulse, her "Oh, yes!" fraught with heavy implications I was too new to grasp. Till now my relations with Barney had been all sweetness and light, but I figured I must now have committed some unpardonable sin, for his scrawled handwriting spelled anger. "Come in!" came the voice behind the door, and I entered to find Rosset agitated.

Fingering a piece of paper on his desk, he nodded two or three times. No gesture for me to take a seat, but a scowl of deep concern. "Your friend Trocchi," he said, "is back in town." Well, better than Mack the Knife, I thought. "He wants to see me." Barney shook his head. "I'm not seeing him. *You* are." I shrugged. I hadn't seen Alex in five or six years, and though we had drifted apart before I left Paris, I still thought of him as a friend and colleague. He and Barney had exchanged a number of letters after I left Paris in mid-1954, mostly about Beckett, and they were cordial. But at his one meeting with the Scotsman, Barney had found him overbearing, even menacing. And that was before Alex had been deep into drugs. Trocchi had dabbled when we were in Paris, but now he was apparently a full-fledged addict, hooked on heroin. "He called about the novel he's writing, an extract of which we published in *Evergreen* a couple years ago that came to us unsolicited, without return address, so we never knew where to find him. Frankly, I doubt he'll ever finish it." Still, I countered, in all fairness we should take a look. "Okay," Barney said, "but keep him away from me."

A couple days later, Frieda announced: "A Mr. Trocchi for you." I picked up the receiver with a mixture of anticipation and slight trepidation. "Dick," he said, "I didn't know you were at Grove." The same voice, warm, friendly, seductive. Time collapsed; I was hooked. He had found a job as a scow captain, plying between Queens and the Hudson, hauling sand and gravel. "I was a valued employee of the Trap Rock Construction Company." He laughed. "You'll recall I'm an accomplished scow man," he said, referring to the hero of *Young Adam*, Joe, whose similar job in Glasgow we all presumed was based on Trocchi himself. The job had given him ample opportunity to write. The new book was set in New York. "I'm calling it *Cain's Book*," he explained. Any biblical connection? I asked. "Of course." From his voice he was the same.

When he entered my office the following Tuesday, he looked exactly the same: imperiously tall, his smile as seductive as ever. Only the eyes seemed different, more sunken, and where they had always been in repose, self-assured, now they darted nervously about from time to time, as if checking the terrain to make sure it was safe. In his hand he was bearing a manila envelope, wrinkled and slightly stained. Thin. I had been hoping for a full manuscript, but this was clearly only a fragment. Suddenly I wondered if Barney wasn't right: he'd probably never finish it . . .

We chatted about Paris, about *Merlin*, about Christopher and Austryn, the former back in England, the latter ensconced in the south of France with his new wife. Patrick was now Paris editor of our old rival, *The Paris Review*. Olympia, while not on the rocks, was in dubious shape, Maurice threatening to pull up stakes and move his operation here. No, I hadn't had any correspondence with him for years. Grove had bought *Naked Lunch* from him, but had no immediate plans to bring it out until the legal waters had been tested with *Chatterley*. "I heard about that," Alex said, nodding. "Brave move . . ." No, Maurice was not paying him any royalties for all the books he had written and translated, roughly a dozen. He couldn't fully blame Maurice for the nonpayment. Two or three years earlier, the French vice squad had walked into the rue de Nesle, seized twenty-five Olympia titles, including *Lolita*, and banned them all. According to Alex, Maurice had sued the government to have the ban lifted, but between the legal fees and the seizure of books he was virtually bankrupt.

Jane? He said they were out of touch. When he saw my expression, Alex hastened to add: "I was the best man at her wedding." Never fantasize about the lives of others: you'll always be wrong.

Alex asked about Jeannette. We had a two-year-old child, a girl named Nathalie, and another babe in arms, Alexander. "Named after me?" Trocchi smiled. "Could be," I said, though I knew it was not. "Fatherhood ain't easy," he added, pulling out his wallet and showing me a picture of a handsome baby boy. "Mark," he said. Then he flipped to a picture of his wife, Lyn. A startling beauty from nearby Long Island. Married on Long Island? I asked. He laughed. "As far away as possible, in Tijuana, Mexico. Lyn's parents did not approve. They'd heard stories about me that probably whitened their hair."

He was back to his life on the scow, the setting for the novel. Lonely but productive. His fellow scow captains a strange, disparate lot, many at rock bottom, either willing to stay there because the job came with a furnished cabin, however spare, or using it as a way station to a better life. His only problem had been the curiosity in some when they had heard the clicking of typewriter keys next door: What kind of man working on a scow would waste his time bent over a typewriter?

"Read the pages," he said, nodding at the envelope, "and tell me what you think."

I pulled out the manuscript. About twenty-five or thirty pages, I calculated. Was this all that the time on the scow had produced? "I'll read them tonight," I said.

He stood, we shook hands. "Good to see you, Dick. It would be nice to work together again."

After I had escorted him out, Barney, seeing me pass his office, gestured me in.

"That took a long time," he ventured. "What's he want?"

"He's back to *Cain's Book*," I said. "He gave me some pages, which I'll read tonight."

"What makes you think he'll ever finish? Have you read that piece in *Evergreen*? If you have, you'll know he's deep into drugs."

"From what he told me today, those *Evergreen* pages are the opening chapter of the book. What he gave me today is chapter 2 . . . Barney, I haven't seen the man in five years, so we have a lot of catching up to do.

Anyway, even if he's a junkie, he can't be any more addicted than Burroughs. And Burroughs can clearly write. The question is, can Trocchi?"

That night I read Alex's pages aloud to Jeannette. She was still intrigued by him; but as someone who loathed the very notion of drugs, she was worried.

Next day I poked my head in Barney's office, told him that the Trocchi was first-rate. Instead of looking pleased, he greeted the news with a frown. We already had *Naked Lunch* under contract. Did we really need another heroin addict on the list? It's very different from Burroughs, I said. Do you want to read the pages? He waved the suggestion aside. Not now, not now. How much is he going to want as an advance? I'm sure not that much. Heroin doesn't come cheap, Barney reminded me. Anyway, remember how long it took Burroughs to write *Naked Lunch*—five years? ten? I'll make most of the advance contingent on delivery, I suggested. He nodded. We settled on an advance of $750, a fraction of what we had paid for *Naked Lunch*. Half up front, the rest contingent on further segments turned in. I argued for more, just a tad, but that was as far as Barney would go. I felt that he would have been pleased if Trocchi turned down the offer and disappeared. See any legal problems with it? Barney asked. I shook my head. Not so far. Good, he said.

Trocchi called. Did he have any more pages? I asked. Yes, another twenty or so. Could he bring them in? What about a contract? I said we'd give him one; we'd discuss terms when he got here. When he arrived, looking more groomed this time, he bore an envelope containing not twenty but only twelve pages. No apparent continuity with the earlier material. If we received only fragments, would they ever fit together? Contract, what about the contract? Did I detect a tinge of panic? More than a tinge . . . I cited the figure Barney and I had agreed on for the advance, then, in a moment of lucidity, aided by the opening lines of *Molloy*—

> There's this man who comes every week . . . He gives me money and takes away the pages. So many pages, so much money . . . When I've done nothing he gives me nothing, he scolds me . . .

—told him we'd be paying in segments. He looked stricken. "That's pretty niggardly, Dick," he said, shaking his head. "It doesn't exactly show a lot of confidence, does it? Even Maurice did better than that."

"I'm afraid so. Part of the problem is that we've got *Naked Lunch* under contract, and Barney's questioning whether we need . . ."

"Another junkie?" Alex finished, looking hurt. "Tell him *Cain's Book* will be as far from *Naked Lunch* as . . . as *Chatterley* is from *Tropic of Cancer*."

"Look," I said, "I'd be happy to go back to Barney and see what I can do, but be forewarned, if he's in the wrong mood, he's liable to say fuck it. Maybe you should shop it around and see if you can come up with some more money. I'd understand."

"The other houses," he said with clear disdain, "are full of shit. They're scared of their own fucking shadow. I've talked to some editors, and they all think I'm a druggie nutcase."

We would pay him the day he delivered. How about today? Could he be paid for the first two installments? He looked desperate and suddenly pathetic. I excused myself, found he could be paid, but only by check. Trocchi shook his head. Cash, he said, he would need cash. I told him he would have to come back tomorrow. Well, could I lend him a hundred dollars? I didn't have that much to hand. Could we go to the bank and get it? I felt trapped, but mostly depressed. Sure, I said, and we walked the three blocks to the Manufacturers Hanover branch at Ninth Street and University Place, where I withdrew the money from my personal account. He clutched it, as a castaway an elusive life preserver, shook my hand warmly, and scurried off—yes, that was the term, his movement now agitated, almost confused. That, I told myself, watching him decamp, was the major difference between then and now: in Paris his pace had been measured and self-assured; today it was hurried, harried, dictated not by an inner rhythm but by some outer imperative.

There were weeks when Alex did not arrive at an appointed hour, nor send any word, and when finally he did appear, it was usually without warning, which made it hard to pay him as he delivered, often pulling me out of a meeting and refusing to leave until the barrelhead had been greened. Barney noted my irritation and told me more than once that I had asked for it. He needled me, too, about the manuscript's snail-like progress, and I had to admit it was frustrating. So many pages, so much money. But, I added, when they came, the pages were invariably good. Will they fit together? Barney wanted to know, doubtless remembering *Naked Lunch*. I said there would have to be some juggling once the manuscript was in, certainly, but a book there would be. A good book. He was reassured, at least momen-

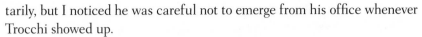

tarily, but I noticed he was careful not to emerge from his office whenever Trocchi showed up.

When on one occasion several weeks had elapsed without word, I became worried and asked several of our mutual New York friends for news of Trocchi. The only one who had heard was George Plimpton, who said Alex had hit him up for small sums—twenty, thirty, once fifty dollars—as advances against a short story he would "shortly" be sending for *The Paris Review.* I asked George how Trocchi looked. There was a pause on the other end of the phone, as if he were searching for the proper words. "Not well," he said. "'Disheveled' I guess is the term . . . I gather you know that he got arrested." I didn't. "I don't know the details," George said.

When at last Alex showed, looking far better than George had described him, I pointedly asked if he was in trouble with the law. Again the hurt look. "Of course not, Dick. Whatever else I am, I'm discreet. Very discreet. I deal only with people I know, who are all trustworthy. Besides, Lyn has been on me to get clean, and I'm working on it." Like all gullible people who want to believe what they know in their heart is a lie, I told him how important that move was, even congratulated him. And, to buttress what he said, the pages he delivered that day were among his best.

Another two weeks went by without word, and with Barney breathing down my neck over the good money I'd thrown out the window for a book that would never be, I decided one afternoon to pay Alex a visit. He lived only a dozen blocks away. I climbed the dreary steps to his door and knocked, thinking as I did what a terrible idea it had been to come, especially without warning. I heard noises inside, a familiar voice asking, "Who is it?" and at the one-word answer "Dick," further scurrying. When the door finally cracked open, Alex appeared clad only in Jockey shorts. Lyn was still in bed. The place was a rat's nest. Clothes strewn about the whole loft, furniture the Salvation Army would have snubbed, the ashtrays filled with cigarette stubs from among which thrust literally dozens of needles. A glass of water and spoon on the bed table. The kitchen sink was filled with unwashed dishes, to which clung remnants of food dating from the Year One. To complete the picture, I stepped, with a loud squashing noise, on a cockroach the size of a mouse. It was one of the most embarrassing moments of my life, and I was about to apologize and beat a rapid retreat when my hosts, who after the unexpected intrusion seemed quite at ease, invited me in as if my visit were perfectly normal. "A spot of tea, old man?"

Trocchi chirped, pulling on a pair of khaki pants and wrestling a sweater over his head. "So nice of you to stop by." I shook my head. "I really can't stay. But since I hadn't heard from you, I began to worry." Now Trocchi apologized, moved over to a long table, swept debris from his typewriter, rummaged among yellow foolscap, and dexterously emerged with a thin pile of typewritten pages. "Voilà!" he said, handing me the manuscript. I thanked him but said I didn't have the cash with me to pay for them. He shook his head, as if that were his last worry, he'd stop by tomorrow to pick it up. The teakettle began whistling, and Lyn, who had by now risen, was rinsing three cups, and we sat down as if to Alice's Tea Party. I felt deep, very deep in the rabbit hole as I struggled for conversation. For it was clear that Lyn, far from easing Alex off the habit, was just as hooked as he. Once again, Jeannette had been right. I was truly sad. Then a terrible thought crossed my mind: Where was little Mark? I decided not to ask.

Standing to leave, I asked when I might expect more pages, and Alex grinned, pointed to the still-half-buried typewriter, and assured me there would be more "within the week," adding, "We're almost there." I now had more than 150 pages, which, according to Trocchi's original assessment some months back, was roughly half the manuscript but which, he now told me, represented a good two-thirds. "I can't really edit it until I have the complete manuscript," I said, lamely I knew, but again Alex assured me he was working every day. Glancing around, trying not to be judgmental, I knew he was lying through his tobacco-stained teeth.

To my surprise, Trocchi began to deliver the rest of the pages on a fairly regular basis. I was delighted, though I learned the impetus was largely that George Plimpton, John Marquand, Peter Matthiessen, and apparently every other soft touch in town had cut him off, so I had presumably become his prime source of income for the next hit. That illusion was shattered the next time I saw George, at a glitterati party at his sumptuous waterside digs on East Seventy-second Street.

I'd known George for the better part of a decade now and liked him immensely. We had become close friends. When we first met in Paris seven or eight years before, his patrician accent had put me off—was this real or affected?—but as the months rolled by, I decided the slightly English upper-class speech pattern was part and parcel of the package: you either took it or left it. I realized that behind the seeming affectation was a serious young man who cared deeply about literature and the world. Still, I often felt oddly alien at his parties, for most of the people there—men and women—seemed entrenched members of the uptown establishment—

literary, political, social—whereas I was a downtown, dyed-in-the-wool outsider.

That night, amid the cocktail buzz, George took me aside and asked me if I'd heard that Lyn was now on the streets. "You mean . . . on the *streets?*" He nodded. "Jesus!" was the only word I could muster. "Not only that," George confided, "this isn't a recent turn of events. Apparently, it goes back as far as Vegas. Maybe before. From what I've heard," he said, "it wasn't Alex who forced her. When they reached a point where they couldn't scrape up enough to eat out in Venice, it was Lyn who suggested they move to Vegas, where she knew she could score . . ." At which he was whisked away to sit down at the piano and, revealing one more talent, tickle out some pretty mean jazz.

33 ∿

Coenties Slip (At Last!)

FOR ALMOST TWO YEARS we had known that suburban life was not for us. On our return from Venezuela with nothing afford-able to be had in the Village and with Nathalie clamoring to be born, we had felt lucky to find our apartment in Bronxville in the nick of time. But now, with our lease expiring, it was time to leave.

Friends and neighbors thought we were crazy. "Two young children," they would cluck, "that's the time people *leave* the city, not rush back to it." For us the only question was where.

Again, serendipity: Jack and Delphine, having decided to forsake Paris at least for a while and, like us, give New York a try, he as an artist with two or three one-man Paris shows behind him, she as a budding actress, had recently found a building in lower Manhattan, on Coenties Slip, a four-story prerevolutionary brick edifice that in its earlier life had been a sail-maker's loft. Jack, Delphine, and their three-year-old son, Duncan, lived on the third floor, and Jack's studio was the top floor. On a weekend in May, with Nathalie and Alexander in tow, we drove the old Studebaker down to look at it, fell immediately in love with the romantic old house, and de-cided on the spot to move there. Its full floor of fifteen hundred square feet was more than double the size of Bronxville. The comforting cacophony of the tugboats plying the waters at the nearby confluence of the Hudson and East rivers, incessantly sounding their horns, and the privacy of the area, which after five was virtually empty as the denizens of the nearby Financial District scurried to their suburban homes, combined to make the place irresistible, especially when we learned that our share of the monthly rent would be $75.

A couple of drawbacks: there was no grocery store within miles, in fact no stores at all. No nipping out to pick up some last-minute item at nine or ten at night. And, oh, yes, the other, minor problem: the building was illegal. A later law allowed AIRs—Artists in Residence—to live and work in some of these buildings, which were specially designated, but that was still a couple years away.

What the hell, it was too tempting to pass up. Move in on a Saturday, when no one was around, which we did with the help of a moving company, the Padded Wagon. The first thing we did, emulating the Youngermans, was rig up an adjustable mirror outside our bathroom window that overlooked the front door, to monitor any visitor. Only friends and neighbors allowed. To all others we would play dead. Cops. Robbers. Firemen. You name it.

We weren't totally alone down there: Ellsworth Kelly had also moved back from Paris and lived just up the street. Also another painter, Agnes Martin, a generation older but still struggling as an artist. Bob Indiana. Across the little park—appropriately named Jeannette Park (which they had unforgivably misspelled "Janet")—that fronted our building was the Seamen's Church Institute, a snug harbor for old or out-of-work sailors, where one could go for a simple but palatable dinner now and then for virtually nothing. If you opted for upscale, there was always Sloppy Louie's up the street a couple of blocks. The Youngermans had invested in a Vespa, stored under the stairs in the first-floor entrance, and twice a week Jeannette and Delphine would straddle the pale green mount and head northward to Canal Street to grocery shop, two pretty Parisian lasses, hair flying in the wind, before long the wonder and envy not only of the lower Broadway merchants but especially of staid Wall Streeters out for a midday stroll, who would pause in their three-piece suits to stare at these two young women careening in their hiked-up skirts through the cavernous avenues of their territory, like alluring aliens from a planet far, far away.

34 ～

The (Over)Heated *Tropics*

WITH *Lady Chatterley* barely out of the gate and still embattled, we had already begun plans for publishing Henry Miller's *Tropic of Cancer,* banned not only here but in virtually every country worldwide. It struck me as an act of near madness, but I toned down my concern and simply suggested to Barney one day that it might be prudent to put Lawrence behind us before committing to Miller. He shook his head, grinned that bad-boy grin, which I had quickly learned meant "I know this is wrong, but ain't we having fun," and said the timing was out of his control. Already at the end of last year, he had been in correspondence with my old friend Maurice Girodias about Miller, he explained, both because Girodias was an old friend of Miller's and because he alone knew of the publishing complexities concerning the rights to *Tropic of Cancer.* When the French publishing giant Hachette had bought Maurice's troubled house, Les Éditions du Chêne, in 1950, they had automatically obtained rights to the *Tropics,* which Maurice had inherited from his father's Obelisk Press. Under that arrangement, neither Miller nor Hachette could sell any rights to the *Tropics* without the other's consent. This already complicated matters, for Miller had a Paris agent, Michael Hoffman, whose opinion he valued and who was not at all sure the time was ripe to have these explosive works published in the States. And just the other day, Barney said, he had heard from Girodias that a copy of *Tropic of Cancer* sent from Paris to an American professor had been released by customs, which could mark a breakthrough, but, Maurice had also pointed out, the attendant publicity might also encourage other publishers, aware of the enormous success of Nabokov's *Lolita* the previous year, to move in on the *Tropics*. So there was no time to lose. However, where Henry Miller himself was concerned, two not insignificant problems had to be faced. First, Henry was now happily ensconced in Southern California, completing a new opus, *Nexus*, but spending most of his time painting, and not at all sure he wanted his banned works published here. Michael Hoffman agreed. All the fuss and furor, bringing Henry back from his carefully chosen wings to center stage, certainly to controversy, if not judicial attack: Did he really need that at this late stage of his life? Second, Henry already had an American publisher, Jay Laughlin of New Directions, who had been faithful to him through the years, though admittedly he had published only the non-censorable books. Miller would have to offer *Cancer* to New Directions first. Nonetheless, Barney had sent a telegram to Miller in late March, offering publication of *Tropic of Cancer* by Grove, with an advance of fifty thousand dollars, huge for us.* On April 4, Miller wrote back thanking Barney but as predicted mentioning his obligation to offer the book first to New Directions, adding that in any event he thought "any attempt to publish these books [*Cancer* and *Capricorn*] was premature." But added that he would take further counsel from Michael Hoffman when he, Henry, was there on the seventeenth.

Five days after that first letter, Miller wrote again, in response to two more cajoling letters Barney had written, one of which enclosed an advance copy of *Lady Chatterley*.

> With your last two letters came one from Girodias (delayed in mails), which made me feel I know you better. Thus far I have heard nothing from either my agent in Paris . . . or from James Laughlin, whom I wrote about your offer. I'll be in Paris on the 17th and will see everyone . . .
>
> This morning Lady Chatterley came . . . Looks good. And it is, of course, a big step forward. But how slowly everything proceeds. The "Cancer" will be 25 years old this September. Soon I'll be dead. I've lived

---

*Huge for anybody: today's equivalent would be roughly a quarter of a million, maybe more.

so long without my rightful earnings I'm used to it now. One has to die first, if you notice, before the ball gets rolling.

I'll write you again from Paris, when I know more . . .

A week later Maurice wrote a long letter to Barney saying he had seen both Miller and Hoffman the day before and again outlining in more detail the Miller-Hachette rights situation. He also raised for the first time the problematic nature of Miller's copyright to these titles in the United States:

> I am not unaware of the copyright situation . . . Probably the best thing you have to do now, before you come, is to write another letter to Hachette . . . outlining the danger of a pirated edition being published at any time in the States, now that the publication of books like "Lolita" and "Lady Chatterley" has changed the standards of censorship in America. They are certainly unaware of the copyright problems (which are very different here). So you should explain to them why the danger is real, and immediate.*

Meanwhile, in Paris, Girodias had met with Miller and his fourth wife, Eve, at the home of Miller's French translator and old friend Georges Belmont. There he pressed Grove's case: fifty thousand dollars was not to be sneezed at, especially since the publisher would hold Henry harmless in case of litigation—that is, Grove would bear all legal costs, indemnifying Miller. Later the next night, after Miller had gone to bed, Maurice took Eve out to a nightclub in Montparnasse, Elle et Lui, where they danced the night away and where, once again, he raised the subject of American publication. She was all for it, she assured Girodias, but she reminded him that where they lived in California, Big Sur, wealth was frowned upon. Most of the residents were there because of the quiet and beauty, and were the *Tropics* to appear, their peace would be lost forever. Already, she said, despite the relative isolation of the place, fans of Henry's work kept intruding—to such a degree that Henry had engaged a friend, Emil White, to fend them off. They would be better off in another town or city, but Henry loved being there and never planned to leave.

It would be another year before the Grove-Miller deal would finally be consummated. More than once over that time, Eve pressed the case with

---

Review of Contemporary Fiction (Fall 1990), pp. 77–78.

Henry. The terrain was further prepared when, the following winter, Miller flew again to Paris, where he consulted with Hoffman before entraining for Hamburg to visit his German publisher, Heinrich Ledig-Rowohlt, the head of Rowohlt Verlag, a convivial, carefree man whom Miller esteemed and enjoyed, for he was not only his faithful publisher but also a reveler, a man of zest and great good humor, who wined and dined his authors with consummate charm and who, to top off an evening, would often in the wee hours rise from his chair, retreat a dozen yards from the end of the table well laden with glasses and bottles, race forward as if heading for a pole vault without a pole, and somersault over the groaning board without breaking a glass or, incredibly, his neck. What other German publisher could offer his well-oiled authors anything close?

Ledig, as he was known, was the illegitimate son of the company's founder who had pointedly retained his mother's name in his surname to let the world know that he was proud of his maternal background. Since he had taken over the publishing house after the war, he had lifted it to new levels, with a keen eye both for young German writers and for foreigners whose work had been ignored or repressed during the long Nazi night, Hemingway for one. His impeccable anti-Nazi wartime credentials had won him the immediate favor of the occupying forces as early as 1945, with the accompanying perks—access to paper, printing and binding facilities, warehouse space—that had enabled him to build the company rapidly into a publishing powerhouse. He was also among the earliest to recognize the need for reasonably priced books in Germany and had started a mass-market paperback line of rare distinction, Rororo. Miller talked to Ledig about his friend and Paris-based English-language publisher, Maurice Girodias, whose joie de vivre he touted, and they decided he should be invited to join them in their Hamburg revels.

Everyone was in a positive and convivial mood, and Girodias again raised the idea of American publication. Henry relented, calling Hoffman in Paris, who cabled Barney in New York, urging him to catch a plane to Hamburg, with a copy of the contract in hand and, of course, a check for fifty thousand dollars. For Grove, whose advances in those days were in the low thousands, or more often in the high hundreds, this was a mighty leap of financial faith. But Barney, unlike Jay Laughlin at New Directions, was ready to bet the house on Henry Miller.

It took Barney three days to arrive in Hamburg, his plane to London having been diverted to Glasgow, where he was grounded for two days before flying down to London and thence to Hamburg. During his forty-eight hours in Hamburg, Barney found a radically changed Miller, no longer glum and negative but cheerful and full of beans, even challenging Barney to a game of Ping-Pong. In the course of two days, the contract was signed, the check handed over, and the future of Grove assured. Surely the publication of *Tropic of Cancer* in America had to be a huge success.

Or were the problems over its publication about to begin?

When they had first met a year or so before, Barney and Maurice, recognizing an instant affinity, had sensed they had much in common both personally and professionally. But theirs was a fragile friendship, born in a mood of celebration, and one that would not long endure. Among other things, what Maurice would soon realize was that Grove's forthcoming battle against censorship in America would, in relatively short order, bring down the embattled walls of his little Parisian kingdom. Olympia's success rested squarely on the still-Victorian attitudes toward sex both in England and in America. As long as anti-obscenity laws prevailed in the English-speaking world, Olympia's increasing output and growing backlist—which in a number of cases now reprinted every few weeks—had a virtual monopoly. Still, on that heady day in Hamburg, as the several parties toasted to the future of the *Tropics* in America, the only clouds on the horizon were those, dark and lowering, that hovered over that harsh northern German city on the Elbe.

35 ∾

Frankfurt bei Nacht

MY MEMORY of the Frankfurt Book Fair, to which I had first gone two years before for George Braziller, was of chilling rain, unfriendly waiters, and the Boschean vision of presumably sane publishers rushing madly to and fro through Halle Fünf—Hall Five—from one appointment to another as if their very lives depended on it, which they probably did. So when Barney announced in midsummer I'd of course be going to Frankfurt with him, I was not overjoyed. On that earlier trip I had been alone, a novice in publishing, with few contacts and only a vague idea of what kinds of books George might be interested in for a house that was still only a gleam in his eye, so I concentrated on books that I thought might work for one of the book clubs, which meant essentially art books. For fun, I tried one or two of the city's underground *Weinkellers*, where by ten or eleven o'clock at night the locals were swilling beer a-go-go and breaking into what sounded disturbingly like army marching songs that sent chills up my spine. Strolling the streets at night, I had stumbled upon a warren of strip joints, smack in the city center, dark and dreary, that struck me as the saddest I had ever seen.* Even the posters

---

*Years later, ten to be exact, when Jean Genet came to New York, he asked Jeannette to escort him to the sex parlors at Times Square, which he declared utterly joyless. But my money's on Frankfurt's warrens.

outside that advertised the delights within made one shrink, literally. My modest hotel near the train station, whose only virtue I could detect was relative cleanliness, became a welcome refuge after my brief nocturnal explorations.

I had been there a full three days before I suddenly realized, upon turning a corner and seeing the colonnaded facade of the Frankfurter Hof Hotel, that I had already passed this way before a decade earlier, on my trip with the cartoonist George Booth through a demolished and devastated Germany that, we both predicted, would never rise again, certainly not in our lifetimes. Well, by God, in nine years it had indeed risen, changed so much that, until the sudden landmark, I had recognized nothing, the rubble having been used to erect a whole new city, stone by stone, though vestiges of its leveled self remained everywhere you looked. Not a handsome city—ugly in fact—but impressive by the speed with which its transformation had occurred. How could this recent wasteland have the temerity, the chutzpah, to host the world's publishers as if the Holocaust had never happened? Why had the victors, France or England, not seized the opportunity to house the fair *chez eux*? Imagine an international book fair under the fair skies of Nice. Even in cloudy Paris or London. But there you are, Frankfurt am Main had seized the day, despite the fact that there was a scarcity of hotel rooms, transportation was hit-or-miss, and the food was at best edible, unless *Wurst mit Kartoffel* was high on your culinary list. The explanation, I was told, was that before the war—or more precisely before Hitler—the most famous international book fair had been at Leipzig, now in walled-off East Germany, so Frankfurt had picked up the tradition as if slipping into new clothes.

Unlike most publishers, Grove had no booth at the fair, but we quickly assumed the role of strolling players, visiting the stands of those we knew or were interested in: Gallimard and Seuil in France; Rowohlt in Germany; Einaudi and Feltrinelli in Italy; Faber and Weidenfeld in England; Seix Barral in Spain. At Faber, I hooked up again with my friend Matthew Evans and exchanged editorial notes. Matthew, the freshest voice in British publishing, who had come to visit me at Grove a few months before, suffered fools poorly and had a great gift for poking fun at the stuffed shirts of his chosen profession. We lunched together more than once, Matthew reserving his caustic wit for the Germans now, wondering what he, or any of us, was doing in this beleaguered land of fog, rain, and rubble.

The focus of the fair in that fall of 1959 was clearly Girodias's Olympia Press, whose discovery *Lolita* was still riding high on the bestseller lists worldwide. No matter that Nabokov had disowned him and was openly refusing to support his lawsuits against the French government in his behalf, Girodias's booth was a hotbed of solicitation and intrigue. What's your next big book? What are you bringing out next season that might work for America? Maurice's faithful assistant, Miriam Worms, we learned, was reported to have been the object of attempted bribes if only she would reveal what Maurice had planned for the fall and winter. She duly reported all this to Maurice, whose chest swelled accordingly and who hoisted himself immediately at least one rung higher on the ladder of self-esteem.

Upon arrival Barney had rented a car, which he used post-dinner to case joints near and far for fun and games, usually accompanied by the other two mad Musketeers, John Calder, the English publisher, and Maurice, with me and one or two other would-be revelers squeezed in. Despite the countless obligations with the German press and booksellers that limited his nocturnal forays, Ledig-Rowohlt was cajoled into coming. At each joint, the obligatory drink or two brought a girl of the night to perch at one's table, offering the bounties of her rarely tempting self, then off again to the next spot until two or three or four in the morning. Inevitably, there came a time when, emerging from some low-down lair even more depressing than the previous, we headed for the car to find it had disappeared. "Are you sure it was down this *Straße*?" "Absolutely!" "Let's check a bit farther along." No Avis. No Europcar. That Hertz! Ha-ha-ha! So down another *Straße*, to no avail. Hey, taxi! Frankfurter Hof, *bitte*! As dawn impinged upon semiconsciousness two or three hours later, a double coffee—which required some doing, for German coffee at the time was among the worst in the world—failed to reveal what had happened to the rented car, whose color and make evaded all our still-addled minds. "Never mind," Barney would mumble as he picked up the phone to report to Hertz that his car had, alas, been stolen. "Not to worry, we'll send another over to you today." So the next night, true to form, having suffered a dozen meetings that morning and afternoon, to discuss books in which we had no interest, or so little it was difficult to stay awake as the earnest presentations scraped across the remnants of our brains, we'd set off, in an Opel or Volkswagen or Ford whose mark we would write down on a scrap of paper to make sure we remembered in the morning, to repeat the Dantesque rounds. By day three I, hitherto of sound body and relatively unimpaired mind, was what is commonly called a wreck, whereas to my barely disguised jealousy Barney seemed fit as a fiddle. I noted that Calder, a gnome of a man whose cherubic and rotund exterior belied a sly and crafty mind constantly at work, looked worse than I, if that were possible. To my dismay, Girodias looked as though he had just won the lottery, and when I commented to Miriam about his disconcerting ability to rebound from a long white night, she simply said: "He has a long history . . . ," which explained nothing and everything. As for Barney, his irritating matinal alertness stemmed, I learned, from his long history of amphetamines. On the last day of the fair, when we were at our lowest ebb, George Weidenfeld collared us at nine in the morning, lording it over us zombies at his impressive stand, with a proposal for a dual history of France and England. The idea was, he enthused, that for the history of England he would have André Maurois, a Frenchman of note, and for the history of France an equally prestigious Englishman. Don't you see, he explained, each of these countries, which have been at each other's throats for centuries, will now have themselves treated and assessed by the other side, so to speak. Objective and prejudiced at the same time. Brilliant, no? Shall I count you in? Barney mumbled something I thought meant no and George assumed was full agreement. Fine! George thundered and reached over to shake Barney's still-sleeping paw, for he later admitted he had forgotten that morning to take his wake-up pill.

Pausing for coffee at a stand directly across from Weidenfeld and Nicolson, we stared into space for roughly a minute until Barney said: "What was George's crazy project?" I laid it out to him, fuzzily but with the general lines intact. "What a fucking stupid idea!" Barney said. "True," I said, "but I think you just shook hands on it." "Jesus, no!" he said. "Do you think he'll *hold* us to it?" I nodded. He ordered another cup of *dreckig* coffee.

"By the way," he said, "any idea where we left last night's car?"

"Not the foggiest," I said.

"Good," he said. "I'll call Hertz and have them send around another so we can get to the airport."

There were a miser's dozen of Frankfurts after that, with a changing cast of characters but similar traps and mishaps, until one day about halfway through the decade we laid down the law: WE BUY NO BOOKS AT THE FRANKFURT BOOK FAIR! We didn't sign it in blood, though we surely should have, for there inevitably came the early morning after the late night when we bought a book, or, God help us, a series of books we should doubtless have avoided like the pest. Still, among all the mistakes, from Frankfurt came two German worthies—maybe more, but these are all I remember without recourse to the archives: Rolf Hochhuth's *Deputy* and Uwe Johnson's *Speculations About Jakob*. It's possible, too, that Friedrich Dürrenmatt, most of whose plays we published starting in 1962, also emanated from the fair, though Dürrenmatt was Swiss, and there is a faint possibility that he came to us directly from Switzerland.

More important than any worthy or dubious acquisitions, however, were the friends one made at the fair over the years, publishers and editors from a dozen countries, though England and France were the sources of far more lasting bonds than the others. The breakfasts, lunches, dinners, and, yes, late, late nights we shared with our growing list of colleagues probably led to our acquisition of authors we would never have published otherwise. With our manifesto to not acquire at the fair itself, we followed up afterward, in quieter moments, when we had a chance to read and ponder before we leaped.

36 ❧

The United States v. *Tropic of Cancer*: Spring 1960

RATHER THAN PAVING THE WAY, the *Chatterley* "victory" actually posed new problems for Grove's plan to publish *Tropic of Cancer*. The federal unbanning of *Lady Chatterley* had sent a message to the arms of government that neither the Customs Service nor the Post Office could or should any longer involve itself in censorship. Fine. But the corollary of that was that now any state, indeed any town or city that took umbrage, could institute a suit, which is precisely what happened. In that glowing spring of 1960, none of us was under any illusion that winning with D. H. Lawrence meant an automatic triumph for Henry Miller. Miller's novels were far tougher to defend than *Chatterley*. Further, while he had many admirers on both sides of the Atlantic, Miller could not be described as a pillar of English literature. However much one admired him, he was a grubby street fighter compared with the English gentleman. We all knew, then, as we geared up for publication the following fall and winter, this would be a difficult fight—though nobody, starting with Barney, had any inkling how long, hard, and financially draining it would be. As with *Chatterley*, the copyright to Miller's works was highly ambiguous. Neither Jack Kahane nor his son had thought to protect the international rights to their authors' works, for their kingdoms by the Seine were self-contained and unforesightful in that respect. We had seen that the minute *Chatterley* was declared not obscene; vultures waiting in the wings had swooped down to feast on the beast, now no longer a dead issue.

Advance copies of *Tropic of Cancer* duly arrived from the printer, clothed in their demure bright blue jacket, and this time, upon careful examination, with no apparent errors to mar their appearance. The introduction was by another eminent critic, Karl Shapiro, whose opening line was meant to elevate Miller to Lawrence status and to warn away would-be censors: "I call Henry Miller the greatest living author . . ." But many people had been frustrated and upset by the *Chatterley* decision, and they were not about to let *Tropic of Cancer* enjoy the same fate. Almost as soon as *Tropic of Cancer* began shipping, there was trouble. Local officials in dozens of states took action against the book, rarely judicial, for a visit or phone call to a bookstore or wholesaler was generally enough to end the sale, assuming it had even started. In Rhode Island, the attorney general asked the wholesalers to "voluntarily" return the book cartons unopened. Thus of the 3,380 copies shipped to Rhode Island, 3,380 came back. In other states, police chiefs, sheriffs, county attorneys, literature commissions (read: censors), or unaffiliated vigilantes pressured stores and libraries not to put the book on sale or remove it from their shelves. In many states, Texas for one, there were seizures, which meant that books were not returned for possible reuse but destroyed. If the publication of *Chatterley* had to some degree slowed the pace of daily work in the Grove office, *Cancer* was, as its name implies, eating into the marrow of our bones. Most of Barney's energy, and a great deal of Fred's and mine, focused on the disturbingly increasing number of court cases, for wherever courageous booksellers stood firm, we had promised to defend them. Often the local defense attorneys required the testimony of some member of the Grove staff or some literary guru—or both—which meant we were sometimes out of the office for days. Our tireless attorney, Rembar, for his part, had no time to defend more than a couple of key appellate cases himself, for he and two colleagues, Shad Polier and Steven Tulin, were too busy preparing a dozen cases at once, counseling, advising, hiring, writing briefs, providing witnesses from coast to coast.

The first case occurred, perhaps predictably, in Boston in September 1961, handled this time for Grove by Ephraim London, who was called back on the scene. Despite London's excellence and the appearance of several impressive witnesses, the court ruled against us in no uncertain terms, the trial judge calling the book "filthy and disgusting," which propelled the case to the Massachusetts appellate court, to be argued by Rembar. His opponent was Edward J. McCormack, scion of a politically powerful Boston family whose uncle was a prominent congressman. Because of the standing of the Massachusetts court, which was held in general high esteem but also known for its conservative stance—one remembers the "Banned in Boston" line that publishers used to their advantage to stimulate sales—if Grove could win here, it might send a strong signal to the rest of the country. On the other hand, Rembar argued in the office one day, it might be better not to win on appeal, for one state's opinion did not necessarily carry weight beyond its borders. I found the idea appallingly intelligent, especially after Rembar gave us the mounting number—and costs—of the litigations still pending or decided countrywide. In Philadelphia, the book had been judged obscene; in Chicago, we had won; in California, there had been two trials: one win and one loss. In Syracuse, New York, three booksellers had been arrested and convicted by a jury of, presumably, their peers. On appeal, their conviction was upheld. And so it went, with our limited resources dwindling day by day. It was imperative, if only for survival, that we somehow get to the Supreme Court. Finally, in July 1962, the Massachusetts appellate court rendered its decision. By a vote of 4–3, it declared *Tropic of Cancer* not obscene. It was an important victory, for the three dissenters had in essence said that this must be settled not in Boston but in Washington. The Massachusetts attorney general, McCormack, had ninety days to appeal to the Supreme Court, but throughout that fall he was engaged in a primary battle for the Senate against the president's younger brother Teddy Kennedy, so we were not overly concerned as the days ticked slowly by. But as they approached the fateful ninety, Barney became stressed out, frantic. Inquiries to the north returned the stunning news that McCormack was apparently so traumatized by his devastating defeat in the Senate primary that he had been rendered politically impotent. So Massachusetts would not bring us to the Supreme Court to try to have that decision overturned after all!

Narrow victories, both in the high courts, both 4–3, first in Wisconsin and then in California, were comforting but, again, got the case no closer to the Supreme Court, for there was nothing for it to rule on. We were now in 1963, two years after the book's publication, and again, as feared, we had had to forsake the hardcover edition and quickly issue a paperback, for the pirates, even more voracious, had profited from the Post Office's non-involvement and the dubious copyright to rush out their own paperback editions. We made some effort to stop them or buy them off, but they scoffed at our threats to sue, for they knew how thin we were stretched fighting the censors, and any moneys we might offer were a pittance compared with their profits from the sales of a million-plus copies. So what if some of their books were returned or destroyed? They had not indemnified the booksellers or wholesalers, so had no legal obligations or costs, nor of course did they intend to pay any royalties to the author. Even allowing for attrition, they were the ones making money hand over proverbial fist, while Grove was reeling.

Our own paperback edition was selling well, but not well enough to cover our mounting legal costs. What's more, many of the now-sixty cases had been instigated on the basis of the paperback edition being available to minors, complicating the legal issue, for while some courts indicated they had few qualms about people with $7.50 to spend for the book, they drew the line at a seventy-five-cent edition, presumably reasoning that at that price not just the elite but "normal" people could be exposed to its filth. Even children, God forbid!

Meanwhile, over these two long years, we had other, non-*Tropic*al fish to fry, other books to edit and publish. And we did, but always with a glance over our shoulders to see if the doors would still open the following morning.

Ironically, the trials of *Tropic of Cancer* ended not with a bang but with a whimper. For reasons unknown, well into 1963 the Supreme Court agreed to rule on a relatively obscure Florida case in which constitutional questions were not involved. Why and how the Court chose it over dozens of others, the record does not indicate, but in all likelihood some of the justices, if not all, had been reading about the endless *Tropic* cases for more than two years and decided enough was enough. If Rembar had been looking forward to trying the case before the Supreme Court, he was sorely disappointed. Almost simultaneously with its decision to take on the case, the Court overturned the negative Florida decision 5–4. Even that momentous ruling was implicit, for the same day it ruled on *Tropic*, the Court tied it to another case, the movie *The Lovers*, and it was on the latter that a real obscenity ruling was made and opinions expressed. It was like gaining entrance to a movie by sneaking in the back door, but at Grove, where we were all exhausted to varying degrees, no one was about to complain.

37 ~

Exit Trocchi

IN DUE COURSE Alex delivered the last pages of *Cain's Book*, and
I settled down to see if and where and whether they fit, for some
batches were unnumbered. The novel consisted of a dozen sections, each with its own epigraph, each self-contained, which made my job
easier.

> My scow is tied up in the canal at Flushing, N.Y., alongside the landing
> stage of the Mac Asphalt and Construction Corporation. It is now just
> after five in the afternoon . . . and the sun, striking the cinderblocks of
> the main building of the works, has turned them pink. The motor cranes
> and the decks of the other scows tied up round about are deserted.
>
> Half an hour ago I gave myself a fix.

That sure as hell set the scene. I shifted some of the other chapters around
till I thought I'd got the order right, then showed it to Trocchi, who had come
to get his last paycheck. He looked through the manuscript, moved two
chapters to different locations, which seemed arbitrary but maybe better,
and pronounced the novel ready to print. When did we plan to publish? As
soon as possible, certainly in the next six months. Yes, I'd show him the
design for the cover as soon as I had it. We both stood, shook hands, then
Trocchi grabbed me in his arms and gave me a bear hug.

I made a copy of the manuscript and gave it to Barney to read. A day or two later he stopped by, tossed the manuscript on my desk, and said: "Well, you could have fooled me. It's damn good. Let's get it out." I asked whether there was any problem, contractual or otherwise, given the similarity of subject, and the fact we had already printed ten thousand copies of *Naked Lunch*, which were languishing in the warehouse while we prepared to publish Henry Miller, who had to take precedence, for, the lawyers all judged, he would be easier to defend than the unknown Burroughs. Barney saw none, although Maurice was pressing even more, threatening to sell *Naked Lunch* to another publisher if we didn't go ahead soon.

When *Cain's Book* appeared in May 1960, it was greeted largely with rave reviews, though a number of the conservative papers saw it as one more flagrant example of Grove Press's efforts to destroy the moral fabric of the country. The *Kansas City Star* called it "an astounding novel," the staid *New Yorker* remarked that it was "ferociously alive with poetry," and the *Library Journal*, as if we had paid them to stimulate sales, called it "just slightly less graphic than Henry Miller." But the best, most generous quotation came from Norman Mailer: "It is true. It has art. It is brave. I would not be surprised if it is still talked about in twenty years." This from a man who viewed his fellow writers as competitors, to be wrestled with and bested to prove that he, Norman, was top dog in town. Or out of town.

I sent the reviews to Alex as they arrived, and he was very pleased. But by this time he had other, far bigger matters to contend with.

One day, not long after *Cain's Book* had appeared, I ran into Ned Polsky, a mutual friend of mine and Alex's, on the street. His opening words were "Did you hear what happened to Alex?"

"So what happened?"

"It seems he went up to score in Harlem—or the Bronx, I'm not quite sure which—in any case, Alex's longtime connection, a Puerto Rican heroin dealer named Wofie. Apparently, the cops had the place staked out, and when Alex came out of the building, they nabbed him, caught him with heroin on him. They said they were going to book him on a charge of possession with intent to sell, which is a serious felony under the new drug laws, you know, you could get the chair for selling heavy drugs. Insane, but there it is. Alex said, 'Hey, I'm just a sorry junkie,' and the cops said, 'We know, but we want you to turn state's evidence against your connection, in which case we'll reduce the charge to a simple misdemeanor.' Alex refused to turn on his supplier, who I guess by now he considered a friend, so they booked him. He's been out on bail—I think Plimpton posted the bond, bless him—but he's coming up for trial and he's scared shitless he'll do time."

"Jesus!" I said. "And I suppose he still claims he's in control, not the drug. What about Lyn?"

Barney generously offered to advance Alex some royalties, which were not due for several months. I tried to contact Alex, but nobody seemed to know where he was. If Lyn's parents knew, they weren't telling, even after I explained I was his editor and friend. All they admitted was that Lyn and Mark had been with them but Alex had flown the coop. I wanted to reach him, I said, to see if I could help, and also to let him know that we were prepared to advance him some royalties, if that would help the cause. But they were adamant: If I was a friend of Alex's, how could they trust me? I got the clear impression they now hated him, would do anything in their power to break up the marriage, certainly do nothing to help.

It was our mutual friend Ned who tracked him down. He had just heard from Alex's court-appointed lawyer, who also couldn't find his client and wanted to make sure he showed up at the courthouse, warning that otherwise he'd be in real trouble, a fugitive sure to do heavy time. "He's hiding out in the back room of the Phoenix Bookshop," Ned said. The literary and secondhand bookshop, down on Cornelia Street, was run by a man named Larry Wallrich, who admired *Cain's Book* and its author and who had said Alex could stay in the back room behind the shop, where there was a cot and toilet, till his worries were over. That afternoon, Ned and I went down to Cornelia Street, after Larry had cleared it with Alex, to find a man who had aged ten years overnight. His eyes were bloodshot, his skin gray as tin. He couldn't sleep; he hadn't had a fix in three days and was desperate to go to Harlem, where he might be nailed again. This "sorry junkie" still saw himself as the savior of some brave new world. What about the trial, which was due to start in two days—was he going to show up? His lawyer needed to know. I'm not sure, Trocchi said. "There's another problem the lawyer doesn't know about. When we were with Lyn's parents, I forged a lot of prescriptions, and there are warrants out for me on fourteen separate charges of forgery. Demerol prescriptions. If the court ever finds out, I'm sure I'll do prison time." We were fighting a losing battle. So what did he plan to do? Leave the fucking country. To go where?

Canada. Easy enough to get past the border there, especially if he used a false name. Should we let the lawyer know? For God's sake, no! But could we tell Plimpton he'd stop by the next day? And could we or George call Leonard Cohen in Montreal to say he'd be arriving by bus, via Niagara Falls? Exact time to follow. Ned proposed coming back down the next night to keep him company, and Alex readily agreed. Both Ned and I urged him to show up in court, for if he fled, he'd be labeled a fugitive and never be able to come back to the States. That seemed to make an impression. If he fled, I said, what would become of Lyn and Mark?

I called Plimpton, always generous to a fault, who was less than enchanted at the idea of seeing him, but his only comment was "He'll probably need bus fare," and then, ironically, "or milk money for his child." And, yes, he would call Cohen, to forewarn him, if it came to that. Was I sure that Alex was really leaving the country? I said he claimed to be still debating, but my feeling was he would flee.

Next day, right on schedule, Alex showed up at the *Paris Review* offices, where, as predicted, he hit George up for the bus fare "and a little more for food on the trip." He told George he couldn't take a normal-sized suitcase, which would arouse suspicion; the last thing he needed was to be searched. Moreover, he wanted to look well dressed and wondered if he could borrow one of George's suits—which of course he'd send back from Montreal as soon as he arrived. George looked dubious, but assented and directed Alex to his walk-in closet. Alex reappeared fifteen minutes later, dressed to the nines, though looking a tad stouter than when he had entered the Plimpton emporium. Quick goodbyes, a hug, with Alex saying he would not soon forget this, and he was out the door. Checking later, George realized that not one but two of his Brooks Brothers suits were missing, as were four of his shirts and several sets of underwear and socks. Stouter? Of course he was stouter! Generous George was furious.*

By the time he called to inform me of the "theft," however, he had cooled down at least a few degrees. He even saw some humor in the flight. "You realize," he said with a chuckle, "I could be arrested as an accessory to the crime. If you think about it, my clothes aided and abetted his clandestine departure from the States."

*There is an account, in a well-meaning but seriously flawed biography of Trocchi published in Scotland in the early 1990s, *The Making of the Monster*, that claims Trocchi "stole" the clothes in George's absence, but Plimpton has refuted that.

When Alex finally got to London, he wrote and apologized to George for running off with a major portion of his wardrobe, promising to send the clothes back at the first opportunity.

Twenty-plus years later, the last time I inquired, the promised parcel had still not arrived.

38 ~

Naked Lunch

THE DECISION to buy the American rights to *Naked Lunch* had taken a lot of guts, for if defending *Chatterley* had bled Grove badly, Miller's *Tropic of Cancer* had us hemorrhaging, as city after city, state after state, attacked and sued, paying little or no heed to the cases that had already been settled in our favor. To compound the problems, Maurice, who had squandered the considerable earnings of *Lolita* on building a lavish nightclub complex, the Grande Séverine, saw *Naked Lunch* as the next pot of gold to save his near-bankrupt enterprise and was threatening to break the contract. The first-printing copies were languishing in the warehouse, for we knew that until *Tropic* was settled, publishing Burroughs would finally burn to a crisp our already-half-roasted goose.

There are various accounts of how *Naked Lunch* first saw the light of day, but one person is clearly involved in all versions: the poet Allen Ginsberg. In the most likely version, Ginsberg, a friend and onetime lover of Burroughs's, had visited him in Tangiers, where he had been living for years, and found his floor littered with papers of all sizes and description, most torn and tattered, covered, as he said later, with rats' leavings. But even in its present state, Ginsberg, leafing through, knew he was onto something special.

He toted the "manuscript" to Paris in the autumn of 1957 and showed it to Girodias, who found it unreadable. "The manuscript didn't make much sense," Girodias wrote later, "due to the deliberate lack of any rule whatsoever in the organization of the text." The Paris publisher was doubtless also put off by the very look of the document, which, he remembered, "was in such a state of disrepair, eaten away by the rats, it was completely dilapidated, collages, bits and snatches . . ."

As Terry Southern remembered it, Gregory Corso, another of the wandering Beats, approached him and Mason Hoffenberg (co-authors of the novel *Candy*, which Grove probably should have published but did not) when they were having coffee at St. Germain des Prés one morning and plopped the manuscript down on the table, announcing that Ginsberg had given it to him and asking that Terry and Mason try it on their (still) friend Girodias, which they did. Perusing the manuscript, Terry relates, Maurice saw there was little or no sex in the first fifteen pages; ergo the book was not for him. When they proudly pointed out to him a blow job on page 16, Maurice scoffed that was not only too little but far too late. Further, he noted, the book was formless, moving skittishly in time and space, whereas his readers wanted clarity, sex on every page, and no ambiguity.

Corso himself, when asked about Mason and Terry's involvement, said that version was all "bullshit," that it was Allen and he who dealt directly with Girodias.

In any event, after Girodias's summary rejection, the indomitable Mr. Ginsberg tried it on his friend Lawrence Ferlinghetti, poet and owner of a first-rate bookstore and small publishing venture in San Francisco, City Lights, who found it not to his liking at all—in fact, to be frank, "disgusting." At this point Allen sent a batch of eighty pages to a friend of his, Irving Rosenthal, who was currently editing the *Chicago Review*, an adjunct of the University of Chicago, who to his great credit immediately understood its importance and courageously decided to publish the extract. However, most university magazines are subject to review by members of the faculty, and they rejected it out of hand. Thereupon Rosenthal, who would later come to Grove as an editor, resigned and started a rival review of his own, with God knows what money, called *Big Table*, and in March 1959, just as we were preparing to launch *Lady Chatterley*, published ten episodes of *Naked Lunch*. The ever-vigilant Chicago postal authorities, alerted by some sixth sense (or an unfriendly faculty member who resented the *Chicago Review* spin-off?), promptly seized several hundred copies, about which there was a stir in the press, so that the rest of the daring ten-thousand-copy print run, whisked to New York and San Francisco by car, sold out upon arrival. So by the late spring of that year, *Naked Lunch* was finally in print. At least in part.

Maurice Girodias was a man not above changing his mind, who knew how to seize an opportunity when he smelled it. With all the publicity Stateside about the book, and the attempted banning of *Big Table*, it began to look for all the world like an Olympia publication. Dealing through the ubiquitous Ginsberg, Girodias paid Burroughs eight hundred dollars for world rights—a mite better than the standard fare for DBs—without a formal contract, of course, and in July the book appeared in all its green-clad glory, number 76 in the Olympia Traveller's Companion series.

At Grove, all the hullabaloo about *Naked Lunch* had not gone unnoticed, and we discussed it at more than one editorial meeting. All we had to go on were the excerpts in *Big Table*, but they were enough. Though *Naked Lunch* was far from an easy read, its fragments coming thick and fast, not always joined at the hip or any other part of the literary body, there were scenes of true brilliance, and humor to rival the best movie slapstick, though here it was clad in funereal black. We knew we had to publish, but we were collectively also aware that the timing was all wrong. Burroughs too would doubtless have to be defended in court.

In Paris, *Naked Lunch*, which had been published in July 1959, had not done much, if any, better than the rest of the line, partly because the French literary press ignored all of Olympia's books and, more likely, because the one-handed reading public for Olympia's works could make neither head nor tail of Olympia's number 76. But Maurice, who rightly sensed that *Naked Lunch* would explode when published in the United States—and would therefore send royalties quickly his way—began, as the months rolled on, to bombard us, first with pleas to make up our minds, then with growing threats. We explained to Maurice that we could never publish *Naked Lunch* until we had won the Lawrence and Miller battles: unlike those two, Burroughs was still virtually unknown in the States, which made his defense far more dicey, for surely we would be accused of riding on those two coattails for simple notoriety and swift financial gain. Finally, in November, we signed a contract and, even though we were unsure when we could actually publish, printed ten thousand copies adorned with a magnificent Kuhlman jacket—to placate Maurice, another act of folly, for funds were low and printers had to be paid within a couple months of completing the job. Despite that act of faith, starting in 1960 and continuing for almost two years, Maurice began first cajoling, then badgering, then threatening to take the book away and sell it elsewhere if we did not publish "immediately." The acrimony culminated in a series of exchanges that should have ended relations, and almost did, until finally Maurice backed down, but only after Burroughs, always the gentleman, had written us a letter of support, for he knew that we were at the breaking point with Miller.

Then, miraculously, in the summer of 1962 a stroke of luck rendered that dispute moot. The English publisher John Calder, with whom we had been in contact over the past year or two because he had been publishing in England several of the same authors as we, including Beckett, and who was deeply involved in the new Edinburgh Festival, invited a number of American writers that year: Norman Mailer, Henry Miller, Mary McCarthy . . . and William Burroughs. In the course of the festival, where Alex Trocchi also appeared prominently, Mary McCarthy declared that Burroughs's *Naked Lunch* was a work of art and he a great writer. That praise from an unexpected, prestigious source, plus the attendant publicity, was enough to convince us the time to publish had come. There was a new lawyer on the case, Edward de Grazia, and, also encouraged by him, we set a release date: November 1962. Unlike the jacket designs for Lawrence and Miller, both plain and understated to undercut any charge of exploitation or pandering, with *Naked Lunch* we decided on a frontal assault. This was a book on and about drugs and the drug culture, explicit, though not blatant, in its treatment of sex, and overtly homosexual when most homosexuals were still very much in the closet. So the jacket was visual, with a spoon, clearly intended for heroin, prominently displayed. Reviews were immediate and, as expected, mixed: we welcomed even the negatives, for they were so virulent that their readers had to be intrigued to see what all the fuss was about. The book went onto the *New York Times* bestseller list and remained there for several weeks. Nary a peep from the Feds or, more important, the locals. It looked as if we might even make some money without siphoning off most of it to lawyers, or having our income pinched by the pirates.

But such was not to be. In January, Boston, that bastion of probity, charged *Naked Lunch* with obscenity, and a long legal battle ensued. Not until two years later—after we had won *Tropic of Cancer* at the Supreme Court level—did the lower court decision came down: *Naked Lunch* was obscene. De Grazia appealed, and in 1966—after almost four years!—the highest court of Massachusetts finally ruled in the book's favor.*

*In his fascinating and nuanced book on the Olympia Press, *Venus Bound*, John de St. Jorre claims that that ruling on *Naked Lunch* effectively ended censorship in the United States. That is only partially correct; though the date of 1966 is right, it was also Charles Rembar's victory that same year at the Supreme Court level, in the case *A Book Named "John Cleland's Memoirs of a Woman of Pleasure" v. Attorney General of Massachusetts*, that literary censorship was effectively ended in the United States. The team of Rembar and de Grazia 2, the Commonwealth of Massachusetts 0.

This said, in reality censorship is never dead. A simple change of regime in any given country can, in one fell swoop, wipe out past gains and reinstate the Deacons of Decency once again.

39 ⤴

Formentor

ONE MORNING in the early spring of 1961, Barney stuck his head in my office and asked if I was free for lunch. I was. Despite the uptown publishing habit of lunching in fancy or favorite restaurants three or four times a week, I preferred to have a sandwich at my desk or grab a hamburger and beer at the downstairs Cedar Tavern. That day Barney also tapped Fred and announced we were lunching at Gene's, a modest but fine Italian restaurant close by on Eleventh Street. The martini for Barney arrived promptly, for Fred a glass of wine, and for me a beer—for all three of us, the better to think more clearly. Barney pulled a crumpled telegram from his pocket, the gist of which was that several leading European publishers were planning a literary prize—Gallimard in France, Einaudi in Italy, Seix Barral in Spain, Rowohlt in Germany, Weidenfeld in England. Would Grove like to be the American partner? It would be a big feather in our cap, I said. Barney, justly proud at the honor, totally agreed. How was it, we wondered, that Knopf had not been chosen, or Farrar, Straus, both bigger and far more prestigious than we?

In all fairness, Barney confessed, the group had apparently first approached Kurt Wolff, the famous German publisher who had come to America before World War II and founded Pantheon Books. With his many European ties and successes at Pantheon, he was the obvious choice. But time had passed him by: Pantheon had been sold out from under him by his partners to Random House, in one of the early mergers that were re-shaping the industry, and though Kurt and his wife, Helen, continued to publish in America through Harcourt, Brace, he did not properly have a publishing house, nor could he as an "imprint"—a new term in the publishing vocabulary for those who had editorial independence within a house but whose other functions, such as production, marketing, and fulfillment, were handled by the parent company—speak in Harcourt's name. It was apparently Kurt who had suggested Grove, for he had seen what we had been publishing over the past few years, much of it emanating from Europe, and was also impressed by the court battles we were fighting.

Was there a downside to joining the group? I couldn't think of any, nor could Fred, but we did have some questions. Was there money involved? If so, how much must each publisher commit to, for from a financial viewpoint we were the walking wounded, to say the least. We were also far younger and smaller than most of the other potential candidates. Where was the prize to be awarded, and when? What kinds of writers did the group have in mind? Barney was elated at the idea of our being included—a finger, as it were, to some of the old-time publishers, none of whom had been especially supportive of Grove's endless legal battles—but at the end of lunch he agreed we needed to know more. It was George Weidenfeld himself who had tendered the invitation on behalf of the group, and it was to him Barney wrote, asking for certain clarifications.

Weidenfeld was swift to write back. According to the plan, he said, the jury, which would consist of two or three writers and critics named by each house, would decide on a short list, from which a winner would be picked at the meeting itself. Or, he amended, *winners*, for the group was divided on one key point: Should the prize be given to an established writer, crowning his or her work—a kind of mini- or pre-Nobel—or to an unknown? If the former, each national jury would debate and decide on a finalist, with each publisher having one vote. After the first round, when it was presumed the list had narrowed, there would be further debate, then subsequent votes till a winner had been picked. At which point, I wondered aloud, would a plume of smoke appear? If the latter, should the prize go to a young writer, someone who had never published before, or someone with only a brief body of work behind him or her, in other words a kind of discovery prize? If this were the route taken, the publishers themselves would be the jury. As for the prize money, it was to be meaningful, though modest compared with the Nobel: in the neighborhood of ten to twenty thousand dollars. Quickly dividing by eight, for there were apparently two or three Scandinavian houses involved too, we saw there would be little financial exposure.

If the prize crowned an established writer's work, wouldn't we for the most part be paying hard cash to promote another publisher's author? Selfishly, what then was in it for us? If the decision was to bring notice to a younger writer, would the same problem not arise if he or she were already published in a given country? Our concerns, we were told, were shared by others, and after further transatlantic exchanges it was decided that rather than slice the child in two, we would have twins. As for a name, it would be called the Formentor Prize, after the site on Majorca where a number of the publishers had met to discuss the idea the year before, and where the first prizes would be awarded this spring, in April 1961. Each winner would receive ten thousand dollars.

We had one further concern: Formentor was on Majorca, which was part of Spain, which was still ruled by the hated Generalissimo Franco. How could we hold an open, freewheeling discussion in such a repressive country? The reply came from Carlos Barral, head of the Spanish publisher Seix Barral and a key instigator of the prize concept. That was the whole point, he said: to have publishers from around the world who were not subject to censorious repression meet and freely discuss literary, and by inference political, matters. The meeting would, contrary to our fears, spotlight Spain's political problems, perhaps forcing Franco, increasingly concerned about Spain's international image, to make some positive changes. Reassuring answers, we felt. Anyway, with these nagging questions settled, we committed, though still pretty much in the dark as to how the whole thing would work. For me, one of the extraordinary side benefits of the prize was that I could stop off in Paris and see Jeannette, who was winding up a three-month concert tour of western Europe. By sheer luck, her final concert was scheduled for Paris on April 21, a glittering event at the Salle Gaveau. Her tour was going splendidly, but I sensed with each succeeding letter or phone call an increasing nostalgia, a longing to see me and the kids. I hired a second babysitter, rallied several friends to spell them on the weekends. Still, I had to break the news to the kids, a task I kept postponing for fear they'd stage a child revolution. Then it dawned on me how to make the announcement: I was going over to Paris to fetch their mother and bring her home! Hurrah for Daddy!

With that battle won, now my dilemma was: Should I surprise Jeannette or give fair warning I was coming? To announce my arrival days before her concert would jolt and upset her. Would it be possible to arrive the *day* of the concert, attend it incognito, then surprise her in the green room? her mother asked. Or maybe even later? There would be, I learned, a gala reception afterward at Maxim's. I landed at Orly early on the morning of April 21, grabbed a cab, and headed to the square Port Royal and to our friends the Manchons. The city, bound in fog, was waking up, the cafés already crowded with blue-clad workers downing their pick-me-up red and office-bound men in suit and tie sipping their morning coffee, the sidewalks filled with well-dressed women on their way to work or escorting their kids to school, all bundled up in coats and scarves, for despite the calendar certifying the arrival of spring, the weather was still gray and blustery. Each bakery we passed sent forth the irresistible odor of fresh-baked bread and croissants. Oh, the sights and smells of the city I loved; even the grinding sounds of green-decked, smoke-spewing buses and, in the distance, the plaintive *bop-ba, bop-ba* two-note wail of a cop car or ambulance brought a thousand memories rushing back. Why had I ever left this magical place? At a red light I glanced at a nearby kiosk, and there, emblazoned in red and black, was an outsized poster announcing Jeannette's concert: "*Sous la Présidence de Monsieur André Malraux, Ministre d'État Chargé des Affaires Culturelles,*" no less. Jeannette had told me of her decision to donate all the proceeds of the concert to victims of polio, which had resulted in Malraux's sponsorship.

As we crossed the city, I saw the same Jeannette poster on virtually every kiosk, which made me feel, for one day at least, as though I owned the place. And to think I might have missed this! Reflexively, I crossed my fingers, for I knew that, however well prepared she was, nerves were forever ready to betray. I remembered reading somewhere a remark from Arthur Rubinstein, who, though he had concertized for decades with total aplomb, said that even in his later years, in the car carrying him to concert halls, he was always overcome with the certainty that his fingers had suddenly turned to spaghetti.

I set off to wander through Paris, down to the quays, where the irresistible attractions of the bookstalls kept me for an hour, maybe more. I had long frequented the *bouquinistes*, always sure I could find some neglected gem, some first edition of a favorite author, and had been rewarded often enough to sustain the habit. That morning, as the early fog lifted and the sun shone brilliantly on the troubled Seine and the once-royal palaces beyond, I sensed it would be my lucky day in more ways than one. So instead of glancing absently at the wares I was passing, I began to scrutinize each display, so much so that the vendor, who normally sat on his folding chair reading his newspaper for the umpteenth time, a *mégot* lingering on his lip, seemingly oblivious of his potential clients, might become suspicious and saunter over: *"Vous cherchez quelque chose de particulier?"* Looking for something special? To which I would respond, *"Une première édition de Proust, par exemple?"* Perhaps a first edition of Proust? Which would generally provoke an outburst of uncontrolled laughter, followed by *"Mais vous êtes fou, non?"* Are you crazy? But that day I was not so crazy, for suddenly, at the fourth or fifth stall, the blue appeared, a blue I had known and coveted for years, a distinctive blue like no other: a copy of Shakespeare and Company's edition of *Ulysses!* With trembling hand I picked it up. Indeed! I leafed through the first few pages. So it was not the first edition but the fourth. Who cared? It came from the hand of the blessed Sylvia Beach! Nonchalantly, I turned it over, saw the cover was slightly torn, and put it gently back among the banal others. I picked another book at random from the pack. I did the same for three or four more, part of my clever ploy, one of them Sartre's *La nausée.* I asked how much, and the vendor named a price more than reasonable, about half the cover price. I said I'd take it, then let my hand hover over several other weathered tomes before returning to the blue, *mon trésor. "Et ceci?"* And this one? *"Ah,"* he said, *"c'est spécial."* That's special. *"C'est de Joyce, vous savez."* That's by Joyce, you know. And he quoted a price well beyond my budget, $15 at the prevailing rates (which would translate into roughly $100 today). *"Ah?"* I said, as if ignorant of the Irishman, feigning to put it back, my mind racing. *"Dommage que la couverture est déchirée au dos."* Pity there's a tear on the back. He picked it up, turned it over, took a final puff of his *mégot*—another would have seared his lower lip—shook his head, and lowered the price by a third. I offered one-half. We settled at 27.50 new francs, roughly $5.50, shook hands, and parted, each sure he had won the day.

I lunched at my old haunt Raffy's, where I was greeted like the prodigal son, though I hadn't been there for years. *Steak frites*, with the same old house wine. I noted to my dismay that prices had escalated sharply. With cheese and dessert, the bill that would have been a dollar in the good old days now came to a whopping three! After lunch, a quick trip around the corner to see Jérôme Lindon, affable as ever, still dressed in his dark suit and impeccable white shirt and tasteful tie, his speech staccato, a Gallic stream rushing down the mountain, bringing me up to date on Beckett. He then thanked me for being involved in the American publication of Henri Alleg's *Question* and filled me in on all the trials—literally—he had been through because of that work: banning, police interrogations, late-night threatening phone calls, even attempts to close him down. He said he wanted to introduce me to his editor, who turned out to be our author Alain Robbe-Grillet, whom I had met in New York the year before. Somehow, Alain had failed to mention his day job—or was it moonlighting?—at Minuit. We had already published two of his novels, *Jealousy* and *In the Labyrinth*, which I found both disturbing and remarkable. After a few minutes in his tiny office, Alain suggested we go have a *pot* at the Deux Magots, where he expounded further on the concept of the *nouveau roman*, a term foisted on him, he said, and several other young novelists, though he insisted they were all quite different and there really was no "school." "Critics," he said, "just love to affix labels to work they don't like or understand."

Suddenly I realized it was after five o'clock and I was due back at the Manchons'. "If only I'd known," Alain said. "Catherine and I would have wanted to come to the concert." He had an invitation from NYU to come to the States for a semester the following year and planned to accept. Did I think it a good idea? Absolutely, assuming it would not detract from his writing. It wouldn't, he assured me. "And this Richard Howard," he asked, "is he good? He seems to translate my books almost before I'm finished, he's so fast!" I assured him Richard was indeed the best. One of my first jobs at Grove had been to edit Richard's translation of *Jealousy*, and I had found it excellent. Further, I assured Alain, where I had a question or quarrel, Richard was always quick to respond or accept. No, believe me, I said, you are well served.

At seven sharp, Jeanne and Frank and I taxied to the Salle Gaveau, where we rendezvoused with Jeannette's parents. There was already a milling throng outside, dressed to the nines. This was a big night for her, in her young career, perhaps her biggest. As the lights dimmed, my heart was so loud I was worried I wouldn't hear the music. Then she arrived onstage, to warm applause, my darling lovely in her long pale pink gown. She looked totally calm. So why wasn't I? She bowed, thrust her fiddle snug between neck and shoulder, nodded discreetly to her accompanist, Thérèse, and after the first notes I relaxed. She was indeed in command, her magnificent tone rich and pure, the audience spellbound. After the last notes there was a long moment of silence, followed by thunderous applause.

At intermission, a furtive spy, I bent an ear to overhear the comments, which ranged from high praise to absolute wonder. Who is this young woman? Where has she been hiding? In America, I understand. But that tone! The Bach . . . I bumped into several people I knew, who had no idea I was coming, and I feared word might worm itself backstage, spoiling the surprise, but apparently not. It took four encores before Jeannette made her final bow. Half a dozen bouquets were rendered by—to me—unknowns. I turned and hugged her mother, who hugged Jeanne, who hugged Frank, who hugged me. Giddy, we all made our way backstage, where a small crowd was already forming. I was last in line. Then she saw me, unbelieving. "You were *here*!" and she rushed into my waiting arms. "Of course, madame. I wouldn't have missed it for the world!" "Why didn't you warn me? Why didn't you—" "I'll explain all that later. And bravo, *mon amour.*" "But who's taking care of the *kids*?" "Catherine, our *fille au pair*, has everything in hand, don't worry," I assured her, but before I could say more, others intruded, postponing my details.

Maxim's owner, Monsieur Vaudable, had closed down the fabled restaurant at ten o'clock for "a private party." In my dark blue suit and modest tie, I felt downscale. White roses on every table, champagne flowing, we finally sat down to a near-midnight supper. Maxim's was where Roszi had solidified her career, for many years the star attraction there. Originally trained as a classical violinist, Jeannette's mother had evolved into the first Gypsy woman violinist who performed to great success in nightclubs. In the late 1930s, she opened her own nightclub on the Champs-Élysées. Vaudable was one of her oldest and greatest admirers, and here was a chance to show her how much he thought of her.

It was past two o'clock when we finally went to bed, euphoric. I suddenly remembered we had to catch a plane for Spain the next morning.

Over our early breakfast, I steered Jeannette to the Formentor Prize, where we were heading. After I reminded her of the concept, she wondered how eight or ten publishers, all from different countries, could ever agree on anything. I was on the American jury. It was because of Beckett, I said: Barney badly wants Beckett to win the prize and knows I'll make a strong case for him. I gave her the rundown on the various juries: for the Italians, Alberto Moravia, Italo Calvino, Elio Vittorini, and a leading Italian literary critic. From Weidenfeld, Mary McCarthy and Iris Murdoch; from Germany, the young but highly regarded poet and novelist Hans Magnus Enzensberger. For our jury, on the West Coast Don Allen had suggested Herbert Gold, who immediately agreed. What about Henry Miller? Invited,

Henry politely declined, but promised he would consider serving the following year if his schedule permitted.

Each publisher got to nominate two candidates for the Big Prize, as we promptly dubbed this wannabe pre-Nobel. So we had begun with a short list of about a dozen, the most prominent of which, at least in our view, were Samuel Beckett and Jorge Luis Borges.

Jeannette and I arrived at Formentor late in the evening. After a nightcap with the other publishers, already there for at least one day at this beautiful five-star resort hotel, we repaired to our room. Waking up early and still in a state of euphoria, I went downstairs and wandered outside under a glowing sun. The steps to the Mediterranean were flanked on both sides by bursts of pink and red geraniums the proverbial riot of color. I rushed back upstairs and pulled Jeannette out of bed; she had to share the beauty and an early-morning swim, the sky above cloudless, cerulean. Magic.

The first day was spent paring down the short list to the two finalists. The perorations supporting each were persuasive and impassioned, but it soon became apparent the prize had a flaw, perhaps not fatal but serious. For both prizes there was a clear division between north and south, the Germanic languages on the one hand and the Romance on the other. With the jury split down the middle, with no apparent give-and-take, I made a strong plea for Beckett's candidacy, giving Borges his due but suggesting that Beckett was the greatest living writer in English, perhaps in the world, comparing him to Joyce but adding (far out on a limb, I knew) that in my humble opinion he would one day rank not only with but possibly *above* Joyce for the depth and diversity of his work. By crowning Beckett, I insisted, we'll send a strong message to the literary world about this prize.

The faces of the Italians, Spanish, and French showed that my words, like those from the other English and American jury members, made little or no impact. The vote—the second round—again ended in a tie. Mixed huddles and confabulations produced no compromise. Finally, reluctantly, the six agreed to disagree: we would split the prize between Beckett and Borges. It was not a happy conclusion, but both were world-class writers, and the choices would still tell the world that this was a serious prize, worthy of attention.

Almost as an afterthought, the Little Prize was awarded to Juan García Hortelano, the Spanish candidate, without dissension and, as it turned out worldwide, without impact.

Despite the north-south schism, and the less than glorious inability to decide on a single winner, the overall impression was that the week had been worthwhile for all parties. For Grove, it had hoisted us overnight to a level of international importance, and both Barney and I felt that from now on it would be easier to do business with our foreign colleagues. As for the money, we calculated that the whole affair, including airfare, hotel, meals for seven—ourselves and the American jury—plus our share of the prize money, came to no more than ten thousand dollars. For a company now used to paying that much for a single Henry Miller court case, it struck us as an outright bargain.

40 ᔰ

City of Night

ᔰ IT WAS DON ALLEN who steered us to John Rechy, from his photograph a handsome, dark-haired, well-muscled young man from L.A., whose first novel, *City of Night*, would, by its subject alone, Don assured us, bring Grove further fame and glory. We suspected it would bring us further court cases as well, and we were already teeming with fame, much of it ill. But we trusted Don, who had nurtured the manuscript over a very long period of time, from its inception as a short story. Like many Grove works, *City of Night* had had its start in *Evergreen Review*, beginning with "Mardi Gras" in issue number 5. Rechy had lived an itinerant life for years, moving from his native El Paso to half a dozen cities in California, to Dallas, to Houston, to New York, and to New Orleans, where he lived for what he termed "an eternity"—several weeks—before returning to El Paso. As Rechy wrote in his introduction to a reissue of *City of Night*, the day after he left New Orleans, on Ash Wednesday, he wrote a long letter to a friend in Illinois describing his life these past few years "traveling back and forth across the country—carrying all my belongings in an army duffel bag; moving in and out of lives, sometimes glimpsed briefly but always felt intensely" and detailing his memories of the Mardi Gras season just past.

In that Carnival city of old cemeteries and tolling church bells, I slept only when fatigue demanded, carried along by "bennies" and on dissonant waves of voices, music, sad and happy laughter. The sudden quiet of Ash Wednesday, the mourning of Lent, jarred me as if a shout to which I had become accustomed had been throttled. I was awakened by *silence*, a questioning silence I had to flee.

Rechy never sent that letter, and a week later found it crumpled in a pocket. He decided to rework his strong memories of the New Orleans moment as a short story entitled "Mardi Gras" and sent it to *Evergreen*. Don Allen read it, liked it, and wrote to Rechy in El Paso saying it was under consideration for publication in the magazine and asking whether perchance it was part of a novel. It wasn't—Rechy had never envisioned writing a novel. John relates that he still had no intention of writing a novel, but he did keep on sending stories to *Evergreen*, which faithfully published them, starting with the summer issue of 1958, six months before I arrived. But publication of new authors in *Evergreen*, at which agents and publishers were now beginning to look more closely, was a double-edged razor: other publishers began to take note of this serious young author, and at least two made him a concrete offer. John, deciding that he wanted to be published only by Grove, wrote to Don informing him of the outside offers. After a hasty editorial meeting, we knew our feelings were, as they say, mutual, and Don was dispatched to John with a contract and a check for the advance in hand. That settled, John still found it impossible to focus, to write a full-length novel, preferring, he admits, reimmersion in his "streetworld." Finally, encouraged by a close friend who can be seen at least in part as Jeremy in the book, John went home to El Paso and began to write every day, as if in a fever, on a rented Underwood typewriter. Each evening John, who was half Mexican, would translate "appropriate" passages into Spanish and read them aloud to his mother, who had no English. She listened carefully and, when he finished, would compliment him on the fine work he was writing. Finally, four years after he had written the letter post–New Orleans, the novel was finished and sent off. Don did a light edit, for the manuscript seemed especially fine and taut, and we cataloged it. Given the title, it was suggested our jacket be a mysterious night shot of a city street. Nothing Kuhlman came up with seemed right, so I toted my 35-millimeter camera, which had seen better days, up to Forty-second Street and, roving the street from Sixth Avenue west, began taking pictures, two or three dozen in all. A couple days later, when they were developed, I brought them into the office and showed them around. Yes, they captured the spirit of the novel: dark city scene, furtive shadows. Sold. Just in time for the catalog.

When John received the galley proofs, however, everything looked "different." The manuscript had seemed fine to him, but when it was typeset, all he could see were errors: wrong words, awkward sentences, clunky paragraphs. He began to correct, at first lightly, then more and more rigorously. He was supposed to return proofs two weeks after receiving them, and when they failed to appear, his answer was "I'm making some slight revisions." Another two weeks, a month. The book would have to be postponed. In San Francisco, Don was put on the case and reported back that, apparently, the revisions were more severe than John had first indicated. Damn! Finally they came to Don: in the text, in the margins, on newly typewritten pages, John had virtually rewritten the book.

Don called to say that he had checked each change carefully, even meticulously, ready to stet anything arbitrary, and found that John's changes were invariably an improvement. I suppose, he said, we'll have to reset from scratch. Don's "hmmm" was nicely ambiguous, but when the galleys arrived, we did reset completely. John, chagrined and not wanting his relationship with Grove to suffer from the start, wrote saying he'd be happy to pay for the changes out of his royalties, as the contract called for. A gesture we politely declined.

Even before it appeared in late spring 1963, *City of Night* went onto the *New York Times* bestseller list, at number 8. One of the first reviews, also prepublication, was from the august *New York Review of Books*, which lambasted it. *The New Republic* was equally negative, but the outrage of both may have helped rather than hindered, for the book quickly moved up on several bestseller lists and remained there for several months. A scandal, to be sure! When will those Grove Press perverts learn to draw the line? As if *Chatterley* and the *Tropics* weren't enough, now *Naked Lunch* and *City of Night!*

Forsooth and gadzooks!

41 ✎

Film

IN 1963, given the growing success of several Grove playwrights—Beckett, Harold Pinter, Ionesco, Genet, Brendan Behan (yes, dear Brendan was back in my life!)—a TV production company, Four Star, approached Grove with an intriguing idea: Why not commission four of your wonderful authors to write TV screenplays? And, by the way, here's eighty thousand dollars to play with. The first person approached was Jean Genet, who firmly said no. But Beckett, Pinter, Ionesco, Marguerite Duras, and Robbe-Grillet—all of whom had recently turned to writing film scripts—said yes. The first one who did was Beckett himself, who sent in a short, complex, but brilliant work that, predictably, he entitled *Film*.

Barney was in sixth heaven; the thought of edging his way back into film delighted him. What's more, Beckett had responded positively to our invitation to come to America to supervise, or at least be present at, the filming, which was scheduled for the summer of 1964. Everyone agreed on the director, Alan Schneider, who had worked over the last several years with Beckett, starting with his direction of *Waiting for Godot*. It was a one-person film, and the obvious first choice was Charlie Chaplin, whose early films Beckett admired greatly. When queried, the Chaplin office responded that Mr. Chaplin did not read scripts. Zero Mostel, another candidate, was not available, nor was Beckett's friend and favorite performer, the Irish actor Jack MacGowran, committed to another film. So the actor chosen, well beyond his best years, was Buster Keaton, whose silent films Beckett had also admired as a young man. At Beckett's behest, Barney and Alan had sought him out in Canada, where he was doing a commercial, and signed him up, and he was due to arrive shortly in New York just prior to shooting. Whether he had read the script or not is uncertain; if he had, it is doubtful he understood it: it was a disturbingly simple plot involving two aspects of the same protagonist, one the perceiver, the other the perceived, the former probing insistently, the latter trying desperately to hide.

Beckett arrived in New York on July 10 and was greeted at the airport by Judith, who escorted him to a private, single-engine plane that gave him a bumpy but blessedly short forty-minute ride out to East Hampton on the tip of Long Island, to Barney's Quonset hut summer residence. Earlier, Barney had asked Milton Perlman, an old friend and for some time now a principal of Grove, whose job it was to administer our too often wayward or antiquated business practices, to be producer, and asked me to be associate producer, a highfalutin title for a job whose main task was to make sure Beckett was happy and well cared for. Perlman had some film experience, but I had none, aside from my endless nights at the Cinémathèque in Paris, where over the years I had probably seen most of the old classics, including all of Chaplin and Keaton.

The weekend in East Hampton, to which Alan Schneider had also been invited, was spent largely discussing the film, but the weather was splendid and there was swimming, lolling about the pool, and playing tennis. Beckett, who confessed to not having picked up a racket for years, was nonetheless tempted onto the court "to take a few swings," first with Barney, then with me. One could see that he knew how to play; his form was good, if rusty, and when the ball came back, it was crisp and for the most part accurate—that is, nicely inside the lines. But to Beckett's growing dismay, he missed every third or fourth ball completely. He kept shaking his head with each miss and finally in disgust left the Har-Tru court, much slower than the grass on which he had played in earlier years, where the bounce is quite different. He muttered about his poor form, but Barney and I both knew that his eyes were largely to blame, for he was plagued with waning eyesight and feared that he might soon go blind.

Barney had scored a major coup in signing up as cinematographer Boris Kaufman, a legend in the business whose career stretched back to working

with Jean Vigo in France in the early 1930s. The cameraman was Joe Coffey, a strapping fellow who also came with high credentials and who, in the
course of the shooting, constantly exuded confidence and good humor as
one thing after another hit a snag. Back in the city, Alan and Beckett
walked endlessly, scouting for locations. Though he was apparently affected
by the heat and humidity, never having experienced the equivalent of New
York summer weather, Beckett never complained. One day in lower Manhattan, Beckett's eyes brightened as we came in sight of a dilapidated old
wall hard by the Brooklyn Bridge. He nodded and indicated that this is
where the opening sequence should be shot, no question. The wall, part of
a building slated for demolition, was pure Beckett: sagging, uneven, its cement flaking and crumbling.

Keaton now in the city, Beckett and Alan paid him a visit in his hotel
suite. Beckett, who had suggested Keaton, looked forward to the encounter with, he confessed, a tinge of nervousness. They arrived, as Alan recorded in the published version of *Film*, to find Keaton watching a baseball
game on television and drinking beer, barely nodding to his two distinguished guests, whose efforts at conversation elicited little or no response.
Finally, they left the room, but not before Beckett, who missed nothing,
observed that he had seen a bit of the ball game, which reminded him of
cricket, though obviously quite different. Which team had Keaton been
watching? he wondered. The Mets, I said. A fairly young team, I said, still
thrashing about. The really good team in New York is the Yankees. Dominant. Would there be time to see a match? he asked. A "game." Ah, yes, of
course. I said I didn't know because of the shooting schedule, but would
inquire.

Shooting began on a Monday, at the outdoor site Beckett had picked
beneath the Brooklyn Bridge. Despite his air of authority, Alan was more
than a bit nervous, because for all his theatrical experience he had never
directed a film before. The morning was also steaming hot. The scene depicted Keaton, dressed despite the heat in a bulky overcoat and a beat-up
hat from which hung a handkerchief, the better to hide from the perceiv-
ing eye, skirting the wall to escape the pursuer, finally escaping into an
apartment building entrance. Take followed take, with Keaton's unflappa-
ble demeanor impressing Beckett more and more as the day wore on. In
and out of Keaton's flight along the wall moved a number of extras, whom
Coffey, following Alan's orders, panned to include. When in the evening
the first day's rushes were viewed, the result was a total disaster. Something called the strobe effect, the result of the panning, made the scene

unusable, painful to watch. Alan was hugely contrite, muttering apologies. Beckett watched impassively; if dismayed, he didn't show it. Shaking his head, Alan declared that the scene would have to be reshot. Barney or Perlman, probably the latter, nixed that immediately: the strict budget simply did not allow it. The day, which had begun with such high hopes and excitement, was ending badly, recriminations alternating with excuses. It was Beckett, emerging from silence, who saved the day. He said quietly, let's simply eliminate that scene, which was meant to establish the two elements of the protagonist, and keep only the image of Keaton along the wall, without the extras.

If gloom and doubt pervaded that first evening, the following days' shooting went almost without a hitch, especially once we were off the street and into the studio on the Upper East Side of Manhattan, where the interior room had been built to Beckett's specifications. Keaton now was more in his element and, Milton suggested, perhaps was even beginning to understand what the movie was all about. At least an inkling. Keaton, in a rocking chair, had to deal with a cat and a dog, whose appearance required multiple takes as he dealt with their unwanted intrusion. After which he artfully covered other intrusive elements that he perceived threatened his being: a goldfish bowl, a parrot's cage, the mirror itself that dangerously reflected his image. Then he removed the staring, godlike image from the wall.

On the second day of indoor shooting, Jeannette joined us, and on a balcony above the set we flanked Beckett, who watched each take with total equanimity, quietly marveling at Keaton's intuitive understanding of what needed to be done, improving with each take, Beckett nodding perceptively now and then when one pleased him especially, his arms leaning on the railing, one hand on each cheek. At one point, gazing down at the set as a new take was being prepared, he turned to Jeannette and, more serious than facetious, said with a sigh: "That room down there. You know, I could live in it very happily." Knowing Beckett, you knew he meant it: if you eliminated the trappings—the parrot and the goldfish, the cat and the dog—that plain, square room down there was not all that different from Beckett's oh-so-plain rooms in Ussy.

One day, as the shooting went on until late in the evening, we ended up at some restaurant near Barney's house on Houston Street, then repaired to his upper floor where there were three or four extra bedrooms. Jeannette and the children had returned to East Hampton for the summer, so I was grateful not to have to taxi home. With dawn not that far off but the house still dark, I saw my door open and a spectral vision framed in the doorway, halting and lame, searching for something or someone. Sleep-walking perhaps. The vision took a hesitant step, then two, into the room, and I realized that it was Beckett, stark naked. "Sam," I said hesitantly. "Dick," he said, "is that you?" I admitted it was, flattered to be chosen, and asked if I could be of help. "You could," he said. "I thought this was the loo. If you could kindly direct me to it." Unsteadily, for it was four in the morning, I left my bed, took hold of his right elbow, and steered him to the door next to mine. The loo.

I had not forgotten my promise to take Beckett to a baseball game. Though my heart was with the Mets, I had hoped that I might show him the best of the sport by taking him to Yankee Stadium. But the Yankees were on the road, so the hapless Mets were all I had. I booked two good seats for July 31, as close to home plate as I could, just down the left-field line. It was a doubleheader, the first game beginning at four, in full daylight. The weather had obliged, so for once Beckett got a taste of a Dublin-like after-noon, cool and breezy. All the way out to Shea Stadium, I had apologized for the team we were about to see, struggling but so often futile. One had to be a die-hard fan not to give up on them, I said as I tried to explain the rudiments of the game. I had seen cricket only twice in my life, both times with Matthew Evans, who had patiently but unsuccessfully tried to unravel the sport's mysteries for me; the only similarity I could detect was that there was a player who threw the ball, damned awkwardly, I thought, and a batter. Beckett listened intently as I droned on, at one point he said he thought he got the general idea, and as we settled into our seats, he con-gratulated me on their choice, so close to the field, for much farther back, he explained, he would have had difficulty seeing. As the game progressed, he asked key questions, wondering why, for instance, when a batter hit the ball so weakly he nonetheless ran as if his life depended on it. And why in the world on what you called a passed ball, the batter didn't run, just stood there. Balls and strikes he understood immediately, and was especially impressed by the blue-suited umpires, who acted with such histrionic au-thority. Surprisingly, and defying all my gloomy prognostics, the Mets not only played well but won the first game.

Almost reproachfully, he turned to me and wondered if they were really as bad as I had made them out. Most of the time, I said sheepishly. Then: "Would you like to go now?" "Is it over then?" he asked. The first game is,

I explained, but there's another to follow. It's called a doubleheader. Is that unusual? Fairly, I said, generally because at some point in the season a game or games had to be postponed because of rain and needed to be rescheduled. "So there's a whole other game?" I nodded. "Then we should stay. We don't want to leave until it's over, do we?" And stay we did, for another three hours, the latter half of which was spent under the lights, where Beckett, even this close, had trouble seeing. Now every time a ball was hit into the outfield, he rose to his feet, pushed his glasses back into his thick shock of hair, and squinted into the night, intent on seeing whether it was a hit or whether, as he reiterated, it would sadly go for naught. Defying me once again, the Mets took the second game as well. As we stood to depart, Beckett said with a sly grin, "Perhaps I should come to see the Mets more often. I seem to bring them good luck."

The last week of his stay, Beckett worked closely with the film's editor, Sidney Meyers, another veteran who, virtually the same age as the writer, shared with him a knowledge and love of music. Meyers was also a connoisseur of painting, and one day he took Beckett to the Met, to view its Dutch collection. But that last week's main pleasure for Beckett was watching Sidney and Alan edit the film, work it into the shape he wanted. On August 6, four weeks after he had arrived in this strange but interesting country, he boarded a plane at Idlewild and headed home, eager to return to the tranquillity of Ussy, where, he vowed, he would remain for as long as he possibly could.

42 ◦

Plays and Playwrights

ALMOST from its inception, Grove had published plays as an integral part of its program, either because a house author had written a play or because, perhaps for the first time, a publisher saw drama as part of literature. At the other end of the spectrum, a few American houses, especially Dodd, Mead, had made a habit of publishing Broadway hits, to capture the moment, and hopefully the theatergoer too. No continuing sale, or very little, after the plays had gone off the boards.

Beckett, of course, was the pedestal on which the drama program stood. And two of *Merlin*'s other discoveries, Genet and Ionesco, had likewise crossed the Atlantic and landed at Grove. Genet's *Balcony* had been translated by good old Bernard Frechtman, who came with the package, and two volumes of Ionesco's best short plays, one brilliantly translated by Don Allen, had appeared the year before I arrived.

In 1959, a Frenchman of Russian birth, Arthur Adamov, whom we also published in *Merlin*, was added to the list with his *Ping-Pong*. Joining him was the wild young Irishman I had known—endured?—in my Paris days, who had spent a memorable week under my rue du Sabot roof, Brendan Behan, whose play *The Hostage* had raised a storm in London the year before. That same year we published *A Taste of Honey*, again by a young Irish author, Shelagh Delaney. According to the account emanating from Britain, Miss Delaney had gone one night to a play by an established play-wright and found it so second-rate she announced she could do far better, went home, sat down, and wrote *A Taste of Honey*.

The following year we added several more to the burgeoning drama list: Genet's *Blacks*; two more volumes of Ionesco, whose plays were beginning to be put on here; and a play by a Spaniard, Fernando Arrabal, called *The Automobile Graveyard* that contained more than a few echoes of Beckett but still had shocked Paris, where Arrabal lived.

Perhaps the most interesting "find" of 1960 was a young American, Jack Gelber. Gelber's play *The Connection* had come within a hair of dying a swift death after the first reviews. But the faltering work, which, as its name implies, was about drugs—not all that surprising, given the mores of the 1960s—got a new lease on life when Kenneth Tynan in *The New Yorker* hailed it as important, indeed seminal. Overnight the play was saved, as people now fought for tickets and trekked downtown to the Living Theatre on West Fourteenth Street to be turned on.

Jeannette and I had seen the play early on, and both of us thought, despite its not-all-that-concealed debt to *Godot*—"Waiting for my Connection"—it first-rate. Grove signed it up pre-Tynan, a mark of trust, and I became Jack's editor and, soon, his close friend. He and his wife, Carol, had, like us, two kids and, thanks to the success of *The Connection*, were now eating on a fairly regular basis.

Many of the new literary plays were beginning to be performed, often to glowing reviews, which stimulated young college professors to adopt them in their drama courses. None became a bestseller, not even *Godot*,* but more and more often as Barney and I sat down to look for reprints, which we did every month, we found we were going back to press with them. It also occurred to us, publishing geniuses that we were, to begin mailing to college professors desk copies of our wares, which resulted in even more frequent reprints on many of the titles.

Several years later, a publishing colleague congratulated us on our "excellent strategy" of publishing drama and finding a market where none had existed before. As with most of what we did, however, there had been no strategy. Still, we had virtually cornered that market, a rich lode, for now new playwrights often did not have to be sought out; they came to us.

---

*By the strict definition that it never made that august list. But by its steady backlist sales over the years, *Godot* was by any definition a bestseller.

Arrabal's translator, Richard Howard, was one of the first people I had met at Grove. He had already translated Alain Robbe-Grillet's *Voyeur*. I edited all of Richard's translations, generally with a very light hand, for I quickly learned that despite the speed of his translations—he often turned them around within a month or six weeks—they were the work of a writer. We too became fast friends and admirers. Richard, openly gay in an era when most homosexuals remained steadfastly in the closet for fear of ruining their lives or losing their jobs, was living with a young novelist, Sandy Friedman, a delight of a man, always cheerful even if stressed or upset. Richard was also a serious poet, and though he earned his living through translations, he spent most of his time writing and reading poetry.

I had a call one day late in 1960 from Robert Hughes, a documentary filmmaker. He had an idea that involved one of our authors, Marguerite Duras, two of whose novels we had published. When we met a few days later, this young man, beneath his silken red hair and unlined face, impressed me with the depth of his knowledge about foreign films. Duras's script for Alain Resnais's superb film *Hiroshima mon amour* was, he declared, a masterpiece. What he had in mind was to cull stills from the screen—not the publicity shots taken on the set—and integrate them into the text exactly where they fell. There are more and more film courses being taught, he insisted, and there's a substantial and growing market for such books. Great, I said. But what about the cost, given the number of pictures—maybe a hundred in all, he guessed, that would grace each volume. We'd do it as an original Evergreen, probably at $1.95. When the costs came in, they weren't outrageous. Barney was all for it, and if this worked, we had a few other art films down the line we could follow up with. We made an arrangement whereby we'd split the modest advance between Hughes and the author. We decided to bring *Hiroshima* out as soon as possible, so that weekend I set about translating the script. At an editing table we watched a projection, Hughes pausing every few seconds to mark on a piece of paper a candidate for a photo. By the time I finished translating a couple weeks later, he had come up with 120 to 130 black and whites, with which we covered the conference table. It took several hours, but by eight o'clock we had laid out the book.

Looking up at the wall clock, I suddenly realized I had not called Jeannette to say I'd be late. I pictured her: carefully dressed and made up—for dinner was a nightly ritual with us—candles lit, wine opened . . . and no loverboy anywhere in sight. This was far from the first time it had happened and, alas, far from the last: the work at Grove seemed to be devouring me, Jeannette had remarked more than once, not so much a complaint as a statement of fact. Though I was ultimately forgiven, forgiveness usually came with the gentle reminder that all I had to do was call and explain. And once again I had not. Better jump in a cab and face the music. The greeting was cold, but when in my excitement I told her how I had spent the day, she immediately—well, almost immediately—forgave me. Still, I knew that I had better start reversing the ratio. Late hours at Grove meant time taken away from not only her but the kids, who too often these days were in bed when I arrived.

Published, *Hiroshima* sold moderately well in the stores, helped of course by the film itself, but as with our drama we mailed copies to every film department in the country, and, little by little, our gem began to be adopted.

With that experiment behind us, we went on to publish several more, including Alain Robbe-Grillet's *Last Year at Marienbad*, again directed by Alain Resnais and starring Jack Youngerman's wife, Delphine Seyrig; François Truffaut's masterpiece *The 400 Blows*, this one starring young, unknown Jean-Pierre Léaud, who turned out to be the son of the Parisian couple I had traveled with in Spain a decade before. We probably would have done many more, but in the midst of all this, in 1963 Hughes was nominated for an Oscar for a documentary on Robert Frost, of which he was the producer. While that honor furthered his career in film, it made him less available for future film-book projects, though we managed a few more: John Osborne's *Tom Jones* in 1964, and Jorge Semprun's *La guerre est finie* in 1967, to name but two.

43 ~

Return to Paris, for Jeannette and Genet

IN THE SPRING OF 1963, Jeannette was invited to tour in Europe, starting in France but on to several cities in Germany—Munich, Frankfurt, Berlin—and London. It was a unique opportunity for her, for though her career was beginning to blossom here, she had, because of her background and training, far greater recognition in Europe. The Paris impresario who had sponsored her at the Salle Gaveau two years before had sketched out an alluring tour for her, which would last three to four months. Knowing how key it would be, she nonetheless hesitated, wanted to decline because of both the children and me. Nathalie was almost five and in her first year at New York's Lycée Française. Alex just turned three. Jeannette's mother proposed to have the children—and Jeannette—stay with her in Paris. "What do you think?" she said. I said the question was now settled, and she had better start preparing for her trip.

I booked passage for them on the SS *America*, but it was with heavy heart that I left the United States Lines office with tickets in hand, proof that I would be without the three most important people in my life for several months. Yet I was all smiles and encouragement as I drove them to the pier on the Hudson where the ship was docked, saw them into their neat little cabin with two double bunks, crushed the munchkins in my arms, and kissed Jeannette a long goodbye. From the pier below, as the ship's whistles announced the leviathan's impending departure and I saw those three on the main deck high above, waving their white handkerchiefs, I tried to smile through my tears, which fortunately were not visible from the great distance between us.

Ever since I joined Grove, we had been publishing eighty or ninety books a year, plus the four issues of *Evergreen Review,* which we considered books, for they were the same format as our paperbacks, in essence anthologies of new works, and were numbered in the Evergreen series. *Evergreen Review* aside, a haphazard mix of hardcover and paperbacks had to follow the normal publishing process from manuscript to bound book, a process that in most houses took roughly the time it took to produce a baby but at Grove generally half that, sometimes less. We were stretched thin, the normal working day ten to twelve hours. When Jeannette and the kids were in Paris, mine stretched even longer, and I was not alone, for often, when I left the office at nine or ten o'clock, Marilynn or Fred was still there.

In the year just past, 1962, we had published eighty titles, which included not only the time-consuming *Naked Lunch* but a novel by a new young author, Robert Gover, *One Hundred Dollar Misunderstanding,* touted to Barney by Henry Miller, and a major volume of stories by Jorge Luis Borges, who had split the Formentor Prize with Beckett. That year also saw the appearance of perhaps our most controversial (though unfraught with legal problems for once) work, *Hitler's Secret Book,* for which Telford Taylor, of Nuremberg trials fame, wrote the introduction, lending weight to its credibility.

Among the plays we brought out, Genet's *Screens* and *The Visit* by a relatively unknown Swiss, Friedrich Dürrenmatt, translated by my old friend Patrick Bowles, added to the fast-growing drama list. Plus a volume of three new plays—*A Slight Ache, The Collection,* and *The Dwarfs*—by Harold Pinter, whom we had begun to publish the year before; Tom Stoppard's latest, *The Real Inspector Hound;* John Mortimer's *Three Plays: The Dock Brief, What Shall We Tell Caroline! I Spy;* John Arden's *Serjeant Musgrave's Dance;* and an American work, Arnold Weinstein's *Red Eye of Love,* which, like *The Connection,* Jeannette and I went to see and were so taken with I told Barney we must publish. He went to check it out, came back, if anything, more enthusiastic than we, and weeks later the published version appeared.

I think it safe to say that by the mid-1960s we had virtually cornered the contemporary literary drama market, not because we had set out to do so with some grandiose plan, but because, having seen our publication of Beckett and Genet and Ionesco, the next generation of playwrights—the Pinters and Stoppards and Gelbers of this world—knew their best chance for publication was with Grove.

One evening roughly two and a half months after Jeannette and the kids' departure, Barney popped his head in my office. "You look tired," he said.

"I probably am."

"Jeannette's tour going well?"

"Winding down. She's got one more concert in Germany, then a big one in Vienna."

"I think it's time we brought out Genet."

"You mean another play?"

"No, the big guy. *Our Lady of the Flowers.*"

I gazed up at Barney with a mixture of admiration and pity. There were still multiple court cases besetting us, which had to be weighing on both his mind and his pocketbook. Yet here he was suggesting we move forward with the Genet novel that was almost certain to bring more legal trouble. It was as if the house were already burning and Barney was handing me another match. But at that point I had not figured out his true, incredibly altruistic strategy.

"The problem is," I said, forgetting all of the above, "the Frechtman translation is piss-poor, and Frechtman still has Jean under his spell."

"You know Genet, don't you? Can't you tell him? Diplomatically, of course."

"Won't be easy. Those novels are Frechtman's lifelines . . ."

"The reason I'm suggesting it—one of the reasons—is that it occurred to me you could kill a couple of birds with one stone: rework the translation with Frechtman, and see your wife and kids in Paris. It would do you, and us, good."

Finally, the light went on, and I was deeply touched. True, he—we— wanted very much to publish the Genet novels, but Barney's timing had much more to do with reclaiming my marriage and my family than anything else. Life without those three had finally gotten to me, and it must have shown.

"Let me write to Frechtman first," I said. "He already knows one of the reasons we haven't gone ahead is the translation. And he knows I'll edit his text whenever we do proceed. I'll tell him by working together—the way Beckett did with me—we'll speed up the process."

Barney nodded, told me to go home, and vanished down the corridor into the night.

Next day I airmailed Frechtman, telling him that we now planned to proceed with *Our Lady* and that to meet our deadline, I'd need to work with him for at least a couple weeks—daily—to edit the translation. The word "edit" was key. Not "retranslate," "edit." Barney had once suggested I retranslate the book, but I knew that would never have gone down. Bernie responded immediately that he welcomed the idea, was free and clear for the next month, simply give him the date. I checked availability and booked a ticket to Paris for the following week. So I called. "Darling, I have terrific news. I'm arriving next Thursday. Yes, in Paris. No, I will be completely independent, working with Bernard Frechtman during the day. Yours at night. Don't tell the kids. I want to surprise them."

It was a gift from Barney I shall never forget. I could have "edited" the Frechtman translation in New York, but he rightly sensed I was nearing the end of my rope. That was one of Barney's often unpredictable generous outbursts.

Overexcited, I didn't sleep a wink on the flight over, felt wonderful at the Orly arrival, grabbed a taxi, and arrived an hour after the kids had left for school. So the surprise was for later. Jeannette's mother, whom I adored, took me aside and said that, however successful and fulfilling the tour had been, she felt, day by day, that Jeannette needed me more than ever, and my arrival could not have been more propitious. When the kids got home to find me seated in the living room, "nonchallently" reading the *Herald Tribune* for the third time, there were shouts of "Daddy! Daddy! Daddy!" that only a parent can appreciate, as two munchkins hurled themselves across the room into my arms. Hugs, kisses, more hugs, then accounting time: "Do you know what they make us do in school?" Nathalie's indignation was palpable, and Alex was nodding even before she outlined the grievance. "They *tie* us to our cots after lunch! *Tie* us! It's awful!" I listened, commiserated, hugged, then tried to explain that there may have been a purpose in this French school madness. Some children—not they, of course—were hyperactive and especially needed a calm moment after lunch. If they weren't confined, they'd be running and jumping around the room so that good children—like themselves—wouldn't be able to rest. Expressions of doubt at first, followed by slightly quizzical looks, as if they were pondering that unlikely possibility. Further, I said, Mother had sent me copies of their homework and writing samples, and I couldn't believe their progress. It was outstanding! Really? Absolutely! Back home, in nursery school or kindergarten, you wouldn't even be printing block letters. Here you're not only writing sentences, but in *script*! What's script? Alex wondered. "Like this, you mean?" his all-knowing sister said, pulling from her knapsack a sheet of lined paper on which, indeed, were fragile but legible handwritten phrases. Hmmm. Maybe *l'école maternelle* wasn't quite as bad as they had thought.

Every morning at nine I took the metro to St. Germain, where Bernie and I met in one café or another and spent the next four or five hours going over the text line by line. Being back there on my old stomping ground made me feel as if I'd never been away. At my most familiar haunts, the waiters remembered me, welcomed me "home," and if I hadn't consciously realized it before, I knew that this was, if not my first, forever my second home. We made progress at roughly fifteen to twenty pages a day, a process sped up by the fact that I had prepared a list of proposed changes before we met. At one point when we were roughly halfway through, Bernie, who had been docile as a lamb till now, in fact thanking me at the end of several sessions for my help in improving Jean's text, looked up through his thick-lensed glasses and said: "I suppose you'll want to be listed as co-translator with me." Accusation or statement of fact? I shook my head. "Bernie, I'm the editor of this book. My job is to make sure Jean's text is as good as you and I can make it. This is a book for the ages, and your translation should reflect that. I have no desire or design to have my name added to yours." He looked as though a great burden had been lifted from his ex-GI shoulders, and without another word on we plowed.

After our first week together, I called Barney and gave him a progress report. "All quiet on the Paris front. I'll bring back a manuscript ready for copyediting. You can schedule the book for next year." And again: "Thanks for dreaming this up."

That fortnight in Paris also gave me a chance to see Jérôme Lindon again, the man I admired above all others in publishing, not just in France, but in the world. We lunched together at a small family restaurant around the corner from Minuit, no more than three doors down from 8, rue du Sabot (where, in a sign of the times, Oscar's primitive-art emporium had been replaced by a Japanese restaurant). We were publishing not only his favorite, Samuel Beckett, but also three or four of his other important writers, including Alain Robbe-Grillet and Marguerite Duras. Duras lived only a couple of blocks away, on the rue St. Benoît, and I paid her a visit after one of my Frechtman sessions. A tiny woman now past her prime if one could judge by the photographs of her prominently displayed around the living room, taken for the most part in Indochina, where she was born and brought up, she was cordial and warm but spent the better part of an hour reinforcing my image of her: bright, dedicated, politically involved, and totally self-centered. I had by now translated two of her works, for which she thanked me, a compliment I would have savored more if she had had more than a shred of English wherewith to judge.

Robbe-Grillet was a whole other matter. When we had first met, I had found him both charming and witty, with a soupçon of malice lurking not far from the surface. Unlike Jérôme, who seemed all business. Alain always had a twinkle, as if one should not take too seriously anything he said or did. He loved to provoke, deflate some academic with an outrageous statement, often about his own work, simply to see how the other person would react. I always sensed there was far more to Alain than met the eye. One of his favorite novels, he admitted early on, was the infamous *Story of O*, intimating that the masochism so thoroughly explored in that mysterious novel—the author of which, ten years after its publication, was still unknown, though theories abounded—was an area that greatly intrigued both him and his wife, Catherine, a small, pretty, dark-haired, vivacious woman full of mystery herself, with whom, rumor had it, Vladimir Nabokov had been smitten when they met. It was also widely bruited about that she was "Jean de Berg," the author of *The Image*, a novel published, oddly, by Minuit, "oddly" because Minuit had never, before or since, to my knowledge published erotica. *The Image* owed much to the practices and principles of *Story of O*, but without the passion, stylistic purity, or conviction.

In any event, catching up with old friends and meeting new added to the wonder and beauty of being back in my almost-native habitat.

44 ∿

Leaving Coenties Slip

THE IDYLL at Coenties Slip ended sadly less than two years after we moved in. Most, if not all, of us in the South Street Seaport area were living illegally, tolerated by some officials who knew the occupants of these weary old buildings were only artists, therefore expendable, ignored by others who, if they tried to expel us, faced going to court. We had hired a feisty young lawyer, Seymour "Si" Litvinoff, who was handling legal and tax matters for a score of artists and writers for a relative pittance, either out of innate benevolence or in the belief that one day these youthful creators would become famous and pay him his due. Ellsworth Kelly and Jack Youngerman were among his clients, as was Terry Southern.

Since we were acutely aware of our building's many violations and the daily concern we might be evicted, Seavers and Youngermans hired an architect to tell us what would bring the building up to code. We loved this unique place and area so much we decided we should try to buy it. Our architect had given us a rough estimate of the house's value, twelve to fifteen thousand dollars, including the cost of necessary repairs. The owner asked for twenty thousand, then quickly dropped to eighteen. The sticking point was: Who would pay to bring the building up to code, without which the sale would not be approved? Finally, we agreed to pay, telling the landlord it would cost us three thousand dollars, which to us meant his selling price should come down to fifteen thousand. He argued for "sixteen thousand dollars," and we agreed to agree.

Litvinoff began soliciting the necessary papers and clearances, and all seemed to be proceeding more or less normally (does bureaucracy ever have a norm?) when Jack and I ran into a new obstacle: the banks. What, a mortgage for a decrepit old building way down near *South* Street? Nobody in his right mind would live there (we could not admit we already did). Not only would we be keeping our beloved building, but we'd be helping preserve a parcel of Old New York. A week later we received an envelope from Chase Bank, which I carried to the top floor, waving it in triumph. "Dear Sirs," it began, "we regret to inform you that, after a careful assessment of your application for a building mortgage at Coenties Slip, your application has been denied." Denied? Could Si find out who the new buyer was? Apparently, the same person or business that had bought our building had been quietly buying dozens of other buildings in the area, most as old as ours, some even older. Historical gems. And, Si added, the plan was to tear them all down.

We suddenly needed to move with all due speed. We scoured the deep downtown, to no avail. In the West Village everything was well beyond our price range. Youngerman had found another loft, half the size of Coenties Slip. Then one morning at work a friend called and said he'd heard of an apartment just put on the market for $154 a month, rent-controlled. Where was it? Upper West Side, Ninety-third Street. Holy tomato! I was reminded of Jeannette's frequent pronouncement that she'd never live in that "combat zone." Without telling her, I subwayed up to see it. A good-sized living room, separate dining room, three bedrooms, decent old-fashioned bath. I knew I wouldn't find anything close, much less better, for the price. Only drawback: the place was on the ground floor, and even in early afternoon the street noise was deafening, radios blasting from a dozen windows, shouts and murmurs from as many neighboring buildings, in English and Spanish. A far cry from the blessed silence of the evening and night downtown, broken only by the comforting call of the tugboats. But life had to move on. I told Jeannette. Where is it? she insisted. Just off Central Park, I ventured. *Where* off Central Park? Upper West Side, I finally admitted. The lease was only for a year, we had no choice. When she saw it, she was placated, but only slightly. "You promise we won't stay for more than a year."

Six months later, Si Litvinoff called us. "You won't believe this," he said.

"The Rockefellers themselves! They're going to locate the world headquarters of the Chase Bank down there, which is why they've been buying up property in the area. As soon as that's made public, can you imagine what each of those properties will be worth? Ten times what they paid for them!" So much for conserving New York's landmarks.

45 ❧

Last Exit to Brooklyn

MY ROUTE TO GROVE almost inevitably took me past the Eighth Street Bookshop, one of New York's best, run by two brothers, Eli and Ted Wilentz. Eli was the more visible of the two, generally the spokesman for his shy and reticent brother, and by now, in 1964, I counted him as a friend. He was a staunch, though worried, supporter of Grove, standing by us as we published book after controversial book, which he would stack defiantly near the cash register or in some other prominent spot certain to bring Lawrence and Miller and Burroughs and Rechy to the clients' attention.

Thus I was startled one morning, shortly before nine, as I was hurrying past the shop, to hear Eli's voice hailing me from the doorway: "Now you've done it! Now you're going to jail!" I'd barely had my coffee, and I was already headed for jail without passing Go?

"Good morning, Eli," I said, turning in my tracks to face him. "What have we done now?"

"*Last Exit to Brooklyn*. The Selby novel. It's really beyond the pale." More than the *Tropics*? I asked. Absolutely, he declared. You mean we're going to be sued again? He guaranteed it. Did that mean he wouldn't stock the book? Of course he would stock it. They would be indemnified, wouldn't they? Of course they would. I asked him what he found so offensive about the book. Certainly not the language? No . . . everything. "It's the most shocking book I've ever read," he ended, and I decided to take that as a compliment.

Arriving at the office, I thought I should report my Eli conversation to Barney, who took it in stride: "They're going to display the book, aren't they?" We had published several sections of the novel in *Evergreen Review*, and the feedback was virtually all positive. Congratulations on discovering a new voice. Shocking but powerful. Perusing again a set of pages that morning, to refresh my recollection, as I had learned to say in court, I found it difficult to believe we'd have legal problems. True, another obscenity trial was wending its way through the courts, that of *Fanny Hill*, published by *Lolita*'s publisher, Putnam, being defended by our old friend Charles Rembar. As of this date, 1964, it was not faring well. A loss for *Fanny Hill* might set freedom to publish back a giant step from the gains of *Chatterley*, Miller, and Burroughs, but for the life of me I could not see it having any relevance to Selby. The language was raw, but far less so than Henry Miller's: street language, that of Brooklyn's lower depths, but of an authenticity no prosecutor could deny. What, then, had prompted Eli's sudden outburst? Leafing through the pages, I came upon "Tralala" and scanned the opening lines:

> Tralala was 15 the first time she was laid . . . Getting laid was getting laid. Why all the bullshit? . . . Tralala didn't fuckaround. Nobody likes a cock-teaser. Either you put out or you dont. Thats all. And she had big tits.

Maybe it was that. Maybe the shock came less from the words themselves than from the cynical, callous attitude of many of the characters, starting with Tralala: you fucked a boy with the same disinterest you displayed in drinking your morning cup of coffee or brushing your teeth. Yes, it was the attitude of these kids that shocked. And of course their age: young people were not supposed to think and act this way. Society would doubtless not go quietly into the night with this one. But rereading random passages that morning, I knew this was a book that had to be published and was eminently defensible, no matter what the cost. The cost . . . Easy for me to say, when I knew all too well the bills that continued to pour in. Still, I was sure that this was a seminal work, both literally and figuratively, one that would endure long after the season's spate of bestsellers had vanished from the earth.

———

Hubert Selby Jr. was a pale, bespectacled young man from Brooklyn who looked more like a librarian than a wild-man writer breaking down still more literary barriers. Shy to a fault, he preferred the shadowy back corridors of literature, apparently intent on avoiding the limelight at all costs. He would describe as he saw fit the sad life and lowlife of Brooklyn whence he came and not worry himself about the reception or repercussions. I became Selby's editor and friend. We worked together closely, spending long hours on his manuscript. I was also delegated to take the photograph *Exit to Brooklyn* that was used for the jacket.

The novel itself, its title a simple roadside sign but, inferentially, one of the most evocative of modern literature, was really a selection of overlapping stories, several of the characters reappearing in minor roles once they had had their brief strut on the stage of his fiction.

It is possible, indeed probable, that of all the books we published that year, *Last Exit to Brooklyn* will best stand the test of time. But for those of us who were in the trenches, there were at least half a dozen others on which we would have placed our money, assuming (wrongly) we had any. That year, 1964, we published far fewer books than had been our wont, either because our finances were too fragile to pay advances for all the projects submitted or because, still with a staff of fifteen, we had yielded to fatigue and overwork. Still, this was the year we published Beckett's *How It Is*, a major new prose piece; two more plays by Bertolt Brecht; William Burroughs's *Nova Express*; Eugène Ionesco's writings on the theater entitled *Notes and Counter Notes*; a volume of poems, *The Dead Lecturer*, by LeRoi Jones, a.k.a. Amiri Baraka; a new volume in our film script series, John Osborne's *Tom Jones*; a third novel by Robbe-Grillet, *The Erasers*; a volume of poems by the Soviet poet Andrei Voznesensky; and young Jorge Semprun's novel *The Long Voyage*, fruit of the second year's Formentor, which unlike the first provided a rich harvest of new fiction, offering the international publishers a fair return on their investment. Not included in the above list was Wayland Young's *Eros Denied: Sex in Western Society*, a work of scholarship and passion that brought the world up to date on the realities of sexual relations.

This was the year, too, when, having published *Our Lady of the Flowers* without (legal) incident, we gave a second blast of the Jean Genet cannon with his equally brilliant, equally provocative *Thief's Journal*. As with *Our Lady*, I went over Bernie's translation with a fine-tooth comb, but by now we could work via the mails, and he was receptive to the majority of my suggestions. If that sounds self-congratulatory, let me quickly add that any kudos should go to Frechtman, for in the reverse situation I am far from sure I would have been as magnanimous.

I'm not sure I was aware at the time, but one of the virtues of working at Grove in the 1960s was the pleasure—privilege, really—of being involved with so many authors who mattered, people whose work you admired and who, in many instances, were—or one day would be—of world stature.

46 ∿

The Grove Method: A Top-Line Approach to Publishing

WE RARELY HAD EDITORIAL MEETINGS at Grove, and in my years there we had never done a P&L—a profit and loss statement—that showed at what point a book would make money, if ever. This admission came as a major surprise to several of my colleagues at other publishing houses, who were obliged to bring their "numbers" to be evaluated at weekly editorial meetings. If the numbers didn't work, they turned the book down even if, as many claimed, they loved the manuscript, swore on the head of their mother that it was brilliant, wonderful, unique. For editors placed in that unpleasant position, the only options were to die or lie, which struck me as unacceptable choices: either you had to slink back to your office in defeat, grumbling about the dunderheaded decision makers who had killed your putative masterpiece, or you took out the template on which the P&L was based, fiddled with the numbers until they *did* work, then re-presented your case to the reigning Caesar who had earlier given you the dumb thumbs-down. A classic case of games people play, and, to me and the rest of us at Grove, a dangerous game to boot: the creative mind versus the bureaucrat, and in that battle you know who always wins.

At Grove, if the manuscript was good, the author serious, the writing (for nonfiction) at least acceptable, you signed it up, especially if the premise was provocative and controversial. Looking back from the vantage point of the mid-1960s at the books we had published since my arrival six years before, I could see several categories that immediately emerged, as if they had been planned, which most of them emphatically had not: Books of controversy first and foremost, which would have to include *Chatterley*, all the Henry Miller, William Burroughs, Jean Genet, Sade certainly, *Story of O*, the John Rechy, *The Deputy*. Next, psychology and psychiatry. Third, books of discovery, that is fiction, drama, and poetry by new authors, a list that would include Shelagh Delaney, Marguerite Duras, Jack Gelber, Eugène Ionesco, Jack Kerouac, Kenneth Koch, Michael McClure, Frank O'Hara, Octavio Paz, André Pieyre de Mandiargues, Harold Pinter, Alain Robbe-Grillet, Tom Stoppard, Alex Trocchi, Arnold Weinstein, Douglas Woolf . . . Since most of these authors were faithful to their publisher, and the publisher faithful to them, each year before we started, we had maybe half the list laid out: new works by our "house" authors. Sprinkle in the works on psychiatry and psychology, and the usual half a dozen relating to the Far East, and there you go: roughly three-quarters of the list was pre-ordained. Which left just enough room for new discoveries without re-course to stodgy meetings. These discoveries came from two sources, our own ebullient editorial brains and our cherished authors, who often wrote suggesting writers they had "discovered." In 1961 or early 1962, Henry Miller wrote to Barney touting a novel called *One Hundred Dollar Mis-understanding* by a previously unpublished young author. The manuscript arrived, and it was indeed funny, irreverent, fresh. We published it imme-diately to considerable success, and the author, Robert Gover, subsequently produced two other novels, not the equal of the first, but full of wit and humor. Samuel Beckett suggested a Frenchman he greatly admired, Robert Pinget, and he too went on the next list. Not that we automatically pub-lished our authors' suggestions, but there was a constant flow to which we paid close attention.

To take a fair example of our decision-making process, one day in 1963 or 1964 I read a French book published by François Maspero, whom I had met a year or two before, entitled *Les damnés de la terre—The Wretched of the Earth*. The author was a black Caribbean-born psychiatrist, Frantz Fanon, who struck me as offering new insights into the hearts and minds of that considerable part of humanity that had been deprived, usually from birth, of basic rights, starting with food and shelter. I discussed the book with Harry Braverman, who joined Grove in 1960, who knew of Fanon and concurred as to his importance. "You and I, Dick, are maybe the only two people in America who have heard of this guy. Of course we should publish him."

I walked over to Barney's office, sat down, a copy of the French edition in my hand, and expostulated for about three minutes on the merits of the book and the author. You think he's that important? Absolutely. Has anybody else read it? No, but I talked to Harry, who knows about Fanon and agrees. Then sign him up. We did, publishing it in 1965 to important reviews, and almost immediately the subsequent paperback became a staple of the backlist. Two years later we published another equally provocative work, *Black Skin, White Masks*, in which he pinpointed the ills besetting the postcolonial world and suggested the remedies needed to cure them.

I never met the man, for he had died young in 1961, but I admired him beyond measure, and after our publication of *The Wretched of the Earth* his widow came to see me in New York to reiterate how gratified her husband would have been to know that his works were appearing in English.

The one book on which none of us would have put our money in the mid-1960s was a manuscript by a Canadian-born doctor out of McGill University, Eric Berne, called *Games People Play*, bearing the subtitle *The Psychology of Human Relationships*. Three years earlier we had published the good doctor's previous book *Transactional Analysis in Psychotherapy*, a specialized work that, despite its forbidding title, had sold reasonably well. I had found Berne an easy author, open to suggestions. I thought we published far too many books on psychology and psychiatry for our own financial good. Despite my reservations, I noted that, increasingly, that category was providing a slow but steady income stream, as many of the titles reprinted and became part of the growing backlist.

With *Games People Play*, however, the doctor was most assuredly suffering from delusions of grandeur, for with his manuscript came a letter stating unequivocally that this work would sell more than a hundred thousand copies, and a print order of that magnitude was strongly recommended. Reading the manuscript, I had to admit it was clearly aimed much more at a general audience than the first book, but the author's expectations seemed so absurd I wasn't quite sure how to answer him, especially after we had more or less decided on a first printing of five thousand copies, based on the first year's sales of *Transactional Analysis*. Publishers of course are generally not bound to inform authors of the exact size of any printings, information they will receive when their biannual royalty reports are sent out.

I simply punted by plying Berne with a number of editorial questions and supplying him with a general idea of the book's schedule. By return came the answer to my editorial queries, followed by an insistent demand to know how many copies we intended to print. The last paragraph of the letter, however, gave me second thoughts, for Berne offered to buy twenty-five hundred copies out of the first printing for his own use. Since authors generally have the right to buy copies of their own work at 40 percent discount, and since *Games People Play* was slated to have a list price—what one pays in the bookstore—of five dollars, I did some simple math and figured that at a cost of a little over a dollar apiece, our total printing bill for seventy-five hundred copies would be virtually covered by his paying us three dollars a book. I showed Barney the numbers, and his response was to wonder aloud if the doctor was good for the promised amount. "I'll make him pay half up front and the second half when he receives the books. Which means we'll have the money in hand before we have to pay the printer."

It seemed that Berne's contribution to fiscal stability, though modest, was a step in the right direction. When the book came off press, to our pleasant surprise the first five thousand copies sped out the door. "Okay," Barney said, "out *our* door, but how about the bookstores?" The sales manager, Nat Sobel, checked a number of retail outlets both in New York and in half a dozen other East Coast cities and reported back that apparently the book was not only selling but selling briskly. "What the hell's 'briskly'?" Barney wanted to know. "Don't you have any *hard* numbers?" Nat did. Pulling a sheet of paper from his pocket, he began ticking off the stores: four out of five here, two of three there, one of three elsewhere . . . on and on. Barney listened impassively, then said: "That's like calling an election when 5 percent of the votes are in." "Still," I reminded him, "Eric's contribution to the first printing paid for the entire cost. So at this point we're way ahead of the game." He nodded, and nervously ordered a second, modest printing of three thousand. By the time that printing arrived a couple of weeks later, more than three thousand orders had been chalked up by the abacus or whatever had replaced it as our counting tool, at which point we had no choice, it seemed, but to order a third, equally modest printing. When that too was gone before the new printing came off press, we consulted and ordered a fourth printing of—dare I say it?—seventy-five hundred copies! Nat made a geographically broader survey, and wherever he phoned, the news was good. The book was still selling "briskly," a term that irritated Barney then as much as the first time, though now he was less pessimistic, for sales were already in the solid five figures.

For the next several weeks, new printings barely kept up with demand, and soon the book hopped onto the *New York Times* bestseller list, where it remained for a record 102 weeks. By year's end we had sold hundreds of thousands of copies, the book had gone to number 1 and remained stuck there.

Waving the paper in my hand the day it first appeared in the top spot, I told Barney there was good news and bad: the good was the book was number 1 in the country; the bad was Dr. Berne had been right in the first place. Barney laughed. "No, he wasn't. He predicted the book would sell a hundred thousand copies. You see how greatly he *under*estimated its potential."

Few of our offerings over the years seemed to recommend themselves to the Book-of-the Month Club, for our editorial approach, and our audiences, were worlds apart. Still, with the bestseller lists to back me up, I sent copies off with a letter suggesting the Berne might just be an ideal choice for BOM. A few weeks later I received a reply thanking me for my submission but, using the standard rejection line, "this isn't right for us." On the first anniversary of its arrival on the *New York Times* bestseller list, however, I took my courage in my hands—a strange phrase, now that I look at it—and sent another copy, with the anniversary circled in red. After the normal, though irritating, delay, word came back that "thank you again, but no thanks." BOM 2, Grove 0.

A full year later, when the second anniversary of the book's bestsellerdom had been reached, I was tempted to try again but thought better of it. Who needed another face slap? Anyway, by then we were preparing a cheap paperback edition, which I figured obviated any chance of a belated book club hardcover. Wrong. One morning I received a call from BOM: Were book club rights still available? They were, I allowed, but I'm afraid you're too late, we're about to release our paperback edition. "That's all right," Mr. BOM intoned, "our audience doesn't care." I reported the conversation to Barney, who at first thought it was a joke. Then, angered by the remembrance of their rejections, he responded with a double expletive, which I leave to your imagination. "Barney," I reminded him, "they're paying a substantial advance, which doubtless, given the timing, they'll never earn out." At which point he acquiesced, and Grove had its first BOM "selection." And again I was wrong: despite the competition of the low-priced paperback, the club not only earned out its advance but kept sending royalties for months on end.

Games People Play was a book that saved our skin, at least for the moment, and also proved how smart you have to be to become a book publisher. Books you swear are going to set sales records stumble and fall, never to be heard from again; books about which you have grave doubts, questioning whether you should have signed them up at all, sell beyond all expectation. That's what makes publishing such fun, and what, so often, makes it hard to get a good night's sleep.

47 ∾

The Autobiography of Malcolm X

HAT MONDAY MORNING was a shocker.

Many people viewed Monday as blue, the first day of a long week in a job most disliked or endured. I can honestly say these last six years at Grove had been endlessly exciting. There were, very simply, no dull weeks. Challenging, yes, but every day seemed to bring forth a surprise, a revelation, an obstacle to be overcome, an accusation to be countered, a financial drama to be coped with. Did that mean automatic stress? Probably. But we were young and certain we were doing something that had an impact, might even change the world, if only a mite.

On that Monday, at six thirty, my usual hour, I stooped to pick up the *Times* outside my door and stood there transfixed. In the center of page 1, the headline read, in twenty-four-point type: MALCOLM X SHOT TO DEATH AT RALLY HERE. Below the headline was a four-column picture of Malcolm, surrounded by aides, on a stretcher being wheeled to the Vanderbilt Clinic a block away from the Audubon Ballroom at 166th Street and Broadway, where Malcolm had spoken at three o'clock as part of the usual Sunday afternoon meeting of his recently founded Organization of Afro-American Unity. Even before I read the article, I muttered to myself, "Bastards!" for I was certain that the killers were members of Elijah Muhammad's Nation of Islam, for which Malcolm had long been the most brilliant minister and spokesman until, a year before, he had broken with it, candidly and bitterly. The break, I knew from my friend Benjamin Goodman, one of Malcolm's closest attendants, stemmed partly from Malcolm's speech roughly fifteen months earlier, known as the "Chickens Come Home to Roost" affair, in which Malcolm, commenting on the assassination of President Kennedy, had intimated—not in the speech itself, which had been cleared with Elijah Muhammad, but in the question-and-answer period that followed— that Kennedy's death was a result of the climate of hate and violence prevailing in America. That might have passed unperceived had he not followed with: "Being an old farm boy myself, chickens coming home to roost never did make me sad, they always made me glad."

That was the remark the papers picked up on, and Malcolm was ordered by Elijah Muhammad to report immediately to headquarters in Chicago, where he was told he would be suspended for ninety days. Malcolm could continue to oversee the daily administration of his mosque, Harlem's Mosque No. 7, but could give no speeches or interviews for three months. Malcolm accepted the order with good grace and later told Benjamin that in all likelihood the Messenger had saved his life, for the outrage occasioned by his remarks made him a likely target for those—and they were legion—who feared and hated the Nation of Islam in general and Malcolm specifically.

But I also knew that Malcolm's remarks that day had finally given Elijah Muhammad the excuse he needed to bring Malcolm down. Permanently. For after twelve years of seeming deference and devotion to the Messenger, Malcolm had become in the eyes of Chicago too big for his breeches. It was Malcolm who so often appeared on television and was solicited for radio interviews and in magazine spreads; it was Malcolm rather than Elijah who had signed a contract with the prestigious house of Doubleday to write his autobiography, and Malcolm may well have sensed a growing jealousy.

What's more, one of the Nation of Islam's basic tenets was marital fidelity, and disconcerting stories had leaked out of Chicago about the Messenger cavorting with a number of the Nation's secretaries, several of whom had mysteriously become pregnant and therefore been expelled from the movement. At first, Malcolm had refused to believe such outlandish tales, surely the work of white devils, but ultimately he confronted the Messenger in Chicago. Elijah had apparently taken him for a private stroll and quoted the Bible at length, citing passages in which Old Testament giants such as Lot and Moses were accused of succumbing to temptations of the flesh. If Elijah meant these remarks as his response to false accusations, Malcolm took them as admissions of guilt. Back in New York, he imparted his increasing disillusion to several of his fellow ministers, at least one of whom reported this back to Chicago. Meanwhile, Malcolm asked repeatedly to be reinstated, but by the end of February, when his suspension was supposed to end but did not, he knew his twelve-year membership in the Nation of Islam was over. For him, it was the bitterest of pills, but being a man of action, and convinced of his importance to the cause of America's twenty-two million blacks, in early March he set up his own movement, Muslim Mosque Inc., headquartered in Harlem. To the press he stated flatly that the rift between him and Elijah Muhammad, for whom he reiterated his respect and devotion, had been engineered by jealous followers who resented their father-son closeness and had poisoned the Messenger's mind.

Most of this I knew from Benjamin, who like many others from Harlem Mosque No. 7 had unhesitatingly joined Malcolm's new venture. They were painfully aware that the road would be rocky and perilous, with only Malcolm's energy, willpower, and intelligence to sustain them. What they did not know, or only vaguely suspected, was that on that fateful day of March 8, 1964, Malcolm had, in proclaiming his independence, effectively signed his own death warrant.

I arrived at work well before nine and went directly to Barney's office. He had the *Times* spread out on the conference table and a radio on. By nine o'clock we had been joined by Fred, Harry, Nat Sobel, the VP and general troubleshooter, Jules Geller, and the director of publicity, Morrie Goldfischer.

With the radio blaring in the background, I yelled, "It had to be Elijah Muhammad's people."

Barney, reading from the *Times*, shook his head. "James X, New York spokesman for the Black Muslims, denied that his organization had anything to do with the killing."

"Of course they're denying it," Harry said. "They have to. But I agree with Dick: often the obvious solution is the correct one."

Barney and Jules were not so sure. They thought the assassination might well have been orchestrated by a government agency, the CIA or the FBI for starters, for Malcolm was viewed by most white politicians—indeed, most whites in general—as an advocate of violence, a danger to society, a demagogue so charismatic and convincing to the nation's blacks that he would be far better dead than read.

"I called Haley twice this morning. No answer."

"To me," Harry said, "what makes it even worse, now we'll never get to read his autobiography."

We knew that for the past year, perhaps longer but especially since his break with the Nation, Malcolm had been working on his autobiography with a man named Alex Haley. Just last week Malcolm had postponed a trip to see Haley in upstate New York, where he had intended to devote two full days to the book. Clearly he was too distracted by the firebombing of his house to focus on anything else.

"Get this," Jules said, reading from the *Times*. "Apparently, the man who introduced Malcolm yesterday closed by saying: 'Malcolm is a man who would give his life for you.' Isn't that a hell of a note?"

The next day, I finally reached Benjamin Goodman, Malcolm's second-in-command. Normally open and friendly, Benjamin now sounded vague. Scared perhaps. This man so close to Malcolm for seven years, who had broken with the Nation the minute Malcolm did, had to be concerned for his own safety.

"Ben, let me ask you: How in God's name did those people get into the hall without being searched? I mean, a twelve-gauge shotgun!"

A long sigh on the other end. "Dick, before I went on, Malcolm was in a state of nerves I'd never seen. At one point as the hall was filling, he turned to me and said, 'Something seems wrong out there.' I think he knew something was going to happen—maybe not specifically, but something. Some of the brothers had pleaded with him to let them frisk everybody coming in, but he refused. 'I'm here among my people,' he told us. 'I have nothing to worry about.'"

I had heard Malcolm speak only once—when Benjamin had invited and vouched for me—and he had both seduced and frightened me. But I knew instinctively that on Sunday afternoon America had lost a man capable of moving the country forward, of healing the race issues as never before.

Three days later Barney called a meeting at 9:01. "I have some interesting news."

We all shuffled in, the same crew that had met to ponder the Malcolm assassination. Barney, with a slight smile of triumph, said dramatically: "Doubleday have renounced their rights to publish Malcolm's autobiography. It seems they're concerned for the safety of their employees. What would keep whoever killed Malcolm, they're saying, from using violence against his publishers? The book apparently attacks the Nation of Islam pretty viciously."

"Then we should publish it," I said.

"Absolutely," Harry said.

Morrie raised his hand. "I second the motion."

"Shouldn't we read it first?" Fred asked—a reasonable question, since three days before we had doubts the manuscript had been completed.

"Who's the agent?" Harry asked.

"Malcolm Reiss at Paul Reynolds," Barney said. Then: "You realize, of course, that if we go ahead, we run the same risk of retaliation."

A collective shrug. "If we miss an opportunity like this," Harry said, "we shouldn't be in publishing."

Days later we owned the book.

A meeting was scheduled with Alex Haley, who turned out to be an amiable, intelligent, slightly overweight black man who had served in the U.S. Navy for twenty years, risen to the rank of chief petty officer, and retired with the goal of becoming a writer and with the luxury of a government pension that allowed him to live frugally and indulge his fantasy, for years if necessary. I had heard Benjamin mention his name, but never in a context that allowed me to picture him. When I met him, I was impressed. No, the manuscript was not completed, he said, but it was well along, their scheduled meeting the weekend of his murder would have been essentially to tie up loose ends.

We'd signed the contract without reading the manuscript, an act of faith. A day or two later, Malcolm Reiss sent down two carbon copies, with the admonition that this was only a draft. We read it immediately and were overwhelmed. Remarkable. Deeply intelligent. Shorn of any self-indulgence. True, it would need work, but the essential was there. The trajectory of Malcolm's life was so dramatic, so unique, and yet so "normal" for all too many American blacks, deprived from birth of any chance of a normal existence, much less fulfilling the American Dream. For me, the most startling moment in his extraordinary journey came when, after more than two hundred pages of heart-stomping adventures and admissions, more than enough to fill a long life, I read: "Tomorrow I shall turn seventeen!"

We decided we had to "crash" the book, that is, cut the normal time between manuscript and finished book by half, maybe two-thirds. Still, the manuscript needed work. Who would edit it?

We debated whether to publish as a paperback original or a hardcover, the former to make it widely available to its core market, which we saw as essentially black, the latter to make sure the book was properly and widely reviewed. The hardcover constituency won out, but the paperback backers were assured we'd issue an inexpensive edition in short order. Finally, advance copies of the finished book, with a list price of $7.50, the lowest we could make it and not lose money,* arrived in the office, an impressive package bearing a handsome photograph of Malcolm, the bearded prophet, on the jacket. Our first printing was ten thousand copies—if that number seems cautious, many stores refused to stock it—and we sat back to await the reviews.

Without question, the greatest Grove accomplishment of that year, 1965, was our publication of *The Autobiography of Malcolm X*.

---

*A year later we did indeed bring out a paperback at $1.25.

48 ~

Story of O

I F EVER THERE WAS a man born to become a publisher, it was Jean-Jacques Pauvert. Attracted to books at an early age, the young Frenchman began to publish under his own name when he was still in his teens. In fact, he was only fifteen when, in the fateful year 1941, when the Nazis did an abrupt about-face and attacked the Soviet Union and Japan bombed Pearl Harbor, he was introduced to the legendary Gaston Gallimard, founder of the Gallimard publishing house, and given a job in its bookstore on the boulevard Raspail. During the later war years, his increasingly sophisticated knowledge of the rare-book market—as many in occupied France with money and no safe place to put it sought financial refuge in first and limited editions—enabled him first to double, then to quadruple, his base Gallimard salary of eight hundred francs a month. Among the bibliophilic treasures that fell into his hands in this troubled time was a three-volume edition, published by Stendhal et Compagnie in the 1930s, of the Marquis de Sade's *Les 120 journées de Sodome*. He dutifully plowed through, but, he later confessed, he failed to understand not only the book itself but also why he was supposed to be reading "this voice that resonated, at times like a thunderclap, at other times soft as silk, with an undercurrent of enormous humor." If that most outrageous of Sade's works confounded him, one must remember he was just sixteen. "So far as I knew," he wrote of the experience, "there was no other example in the history of literature—or writing—of these gigantic indecencies, these outrageous obscenities, these multiple, methodical, atrocious details." It would have been disconcerting no doubt if his reaction had been different. Still, the memory of that teenage encounter implanted itself in his brain, where it lay dormant for the next six years.

At the bookstore he met a number of authors, mostly published by Gallimard: Raymond Queneau, Marcel Aymé, Henry de Montherlant, Jean-Paul Sartre, and—most important, though obviously he was unaware at the time—Jean Paulhan, the éminence grise of Gallimard. Paulhan was much taken by his young colleague's enthusiasm, precocious knowledge of books, and disposition, and over the next few years he welcomed Jean-Jacques into his open "editorial" meetings at Gallimard's literary magazine, *La nouvelle revue française*, or *NRF*, where the state of literature and politics—in France they are inextricably entwined—was examined and dissected.

Intrigued by his early reading of Sade, but knowing little about him, Jean-Jacques set out to learn more, to ferret out lesser-known texts by and about him, starting with Eugen Dühren's *Der Marquis de Sade und seine Zeit*, Maurice Heine's editions of selected writings, Paul Bourdin's *Correspondance inédite du marquis de Sade, de ses proches et de ses familiers*, and above all Guillaume Apollinaire's *L'oeuvre du marquis de Sade: Pages choisies*, in the preface to which the poet declared:

> It strikes me that the time has come for these ideas that have been ripening in the unspeakable atmosphere of the restricted sections of libraries, and this man who was completely forgotten throughout the nineteenth century might well assume a dominant position in the course of the twentieth.
>
> The marquis de Sade, the freest spirit that ever lived, also had very special ideas about women, whom he wanted to see as free as men.

Ideas that had a profound effect on the fledgling publisher. Who was this man whose very name sent people into paroxysms of rage on the one hand and elicited such ecstatic praise on the other? Rebel? Revolutionary? Visionary? Madman? Perhaps all four. The more he read and the more he learned about this "monster author," the more he was beguiled. Was this not an opportunity for a young publisher? If, as Apollinaire had proclaimed, he was the freest spirit that ever lived, should he not be unshackled for the world to judge? By 1948, having read all there was to read by and about the man, Pauvert made up his young mind: he would devote himself to resuscitating Sade, would publish all his work, no matter how long it took or whatever obstacles, including the threat of confiscation, even prison. And, most daring of all, he intended to publish Sade not clandestinely, as others had before him, but with his imprint and address openly and proudly affixed to the cover. When he made this life-altering decision, Jean-Jacques Pauvert was all of twenty-two.

Flash forward six years. The more-than-decade-long friendship between Jean-Jacques Pauvert and Jean Paulhan had not only endured but flourished. Pauvert still frequently showed up at Paulhan's weekly Wednesday meetings at Gallimard, and Paulhan, aware of Pauvert's commitment to Sade—which had already resulted in his publication of several volumes, each the subject of legal proceedings—increasingly admired the young man's pigheaded courage. The two often lunched together, and on more than one occasion Paulhan alluded to a mysterious manuscript that had come across his desk that he found "quite extraordinary," a term he rarely employed. Somewhat irritating, in the absence of the manuscript itself, was Paulhan's reiterated statement that Jean-Jacques would be the most likely publisher for it—in fact, the only one daring enough to take it on. His own house, Gallimard, Paulhan confessed, had had first crack at it, dithered for a year and a half despite his own oft-voiced enthusiasm, and finally turned it down, Gaston Gallimard having cast the deciding negative vote after one member of the editorial board had told him, "Gaston, at your stage of life you don't need to be publishing *pornography!*" All of which further whetted Jean-Jacques's literary appetite. Repetition being the mother of lassitude, however, Jean-Jacques stopped saying he'd be only too happy to read it. Until one glacially rainy night in December 1953, or January 1954, as Pauvert relates, he was walking along the rue Jacob when he ran into Paulhan, who suddenly announced: "You know that manuscript I've been talking to you about, well, I've got it with me!" Jean-Jacques showed little enthusiasm, but Paulhan literally thrust the rain-soaked envelope into his arms and assured him it would be worth his time.

At home, after dinner Jean-Jacques opened the packet to find a short note from Paulhan saying that unless he was badly mistaken, this was a work that would have an important place in the history of literature, adding that, despite the few corrections in the margin in his hand, the book was in no way his but the product of a very talented, special woman who was choosing to remain anonymous and publish under the pseudonym Pauline Réage. Jean-Jacques noted the intriguing title, *Story of O*, and began to read. At one in the morning he finished and woke up his wife. "Breathtaking," he said. "It's MY book. The book I've been looking for all these years. True, I'm the publisher of Sade. But it's with *Story of O* I'm going to make my literary mark."

Early—too early—the next morning he phoned Paulhan, apologized for waking him up, and announced he was ready to make a contract. When could he meet the author? A few pre-coffee wheezing coughs on the other end, and the Gallimard éminence grise was forced to confess that the author had already signed a contract with another publisher. What? That was not *possible*! Then why had Paulhan given him the manuscript *after* the fact? It was *his* book. As Jean-Jacques describes it, visions of guns and knives swam through his head, of poisons that, drop by fatal drop, would do in this interloper, whose name he finally extracted from his by now thoroughly cowed friend. Paulhan tried to explain that he had given the manuscript to Pauvert because he thought the man who had contracted for it might be having second thoughts. The publisher in question was the very proper Monsieur René Defez, owner of Éditions des Deux Rives. "That gentleman currently has some serious problems with the government," Paulhan explained, "and may not want to add to them with *Story of O*. Perhaps you can work something out with him."

Defez's problem, it turned out, was an explosive book he had recently published, *Le trafic des piastres*, exposing corruption not only at the highest levels of the French government and military in Indochina but reaching as well into the Paris parliament and, apparently, even the inner circle of the French president. Defez's home and office had been burglarized, and he was currently the subject of several indictments. To Jean-Jacques's urgent inquiries, Monsieur Defez responded, "Oh, yes, you mean Madame O, the little porno novel Paulhan laid off on me. You really want it? I paid a hundred thousand francs for it. Pay me back the same amount and the contract is yours." Fortunately, Jean-Jacques had brought along his checkbook, and he complied without hesitation. Later, he had second thoughts: Why so precipitous? The man was so clearly no longer interested in the project that if he, Jean-Jacques, had bargained a bit more, Defez would probably have let it go for nothing. Ah, hindsight . . .

Now his only concern was how he would cover the check, for he had known as he wrote it that the account was virtually empty. So what? He'd find the funds somehow. Meanwhile, he had his book. Nothing else mattered.

Enter (once again!) Maurice Girodias. By the spring of 1954, both Jean-Jacques's office on the rue des Ciseaux and Maurice's sublet on the rue Jacob having become too small for them, they decided to join forces and share a large office at 8, rue de Nesle, off rue Dauphine. Given their new proximity, it was only normal that Jean-Jacques tell Maurice about his exciting discovery. Girodias asked to read the manuscript and decided it would fit nicely into Olympia. There was never a formal contract between them for the English version—Girodias was suspicious of paper trails, for they could be trod against him—but it was verbally agreed that Olympia could print no more than three thousand copies and that the translation would be undertaken by Girodias's brother Eric, an excellent translator. To capitalize on the uproar that Maurice presumed would greet *O*'s publication in French, he decided his English version had to appear at the same time. But Eric was busy with another project, and all the tried-and-true members of Maurice's translating stable—Trocchi, Wainhouse, Logue—were otherwise engaged, so he turned to that relatively new Merlinite in Paris, Baird Bryant, who swore he could meet the deadline. What he failed to divulge was that his French was, to be generous, limited. When Baird delivered the manuscript and received his standard six-hundred-dollar fee, Maurice may or may not have read it. If he did, he failed to correct even the most egregious errors, for the French publication date in June was fast approaching, leaving him, in his mind, no choice.

The French book, clad in its demure yellow cover and proudly bearing the name and address of its publisher (anyone who wants to pursue me knows where to find me)

A SCEAUX

CHEZ JEAN-JACQUES PAUVERT

MCMLIV

arrived from the printer to almost no bookstore orders. No problem: wait until the reviews, pro or con, it matters little, start appearing. Wait for the uproar. One week, two weeks, three weeks, four. Not to mention five, six, and seven. The only review to appear was a notice in *Dimanche-matin* on August 29 that, while positive, compared *O* to the Song of Songs, perhaps more aptly to the tale of Tristan and Isolde. Not exactly selling copy, and besides nobody read *Dimanche-matin* anymore. The only person regularly depleting stock was Jean Paulhan himself, who kept writing and asking for "ten copies if you please"; "six more if you don't mind"; "can I have a few more? I assure you they will be put to good use." In short, no movement. No uproar. No sales.

Part of the problem was that a few months before O's publication, another novel appeared, written by an unknown teenager named Françoise Sagan, that took Paris—and later the world—by storm: *Bonjour tristesse*. It was shocking in an undaring way, a book you could discuss openly without fear of opprobrium. By year's end, *Bonjour tristesse* had sold over a million copies. Counting, Jean-Jacques figured maybe a thousand of O had shipped, but that probably included Jean Paulhan's "promotion" copies.

That lack of critical and commercial success did not, however, deter the judiciary, for someone in high places either had read the book and been shocked or had been told it was truly scandalous. Further, this female Sade had to be uncovered and chastised before she sapped the moral fiber of the nation. Both Pauvert and Paulhan were summoned separately by the Brigade Mondaine. The publisher, for whom such inquests were by now old hat because of the Divine Marquis, admitted he indeed knew the author. Yes, she was a woman, though she had used a pseudonym. Yes, he had a good and valid contract. No, the police could not see it. His defense, in short, was that such information between publisher and author was privileged, as was that between a lawyer and a client. Stymied, the inspector stood, shrugged, and the two shook hands. Pauvert 1, Brigade Mondaine 0.

Jean Paulhan, suave and imposing, took a different tack. Yes, he was fairly sure he knew who the author was, and, yes, he was prepared to reveal her identity. Good! Now we're getting somewhere! One person frequently mentioned, Paulhan averred, was Lucie Faure, the wife of the prominent politician Edgar Faure. Another name bruited about, he had to confess, was that of Louise de Vilmorin, a lady well-known in high circles, a woman of considerable wealth and standing. He could go on, he said, but didn't they see the problem: Sullying the name of ladies who might well be innocent? All of whom were well connected? What gentleman would ever stoop that low? The inspector(s) nodded in agreement. Indeed. Many thanks, Monsieur Paulhan, for all your help . . .

A faint ray of light in the darkness of O came early in 1955, when the novel won the Prix des Deux Magots, a literary prize started before the war that counted among its laureates the highly regarded Raymond Queneau, author of *Zazie dans le métro*. It was, as Pauvert noted, not the Goncourt, France's most prestigious literary award, but it was notice of the book's existence.

Another push came roughly a year after publication, when two extremely laudatory reviews finally appeared, one in *Critique* by André Pieyre de Mandiargues, the other by Georges Bataille in *La nouvelle revue francaise*. Both reviewers were friends of Pauvert and Paulhan, so there was a touch of *copinage*—cronyism—in their praise, but nonetheless it brought the book to the attention of a wider audience. Still, it would take years before word of mouth, aided and abetted by the continuing curiosity and controversy about who Pauline Réage really was, brought Jean-Jacques's prescient prediction to reality. Into each copy of the original edition he had inserted a card that read: "*Story of O*, we assure you, is a book that will make its mark in the history of world literature."

Today, more than fifty years after its publication, that assurance to the reader has been borne out. Far more copies of *Story of O* have been sold worldwide than, with all due respect, Françoise Sagan's *Bonjour tristesse*.

I did not meet Jean-Jacques Pauvert until the early 1960s, but I had taken note of his courageous commitment to Sade over the years and followed the vicissitudes of *Story of O*, which he published the last year I lived in Paris, 1954. From a scandal virtually ignored at first, *O* by slow degrees, mostly by word of mouth and then increasingly from heated controversy— for the feminist movement of the 1960s branded it as pandering to male fantasies, and more than a few swore the book, which details a beautiful woman's total and willing subjugation to male sadists, had to have been written by a man—became a worldwide success. That *O* was (or purported to be) written by a woman without doubt contributed to its ultimate triumph. But unquestionably, two other elements helped: the preface by the literary icon Jean Paulhan, which even the most vehement detractors could not ignore; and, even more important, the quality of the writing itself, for the prose of the novel was shot through with stunning, if often painful, images, which after the initial shock imbued it with a mystical aura—even a religious one, for in O's suffering and subjugation some found parallels with the blessed martyrs, even with Christ.

I had first heard of the novel not from Pauvert but from Girodias's English-language edition, which appeared the same year as the original French. Reading it, I wondered what all the fuss was about, why critics— even those who condemned its content—raved about its prose, its purity of style, for in the Olympia version the prose was so stilted and awkward I dismissed it as the trash it actually wasn't.

Barney and I discussed the book briefly my first year or two at Grove, and I was dismissive, scoffing at the French literati who were still claiming it was a classic. Only when I finally read the French did I understand that the problem lay not with Pauline Réage but with Olympia's unnamed translator. Not only had he (she?) massacred the style, but the mistranslations, the howlers in the Olympia edition, were as frequent as they were egregious. After I revised my judgment, we approached Girodias about the English-language rights, which he said he would be happy to sell us if, to be sure, the price was right. To make a contract, however, we needed proof that he, not the French publisher Pauvert, owned the foreign rights. Ah, what suspicious types these Americans! Will my word not suffice? No, my dear Maurice, it will not. A simple copy of your own contract will be fine. Sputter, sputter, foil and fumble. You must understand that in France a simple handshake seals a deal. But this is America, my dear friend, where pen and ink are more in fashion. Further beating around the bush. It occurred to us finally what should have occurred to us immediately, namely, that the man had no foreign rights and maybe no rights at all. A letter to Monsieur Pauvert confirmed that Olympia had never had a contract, its "rights" restricted to a single modest printing of three thousand copies, which of course Maurice had immediately violated by printing almost twice that number. When he had been put on notice never to print more, he had simply changed the title to *The Whip and the Lash* and gone back to press. Further—this according to Jean-Jacques—the author, herself a critic and highly considered translator, had been so appalled by the Olympia version she had written a letter of protest to Jean-Jacques:

> *Dear Friend:*
> *You know as well as I that if we agreed to authorize a printing of only 3,000 copies (not a copy more!) of the translation of* O *by Girodias, it was before we had a chance to see the translation. I was horrified by the translation. It is uncommonly vulgar and completely denatures the character of the book. Under no circumstances can it continue to be sold, and I hereby authorize you to take whatever measures are necessary to stop its sale.*

With the issue thus clarified, we contracted with Pauvert for the English-language rights. In all fairness, after Madame Réage's letter of protest, Maurice had hired someone to clean it up, and the resulting version was far better. But given the rift between Maurice and Jean-Jacques, there was no way we could refuse to deal with Girodias contractually and at the same time ask to use his new translation. In fact, a basic condition of buying the English-language rights was Jean-Jacques's stipulation that we commission a new translation. By now, he and Maurice were in open war.

We had talked about *O* with Pauvert, first in Paris in the spring of 1963 and again at the Frankfurt Book Fair that fall. From our first meeting, I found Jean-Jacques a delight, a totally positive spirit, whose almost handlebar mustache quivered with pleasure whenever he smiled or laughed, which was often. His close colleague Jean Castelli, who managed the company and handled foreign rights, was a perfect "second," almost as charming and energetic as his boss.

"O . . . ah, O . . ." Then the smile. Of course he would like us to have it, but there was a problem: "Monsieur Girodias. Olympia and Grove. Weren't we in bed together? After all, Casement, Burroughs, Miller . . ."

Jean-Jacques had a point, starting with the Casement diaries.*

Henry Miller for another, not to mention *The Olympia Reader*, on which Girodias was counting to make himself rich once again (the fruits of *Lolita*

---

*The full title for which was *The Black Diaries of Roger Casement*. Casement, born in 1864 in Northern Ireland, joined the British Civil Service and served with distinction as consul in a number of African countries, where he discovered and exposed the lamentable conditions used by virtual slave labor in the mines and on the plantations of the Belgian Congo, for which he was knighted. At the outbreak of World War I, he joined the Irish independence movement, therefore allied himself with Germany, where he moved. In the spring of 1916 he landed on the Irish coast from a German submarine, was captured, and was sent down to London, where he was tried for high treason, condemned to death, and—despite serious diplomatic efforts to save him, not only from his native Ireland but from Britain and the United States—hanged himself in the summer of that same year. Since then, questions abounded about the diaries Casement had kept, some people questioning their authenticity and claiming they had been fabricated to help the prosecution, for Casement was homosexual and the diaries contained explicit sexual descriptions in an era when homosexuality was still very much anathema. Unlike so many of his other books, where often he sent them to press without even a cursory look, for the diaries Girodias acted as editor and, together with his secretary, Miriam Worms, fashioned a strong volume out of the raw material. We—Grove—had published it the year I arrived. Barney—half Irish himself—loved the book almost as much as Maurice did, for as both gentlemen have admitted, in Casement they saw many personality traits they saw in themselves. The book was a nonsuccess commercially on both sides of the Atlantic.

now squandered). Anything we did together, we insisted, was on a book-by-book basis.

The truth was, Maurice was furious with us for negotiating with Jean-Jacques rather than with him for the English-language rights to *O*. "There goes, under my nose, another book for which I have fought like the devil," he would write to his New York lawyer. "Of course, Jean Jacques needed the couple of thousand dollars Barney presumably paid for the contract, and he just dismissed me as a negligible quantity." For the last year or two, relations between Grove and Olympia had in fact been fast deteriorating, for the simple reason that each court case we won, bringing down the walls of censorship, made us—and everyone—freer to publish without restriction, which meant that Maurice's little empire of forbidden work was shrinking daily.

Contractually, we would have to translate from scratch. I wondered whether Richard Howard might take it on, but he was busy with other work. Barney suggested Patsy Southgate, for he thought the novel should be translated by a woman. Patsy, a beautiful young woman whom I had met briefly in Paris when she was married to Peter Matthiessen and had become a friend, politely declined, not on grounds of morality, though she found the book disturbing, but because, she said, she was then concentrating on her own writing, having recently published a superb story in *Evergreen*. And then one night, close to dawn, it came to me as if in a dream: I knew whence the author had derived that name. And, almost at the same time, I had solved the code name of the translator.

Barney asked me to translate *O*, and I accepted. I became "Sabine d'Estrée."

The author's name including coded clues to the real author's identity, I felt that it was imperative to play along and create a code for the translator's name as well. It was equally important to have the translator be a woman. I had a lot of fun searching for a name when I came upon "Sabine," Jeannette's middle name. As for d'Estrée, "Sabine astrayed" . . . evolved into "d'Estrée".

We all swore to secrecy, including Pauvert and Jeannette, and so it remained for several decades. The literary world, meanwhile, went into contortions and speculations to try to unlock the code and expose the name of the translator, each time making me smile.[*]

---

[*]In his well-researched book *Venus Bound*, John de St. Jorre names me as the translator of *O*. Though he is not absolutely sure, he says that if "money were to be wagered I

Once again, we wondered, would the censors move in with fangs bared, for though the barriers were crumbling, this could well be perceived as even more shocking than Miller. Sadomasochistic to say the least, though a case could be made that O, in all her tribulations, was almost saintly in her response to her torturers, to be compared to the early Christian martyrs. I suggested this potential defense to Barney and Fred one morning. Double head shakes. Then what we should do is run the opening section in the magazine and see the response. Double nods. A brief introduction to that scene was added, which we ran with the partial translation in *Evergreen Review* 31 in the fall of 1963 and waited. If we anticipated howls of anger or disgust, we were disappointed. Still, maybe they'd come when one had the whole book. Censorship may have been on the ropes, but it was far from knocked out. We knew, too, that O had been censored in France—copies of the Olympia edition had been seized shortly after publication, both Girodias and Pauvert questioned by the Brigade Mondaine, as were several of the putative authors. When, however, it turned out that some of the suspects were women of prominence, the investigation was quickly dropped. Someone high up in the government, it was rumored, had given the order to cease and desist. Still, Paulhan had to hire a lawyer to defend himself and the book, and when later he was nominated to a seat in the Académie Française, those who opposed his inclusion among France's "immortals" surreptitiously placed a copy of O on every academicians chair, to sway the vote. The tactic backfired, and Paulhan was elected without further incident.

The novel would shock, we knew (or hoped), but we were weary of lawsuits and discussed how best we might avoid them in this instance. Customs was no longer a force of censorship, but, we recalled, it was New York customs, in the person of Deputy Collector Irving Fishman, who had declared *Lolita* not obscene when an Olympia copy fell into his hands. Why not try that route again? We asked Pauvert to mail us several copies, which predictably were seized at the border. On appeal, that same Mr. Fishman declared the book not obscene and released the copies. So far, so good. Nonetheless, as a safety measure, we decided to add to Monsieur Paulhan's introduction another essay by one of our authors, André Pieyre de Mandiargues, which in essence was a laudatory review he had written

would place mine unequivocally on the Seavers [meaning me and Jeannette]." I say: John, if you can break the code of the author's name and that of the translator, you will know for certain the identity of both.

of the work in France. Again, to avoid any appearance of appealing to prurience, we clothed the novel in a pristine white jacket, with the title set in a modestly small typeface framed by a discreet rule, repeated the title on the verso, but otherwise left this free from any copy save, at the bottom, a line taken from the movie industry—"The sale of this book is limited to adults"—and sent it into the world. By now, bookstores had grown used to the annual Grove Press shocker, were generally impressed by the way we defended them, and were less prone to take none or to conceal our dubious wares under the counter. A few days after O arrived in the stores, I visited half a dozen in the New York area and saw, in most instances, the novel openly—may I say proudly?—displayed. Another small step for man- (and woman-) kind.

Much to our surprise, the reviews were mostly favorable. The book-bible *New York Times Book Review* assigned O to Albert Goldman, a Columbia professor of English, who wrote:

> *Story of O*—notorious as an underground novel, remarkable as a rare instance of pornography sublimed to purest art—appeared first under mysterious circumstances in Paris in 1954. Bearing the name of an unknown, presumably pseudonymous author, Pauline Réage, and the endorsement of an eminent critic, now a member of the Académie Française, the book was greeted with a mixture of respect and perplexity . . .
>
> *Story of O* is neither a fantasy nor a case history. With its alternate beginnings and endings; its simple, direct style (like that of a fable); its curious air of abstraction, of independence of time, place, and personality, what it resembles most is a legend—the spiritual history of a saint and martyr . . .
>
> Despite its sensational action, O's history maintains the sweetly solemn tone of a female martyrology. This paradox is representative of the book's imaginative texture, a tissue of intricately woven ironies whose consolidating theme—implied by the religious symbolism of the convent like schools, the iron ring, the flagellations—is a perversion of the Christian mystery of exaltation through debasement, of the extremity of suffering transformed into an ultimate victory over the limitations of being . . .
>
> O comes to embody all three aspects of feminine being symbolized by the triskelion—the modest maiden (Diana), the inviting woman (Luna) and the sinister crone (Hecate).

In one fell swoop Professor Goldman, in our most important print medium, had outdone both Messieurs Paulhan and Pieyre de Mandiargues in endowing O with an almost mythological respectability. Predictably, the book went onto the *New York Times Book Review* bestseller list and remained there for weeks.

49 ✌

Grove Goes Public

As the man—or woman—said, "I've been poor and I've been rich, and I can assure you, rich is better." Or words to that effect. At Grove we were all earning a living wage but little more, and if ever we were tempted to join a larger house at considerably more money, the response was almost inevitably "We're having too much fun here." True, Barney was often irascible, a control freak, most of the time manic, prone to panic attacks, reveling in unfairly pitting one so-called executive against another—his method, we surmised, of testing our mettle or seeing how far we could be pushed, for there was a sadistic element in his makeup, in stark contrast to his innate generosity. In all fairness, the brunt of our financial strains lay on his none-too-broad shoulders, for he and his mother owned all the stock of Grove, and when losses occurred, as they often had, it was from their pockets the deficit had to be made up.

For the three years between 1962 and 1964 we had been in a Sargasso Sea financially, with sales stagnant and profits, when they came, minimal. In 1962 we had lost roughly $400,000 on sales of slightly over $2 million, largely because of the soaring costs of the lawsuits.* I remember one day that year when Barney disappeared in late morning and reappeared just before five, saying he had spent the day with some people on Wall Street.

---

*In today's terms, one should multiply by roughly five or six.

"To raise money?" I asked. He nodded, said, "No takers," shrugged, and disappeared into his office. I had always heard that the extent of his inherited wealth was exaggerated, though it stood him in good stead in obtaining bank loans and printers' credit, but that day I had my first inkling the pockets were really not all that deep. Later I learned he had ventured to the Financial District not to raise money but to try to sell the company. Anyway, the next two years, though our sales were at a virtual standstill—down a bit in 1963, up a bit in 1964—we managed to turn a profit, slight but reassuring. The next year, thanks in part to several bestsellers, including the irrepressible *Games People Play*, our sales soared by almost 50 percent, with a substantial profit. Nineteen sixty-six saw another 20 percent increase in sales, as the growing backlist, aimed at schools and colleges—with Jules Geller bombarding academe, especially the younger professors, with reading material and teachers' guides—kicked in and accounted for roughly 30 percent of the business, and another sizable profit. That year, too, we started a book club, which by year's end had seventy-five thousand members, while the large-format (*Playboy* size!) *Evergreen Review* circulation soared from 35,000 in 1965 to 120,000. Add in Cinema 16, purchased from Amos Vogel in late 1966, an eclectic library of art films, documentaries, and film classics aimed primarily at schools and colleges, and the acquisition of three major feature films—including *Finnegans Wake*—and we began to look like a multipronged media company, constantly ahead of the curve and sufficiently attractive to draw the attention of Wall Street.

"How would you feel if we went public?" Barney tossed out one day around the beginning of 1967. "They're talking about making a public offering in June or July of 240,000 shares at somewhere between six and ten dollars a share. That would net us well over a million dollars at the very least and ease all the financial pressures we've always had. Money to expand. Buy more and better books. Some feature films. Another book club?"

Who could say no, especially when we learned that members of the executive committee would all receive shares. Not options: shares. If there was a gimmick, we didn't see it.

I can't say the place swarmed with due-diligence snoopers, but our accountant Joe Warren made available to the underwriter the company's results for the last five years and a fair estimate for 1967, which looked—to borrow a word from the late great Terry Southern—fab. Proper papers were drawn and duly registered. We were happy to see that several of our suppliers, including printers and paper merchants, who had, not all that long ago, asked us to pay a portion of our bills up front, had jumped on the bandwagon. Finally, on July 7, 1967, each of us received four thousand shares at the offering price of seven dollars per share. It didn't mean we were suddenly rich, but with gas at roughly thirty cents a gallon, milk at a few cents a quart, and my Central Park West rent $354 a month, it made us all feel less poor. Despite ourselves, we checked the NASDAQ numbers each day as the price of our stock soared, first to ten, then to fifteen, then to twenty, and well above. Morrie Goldfischer, whose sense of humor was pervasive, made an almost daily joke of our sudden riches. Holding *The Wall Street Journal* open to the NASDAQ page, he would sidle up and whisper, "See today's quote? Another two grand in our pockets. Not bad, eh?" Suddenly we were rich, not superrich, but seemingly rewarded for our several years of sweat equity. Except . . .

Except that we learned, later rather than sooner, that ours was "letter stock" and could not be traded for an extended period of time. While many of our investors bailed out, doubling, trebling, and in some cases quintupling their investment, we could only watch and wait. Barney had never told us of this restriction, and the disillusion was apparent in the office, especially when we saw the frenzied stock soar as high as forty at one point, making us each worth roughly $160,000—on paper—ten to fifteen times our annual salaries. If we had had a watercooler, Grove stock, not exciting new manuscripts, would have been the constant subject of our conversations. Furthering our concern, we knew from our internal numbers the stock was clearly overpriced, and indeed soon it began to drift downward. By the end of the year it had stopped drifting and plummeted to nine, at which point a number of brokers recommended it as a no-brainer "buy."* As we watched its downward spiral, all we could do was sit on the sidelines and hope. For believers, pray. Hey, at nine, it was still eight thousand dollars more than our purchase price. The original plan was to sell your stock at some heady price, pay off the loan, and pocket the proceeds. In my case, I had borrowed the twenty-eight thousand dollars from a Connecticut bank, the loan co-signed by my father, who as the stock ascended complimented me on my astute buy. But even that was qualified. "I didn't know you had any business sense," he would say. "I guess I was wrong." But then he too noted the drift and ceased his encomiums, his expression, if not his words, indicating: "Well, I guess I was right in the

---

*By "no-brainer" I refer to the contents of the craniums of those brokers who, without doing their homework, were still recommending the stock at that point.

first place." Still, the Connecticut bank so far had shown no sign of worry. But if the stock drifted much further . . .

When finally we were free to sell, the stock had reached a point somewhere below a dollar a share. Should we hang on to it, hoping it would rebound? What at this point did we have to lose? Another four thousand dollars, it turned out. When finally I did sell—the bank's patience was not unlimited—the loss was virtually the entire "investment." It was a harsh introduction to the vagaries of the stock market, as well as a concrete example of the law of gravity.

So, I've been poor and (on paper) rich, and, believe me, poor is better. Far fewer night sweats. Far fewer heartbreaks. Far fewer scowling faces.

50 ∿

Genet Comes to America

THE YEAR 1968, again having no alternative, dawned on a note of mingled hope and despair. The turbulent 1960s were winding to a close—or so it seemed. In fact, the worst—or best, depending on your viewpoint and political bent—was yet to come.

The United States was still bogged down in Vietnam. What had earlier been termed JFK's war was now Lyndon Johnson's, and that albatross was weighing ever more heavily round his thick Texas neck. Quagmire abroad was matched by increasing resistance to that "pointless, hopeless" war at home. And the naysayers and protesters could no longer be labeled by the administration as hippies and druggies (weren't they the same, after all?), Commies and pinkos, Beats and bohemians. Middle-class Americans were joining the marches and signing the petitions, and even American corporations—perhaps for their own venal reasons, but nonetheless—were alerting Washington to the fact that continued, unqualified support of the war was not a given.

It was an election year, and the mood of the country did not seem to bode well for the incumbent. Taking political advantage of the nation's growing winter of discontent, voices of opposition were gathering political strength as the primaries began. One man in particular, the senator from Minnesota Eugene McCarthy, surrounded by a band of exuberant, youthful cohorts, was focusing on the folly of the Vietnam War in particular and, to judge by the polls, gaining in popularity week by week. The greatest political enigma of the moment was the carpetbag senator from New York, Robert Kennedy. Where did he stand on the key issues? Would he or would he not challenge a president he clearly loathed but till now had backed for a second term? As for Lyndon Baines Johnson himself: Would he or would he not run again? If he did, the Democratic nomination was his. But in the late months of 1967 and the early months of the new year, he had been pointedly, and eloquently, silent on the subject.

For their part, the Republicans seemed intent on nominating that all-time loser, Richard Milhous Nixon, the man who had lost the presidency by a whisker—no, a shadow—to JFK in 1960, then followed up that painful loss by failing in his quest to unseat Pat Brown two years later for the governorship of California. Early in 1968, the New Hampshire primary shocked the country—and the politicians. Gene McCarthy and his youth brigade's unexpected vote total at the Democratic primary led Johnson to withdraw from the race. The message was clear: in 1968, politics as usual was an endangered species. But even before McCarthy the Good had had a chance to savor his victory, Robert Kennedy, the Great Vacillator, made a decision: it was time to join the race. The detested LBJ was indeed vulnerable. McCarthy had shown the way, but he, however worthy, was vulnerable, too. Once the vaunted Kennedy machine revved up, Gene's guys and dolls would be revealed as the rank amateurs they doubtless were. Tough, the cries of foul play. Be damned, the accusations of callow opportunism. There was a dynasty to be protected and prolonged. Camelot was not dead after all.

In a stroke of journalistic brilliance—madness?—*Esquire* magazine, sensing that the Democratic convention in Chicago might well be a historic event, invited three world-famous writers, all published by or associated with Grove, to cover the convention: the satirist Terry Southern, author of *The Magic Christian*, "the author most capable of handling frenzy" (*Esquire*); William Burroughs, author of *Naked Lunch*, the nightmarish work that had propelled him from the North African expatriate drug scene to *New York Times* bestsellerdom; and Jean Genet, playwright, novelist, ex-convict, and homosexual, author of two long-banned works we had recently published in the United States, *Our Lady of the Flowers* and *The Thief's Journal*, a man dubbed by the State Department as "undesirable" and, as we have seen, by the French philosopher Jean-Paul Sartre as "Saint Genet" (take your pick). And to round out the fearless threesome, *Esquire* assigned the journalist John Sack to cover the convention from the police point of view. Not quite equal time, but still . . . Whether it was the publisher, Arnold Gingrich, or the editor Harold Hayes who dreamed up the idea, it was an act of inspired madness. For even *Esquire*, which early on modestly proclaimed that it "required no special wisdom to foresee that the Convention of the Democratic Party in Chicago was likely to transcend the limits of ordinary politics," could know that those five days in the Windy City would turn into a lopsided mixture of theater of the absurd, Grand Guignol, and pure tragedy, into an event that the respected newsman Eric Sevareid would later term "the most disgraceful spectacle in the history of American politics."

At seven o'clock on Sunday morning, August 18, the phone rang in our ramshackle but beloved former horse barn on eastern Long Island, where we spent most weekends. I picked up the receiver, wondering who could be calling at this ungodly hour.

"*Allo.* Dick *Sivère?*"

My name all right, but with a decidedly French tilt.

"Jean here. Jean Genet."

"Jean! Where are you calling from, Paris?"

"No, Canada. I'm on my way to New York."

"Great. So you got your visa after all."

"Not exactly. I'll explain everything when I see you. I should be there in a day or two."

"Shall we get you a hotel?"

"Yes, I'd appreciate that." Pause. "Uh, Dick. Nothing too fancy. But as close to Forty-second Street as possible."

"Okay. I'll call you back to let you know where you'll be staying."

There was a pause. "You can't," he said. "I don't have a phone here. When I get in, I'll come down to Grove, and you can direct me from there."

I knew that Genet had no fixed abode, that wherever he went he preferred hotels, and the more frugal the better. Jail had doubtless given him a taste for the spare. He had written eloquently on the terrors of long-term convicts emerging from prison to "freedom," described how difficult it was to adapt to the world you had dreamed of rejoining, and theorized that ex-cons felt comfortable only in prisonlike surroundings. Thus his penchant for cell-like hotel rooms.

I called Barney in East Hampton to inform him of Jean's impending arrival and to settle on a hotel.

Jean's enigmatic remark about his visa reminded me of the story he had told me about his previous encounter with American officialdom four years before.

In the early 1960s, several of Genet's plays, including *The Maids*, *The Balcony*, and *The Blacks*, had been performed in New York to great success, and we had published them as Evergreen paperbacks. By 1964, two of the plays had been performed a thousand times, and to celebrate that twin event, the producers and Grove had jointly invited Jean to New York. Genet went down to the American consulate on the rue St. Florentin and duly filled out the necessary forms. He was then called in to the vice-consul's office, where he was asked a number of weighty questions, the most important of which was: "Are you now or have you ever been a Communist?" To which Genet truthfully said, "No." He had in fact briefly been a Trotsky-ite, but certainly that did not qualify, did it? (I later asked Jean what he would have answered if the man had asked him whether he was a homosexual, fully expecting him to tell me that he would have lied. But Jean rarely gave you the expected. He simply said: "But he didn't ask me.") Whereupon the vice-consul stamped his passport with the American visa and Jean returned to his lodgings, a fairly remote Paris hotel.

A few hours later the landlady yelled upstairs: "Monsieur Jean, you have a phone call!"

Most no-star Paris hotels in those days had but one phone, down in the owner's office. Jean did not receive all that many calls and wondered who it could be.

"Monsieur Genet," the voice on the other end began, "this is the American consulate."

This was not the voice of the man who had stamped his passport. Genet assumed it was the man's superior, probably the consul himself.

"I wonder if you'd mind stopping by the consulate," the man went on.

"Of course," Genet replied. "May I ask why?"

"I'm afraid we've made a mistake in giving you a visa. Could you kindly bring your passport back so we can correct the error?"

Genet remembers thinking that the poor vice-consul, doubtless a semi-literate who had never read his work and had no idea what a threat Jean was to the fabric of American society, would probably be soon on his way to the U.S. equivalent of diplomatic Siberia. Visibly, the man on the phone was better read.

"Monsieur," Genet said, "when I needed a visa, I came to your embassy to get it. If you want it back, you can come here and get it."

There was a pause.

"You should know that even with that visa in your passport, they'll stop you at the border," the consul said. And with that he hung up.

After that exchange, Genet decided he didn't want to go to the United States. Jean never knew why the reversal, but he assumed it was either his homosexuality, his status as ex-convict, or, most likely, the fact that Grove at the time was being harassed by a whole panoply of would-be censors for its scandalous publications, from D. H. Lawrence to Henry Miller, William Burroughs to, yes, Jean Genet himself.

This time, Grove decided to take the matter into its own hands rather than leaving it to the Paris bureaucrats. Barney had a relatively highly placed friend in Washington to whom he wrote several letters. The replies, when they came, were politely evasive. He would look into the matter. He would see what he could do. He understood that Mr. Genet was a writer of world stature. There were proper channels, however, as he was sure Barney would understand. *Esquire*, having concocted the triumvirate, seemed vague on the matter. If the threesome was reduced to a duo, so be it. Perhaps it was feeling blinded by its own brilliance, and having second thoughts. Irrespective of Chicago, we at Grove very much wanted Genet to come for our own selfish reasons. His works, both fiction and drama, had been well received and highly praised. And for once, despite the usual alarms, neither of his novels had been attacked by the censors. With Genet, there were no court cases to gobble up the proceeds.

As July waned, we had to admit defeat and inform Genet that we had struck out in Washington.

"Don't worry," he said. "I'll take care of it myself."

I wondered just how he would take care of it.

The next morning, Jeannette and I took a taxi from our Central Park West apartment to the Biltmore.

The cherubic bad boy's (at fifty-seven) only baggage was a tiny briefcase hardly capable of holding toiletries, much less a change of clothes. I knew from my earlier meetings with Genet in Paris, and from talking to Bernie Frechtman, that he generally traveled light. But *this* light?

"Did you leave the rest of your baggage at the station?" I asked hesitantly. Genet looked at me as if I were mad.

"This *is* my baggage," he said with the trace of a smile, pointing to his briefcase. And indeed, for the next ten days, when we lived in close proximity and—as will be seen—in virtual intimacy, Jean needed no more than the contents of his satchel.

I had forgotten how cherubic-looking the man was. Pixie-like. No more than five feet five or maybe six. His pate was all but bald, with a small snow-white patch of hair just above the slightly protruding ears. And his eyes: pale, pale blue. But it was not so much the color that made them distinctive as the intensity with which they fixed on you. When he talked to you, you were the only person in the universe. Few people in my life have ever made me feel that way—Beckett was one—it is a rare quality.

After lunch, on our way back uptown to the Biltmore, I asked Jean why he had gone first to Canada instead of directly to New York. I wanted to get the lowdown on the visa. Jean responded by reminding me of the fiasco at the American consulate, saying that he had decided never to make that mistake again.

"I'll tell you the whole story," he said. "But you must promise not to tell *Esquire*. Otherwise they may get nervous and decide not to send me to Chicago."

I solemnly swore.

"We French don't need a visa for Canada," he said. "And since I know the border between Canada and the United States is lax, I figured if I went to Canada first, I'd find a way across the border."

"And how did you?"

"The second day after I arrived in Montreal, I was walking down the street when a young man came up to me and asked very timidly if I was by chance Jean Genet. When I admitted I was, he said he had read my work and seen two of my plays and could he do me the honor of showing me the city. Which he did for the next two days. I told him I was going to New York and didn't have a visa. 'That's no problem,' he said. 'I'll drive you across the border to Buffalo. You can take the train from there.' If the border guards asked, he'd pass me off as his uncle. But at the border they just waved us through. And," he said triumphantly, "here I am!" His delight at fooling the American customs was almost childlike.

"But, Jean," I said, always the worrier, "that's all right for New York. In Chicago, though, there's going to be a lot of document checking. And the rumor is, Mayor Daley's got the Chicago police force on full alert. What if you get arrested?"

He shrugged, and I realized that for Genet the threat of arrest ranked far down in his grab bag of concerns. Still, it worried me, for I knew Jean had a long record, dating back to before the war, for theft, desertion, embezzlement, not to mention "public offense to decency." But these petty imprisonments paled before the outrage his openly erotic, homosexual novels had caused in France, starting with *Querelle de Brest* and, later, with *Our Lady of the Flowers* and *The Thief's Journal*. Years before, in Paris, Jean had also confided to Jeannette and me, at an evening with our close friends Monique Lange—who perhaps knew Jean better and longer than virtually anyone—and the Spanish novelist Juan Goytisolo, that in 1938 he had been a member of the Trotskyist Fourth International. However short-lived and superficial his involvement, that gave him the added label of "Commie."

Given the incident at the American embassy in Paris, I had to believe that some worthy branch of government in Washington—probably the FBI—was privy to this information.* Once we had arrived in Chicago, Jean's presence there was bound to be noticed immediately, if not sooner, by at least one member of the fifty-thousand-strong contingent of police, U.S. infantry, National Guardsmen, FBI, and Secret Service agents on hand to maintain disorder.

We went to lunch the next day, and at Jean's insistence sat outdoors at a sidewalk café under a searing August sun. Inside, I knew, the place was mercifully air-conditioned, but Jean would not be swayed. "Inside, we see nothing," he explained. "Here, we're part of the city." Despite the heat, Jean wore the same clothes throughout his stay: beige corduroy trousers, a light cotton shirt open at the neck, and a suede jacket of gracious origins but which had seen better days. Blacks sashayed past wearing tight-fitting pants. Jean eyed them with open pleasure.

"*Les fesses américaines,*" he muttered, shaking his head. "There's something different, *very* different, about American buttocks." He followed their undulations down the street until they disappeared around the corner. "New York," he said, "reminds me of a colonial city. It *is* a colonial city!" Just then a garbage truck rolled by, stopping directly across the street to gather its loot. All three of the sanitation men were black, well muscled, and two of them were bare chested. Jean could not contain himself and

---

*Actually, when finally released, the FBI file on Genet ran to more than five hundred pages.

called over to the men in French, praising them for their rhythmic labors and gleaming chests.

"Jean," I said, "I wouldn't. I mean, they might not understand . . ."

"Don't worry," he said with an irresistible grin. "They understand."

And indeed, all three waved back across the street at us and laughed broadly as the truck pulled away. I was beginning to believe that Jean's innate charm and openness were like an invisible, protective wall around him, fending off all harm. That thought came back to me a few days later in the midst of the Chicago madness.

At Genet's request, *Esquire* had hired Jeannette and me to squire him around New York and Chicago and to be his official translators. On Friday, the day before our flight to Chicago, Jean asked Jeannette to take him on a sightseeing tour of Forty-second Street. He'd heard a lot about the movies and peep shows of the area and wondered how they compared with the French equivalent. For an hour or two, Jean explored the lower "porno" depths of Manhattan with Jeannette in tow, emerging from each successive shop looking more and more gloomy. He shook his head.

"These places are grim," he told Jeannette. "There's absolutely nothing erotic about any of them. Not that the French equivalent are much better, but at least the performers have some wit. Here everyone looks mechanical, depressed. These places are so dismal. Sex should not be dreary, it should be fun. I do not detect any trace of joy here. Let's go back to the hotel."

That afternoon we paid the obligatory courtesy call to *Esquire* at 488 Madison Avenue. Harold Hayes oozed Southern charm, asking Jean with a broad smile what he thought of America. Since I knew pretty well the answer, for Jean's preconceived notions of this country were well-known— he found it racist, overbearing, a potential danger to the world by its military arrogance and might, coupled with a naïveté that allowed itself to get involved in stupid, winless wars, for example, Vietnam—I feared he might blow the deal on the spot, for candor was one of his many dangerous virtues. Jeannette and I were once again fooled by him, taken aback when he declined to respond, merely saying that as a guest of America he preferred not to abuse its hospitality, that he would doubtless have a fairer impression post-Chicago. One of the editors, whose name I had not caught, assured Genet that he was among friends and should feel free to speak openly. Didn't the fact that the magazine had chosen him to cover the convention signal its openness to controversy? Jean, changing moods, said, "Oh, no, you chose me because of my name. Pure snobbery!" Which sent an immediate chill throughout the already-air-conditioned room.

The young, simpatico editor John Berendt was the *Esquire* staff member assigned to (e)squire us through the shoals of Chicago's windswept waters. Affable, attractive, and efficient, he handed us our press credentials and plane tickets. He'd be flying out a day ahead. With us on the flight was my old friend Terry Southern. Bill Burroughs, coming from London, and the seasoned journalist John Sack, coming from God knows where, would join us later in the day.

On the plane to Chicago, we tried to brief Jean on the current state of American politics, reminding him of the difference between Republicans and Democrats (Genet: "There isn't much, right?"), the discontent among the young, the dark horses among the Democrats who might have a chance of upsetting Hubert Humphrey. Genet cut us off.

"With young Kennedy dead, the only one with a chance is McCarthy, no?" he said. "And as I understand it, he doesn't stand much of a chance. The party doesn't like him. Is that true?

"And how did this fellow Nixon get nominated? He's such a bad person. Does America like bad politicians? In France, all politicians are bad. But here I thought you had some good ones."

Not many, we admitted, but Gene McCarthy stood head and shoulders above the rest.

"You seem to shoot all the good ones. Will McCarthy be in Chicago? He won't win, but I'd like to see him."

Yes, McCarthy was due in on Sunday, and we planned to see him.

"Anyway," Jean said, "it doesn't matter. I plan to write a piece as seen through the legs of a Chicago policeman."

I wasn't sure I understood.

"There are going to be a lot of policemen in Chicago, right? Maybe thousands? The policemen will be between us and the politicians. So if you want to write about the politicians, our viewpoint will be from *behind* the police. I'll write the piece from behind a Chicago policeman. Maybe from between his legs."

Hmmm, I thought. This could be truly interesting . . .

On Friday, Grove gave a lunch for Genet in Barney's office above the Evergreen Theater on Eleventh Street. Most of the conversation focused on the events-to-be in Chicago. For days, the newspapers—and especially television—had been enumerating the various "outside" (read: unofficial) disruptive forces that threatened to turn the host city into a Roman circus. A number of countercultural organizations had issued a clarion call to their constituents to show up in Chicago to be both seen and heard: flower children, peaceniks, hippies, yippies. Dave Dellinger, editor of *Liberation*, a leading figure in the movement to end the war in Vietnam, who the previous fall had led the highly successful and politically effective Pentagon march, would be coordinating similar marches in Chicago, it was reported. The SDS—Students for a Democratic Society—were expected in force. The yippies, led by the stalwarts Jerry Rubin, Abbie Hoffman, and Ed Sanders, were said to be bringing, appropriately, a pig to Carl Sandburg's "hog butcher for the world," not for slaughter, but for nomination. In their eyes, nominating a 150-pound porker for president made fully as much sense as naming a Humphrey of roughly equal weight to the ticket.

The country was still in shock over the assassination two months before of a second Kennedy: Bobby, however controversial and disliked by some, had gained immediate stature from martyrdom, and his shadow lay broadly over the next week's events. After his primary victory in California, Bobby had become a viable alternative to Hubert Humphrey. Much of the protest in Chicago was aimed at the notion of a closed convention, that Humphrey the Handpicked was not only a shoo-in but, symbolically, the assurance that the Vietnam War would continue and probably escalate. Gene McCarthy would be there, but Bobby Kennedy had effectively hobbled his candidacy, and the senator had nowhere near the votes necessary to make it a contest.

All the media hoopla predicting the breakdown of law and order prompted Mayor Richard Daley to reassure his fellow Democrats that their convention site would be made safe and secure. The twelve-thousand-strong Chicago police force, beefy and blue, was on full alert and prepared to handle any situation that might develop. Besides, as backup, there were always five thousand members of the National Guard, four thousand Illinois state troopers, six thousand American soldiers in battle uniform, not to mention swarms of FBI and Secret Service agents. All of which must have been most reassuring to the delegates.

Given the subtleties and idiosyncrasies of the American nominating process, plus the extraneous, contradictory elements of this year's convention, I had assumed as I translated the gist of the conversation to Genet that most of it was over his head. Again, I had underestimated the good gentleman.

"The children are fed up with the old farts in power," he concluded. "Your Vietnam is our Algeria. To me, all this sounds like April in Paris."

He was referring not to the romantic song but to the events four months earlier that had brought France to a virtual standstill and forced an entrenched government out of office. Genet, it turned out, knew a lot more about politics, especially their inner workings, than *Esquire*, or any of us, had ever suspected.

Genet reiterated to everyone around what he had confided to me the day before—he planned to write his piece by viewing events through the inverted V of a Chicago cop's thighs!

"But last night," he said, "I watched your television, and it showed some of those *flics* [cops]. The thighs are still important, but I was also impressed by their bellies—they wear their belts and their revolvers *beneath* their bellies. And the visors: they all wear visors that cover and shield their faces. You cannot see their eyes, but they can see you. So I shall perhaps write each day not only from between the thighs but also from the viewpoint of the bellies, the visors, the revolver."

Somehow, Genet knew that Barney was from Chicago and had asked him at our Friday lunch if he was going, too. Barney had responded that unlike Jean he didn't have a specific purpose that would justify his going.

"The purpose," Genet said, "is to be there, no?"

Barney said that he had to go to the country—East Hampton—that afternoon but that he might well fly out Saturday or Sunday.

51 ❧

The 1968 Convention

DRIVING IN FROM O'HARE AIRPORT next day, we were all struck by the desolate, empty outskirts. A vision of utter poverty, neglect, despair.

"Where are all the blacks?" Genet wanted to know. "If this is where they live, I can't imagine some people aren't out in the streets."

Occasionally, at a street-corner grocery store, a few blacks were hanging out, but Jean was right: Where *was* everybody? Maybe, I figured, the massive presence of the police throughout the city was an inducement for them to stay inside. But Jean was unconvinced.

We checked into the Chicago Sheraton on North Michigan Avenue and agreed to meet at six o'clock in the Downstairs Lounge to make plans for the next five days. That evening we were scheduled to meet Dave Dellinger and hear what he had to say. Then, after dinner, off to Lincoln Park, where most of the protesters had gathered. By this time there were several thousand of them, and without a hotel room to be had in the city, most had come prepared to camp out in Lincoln Park throughout their stay. But that afternoon Mayor Daley's office had thrown down the gauntlet by announcing that Lincoln Park would be closed at 11:00 p.m. Everyone would have to be out by the curfew or suffer the consequences.

Burroughs, who had flown in from London that afternoon, joined us in the bar, dressed, as always, more like a Midwestern banker than the true revolutionary he was. Tall, thin, and with a deadpan face that would have given Buster Keaton a good run for his money, Burroughs was the authentic black sheep of the famous family that gave its name to the adding machine and computer company. I had been his editor at Grove for several years now, and we had become good friends. I liked and admired him immensely and felt—as I feel today—that he was a major, if much misunderstood, writer, one of the great experimentalists of our time. Still, he remained to me an enigma: the exterior was impeccable in look, dress, and manners; the inner man was a nexus of high subversion. Not since Sade, in my view, had a writer used more effectively and tellingly an addiction, an obsession, as a creative springboard to inveigh against the clichéd world of the dull, the hypocritical, and the pretentious.

He and Genet had never met, but each knew—and admired—the other's work. It was obvious they struck an immediate bond, and for the next two hours we exchanged ideas and formulated plans, some serious, some mad, all impractical, since we had no idea what awaited us in the streets. If Berendt was nervous about his charges' disparate fantasies, he did not show it, even as drinks flowed and exchanges became less and less coherent.

Burroughs announced that Allen Ginsberg was in Chicago for the "events" and wanted very much to meet Genet. Allen had come, convinced that, using a method of chanting he had learned in India not long before, he could calm the troubled waters and help prevent violence.

A little before eight, Jeannette, Genet, and I drove over to Dave Dellinger's Peace Headquarters. His "peace room" was a nearly empty, poorly lit place with glassless windows covered with torn plastic that flapped in the night wind.

"We're not seeking a confrontation," Dellinger said before anyone had even had a chance to ask a question. A gentle but imposing man with graying hair, he looked more like presidential timber than any of the candidates from either party, with the possible exception of Gene McCarthy. His "staff" seemed to consist mainly—or perhaps solely—of his son Ray, clad in khaki and wearing a blue beret, who hovered protectively over his father. "We're here simply to protest the foregone conclusion that there is no alternative to Humphrey. And of course to express our continued opposition to the war in Vietnam." Did he think there was going to be violence? asked Genet. Would the Chicago police attack young people—those

Genet called the "gentle children"—in the park? "I can only hope the mayor's office would reconsider its position," Dellinger replied. "Maybe Mayor Daley will realize that the best way to deal with a situation like this is to accommodate it, not defy it," he said.

We were then invited to join Dellinger in the protest march scheduled for Wednesday. I translated the invitation for Genet, telling him that, however peaceful the intent, there could well be violence, probably arrests, and reminding him that he had no visa.

"Of course," he said. "Of course we will march."

Allen Ginsberg was staying at the Lincoln Park Hotel, just opposite the park itself, which was our next nonmilitary objective, so we decided to drive over, take the pulse of the park, and see if we could find Allen. I was elected by unanimous vote to do the driving, doubtless on the basis of my long experience in manning getaway cars. Allen was not in his room, we were told, but might be in the park. He had been seen leaving, carrying his instrument. When I translated this for Genet, he smiled malevolently and said, "I certainly hope so."

"Hope so what?" I asked.

"That he's taken his instrument with him," he said.

"The man's referring to a *musical* instrument," I said.

"Ah!" said Jean. "I thought he meant *the* instrument."

We arrived there about 10:00 p.m. to a menacing sight: hundreds of blue-clad policemen equipped with billy clubs, Mace, gas masks, and riot guns lined the sidewalk circling the park, which was pitch-dark except for a smattering of bonfires here and there. The police, as Genet had imagined them, were beefy and bellicose, the terms are not too strong, and standing among them, like some huge, quiescent, prehistoric animal left over from a grade-B movie, was an armored vehicle on top of which sat a bank of darkened searchlights. Near the vehicle stood a cop with a bullhorn: "This is the final warning. Clear the park. The park will be closed at eleven o'clock. Anyone remaining will be subject to arrest."

In the distance, we spotted Ed Sanders, a writer and member of the rock group the Fugs, slinking along the edge of the park just beyond the grasp of the blue-clad finest.

Terry, always the wit, shouted out to him: "Hey, Ed! Where's that loony fruit Al Ginsberg?"

Ed stopped in his tracks as though pierced, turned, and glowered in the direction of the offending voice, ready to do battle or flee, as reason dictated. Then he saw it was only our wacko group.

"He's doing his thing," Ed told us, "over by that fire."

His "thing" was chanting the word "om" over and over in the darkness, accompanying the chant with a portable harmonium (his instrument). The oms varied in tone, intensity, pitch; some were staccato brief, others drawn out for several seconds. Seated around him were a couple hundred people, most echoing his chant, others immersed in presumably peaceful thought. Nearby, a group of blacks was playing a flute and bongo drums. Not long before, we were told, as the bullhorn threats grew more strident, rumors had begun circulating that the police were moving in, and some people had panicked. Allen's om-ing, however, had had a calming effect, and from a very small circle of thirty or forty, his disciples had grown impressively.

As we approached, Allen saw that Saint Genet was among us. He broke off his chant, came over, and prostrated himself before the master. Jean, seemingly neither surprised nor embarrassed, merely smiled. In fact, I suspect that the completely surrealistic world into which he had landed had by now inured him to virtually any surprise. We sat down with the protesters—numbering by now more than a thousand, I would guess— and began chanting with the best of them. Genet seemed especially delighted by the nocturnal gathering and chimed in his om-ing in perfect pitch.

It was by now past eleven, and although the bullhorn warnings continued unabated every few minutes, we had begun to take them for idle threats. Maybe Mayor Daley had finally been touched by grace.

But no.

Terry Southern described the next half hour's events with his usual understated acumen:

Burroughs looked at his watch, and with that unerring awareness of which he is capable, muttered, "They're coming." At that instant, the banks of searchlights blazed up on the armored van which was already moving toward us. Fanned out on each side of the van were about a thousand police.

"Well, Bill, I think we'd better pursue another tactic," I suggested, getting to my feet. What the hell, we were supposed to be here as *observers*, not as participants in any of Allen's crackpot schemes. That the entire reportage team should be busted the first time out was unthinkable.

Genet was the most difficult to persuade, but finally, on Ginsberg's insistence, we all went up to his hotel room.

There, all inhibitions gone (if ever there had been any), Allen knelt in front of Jean and kissed his feet. "I have read *Our Lady of the Flowers*," he said, still on bended knee, "one of the great works of the century. And you, monsieur, are a great saint."

That night, on television, America saw its children being clubbed, beaten, kicked, maced, and gassed as the rampaging Chicago cops advanced, in a pincer action, on both sides of the armored van's searchlights. It was, to Americans unused to civil violence, who believed that such confrontations between police and civilians were a foreign vice, a shocking sight. But as always television is a filter as much as a recorder; most of the time it creates a distance between viewer and event. Having lived that event—and the even more violent nights that followed—I can attest to the difference. One point, among many others, that television failed to capture that night was the fact that by employing a pincer movement, the Chicago police had no desire to clear the park. They wanted to club the kids. For as the crowd dispersed and headed for the park's fringes, presumably leaving the cops behind, it found itself facing another equally menacing phalanx of blue at the park's exit. Thanks to Terry's perspicacity, and Allen's kind hospitality, we were a few dozen steps ahead of the crowd and reached the edge of Lincoln Park before the pincer movement took its toll. Again, Terry Southern:

> Near the street, I glanced back in time to see [the cops] reach the place where we had been, and where a dozen or more were still sitting. They didn't arrest them, at least not right away; they beat the hell out of them— with nightsticks, and in one case at least, the butt of a shotgun. They clubbed them until they got up and ran, or until they started crawling away (the ones who were able), and then they continued to hit them as long as they could. The ones who actually did get arrested seemed to have gotten caught up among the police, like a kind of human medicine ball, being shoved and knocked back and forth from one cop to the next, with what was obviously mounting fury. And this was a phenomenon somewhat unexpected, which we were to observe constantly throughout the

days of violence—that rage seemed to engender rage; the bloodier and the more brutal the cops were, the more their fury increased.

NOTES FROM CHICAGO DIARY

Sunday, August 25. Morning.

About eight o'clock, awake but before we are out of bed, a knock on the door. It is Jean, asking to come in. I open. The mischievous gnome, whose room is a few doors down, is wearing a Japanese-style kimono and bearing a sheaf of paper in his hand. Jeannette pulls the covers a bit higher as I stammer apologies for being a slugabed. Jean's speech more than a bit slurred—not from drink, but from Nembutal, I had been told by Rosica,* which Jean takes to sleep. He wants to read us his first day's reportage. I sweep him in with a grand, princely gesture. Jean heads not for the chair but straight for the bed and crawls in beside Jeannette, patting the sheet beside him, a clear invitation for me to join. Rub-a-dub-dub. In I go. Jean begins to read:

THE FIRST DAY: THE DAY OF THE THIGHS

The thighs are very beautiful beneath the blue cloth, thick and muscular. It all must be hard. This policeman is also a boxer, a wrestler. His legs are long, and perhaps, as you approach his member, you would find a furry nest of long, tight, curly hair . . . A few hours later, about midnight, I join Allen Ginsberg in a demonstration of hippies and students in Lincoln Park: their determination to sleep in the park is their very gentle, as yet too gentle, but certainly poetic, response to the nauseating spectacle of the convention. Suddenly the police begin their charge, with the grimacing masks intended to terrify; and, in fact, everyone turns and runs. But I am well aware that these brutes have other methods, and far more terrifying masks, when they go hunting for blacks in the ghettos, as they have done for the past 150 years. It is a good, healthy, ultimately moral thing for these fair-haired, gentle hippies to be charged at by these louts decked out in this amazing snout that

*Rosica Colin, Jean's longtime literary agent.

protects them from the effects of the gas they have emitted . . .
The person who opens her door to receive us as we try to escape
from these brutes in blue is a young and very beautiful black
woman. Later, when the streets have finally grown calm again,
she offers to let us slip out through the back door, which opens onto
another street: without the police suspecting it, we have been
conjured away and concealed by a trick house . . .

Sunday Afternoon

We drive out to Midway Airport to cover Gene McCarthy's arrival. Jean is especially intrigued to see this "outsider," the decent
alternative to the rigged convention. Several thousand people have
gathered—still, a numerical disappointment, I would think—but
their colorful, flower-bedecked signs, WE WANT GENE, are waving
rhythmically, as if a sea of windblown flowers. Three platforms—
actually the empty beds of trucks—are gathered in a semicircle. On
one, a rock group; on another, a brass band. McCarthy's plane is
about half an hour late. Finally it arrives. Gene, smiling broadly,
descends and scrambles up onto the empty platform. Jean remarks
on how little police protection there is for him. Virtually none, in
fact. McCarthy begins to speak, but no sound emerges from the
mike. Dead. Gentle tapping fails to bring it to life. Jean murmurs:
"Sabotage?" Realizing how often he is, with a single word or thought,
prescient, I wonder if he isn't right. McCarthy hops over onto the
platform of the rock group—no power there either. Ditto the brass
band. He returns center stage, and there, miraculously, sound has
been restored. He is tall, with a generous shock of gray hair, and a
smile that ought to win millions of hearts and, more to the point,
votes. I translate for Genet as he speaks. He is here not as a spoiler
but as a winner. He will not be denied his final effort to turn the
convention around. It has been a long and difficult eight months,
but he has voiced an alternate opinion and been heard. The convention cannot ignore your—he is referring to the crowd—demands.

GENET ON GENE:

As McCarthy leaves the speaker's platform, it seems that no one is pro-
tecting him, save for the sea of flowers painted by the hope-filled men and

women . . . In order for McCarthy to arouse such enthusiasm, what concessions has he made? In what ways has his moral rectitude been weakened? And yet the fact remains that all his speeches, all his statements, reveal intelligence and generosity. Is it a trick? . . .

> I realize that in his mind, as in his writing, Genet is relentlessly probing. He has seen and lived too much, and is too brilliant, to accept any surface for what it seems. Especially in politics. But also in most other life situations. His attitude is not to be confused with cynicism, an entirely different stance. No: instinctively, he likes McCarthy; but, automatically, he is searching for the flaw, faint or fatal, the secret motivation, the person behind the mask.
>
> Seduced by the man, and hoping to learn more about this "outsider," Genet asked if we could interview McCarthy, whose headquarters we had learned were at the Conrad Hilton Hotel. When we arrived at the fifteenth floor, the senator was not there—otherwise engaged, we were told—but would be available later. He would be informed of our visit. Again, Jean, impressed by the youth of McCarthy's faithful, tugged my sleeve and said, "I thought all presidential candidates had police protection. Not one in sight, no?" And indeed there was none.

Monday, August 26. Morning.

Eight o'clock. Knock on door. This time we are prepared. Again, kimono-clad Jean crawls into bed, unfolds his blue-lined sheets of paper, and begins to read.

THE SECOND DAY: THE DAY OF THE VISOR

The truth of the matter is that we are bathed in Mallarmean blue. This second day imposes the azure helmets of the Chicago police. A policeman's black leather visor intrudes between me and the world . . . Supporting this visor is the blue cap—Chicago wants us to think that the whole police force, and this policeman standing in front of me, have descended from heaven—made of a top-grade sky-blue cloth. But who is this blue cop in front of me? I look into his eyes and I can see nothing else there except the blue of the cap. What does his gaze say? Nothing. The Chicago police are, and are not. I shall not pass . . .

I listen intently as Jean reads. The Chicago police as Mallarmean blue? I wonder how *Esquire* will cotton to that wool. I have to assume, though, that if a magazine makes the mistake of inviting genius to grace its pages, it cannot be too upset or shocked by the results. And I marvel that Jean will, as he had warned, write his piece from the viewpoints of the policeman's various body-and-uniform parts. While he had never set foot in Chicago, never seen a Chicago policeman in the flesh, I suspected that he knew before coming exactly how—and probably what—he would write.

Music, we learned, was one of Genet's abiding passions. His knowledge of music is encyclopedic and profound, his insights original. In the middle of the political maelstrom Jean and Jeannette abandon themselves to the subject they both love. I listen with a mixture of awe and humility. Where, I wonder, did Genet acquire his musical expertise? Jeannette tells him of her plan for a recital to give back in New York that fall. Although she had been trained as a classical violinist, jazz had always been part of her musical landscape. For the past several months she and several talented jazz musicians had been "jamming" together. The drummer was Jack DeJohnette, the pianists Keith Jarrett and Chick Corea, with three other jazz musicians. When Jeannette mentioned to Genet her plan—innovative at the time—to divide her forthcoming concert between classical and jazz repertory with the appropriate change of costume, Jean got very excited and appointed himself on the spot her production and stage manager. We knew of Jean's involvement in the theater, but his musical erudition was a revelation to us both.

Late morning, we all head for Lincoln Park. The yippies are out in force, unfazed by last night's clubbing and gassing. In fact, the events—probably due to television coverage—have galvanized other forces to join them, including the clergy, who promise to be out in force next time. The yippies proudly display their candidate, the Pink Pig, which they keep in a burlap bag. Burroughs, believing in fairness and equal time, records the pig's snorts and squeals, which he'll doubtless later splice in some kind of cut-up masterpiece into the cops' threats, the delegates' speeches, the blaring music.

Monday Afternoon

Jean, Burroughs, Terry, Allen, Berendt, Jeannette, and I—plus a new member of our sexy septet, the Beatles' photographer Michael Cooper—head out in two cars for the Convention Hall. Trouble parking, as interdictions abound, and the good citizens of the area, suffering from a severe case of hippie phobia, scream at us, "Don't you park in front of my house! I'll call the police!" Can't totally say I blame them from the looks of us, not to mention the hippie mayhem they witnessed on television last night *that was coming mighty close to their hallowed homes, by God!* As for appearances: Genet as described. Allen bushy. Terry scruffy, despite his protestations to the contrary. Yours truly not exactly a fashion plate either. And to top off the sartorial nightmare, Michael Cooper was decked out in a basically purple outfit—including the hat—with one pant leg blue with white stripes, the other red with polka dots. Shoeless to boot. Only Jeannette, Burroughs, and Berendt lend a modicum of decorum. Not enough, I fear, to offset the others in the eyes of the police swarming around the Convention Hall. In circling to land our outer-space vehicles ("Why," Genet wonders out loud at one point in our travels, noting the model name of our rented Ford, "would anyone name a car 'Galaxie'?"), we see the convention area looks more like a military installation, an armed camp, than the center of the democratic process. Three rings of barbed wire, the outermost a good quarter mile from the entrance, and at each barrier a checkpoint manned by a phalanx of Chicago's finest. Jean has altered my optic, I can no longer refrain from checking out the cops' bellies and thighs. Precisely as described, to a man. Meanwhile, "concentration camp," Jean keeps muttering, appalled by the quasi-military surroundings. Trepidations for my charge. There is no way Genet is going to get through all three checkpoints unscathed. I picture him handcuffed and shackled. "Officer, you don't understand. This is one of the great writers of our time. His ID is back at the hotel. You can't arrest him." Burroughs, on the contrary, pleased as punch, reveling in the moment. His normally deadpan face creased with a visible—yes, visible—grin. Armed with his ubiquitous tape recorder, Bill keeps it running full tilt at each checkpoint, as the cops question us at length about our race, religion, professional purpose, and planet of origin. Burroughs, staunch proponent of the cut-up method of writing, doubtless gathering material for future work as well as recording the historic moment. A double whammy, or How to Turn Impending Disaster into Creative Delight.

Miraculously, after proving all our press credentials are in order, we get through the first two checkpoints. But at checkpoint three, we realize the outer Boys in Blue were simply passing the buck. The real test was upon us. At the inner circle, an unusually bulky lieutenant stops us cold. Berendt the Normal draws himself up full height. "These are bona fide *Esquire*-accredited journalists," he says firmly. Slight quaver. Wait here. The lieutenant disappears and returns shortly with a gray-flannel human, indelibly stamped National Security, Secret Service Division. Carefully checks all of our press credentials. Then IDs, one by one. I hold my breath. This is it: Genet's outlaw status will inevitably be revealed. No visa, no washy. *Juzgado*, Jean baby. But when Secret Service comes to Genet, instead of asking for his ID, gray flannel pauses, looks, smiles, then thrusts out his hand and vigorously shakes Jean's. Has he by chance recognized him? I doubt it. Still, there is no other explanation. As for Jean, he looks disappointed. In any event, his magic has worked once again. Secret Service to lieutenant: "They're okay. Let them through." Disbelief from the Blue, but only a slight shake of the head as if to say, "Your responsibility, hotshot."

Inside we mount to the rafters. Speakers droning. Flags waving. Music blaring. Party-hatted delegates swaying. Burroughs madly recording. Jean more upset by the minute. We endure for an hour, maybe an hour and a half. Terry: "The fix is in. Let's get outta here." Unanimous agreement. Our return to the hotel quietly depressed, as if some new low point of the trip has just been witnessed. What has been happening in the streets was of no consequence to the people inside the Convention Hall. This could be Any Convention, Any Year.

Tuesday, August 27. Morning.

Knock, knock.

"Who's there?"

"Jean."

"Jean who?"

"Jean Genet."

"*Ne vous gênez pas.* Come right in!"*

Our now-routine morning journal. Jean's voice thicker this morning—one sleeping pill too many?—but his prose just as lucid as ever.

THE THIRD DAY: THE DAY OF THE BELLY

A policeman's beautiful belly has to be seen in profile: the one barring my route is a medium-sized belly (de Gaulle could qualify as a cop in Chicago). It is medium-sized, but it is well on its way to perfection. Its owner wheedles it, fondles it with both his beautiful but heavy hands. Where did they all come from? Suddenly we are surrounded by a sea of policemen's bellies barring our entrance into the Democratic convention. When I am finally allowed in, I will understand more clearly the harmony which exists between those bellies and the bosoms of the lady-patriots at the convention—there is harmony but also rivalry: the arms of the ladies of the gentlemen who rule America have the girth of the policemen's thighs . . .

I wonder if Jean will give, in his early wake-up report, his reaction to yesterday's near slammer miss at the convention. He promptly does:

The chief of police—wearing civilian clothes and his belly—arrives. He checks out our passes, our identification, but, obviously a man of taste and discretion, does not ask to see mine. He offers me his hand. I shake it. You bastard . . .

Genet takes his Miraculous Protection totally for granted.

*A bad pun, but one that delighted Genet. Because of his daily matinal door knocks, we said he reminded us of a (bad) American joke series, namely, the antique "knock, knock" jokes. The pun here is on Genet's name and the similar-sounding French verb, *gêner*, literally to embarrass or inconvenience. Thus, *"Ne vous gênez pas,"* which freely translates as "Be my guest" or, in this instance, "Come right in."

Tuesday Afternoon

Back to the convention. Security no problem, our previous day's entrance assuring us reentry with no questions asked. The *Esquire*-appointed freelance photographer, Jack Wright, having been summoned east on another (more important?) assignment, Berendt asked if any of us stalwarts had photographic knowledge or experience. Silence all around. Stupidly, I admitted to having, in my Paris days, accepted two magazine assignments to North Africa, which included taking the pictures. The job, alas, was mine. He handed me the Leica, which Wright had magnanimously left behind. For the next three days, I took eight rolls of film, focusing on our hardy group in perilous situations (at the Amphitheatre, on the streets, at the Coliseum, in Grant and Lincoln parks). Superb all, I am sure, except for a slight mishap, to be acknowledged later.

The convention still a preordained bore, we stayed but an hour. Then off to Lyndon Johnson's Unbirthday Party at the Chicago Coliseum, organized by Jerry Rubin and the yippies. "Ah," breathed Jean, "how much better the air is here." Perhaps a political contrast, but more likely referring to the stench around the convention center, which was hard by the storied Chicago stockyards. Later, Jean would describe the occasion at the Coliseum: "Part of America has detached itself from the American fatherland and remains suspended between earth and sky."

Tuesday Night

Back to Lincoln Park about eleven. Different feeling in the air. About twice as many people as on Sunday, we estimate, and two or three times as many bonfires in the night. Priests and ministers, true to their word. A large wooden cross has been constructed in the middle of the park. A fair number of men wearing hard hats and helmets; several dozen medics in white, with Red Cross armbands. Allen is worried: no amount of chanting will prevent violence tonight. Palpable tension in the air, not here on Sunday. And tonight, a great many more cops out. Is it my imagination, or do they all seem bigger? Taller? Stouter? Another difference tonight, journalists everywhere. Recognizable media figures milling about.

I note, among others, the impressive silhouette of Clive Barnes of *The New York Times* seated on the grass not far away. Sent to cover the Living Theater no doubt. No: the theater of the absurd. Will they—the media—deter violence? Bashing kids is one thing; bashing journalists quite another. Still, the word is that Mayor Daley has not changed his tune. On the contrary.

Again the repeated bullhorn warnings, for well over an hour. Shortly after midnight, cops begin moving in, shoulder to shoulder, riot guns at the ready, gas masks donned, preceded by a car filled with four cops wielding shotguns. Someone tosses a stone, or a brick, at the lead car, breaking the windshield. All hell breaks loose. Tear gas, ten times worse than before. The cops charged, both to relieve their colleagues in the car, who were surrounded by furious protesters twenty or thirty strong, now rocking the vehicle back and forth in a clear attempt to overturn it, and to track down and club the unwelcome intruders.

The first night Terry had suggested a tactical retreat on the premise that it would be unconscionable for such a prestigious reporting team to be wiped out so early in the game. Tonight, when we saw the brick-through-windshield, he again uses good common tactical sense by suggesting that valor will best be served by rapid strategic withdrawal. We flog our way through tear gas, coughing and stumbling, but finally reach the presumed safety of the street beyond the park. Hundreds of demonstrators pound toward us, heading the other way. "Run!" a girl shouts as she passes. "They're coming from that direction!" and she points away from the park in the direction where we thought safety lay. And indeed, lumbering toward us was another wall of blue.

"Shit," Terry hisses.

"Hmmm," Burroughs observes.

"*Qu'est-ce qu'il y a?*" Jean wonders. What's happening?

We start back up the street, but realize that's No Exit.

"In here," I yell, and we all pile into the hallway of a house, move as far to the back as we can, and crouch down.

Jeannette, who as a little girl had lived through the German occupation of Paris, daily bombings, and more than once seen German soldiers running through the streets in pursuit of their prey, has a seizure of déjà vu. Trembling, uncontrollable trembling. I put my arm around her, but the trembling only increases.

Through the glass hallway door we see the cops thundering past and for a moment think we are safe. But then we hear them next door and realize they're routing out the recalcitrants and beating them unmercifully as well. Moments later, in rush four cops, clubs raised. Jean was closest to the street door, therefore first in line to be clubbed. As the cop raised his billy to hit him, Jean simply looked at the man—I dare say straight in the eye—and for several seconds the club remained poised above his head. Then, slowly, he lowered it, as if his arm had been tugged downward by some invisible, omnipotent, doubtless Genet-inspired force.* "All right, you Communist bastards," another cop said, "get the hell out of here." And with that they prodded us out into the street, back into the Coliseum, where we felt like early Christians— understanding for the first time why the man we were escorting had been called Saint Genet. Through a labyrinth of side streets, we make our way—not proudly—back to the hotel.

Wednesday, August 28

Dave Dellinger's Peace March had evolved into a demonstration in Grant Park, for Mayor Daley has not only refused to grant a permit but brought in the National Guard to buttress the beleaguered police. It is the Guard that blocks our path, standing across the proposed line of march. Unlike the mayor's Bellies in Blue, these young men, half the age of the police and in most instances half the girth, look slightly uncomfortable, as if they would prefer to be elsewhere on this sweltering August afternoon. Our heavily literary, notably unmuscular group has been invited to be in the front, among the leaders of the march. We link arms and move slowly forward, noting with unease the bayonets gleaming in the bright sunlight before and beside us. We shuffle, mark time, stand still. Finally, after a long wait, we repair to Grant Park, where a stage has been set up. Singers strum guitars and sing of peace and brotherhood. Brightly colored balloons ascend into the cloudless sky. Speeches fill the afternoon air, distorted by less than perfect

*John Berendt remembers the moment quite differently and, alas, far less romantically. He recalls pressing Genet against the wall and shouting to the cop, "Stop! He's an old man! Don't!" And he didn't.

sound equipment. But we know the message. Shrill attacks on the unnecessary violence. Ringing denunciations of Mayor Daley. Equally scathing assaults on the official convention and the Democratic Party, purportedly the party of the people but obviously blind to the hue and cry of the country's youth. Humphrey derided. The shamefulness and stigma of Vietnam.

Vendors sell hot dogs and hamburgers, Coke and Pepsi. If you close your eyes, the odiferous afternoon makes you think you're at a July Fourth picnic, or out at the ball game, rather than taking part in high political drama. One group decides to set out on a symbolic march to the Chicago slaughterhouse. As we had earlier, they lock arms, eight abreast, and begin their peaceful walk, this time the front line made up of a group of blacks. Like us, they are blocked, this time by the Blue. Unlike us, they continue walking, straight toward the blue line, which stands fast. Then, again, the tear gas and the blue line advances, clubs flailing. This is no Fourth of July. No ball game. It is late August in Chicago, 1968.

Thursday, August 29

One presidential candidate not invited to the convention was the comedian Dick Gregory, who in Chicago is dead serious. Angered and frustrated at the city's refusal to grant permits to marchers, Gregory has a brilliant idea. "Come on down to my house. No one can stop me from inviting you to a party." Genet was delighted at the ruse. A man of great wit and humor himself, he responded immediately to the same quality in others. Here is Jean on that last day's invitation to the ghetto:

Dick Gregory is inviting his friends—there are four or five thousand of them in Grant Park—to come home with him. They won't let us march to the Amphitheatre, he declares, but there's no law that says you can't come on down to my house for a party. But first, he says, the four or five policemen who have stupidly allowed themselves to be hemmed in by the crowd of demonstrators must be freed . . . Gregory explains how the demonstrators are to walk, not more than three or four abreast, keeping on the sidewalk and obeying the traffic lights. The march may be long and difficult, he says, for he lives in the black ghetto of South Chicago. He invites the two or three who had earlier been beaten by the cops to head the march, for he figures the police, whose job it is to stop the march, may be less brutal with them.

We walk along the hedge of armed soldiers.

At long last, America is moving.

Anyone who doubts the prescience of Jean Genet should read the opening of his last day's report:

Is it necessary to write that everything is over? With Humphrey nominated, will Nixon be master of the world?

We flew back to New York Thursday afternoon. At the airport, an *Esquire* limousine was waiting to take us to a site in the Bronx where the cover-story photo was to be shot. No one had the foggiest notion what the cover shot was supposed to be, except that *Esquire's* Chicago Four would be in it. We arrived at a desolate, deserted street, paved in brick, where a photographer awaited, together with a young male model who looked as if he had been dragged through the streets of Laredo by a posse of Western bad guys before being deposited in the Bronx. The photographer was perched a story above the street. The model was lain with his face down on the curb, his torso on the street, his legs on the sidewalk, his body and the surrounding pavement appropriately drenched in ketchup, which the photographer's lens would pick up as blood. Genet, Burroughs, Southern, and John Sack surrounded the pseudo-hippie—was he dead or merely sorely wounded, this victim of Chicago's mindless violence?—staring upward, with looks of accusation, at the offender, presumably Mayor Daley. Or Hubert Humphrey.

After the photo session, the car drove us back to Manhattan. Genet was beside himself.

"I detest sham," he said, shaking his head. "Chicago was one thing. At least there you were a real participant. But this . . ." I conveyed Genet's thought to Berendt, who, as always, was understanding, a calming influence. He asked that I try to explain to Jean that there was no way in the madness of Chicago that they could have taken a picture that would properly convey the scene as, he hoped, this simulated version would. Jean, not satisfied, simply shook his head.

The word "picture" gave me a start. For in the rush and tumble of Chicago, somewhere Jack Wright's camera and my eight rolls of film had gone missing. Would everyone please check his bags and see if by chance they had its precious—nay, irreplaceable—material . . . Nothing. I knew Jack Wright was far from well-heeled and vowed to have *Esquire* reimburse him.

52 ᕉ

And Now for My Fee

JEAN HAD AGREED to write two pieces for *Esquire*, one of which, "The Members of the Assembly," he had finished before he left Chicago. The other, entitled "A Salute to a Hundred Thousand Stars," was in rough draft, and Genet said he would finish it that afternoon, since he wanted to leave New York on Saturday. I had already translated the first piece before leaving Chicago, since *Esquire* was on a tight deadline, and promised Harold Hayes that I would translate the second piece over the weekend if Jean gave it to me by the end of the day on Friday. Financial agreements on Jean's Chicago trek had been made between *Esquire* and Jean's agent, Rosica Colin. Jean was to be paid in dollars, in cash. I turned in the first piece that same afternoon, later calling Hayes to say Genet was leaving town the next morning and would like to be paid.

"He'll be paid when both pieces are turned in," Hayes said.

"You already have one to hand," I said.

"And the other?"

"For Chrissake, Harold, we just got back, from five rather harrowing days, I might add." I felt like asking Hayes how he had spent the past week—nothing dangerous, I trusted—but refrained. "Jean's finishing up the second piece as we speak, and I promised Berendt you'd have the translation Monday morning. I'd say that's pretty fast."

"I repeat: he'll be paid in full when we have his pieces in full. Since we have one, he can pick up half his fee this afternoon."

I was furious. And ashamed, for it was we at Grove who had encouraged both Genet and Burroughs to accept the job. But I was dealing with a brick wall. Or someone with a brick for a brain. Or someone whose epithet rhymed with brick. I made one final, humiliating plea.

"Harold, I'm not sure you heard me. Jean is leaving tomorrow for Europe"—I refrained from saying he'd be leaving, precariously, via Canada, assuming he made it across the border without getting arrested—"and the agreement was he's to be paid in cash, I believe."

"If Genet wants the first half of his fee, he can pick it up this afternoon at the office." Click.

For a moment, I became a Chicago cop, blind empathy, with a murderous urge to use my club. But I figured there was no use sparing Genet the solemn truth. The vision of genius laboring away in his hotel room on a piece for which he probably would not be paid struck me as the depths of the absurd. I grabbed a cab to the Delmonico and shot up to room 911. There he was, seated at a tiny desk, his neat blue-penned script covering a schoolboy's lined white sheets.

"I've just finished," he said, clearly pleased with what he'd written. "Shall I read it to you?"

"Please do . . . But first I should tell you . . . I just got off the phone with Harold Hayes . . ."

"I never liked that man," he said. "When I first laid eyes on him in Paris, I didn't like him. Did you tell him I needed my fee today?"

"Yes, we can go pick it up right now. The only thing is"—I saw Genet lock his blue eyes on my embarrassment as if he knew in advance what I was going to say—"they're only going to pay you half your fee now."

"Did you tell them I'm leaving tomorrow?"

"Yes, of course. He wouldn't budge. They say they only have one of the two pieces."

"Here's the other one," Genet said. "I'll give it to him when we go there."

At the *Esquire* offices there was an envelope for Jean. He opened it and counted the money. Nineteen hundred dollars.

"That's only half," he said to the receptionist in French. She smiled at the cute man, but the cute man wasn't smiling back.

"I want to see Hayes," he said. I passed on the message.

"I'm sorry, Mr. Hayes has gone for the day."

I passed on the message.

Genet, without missing a beat, reached out and picked up the envelope containing "A Salute to a Hundred Thousand Stars" and stuffed it in his pocket. "Tell Mr. Hayes when I get my full fee he can have the second piece," he said. I passed on the message.

Back in his hotel room, Jean took the pages and slowly, methodically ripped them lengthwise into a dozen pieces, tossing strips into the wastebasket.

I watched, increasingly ill as I saw the shattered manuscript disappear. "Why the hell did you do that?" I said querulously.

"They'll never pay me," Jean said. He paused. "Did you ever notice," he said, "that when there's a difference between people who have money and those who don't, it's always the former who win? I've never known it to fail."

Friday Night, August 30

Jeannette was preparing a farewell dinner at our house for Jean, Barney, and some other Groveniks. I was not looking forward to it now, since Jean's foul mood was sure to permeate the celebration. But again I was wrong. If he was disturbed or angry—and I knew he was—he never let on, and the evening was a resounding success. In fact, I had never seen Jean in finer form, regaling us with stories of the past week.

What was the high point of Chicago?

"My meeting with the Black Panthers," he said, almost in a rush.

"On Tuesday—no Wednesday—we went to a Free Huey rally in Grant Park where I met Bobby Seale, David Hilliard, and a third Black Panther leader whose name I didn't catch . . ."

"Wendell Hillard," I supplied.

"Right. Anyway, Seale gave this impassioned speech in which, if I understood Dick's translation, he suggested the White House be painted black. What a splendid idea!"

Laughs all around.

"But I shook all three hands and told them I was with them in their struggle . . . And if one day they needed me, I'd come back."*

---

*True to his word, Jean did come back a year and a half later, in March 1970, and involved himself deeply in the Black Panther movement.

The rest of the evening focused on the future, the upcoming Humphrey-Nixon race, about which Genet opined that it really didn't matter who won. "They were both *connards* [assholes], were they not?"

At one point, he turned to Barney and said, rather gently, I thought, "You missed a great event in your hometown. I thought you were coming on Saturday," his blue eyes boring into Barney's.

"I know, I know," Barney said. "Actually, at one point Saturday morning I got in my car in East Hampton and headed for the airport. But after a few miles I turned back. I don't know why." It was one of the few times in my long acquaintance with Barney that I saw him truly contrite.

"A shame," Genet said. Barney, for whom "contrite" was a foreign word, lowered his head. "You missed a great event."

Which ended the evening.

Before exiting Jean's hotel that afternoon, I had been determined not to leave the despoiled manuscript behind. On the pretext that I had left something in the room, I went back up and rescued the remnants.

The following evening, Jeannette and I drove Jean to LaGuardia, where, without further incident, he boarded a plane for Montreal. He had been in America less than two weeks, but as we headed home from the airport, we both had the feeling we had just lived a mini-lifetime.

"Why 'mini'?" Jeannette laughed. "It seemed pretty 'maxi' to me."

That Sunday, I managed to stitch the scraps together with Scotch tape, translated them, and sent the piece off to Harold Hayes with a note. Not surprisingly, I never got a reply.*

For several weeks I pursued Jean's lost cause and also tried to get Hayes to reimburse Jack Wright for his missing camera. Jack was a friend of Terry Southern, who sent a barbed wire or two on Wright's behalf as well. Finally, with Hayes's continuing silence ringing in my ears, I wrote to the publisher, Arnold Gingrich, on December 27, in a post-Christmas Dickensian mood of ill humor. On December 30, Gingrich wrote back:

> *In Harold's absence . . . I can only give my impression of why you may have failed to hear from him.*

---

*Later Genet's agent, Rosica Colin, told me, however, that she had received, on Jean's behalf, a portion of the fee agreed upon for the second piece, together with a standard rejection letter.

I got the feeling that Harold was up to here (!) on everything to do with Genet, after paying the horrendous bills that his presence incurred. This involved, as you know, not only expenses for Genet and you and your wife, but also a substantial payment for an additional piece, which turned out to be such a calculated piece of effrontery that Harold could only assume it had been written as a deliberate put-down.

Harold paid and paid and paid until he reached a point at which—I take the liberty of guessing—he would have turned down Jesus Christ himself if he had asked him to lend a hand at carrying that heavy cross up the Golgotha Hill.

If my impression is wrong, I am sure Harold will correct it upon his return.

> *Yours always sincerely,*
> *Arnold Gingrich*
> *Publisher*

On January 15, with still no word from Hayes, who, it could be presumed, had returned from his "absence," presumably self-imposed, I wrote Gingrich back. I first reminded him that Genet, a spartan soul, incurred costs in New York, before and after the convention, of a grand total of three hundred dollars. If that was excessive, he and I should sit down and re-define the term. As for the fee, that had been agreed between Hayes and Rosica Colin, so no surprises there, as none for our translation fee, which had been proposed by Hayes. My strong suspicion was that the magazine's anger was directed not at Genet's expenditures—which at any calculation had to be termed modest—but at his politics. I closed:

> I am certain that Genet never made any bones about his feelings on the Vietnam War before he came here, and while *Esquire* has every right not to like the piece he wrote, it was most certainly not a calculated piece of effrontery, and I know that Genet takes the piece quite seriously. I gather, in fact, that it is being published in two or three major European publications.
>
> What I am saying in effect is that, if Harold "paid and paid and paid," to the best of my knowledge he did not pay for anything, or at any rate, that he had not contracted for.

The night of our farewell dinner for Jean, I had taken Barney aside and told him the story of *Esquire's* reneging. He was as appalled as I, upset for

Jean, and impressed by his good front throughout the evening. He also had an immediate and generous solution. If *Esquire* turned the piece down, we'd publish it in *Evergreen Review* and pay Jean the *Esquire* rate—which was five or six times ours. In due course, the piece appeared in *Evergreen Review*, which pleased Jean no end when I sent him the issue.

Strangely, he never asked how "A Salute to a Hundred Thousand Stars" had made it from the wastebasket of his hotel room to the pages of *Evergreen Review*.

53 ~

Goeth Before a Fall

BY 1968, Grove had tiptoed into film, having purchased, in addition to Amos Vogel's Cinema 16, a smattering of feature films, as well as producing Beckett's *Film*. It was a minor part of the Grove business, but it occupied a special place in Barney's heart.

Flash back to the Frankfurt Book Fair 1967. At the fair that year were a curious couple, Eberhard and Phyllis Kronhausen, whose book *The Sexually Responsive Woman* we had published a few years earlier. The Kronhausens, it was rumored, advised a number of Hollywood stars on how to broaden, and presumably enrich, their sex lives. Why they were at the fair I cannot remember, but I suspect to flog their latest opus to foreign countries.

On the second day of the fair, Barney showed me an article in *The Manchester Guardian* that had been brought to his attention about a recently released Swedish film, *I Am Curious (Yellow)*, the subject of enormous controversy for, the article said, its blatant sexuality. Wasting not a moment, Barney sought out the head of the leading Swedish publisher Bonniers, who knew all about *Yellow*, called the foundation that had made it—for it turned out to be a nonprofit venture—and arranged for a screening. Because we had meetings prescheduled months in advance, there was no way Barney himself could go to Stockholm till after the fair. Wait a minute: What about the Kronhausens? Excellent idea—with one exception. Before the

K-couple undertook the burdensome task, they made Barney sign a letter specifying that if we took on the film, they would get 10 percent of the proceeds. I had known that Barney was at times generous to a fault, but what a fault, this! Ten percent for *viewing* a film, all expenses paid? They reported back that the film was "pretty good," hardly a glowing recommendation, but Barney, now convinced this was made-to-order Grove, hopped on a plane to Stockholm as soon as the fair was over, viewed it with his wife, Christine, and bought it on the spot for a hundred thousand dollars (well over half a million in today's dollars).

First, it wasn't by any stretch pornography; in fact, it was a serious work about class struggle, about a young girl being exploited by her boyfriend, about women's rights. But it *was* titillating, probably what would today be labeled soft porn, and came with a huge aura of controversy. Back in the office, when Barney reported the purchase, there was considerable head shaking, for we were still pretty pissed and beleaguered financially. If the film bombed, would there still be a Grove? From a legal point of view, it sounded as if it was going to be déjà vu Henry Miller all over again, for this time, assuming we got the damn thing through customs, we would have to offer indemnity to all theaters that booked it. Some copies had been smuggled in through Canada, but though these were useful for in-house screenings, no commercial exploitation could occur until customs officially released it. The film was seized at the point of entry, in the instance New York, and held under lock and key at the customs house at the corner of Houston and Varick streets. Several of us made the pilgrimage to visit our prisoner and plead its case, until it was finally released under threat of suit. An empty victory, for the legal fun was about to begin. It was not until March 1969, a year and a half after its Swedish release, that the film finally opened in the United States. Predictably, many theaters refused to book it, even with the promise of indemnity, so that in dozens of cities we rented empty theaters and hired local staff to show it. Time and again we were arrested and the theaters shut down, until one day Ed de Grazia, who was handling the legal end of the project, had the brilliant idea of hiring local attorneys *before* the film opened, their fees to be 10 percent of the box-office take. Wherever that tempting offer was seized upon, there were no lawsuits, but still a bucketful were wending their way expensively through the courts. Offsetting this, wherever the film was shown, the lines were long, as theater after theater reported sold-out performances around the clock. The Grove Press coffers were daily filled to overflowing, a new experience. Even so, there were many hands in the Swedish cookie jar. Unlike the major film distributors, we had no means to audit a theater's gross for any given day or week, so were dependent on the honesty, integrity, and moral compass of theaters throughout the land.

Wherever we lost in court, we appealed, for we needed a final ruling, which could come only from the Supreme Court. The first case to make it there was a Maryland lawsuit, where we had lost twice, in the lower court and on appeal. At the Supreme Court, however, we judged our chances good, both because the court was fairly liberal and because one of the justices, William O. Douglas, had been published in *Evergreen*. His book *Points of Rebellion*, a chapter of which we had excerpted, had made an astounding statement; namely, it asserted a citizen's right to protest, or even revolt, against a government that does not fairly or rightly represent him or her. Pretty daring, in the midst of the Vietnam War. So daring, in fact, that there was a movement afoot to impeach Douglas. As part of that process, Congressman Gerald Ford had brandished on the floor of Congress the copy of *Evergreen Review* containing Douglas's piece—a magazine he labeled "pornographic"—and declaimed, "This is the kind of magazine that publishes Justice Douglas!"

When the *I Am Curious (Yellow)* case was finally heard, Justice Douglas recused himself because of his association with, or appearance in, *Evergreen Review*, as a result of which the decision came down 4–4. In other words, we lost. But by then the film had more or less run its course, having been shown in every major city in the country, and having contributed huge (by our standards) numbers of dollars to our dear, no longer (for the moment at least) financially fragile company. But beware of unexpected successes, for, we were learning, they are often the breeding ground of future failures.

If 1968 was the year of revolt and revolution in many countries of the Western world, for us at Grove 1969 was the year when, our coffers for once reasonably full, we published a record number of titles, both FOAs (Faithful Old Authors) and a bumper crop of new. Thanks especially to *I Am Curious (Yellow)* and to a far lesser extent its companion piece, *I Am Curious (Blue)*, the company had grown exponentially, not rationally, but more or less like Topsy. From 20 or so employees half a dozen years before, our weekly payroll now numbered close to 150, housed in our spanking-new building on the corner of Bleecker and Houston streets, plus our warehouse and book club premises over west on Hudson Street. A dream come true, yes? A nightmare in the making, if truth be known. In our gleaming new office, which one entered through a massive arch in the shape of a capital G, the top executive floor had been laid out with Hollywood in mind: posh everywhere. Barney had gone all out, hiring architects and interior decorators—friends all, so he could feel in his heart of hearts he was not only building an office building worthy of our new wealth and status but helping out buddies as well. The executive offices were spacious, filled with ultramodern furniture that bespoke not nouveau riche but dirty rich (according to our detractors, who were legion), whereas on the floors below and at Hudson Street, hoi polloi were granted warehouse furniture. To make matters more divisive, in outfitting the new building, Barney had decreed an executive elevator accessible only to the top-floor staff. The book club employees worked for sums ranging from seventy-five to eighty-five dollars a week in jam-packed cubicles, breeding resentment and discontent. The ultimate irony: Grove, a liberal institution prone to shaking up the establishment, was, in its fervor to grow, in danger of turning into the establishment itself.

Nonsense, we kept telling ourselves, we were still publishing good books (though perhaps not as timely and provocative as in years past). Or were we? Among other things, we seemed to be increasingly infected with a serious case of Anonymous, as book after book from Barney's cache of old-time erotica made its way from his private library to our very public lists. Of varying quality, some were quite charming, dating from the Victorian era or the early part of the twentieth century, when surface mores of utter probity gave way to man's apparently insatiable desire to document and express repressed sexual fantasies. No fewer than ten of these titillating gems appeared the last gasp of the 1960s, ranging from *Miss High-Heels* on the Zebra list at $1.75 to *Venus School-Mistress*, a Grove Press hardcover at $5.00. Nothing to be proud of, to be sure, but who could dispute Barney when, wielding pencil and paper, he showed the break-even point to be only a few hundred copies ("Look, no royalties!") and the profit margins enticing. After more than a decade of bringing hundreds of new voices to the world, including dozens of poets at a time when most publishers were dropping them as unworthy of their investment, who could condemn a handful of old-time erotica?

Offsetting, or overbalancing, the Victorian erotica were a relatively rich harvest of the FOAs: new works by Beckett, Burroughs, Ionesco, Pinter, Julius Lester, Jack Gelber, Rechy, Pablo Neruda, the Polish novelist Witold

Gombrowicz, and three further volumes in our film-book series, Kurosawa's *Rashomon*, Truffaut's *400 Blows*, and Antonioni's *L'avventura*—enough good works to reassure us we were not sliding down the slippery slope of exploitation.

One of the titles of which we were especially proud was by Jim Haskins, entitled *Diary of a Harlem Schoolteacher*. The Haskins was important, revealing firsthand the problems of teaching in inner-city schools in the 1960s, mirroring the despair of so much of the Harlem population. The book came out to good reviews, the sales were modest but continuing, and next year it would become an Evergreen paperback, where its more modest price would presumably find the audience for which it was intended. By Grove standards, noncontroversial.

The last week of March, I opened a letter whose return address was Coca-Cola USA, in Atlanta, Georgia. Neatly typed, surely by an executive secretary of impeccable credentials, the letter read:

Dear Mr. Seaver:

Several people have called to our attention your advertisement for Diary of a Harlem Schoolteacher *by Jim Haskins, which appeared in the* New York Times *March 3, 1970. The theme of the ad is "This book is like a weapon . . . it's the real thing."*

Since our company has made use of "It's the Real Thing" to advertise Coca-Cola long prior to the publication of the book, we are writing to ask you to stop using this theme or slogan in connection with the book.

We believe you will agree that it is undesirable for our companies to make simultaneous use of "the real thing" in connection with our respective products. There will always be likelihood of confusion as to the source or sponsorship of the goods, and the use by such prominent companies would dilute the distinctiveness of the trade slogan and diminish its effectiveness and value as an advertising and merchandising tool.

"It's the Real Thing" was first used in advertising for Coca-Cola over twenty-seven years ago to refer to our product. We first used it in print advertising in 1942 and extended it to outdoor advertising, including painted walls—some of which are still displayed throughout the country. The line has appeared in advertising for Coca-Cola during succeeding years. For example, in 1954 we used "There's this about Coke—You Can't Beat the 'Real Thing'" in national advertising. We resumed

national use of "It's the Real Thing" in the summer of 1969 and it is our main thrust for 1970.

Please excuse my writing so fully, but I wanted to explain why we feel it necessary to ask you and your associates to use another line to advertise Mr. Haskin's [sic] book.

We appreciate your cooperation and your assurance that you will discontinue the use of "It's the real thing."

Sincerely,
Ira C. Herbert

Convinced that Mr. Herbert, or Coca-Cola, had gone frigging mad, I took the letter in to Barney. "What the hell's wrong with you?" he asked, before my belly laughter reassured him. I handed him the letter, which he read as carefully as if it contained yet another threat of lawsuit, then he too burst out laughing. "I assume you're not going to let this pass," he said. "I'll show you my response," I said.

Next morning I sat down at my trusty manual typewriter—I had not yet mastered the complex technology of the IBM Selectric—and replied thus:

Mr. Ira C. Herbert
Coca-Cola USA
P.O. Drawer 1734
Atlanta, Georgia 30301

Dear Mr. Herbert:
Thank you for your letter of March 25th, which has just reached me, doubtless because of the mail strike.

We note with sympathy your feeling that you have a proprietary interest in the phrase "It's the real thing," and I can fully understand that the public might be confused by our use of the expression, and mistake a book by a Harlem schoolteacher for a six-pack of Coca-Cola. Accordingly, we have instructed all our salesmen to notify bookstores that whenever a customer comes in and asks for a copy of Diary of a Harlem Schoolteacher *they should request the sales personnel to make sure that what the customer wants is the book, rather than a Coke. This, we think, should protect your interest and in no way harm ours.*

We would certainly not want to dilute the distinctiveness of your trade slogan nor diminish its effectiveness as an advertising and merchandising tool, but it did not occur to us that since the slogan is so closely identified with your product, those who read our ad may well tend to go out and buy a Coke rather than our book. We have discussed this problem in an executive committee meeting, and by a vote of seven to six decided that, even if this were the case, we would be happy to give Coke the residual benefit of our advertising.

Problems not dissimilar to the ones you raise in your letter have occurred to us in the past. You may recall that we published Games People Play, *which became one of the biggest nonfiction bestsellers of all time and spawned conscious imitations (*Games Children Play, Games Psychiatrists Play, Games Ministers Play, *etc.). I'm sure you'll agree that this posed a far more direct and deadly threat to both the author and ourselves than our use of "It's the real thing." Further,* Games People Play *has become part of our language, and one sees it constantly in advertising, as a newspaper headline, etc. The same is true of another book we published six or seven years ago,* One Hundred Dollar Misunderstanding.

Given our strong sentiments concerning the First Amendment, we will defend to the death your right to use "It's the real thing" in any advertising you care to. We would hope you would do the same for us, especially when no one here in our advertising agency, I am sorry to say, realized that you owned the phrase. We were merely quoting in our ads Peter S. Prescott's review of Diary of a Harlem Schoolteacher *in* Look, *which begins "*Diary of a Harlem Schoolteacher *is the real thing, a short, spare, honest book which will, I suspect, be read a generation hence as a classic . . ."*

With all best wishes,
Sincerely yours,
Richard Seaver

I fully expected a tart response from Mr. Herbert or, God forbid, an even higher Coca-Cola executive threatening me, or Grove, or both, with a million-dollar lawsuit, or even bodily harm. After all, our mere plastering of Che Guevara's poster throughout New York, to forewarn its denizens of the impending arrival of excerpts from his diaries in the next issue of *Evergreen Review*, had prompted anti-Castro Cubans to lob a bomb into our premises at 64 University Place. Imagine, we thought, what an ever more powerful organization such as Coca-Cola might dream up as retaliation for our having borrowed—nay, usurped—its precious slogan. We put the staff on red alert, a move that perhaps saved the day, for if the Atlanta headquarters had planned an assault, its knowledge that we were all at our battle stations (for its spies, generally disguised as Coca-Cola truck drivers or deliverymen, were everywhere) doubtless deterred them.

In any event, at the dawn of the 1970s, we had far more serious matters to contend with.

The April 1970 issue of *Evergreen Review* had on its cover a fully clothed, futuristic male, looking for all the world like an astronaut–hockey player, complete with shoulder pads, a helmet, a Rangers jersey, gloves, and a hip-holster pistol. In his arms—one hockey glove grasping the midriff, the other the wrist—Mr. Freedom (for that's who our hero was) held a scantily clad, sequin-spangled red-white-and-blue redhead, whose open mouth could just as easily be construed as a cry for help as a moan of ecstasy. Let the beholder decide.

The magazine cover, intriguing in itself to most, was also a prime example of Grove's new internal synergy (a word we actually used in our discussions of Grove's future, God help us all!). Not only did it supply grist for the *Evergreen Review* mill, it also served as the poster for the U.S. release of the Grove film, *Mr. Freedom*, a not-too-subtle satire on America as it moved out of the turbulent 1960s. A scathing attack on American foreign policy, especially its "vulgar and grotesque" involvement in Vietnam and the Strangelove notion that democracy had to be brought to the rest of the world, even at the cost of destroying it, the French-made film was written and directed by the ex-patriot (*sic*) William Klein. It starred John Abbey as Mr. Freedom; Delphine Seyrig (who had been propelled to cinematic stardom as the Garboesque lead in Alain Resnais's *Last Year at Marienbad*) as Marie-Madeleine, organizer of the Whores-for-Freedom network; Donald Pleasence (whose voice and accent bore an uncanny resemblance to Lyndon Johnson's) as Dr. Freedom, the mad mastermind behind the movement to save the world from anti-freedom infiltration; and Philippe Noiret as Moujik Man, Russia's answer to Mr. Freedom.

On the surface it was a perfect vehicle for the Grove Movie Machine: irreverent, sexy, outrageous, politically pointed, a no-holds-barred attack on the establishment. Unfortunately, its script, dialogue, and direction, alas, were sufficiently amateurish to give film critics a golden opportunity to lambaste it.

The rest of issue number 77 was vintage Grove. In addition to a cover tie-in interview with William Klein about the making and meaning of *Mr. Freedom*, there was a storyboard sequence using stills from the movie. The lead article was by the black writer and activist Julius Lester, whose *Look Out, Whitey!* we had reprinted. Entitled "The Black Writer and the New Censorship," it attacked the white-dominated book-publishing industry for its sorry record of not publishing black writers and, even more egregious, its seeming refusal to hire black editors. Although Grove had published a number of black writers—Frantz Fanon, Malcolm X, LeRoi Jones, a.k.a. Amiri Baraka, Julius Lester himself—as a percentage of our lists, blacks were underrepresented, so in effect Julius's piece was as much an attack on Grove as it was on the industry as a whole. I thought the piece important and right-on, but as Julius's editor I felt I should discuss it with Barney. He read it with an increasingly black (no pun) scowl on his face, then said: "Do you really think we should publish this?" "Absolutely," I said. He nodded. "Okay. Let's make it the lead article." That's what endeared Grove to me, I reminded myself. What other house would have opened its editorial pages to a voice whose slings and arrows were aimed directly at its heart? The issue also contained Tom Hayden's "Repression and Rebellion," his response to being convicted in February by a Chicago jury "of having crossed state lines to incite rioting" during the 1968 Democratic National Convention; Nat Hentoff's "Keeping Ecology Alive," a call to arms to save the planet long before that cause became fashionable; and, most important, the aforementioned chapter from Justice Douglas's then-forthcoming book, *Points of Rebellion*, entitled "Redress and Revolution," which echoed the antiestablishment themes of Hayden and Hentoff, likening the political climate of Washington at the turn of the decade to that of King George of England at the time of the American Revolution. Attacking the Pentagon, the highway lobby, and the CIA, Justice Douglas stopped just short of calling for a new American Revolution. Pretty heady stuff, we thought, coming from a member of the Supreme Court, though clearly his views did not constitute a majority opinion.

As we entered the 1970s, we were still offering up the same combination of provocation, social consciousness, and (tasteful?) sex that had served us so well during the previous decade. Thumbing your nose at the establishment (Klein) as you taunt the censors (Freed) and proselytize (Douglas, Hentoff) was no simple task. But somehow Grove and *Evergreen* had mastered it, and the combination was still working on all cylinders.

Or was it?

54 ⤴

Fur, Leather, and Machine Workers, Arise

NE DAY in early April 1970, about the time Mr. Freedom was hitting the stores and stands, Barney and I arrived back at Grove after lunch to see two scruffy young men, barely out of their teens to judge by their zit-scarred faces, entering the building. They were clothed, if that is the proper term, in jeans and jackets so tattered your eyes automatically shifted downward in search of the mendicant's paper cup. But if they were juvenile bums, why did they disappear through the magic G into the building?

"Who are those two guys?" Barney growled.

"They work here," I said, vaguely remembering them.

"Who for?" he rightly wanted to know.

"For Myron. In the book club."

"Do you know their names?" Barney insisted. I was afraid he would ask that. "As the number-two person in this company, shouldn't you know the names of all the people who work here?" Before I could answer, he added: "The fact is, *I* don't know the names of half the goddamn people here anymore."

"Me neither," I confessed.

"Well, that's not a good situation," Barney muttered.

Fortunately for our mood, the ever-cheerful Frieda, perched atop her swiveling stool behind the giant new switchboard, looking more and more like a Kewpie-doll space cadet in *Star Trek*, greeted us with a warm "Hi, Barney. Hi, Dick. I have a stack of messages for both of you." But as we entered the executive elevator, both of us felt an uncomfortable twinge at the memory of the two bedraggled persons who had preceded us through the big G. Grove was changing—had changed over the past three or four years; that was undeniable. Had we grown too fast? And was this building, fruit of our one conservative decision to channel our windfall *I Am Curious* millions not into speculative new book titles but into real estate ("you can never lose putting your money in real estate," an adviser had assured us), had this become a dangerously divisive element? Though he was silent, I suspected the same questions were going through Barney's mind, too.

On Wednesday, April 8, 1970, a young woman who worked in fulfillment for the book club ran into Martin Quayle, the Grove comptroller, in the downstairs hallway.

"Oh, Marty," she gushed, "we've just had the greatest organizing meeting!"

Not quite sure he had heard correctly, Quayle, feigning pleasure at the news, probed a bit. "Oh, yes, where was that?"

"At union headquarters on Twenty-sixth Street, of course. Where do you think?"

Union headquarters, it turned out, was that of the Amalgamated Meat Cutters and Butcher Workmen of North America—at first glance, or even second, a totally unlikely bedfellow for an avant-garde publisher, or any publisher for that matter. Grove's warehouse had already been organized two or three years before with no opposition and no subsequent problems. But the notion of unionizing book publishers' editorial, or even sales and marketing, arms had always struck industry executives as nonsensical. Absolute freedom editorially—to pick and publish the books you want—was the sine qua non of the business. How would a unionized editorial staff handle a manuscript attacking the labor movement? Or a book supporting a political candidate anathema to the AFL-CIO, of which the Fur, Leather, and Machine Workers—the union that had taken over Grove—were part? Or, God forbid, a vegetarian cookbook?

If Quayle's information proved correct, that Grove was threatened with an attempt to be unionized, why in the hell the Fur and Leather boys? Had they run out of butcher shops, hog butchers for the world, sheep, and beef? Whatever the reasons for their expansionist ambitions, further probing revealed that they had formed within their union a Publishing Employees Organizing Committee. One small leap across a meadow of sheep or cows and, voilà, you land squarely in Bookland. It made all sorts of sense, if you didn't think about it.

But why us? Because we were known to be liberal, therefore pro-union, therefore unlikely to resist their efforts? Because we had grown so fast that the union knew we had scads of new, low-paid employees, always a fertile ground? Because, the more paranoid among us deduced, the government, weary of our parries and thrusts through the years, had co-opted the union into making its frontal attack, all expenses paid by some shadow organization in Washington? That was Barney's firm belief: for years he had been convinced that there was a mole among us, reporting to the FBI or CIA or whatever antisubversive agency to which he (she?) reported. If most of us old-timers tended to chalk Barney's conviction up to paranoia, we also had to remember that we were the only American publisher in history to have been bombed. What's more, the same anti-Castro people who had tossed a fragmentation grenade into our second-story window two years before, destroying the production department, had that same night bombed half a dozen other sites in the city, yet when arrested and brought to trial, they were let go, a bizarre carriage of non-justice sufficient to make the healthiest mind paranoid.

In any event, the rumor of the union meeting was soon confirmed: not only had the Fur and Leather boys formed a publishing committee, but several disgruntled Grove employees had already rushed to embrace it. Barney was livid. "We haven't got enough problems around here without this!" he growled. He had a point. After three or four years of one victory after another, some Pyrrhic, some real, both in the courts and in the market-place, there were increasing signs of strain within the company. The seemingly endless flood of moneys from I Am Curious (Yellow) and (Blue) was finally slowing to a trickle. The cost overruns on the new Mercer Street building had been staggering. The book business in general was stagnating. Our three mass-market lines—Black Cat, Zebra, and Venus—were not selling through as well as we had planned, and the returns were fast eating up the receivables. More, the so-called synergy between the book club and the publishing arm was increasingly tenuous.

But without doubt our greatest sin had been expanding too fast. Still tiny by corporate America's standards, we had nonetheless more than qua-drupled sales over the past three or four years. Spurred by the fact we were a public company, traded on the NASDAQ exchange, we felt for the first time the need to grow, if only to keep up with our image as "a smart little company that could do no wrong," as one misguided broker had dubbed us, either because he really believed it or, more likely, because he was touting us to his clients as the newest way to get rich overnight. In any event, in this cruel month of April 1970, our new thirty-two-thousand-square-foot building housed only half the total staff. The editorial department, for years two and a half strong, now counted a dozen more-or-less full-time employees.*

Throughout most of its existence, Grove had knowingly and willfully chosen to ignore organization charts detailing lines of authority. Since for years many of us had worn several hats, often as many as six or seven, it was hopeless to try to draw up such charts, much less implement them. When an urgent need appeared, anyone qualified, even peripherally, stepped in to plug the gap. Though hired as managing editor, a job in most publishing houses meant to keep the flow of manuscripts on track, I soon became co-editor with Barney of *Evergreen Review*; editor in chief of the book division; production director for several months after Richard Brodney departed; sales rep for part of the northeastern territory when our commission rep for that territory suddenly resigned; head of inventory control, making certain our growing backlist was never out of stock; and design consultant with Barney for our covers and jackets, liaising for years with Roy Kuhlman. That for starters.

Strategic plans and five-year forecasts, which I heard some of my uptown colleagues rhapsodizing about, seemed to us useless, if not risible. How could we, or anyone, in good faith make such futuristic predictions for 1972 or 1973, much less 1975, when we hadn't the foggiest notion what we would be publishing in those years? We recognized that book publishing is by its very nature a seat-of-the-pants business, where instinct and intuition must reign. Unlike the larger houses, several of which were owned by corporate masters, we had no imposed mandate to grow by 5 or 10 or 15 percent per annum. If we survived and paid our bills, and hopefully did

---

*"More-or-less" because at Grove some of the editors who were considered full-time worked part-time at their request, and some worked partly at home because of domestic needs. In short, in keeping with its liberal practices of the past, in its new, larger incarnation it did its best to accommodate its employees' personal schedules. Another tactical error, for that effort at accommodation, in retrospect, was barely, if at all, appreciated.

right by our Faithful Old Authors and introduced to the world new voices, that was enough. That philosophy had served us well in the past and would, we firmly believed, in the new decade as well.

But the hard fact was, Grove *had* changed. When we were small and squeaking by, it was all for one and one for all. No one was making much money, so who was there to envy? We were all making a decent wage, but the whole point of being at Grove was that it was exciting. And freewheeling. Bombs away and a laugh a day . . . Throughout the 1960s, we had the feeling we were shaking up the gray-flannel establishment and striking a chord among members of the younger generation, many of whom, judging by their letters, were telling us we had changed their lives.

The world too had changed, more than we realized. Our battles against censorship, our espousal of writers the establishment had hitherto disdained, had opened the doors, if not the minds, of other publishers, far more ready now to take on authors and subjects that had previously been taboo. Our piddling advances to authors only too happy to be published at all in the 1960s now began to look like what they were—piddling—with larger houses ready to offer several times what we could or would muster. Too, women's liberation was forging to the forefront of people's consciousness, and we who thought of ourselves as liberators were now being viewed—by a minority, perhaps, but a very vocal one—as repressive. Or worse: exploiters of women. But as the news that day of the unionization attempt reached us, we were only vaguely aware of these sea changes, if at all.

Barney opened our hastily convened executive committee meeting on an unusually quiet note: "What the fuck are the Fur, Leather, and Goddamn Machine Workers doing trying to organize Grove? It makes no goddamn sense!"

Indeed it did not. Why, we wondered, not the bigger houses? Random House? Simon and Schuster? Doubleday? Ten times as many employees as Grove. Harper had an in-house union, someone remembered, but it was a rather benevolent, nonthreatening group whose main goal was to make sure middle- and lower-rank employees got their fair share of benefits.

"We still don't know whether this is anything more than a probe," said Jules Geller, the authority among us, for in the 1930s he had been a union organizer in the Midwest. "Just because the union met with a few employees doesn't mean they'll make an all-out attempt."

"Do we know who went to the meeting?" Barney wanted to know.

"Several from the editorial department, I'm sorry to report." I had asked around as soon as I heard the news. "Robin Morgan for one. Cicely Nichols. And I think Mary Heathcote . . ."

At the last named, Barney winced, for she was a friend whom he had urged me to hire. "I never liked that Robin Morgan," he said. "She always struck me as a troublemaker. But Mary . . ."

"Ward Damio was there," Fred put in.

"Oh, God, *him!*" Barney hissed.

Damio was a young man with a big motorcycle. In any other company, he would have been a misfit. At Grove he was just another employee who was somewhat different from the other different employees. Well, not quite. He worked for Myron Shapiro in the book club, but his job performance, according to Myron, ranged from perfunctory to near zero. The black-leathered, chain-bedecked Damio lavished most of his time and love on his cycle, leaving little time or energy for work. No one had to clock him in or out of the office: the roar and screech of his cycle indelibly marked his comings and goings.

"What the hell was Damio doing up there?" Marty asked. "Or did he think the 'Machine' in the union's name referred to his motorcycle?"

"It gave him an excuse to cycle up to Twenty-sixth Street?" Morrie suggested.

"Also got him out of work for a couple hours," Barney growled.

"Can't you control your employees, Myron?" Jules asked, only half jokingly, for I knew there was no love lost between the two.

"Up yours, Jules," Myron responded icily, his Trotsky chin whiskers bobbing furiously.

If there's trouble in the ranks, I remember thinking, the executive committee is not exactly a peaceable kingdom either.

As best we could make out, most of the people who had attended the union meeting had done so in support of the peons on the ground floor and at Hudson Street. Conversations with several confirmed that if they went, it was to help right a perceived wrong, namely, to have the salaries of Myron's slaves raised from seventy-five dollars to eighty-five dollars a week. If you thought about it, they were acting in true Grove tradition. But the message received was quite different. Regardless of motive, these people were in Barney's mind traitors. For him, Grove was not just a place of employment, it was a *cause*, and those who betrayed it should be hanged from the yardarm.

"Well, I can tell you one thing," he said grimly. "I intend to fight this to the death. If ever Grove is unionized, it would spell the end of the company."

"Careful," Jules warned. "You can't take any action against the people you know are pro-union, or attended union meetings. We'll be monitored."

"But that's true only when there's an official organizing drive going on, right?" Barney said.

"Yes," Jules said, "that's true."

"So if we ever wanted to fire people, now would be the time, right? As I see it, we have a very narrow window of opportunity."

Jules shook his head. "They'll still try to prove there's a connection between our knowledge of the union activities and the firings. They'd probably take us to arbitration."

"But they couldn't *prove* there was a link, could they?"

I glanced over at Barney. His forehead was knit in a deep scowl, and his tight lips looked like the proverbial seamless scar. He was as white as I'd ever seen him. This was, I knew, the pre-explosive Barney.

"Why don't we try to find out more before we go off the deep end?" I ventured, suddenly seeing half my editorial staff gurgling down the drain.

Barney looked over at me as though I had lost my mind. Fact was, I didn't really believe my own words. I had the sinking feeling we were already well into the deep end.

That night when I arrived home—late as always—the children were long in bed and Jeannette looked as though she would have my head if she could remember where she had put the ax. But when she saw my face, she suddenly softened. "Trouble in paradise?" she asked.

I nodded, then filled her in on the day's events.

"So what's the solution?" she asked. I told her Barney's plan was to fire several people immediately, before the organizing drive began. "But won't that be obvious?" she insisted. I nodded. "Wouldn't it be best just to go through the process? There are enough sane people at Grove to vote against it, aren't there?" I agreed and said I had made that suggestion at today's meeting, to no avail. "How long would the whole unionization process take?" she persisted.

"Two or three weeks, maybe a month."

"Then you should definitely go through with it," she concluded. "Wait and see, if you fire all those people, all hell will break loose. What's more,

I can just see you coming home two or three hours later every night, with as much work as ever and three fewer editors to do it. As it is, you don't see your children half enough. Not to mention me . . . You know, darling, I swear you love Grove more than you do me."

Game, set, and match.

Next morning the tension at Grove was palpable and mounting. The pro-union folk knew that we knew, and the scornful looks we received as we entered the sixth-floor elevator could have killed. Another hasty meeting was called. Buttressed by Jeannette's compelling arguments the night before, I made a last-ditch plea not to fire people until we'd gone through the unionization process, which I proclaimed we would surely win.

"And if we lost?" Barney said.

"Dick's right," Jules said. "I've checked, and this will be all over in roughly two weeks. Maybe sooner. If we fire these people now, God knows the price we might pay."

"And if we lost?" Barney said again.

"Jules and Dick are right," Morrie said. "Firing people now will swing more votes to the union, that's for sure."

"And if we lost?" Barney insisted. At which point we knew our advice was immaterial. The kid who owned the football dictated how and where the game would be played.

Further discussion about who had to go wavered between eight and fifteen, until we settled on nine.

"I assume we should inform them on Friday," Jules suggested.

"Friday, hell!" Barney objected. *"Tonight!"*

"What if, when we tell them, they refuse to leave the premises?" Morrie asked.

"That's a distinct possibility," Jules said. "A sit-in might be joined by a lot of others."

"We'll do it by Western Union," Barney said. "A telegram informing them they're fired and are not to set foot here again. But at least three, starting with Robin, I want out of here today."

There was heated discussion about both the timing and the draconian telegraph method, but again Barney was adamant. That day, April 9, and the next, pink slips in the form of yellow Western Union telegrams arrived at all nine employees' homes. It was perhaps a needlessly cruel way to go about it, but Fred and Barney were scheduled to leave for Denmark that weekend to view some more Scandinavian masterpieces for the already-overburdened Grove film archives and wanted all this out of the way before they departed. We who were left behind had the job of coping with the repercussions. I had mixed feelings about both the firings and the way they were handled. I also remembered Jeannette's prescient thought that with four of the nine beheadings from the editorial department—for in addition to Robin, Cicely, and Mary we had let go a first-rate young editorial assistant, Beverly Ravitch—my life was going to be sheer hell. I sensed, too, that there would be serious consequences of the late-night telegrams. Over the weekend I conjured up in my mind several scenarios, but none was even close to what actually came to pass.

Monday morning, up at dawn after a second sleepless night, I arrived at the office well before nine to find the place seething. A couple dozen people—mostly Grove employees, to judge from a cursory look around—were milling about outside the building, talking, arguing, several handing out broadsheets. Someone pressed one into my hand as I passed. It was a one-page mimeographed sheet whose headline read: WOMEN HAVE SEIZED THE EXECUTIVE OFFICES OF GROVE PRESS. I glanced up at the sixth floor: a red and white banner floated from one of its windows. Inside the building I found a magnified repetition of the scene outside: employees arguing in the corridors, shouting, gesticulating wildly, threatening. From what I could gather, about half an hour earlier a number of women, parading under the banner of the Women's Liberation Front, had arrived, taken the executive elevator to the top floor, and locked themselves in Barney's office. They had blocked off access to the top floor by shoving desks and chairs and files against all the doors. Myron, on the floor below, I found wringing his hands. Jules, Morrie, and Nat were huddled at a nearby window, talking in hushed tones.

"They want to meet with Barney and won't leave till he sees them," Myron said.

"Didn't you tell them he's out of the country?"

"They won't talk with me. As soon as I say who it is, they hang up."

"Shit! Does anyone know where Barney's staying in Copenhagen? Where's Judith?"

The triumvirate by the window joined us. "Anybody know where Barney is?" I repeated, and all shook their heads. Judith was not yet in, and she alone knew his hotel. Meanwhile, I figured we'd better go up to the top floor and break in. Jules shook his head. "We've already tried that. They've got the top floor pretty well barricaded. Anyway, I've told them Barney was in Europe. They told me in that case they'd only talk to you."

"Any tactical suggestions?" I asked.

"Try to find out what they want."

"I know what they want. Have you seen the broadsheet? They want editorial control of all Grove publications, a few million dollars for assorted causes, a day-care center for children. God knows what else."

There was a stairway from the fifth to the sixth floor, which we climbed to find, as expected, that door too was barred. Three of us tried to force it open, but it wouldn't budge. "Probably bolted from the inside," Jules said, and an examination of the safety door one flight down showed one could lock it from within.

"Do we know who's in there?" I asked.

"The only one we know is Robin Morgan," Morrie said.

"Any other Grove employees?"

"None that we know."

"How many in all?"

"About ten," Jules said, "according to those who were here when they arrived."

We climbed back up, and I shouted through the metal barrier. "Robin, this is Dick. Tell us what you want." Silence. I tried again, even louder. Even louder silence.

"I don't think they can hear you," Jules said. "Why don't we try to call them on the intercom."

Back downstairs, I dialed Barney's number, and a dulcet voice replied, "Women's Occupation Forces. Who's this?"

"Dick Seaver." Pause. "Is Robin there?"

"Just a minute." A few seconds later Robin came on.

"What in the hell do you think you're doing, Robin?" Across the room I could see Jules gesturing for a softer approach.

"We're demanding that Grove give us editorial control. You all have made millions exploiting women. It's time you paid us back. All your pornographic films and books degrading us . . ."

"Come on, Robin," I tried. "Let's be reasonable. Give us a list of your demands and we'll see if we can meet any."

"First of all, all those who were fired must be reinstated."

"How many Grove employees are up there with you, Robin?"

"None of your business, Dick. Furthermore, if you don't meet our demands, we'll destroy all the Grove Press files."

Suddenly a vision of the precious correspondence—Beckett's, Genet's, Pinter's, Burroughs's, Ionesco's, Miller's—going up in Nazi-like flames nearly made me sick to my stomach.

Robin must have been reading my mind, for she went on: "And we're serious about that. Read the broadsheet carefully. It's all laid out there."

I looked down at the paper I had grabbed without really reading it. Even at a glance I could see the absurdity of the demands, which the broadsheet labeled "just conditions," the first of which was that Grove cease all publication of books and magazines, and the distribution of films, that degrade women. In other words, censorship again, this time not from the customs or postal authorities but from a band of perhaps well-meaning, but sadly misguided, women. As soon as the thought passed through my mind, I regretted giving them the benefit of the doubt. Well-meaning, my foot!

"I'll call you back in a few minutes," I said to Robin.

I looked around at my esteemed colleagues, none of whom I had to brief, for I had had Robin on speakerphone. We all had copies of the broadsheet. We were guilty of "oppressive and exploitive practices against our own female employees." Nonsense! Women employees at Grove in key positions of editorial, production, and marketing were legion, and our work hours (thirty-five per week), medical benefits, vacations, and holidays were well above industry average and always had been, even in times of financial stress, which were many. "A 24-hour free childcare center controlled by women"; a fund for recently divorced women "to help them get back on their feet"; a fund to establish abortion and birth-control clinics; "a bail fund to free each month a minimum of 100 'political prisoners' [read: prostitutes] from the Women's House of Detention"; finally, "women must control 51% of all decisions, editorial and otherwise."

I looked up, as did almost simultaneously the other four gathered there.

"I knew Robin was a pain in the ass," Jules offered, "but I didn't know she was stark, raving mad."

"If I understand correctly," I said, waving the broadsheet, "there are a dozen or so women up there, and the only Grove employee is Robin. So what's this shit about her speaking for all women employees at Grove? In my experience, nobody even takes her seriously."

"More to the point," Jules said, "do you think they're crazy enough to actually destroy those files?"

Everyone nodded.

"Jesus!" I said. "Those files are priceless. Grove's whole history is there. Somehow we've got to break in."

"How?" Morrie said. "They've blocked off the elevator, and we've seen we can't budge the safety door."

"Through the window?" Myron suggested, and I could just see him—or any of us—scaling the vertical brick wall à la Spider-Man, breaking a window, presumably with an elbow, scrambling in through the shards, and, if not yet bleeding to death, taking Robin in a stranglehold. At the very least, seven years for assault and battery. Seven years?

Just then Judith arrived, flustered but still cogent enough to give us Barney's telephone number in Copenhagen. While Frieda was putting through the call, I asked Judith what she knew of Barney's schedule, for in Europe it was now past mid-afternoon. He's booked solid, she thought, but should return to the hotel before dinner. Eventually, I reached the concierge, found that Mr. Rosset was indeed out, and left a callback message. I didn't use the word "urgent," for fear he would panic, but I did say "important."

I got Robin on the phone again and told her we couldn't reach Barney, but had left word for him to call as soon as possible. Meanwhile, under no circumstances should they destroy property; among other things, that could get them serious jail time. I had no idea if that was consistent with the law but hoped it might deter them at least momentarily.

Meanwhile, we all went back downstairs and told people everything was under control, please get back to work, but few seemed inclined to do so.

Around noon our time Barney called. It was Judith who answered. "How are things?" he said.

"Fine," she lied, "the only thing is, I'm not in my office. I'm down on the fifth floor."

"Why?" Barney wondered.

"Because the sixth floor is occupied by a women's liberation group."

"A what!" he yelled. At which point she handed me the phone, and I filled him in on the morning's—now afternoon's—events.

"And they're threatening to destroy the files?" he screamed. "Get them out of there!"

"The elevator's cut off, and the back stairs are blockaded and locked from the inside."

"Then go in through the skylights," he advised, forgetting there was no access, except from the top floor, to the roof. Maybe we could use sky-hooks, I remember thinking, a faint remembrance from my callow youth when as an eight-year-old at summer camp I had been told, and firmly believed, that the heavens were held up by these magical skyhooks.

"Do any of you other geniuses over there have any ideas?" he bellowed, referring to the august executive committee hovering around the phone.

"We could call the cops and have them evicted," Jules the Wise suggested.

"That's the stupidest idea I've ever heard!" the voice-across-the-water replied. "How many times have we been arrested over the years? Two hun-dred? Three hundred? Grove resorting to the police? They'd laugh in our face!"

Clapping my hand over the phone, through which nonetheless some high-pitched sounds still sputtered, not unlike those emitted by a stuck pig, I asked the now-stymied committee if it was time to impart to Barney the rest of the bad news: that, downstairs, the place was being picketed by several hundred people, both employees and union sympathizers, which, while not as immediately threatening as the women upstairs, was an in-creasing pain in the ass. And Barney was conveniently forgetting that his mass firing of nine people two days before his departure was the cause of all this, for we had also learned that Henry Foner, the union president, had just filed an unfair labor practices complaint against the company. I decided not to draw this causal connection, but the consensus was we'd better tell him, in this upstairs-downstairs drama, about the shenanigans on the sidewalk.

"Fuck the pickets!" he said. "It's the Grove archives that have to be saved. Call Rembar and then phone me back."

Rembar, the voice of calm, listened quietly as we outlined to him the sequence of events, starting with the threat of unionization—of which, it turned out, he was aware—the Thursday and Friday night massacres, the pickets downstairs, the occupation upstairs, coupled with the serious threat to the Grove Press files, and Barney's presence in a land far, far away.

"Call the police," he said. "You have no choice."

We conveyed Rembar's advice to Barney, who said, obviously forget-ting his violent reaction to that same piece of advice from Jules only half an hour before, "Of course that's what you should do. What the hell are you waiting for?"

We decided the police needed only the short version, not the background that presumably had precipitated the occupation. Trespassing. Breaking and entering. Threatening destruction of company property. That was all they needed to know. Within half an hour a considerable blue contingent arrived, preceded by the scream of sirens, which swarmed through the jeering picket lines and arrived battle ready on the fifth floor. On the intercom, they ordered the women to surrender. If they did not, they would be charged not only with illegal trespassing but also with resisting arrest. To our great surprise, the occupation forces reacted not with a bang but with a whimper, unlocking the elevator and surrendering almost meekly, though several, when they arrived downstairs, lifted their fists heavenward, to which the pickets responded with shouts of encouragement and support.

Among the pickets we noted a couple of dozen Grove employees, bearing signs one more ridiculous than the other, making demands they doubtless did not believe in and knew could never be met. When and why, I remember wondering, did an individual abdicate personal responsibility and join the mindless herd? But what galled me and the other Grove executives even more was the sight, among the pickets, of a number of our publishing colleagues from other houses, people I had thought of as friends. One, Aaron Asher, to whom I was—or thought I had been—especially close, was chanting with the others as they slowly circled back on the Mercer Street sidewalk. I sidled up to him and asked him what the fuck he thought he was doing. He gazed at me imperiously and said that he fully supported women's lib and had heard of the unforgivable way we had fired our editors. "I thought we knew each other well enough," I said, "that you might have called me and found out the facts before you did this." He shrugged and made his way slowly round and round, and where he might have stopped nobody knows.

Studious, bespectacled John Simon of Simon and Schuster (no relation) was also there being interviewed, a microphone pressed close to his fast-moving lips. From what I could catch through the noise, he was accusing us of treating our employees as if this were the seventeenth century. Really! There were no yellow telegrams way back then, you jerk! Besides, I thought, I'll match our employee benefits against yours any day. Short, paunchy, lightly bearded André Schiffrin, the head of Pantheon, was also present, only too happy to be interviewed by the ever-vigilant press. What he was stressing, if I understood correctly, was the irony that Grove, which had fought so hard for freedom of speech through the years, was now denying it to its own employees. André, you are absolutely right, and may you side with women's lib when they come and occupy *your* premises.

Even more galling was the sight of several of our authors, including Ed Sanders, Calvin Hernton, and, to my special chagrin, Julius Lester, an author I greatly esteemed. I walked over to Lester, ignoring the taunts and jibes of Damio and half a dozen of his cohorts (three of whom I swear I'd never seen), and stuck out my hand. There was a moment's hesitation, then he took it. Black on white. "Julius," I said, "do you trust me?" "Implicitly," he said. "Then when I tell you what Robin Morgan is doing is wrong, terribly wrong, will you leave the line?" He looked me square in the eye. "Sorry, Dick," he said, "I believe in women's lib." "So do I," I said. "But not in Robin Morgan and what she's up to. Do you know that none of the women up there, except Robin, are Grove employees?" "True? I was told they *all* were." "And they are threatening to burn or destroy our editorial files . . . including yours. Does that sound like the Ku Klux Klan to you? Or Nazi Germany? It does to me." We moved aside from the chanting crowd. "Julius, follow your conscience, but I at least wanted you to know the facts. Call me in a day or two and I'll give you the full gory details." And I turned and walked away. At the big G entrance, still under allied control, I looked back and saw Julius had quietly left the picket line and was heading north.

By mid-afternoon the crowd had dispersed, but any notion of returning to work was lost. Ward Damio was trying to organize a meeting with other employees on the first floor. Myron ordered them to go back to work, but they refused. After a long phone call to Copenhagen, he reported that Barney would be back next day and would hear their grievances. Barney had also apparently authorized Myron to go down to the precinct and press charges against the arrested women. There he asked the judge to set bail, on the premise that if released they would try to reoccupy the Grove offices. The judge said no and released them on probation.

Heading home that night, I had the sinking feeling that this had been by far the worst, perhaps most fateful, day I had ever endured at Grove. Straphanging on the shuddering C train north, I also hated myself for toting all this daily garbage back into our hallowed halls, for despite my efforts to separate day from night, work from family, it was becoming harder and harder to do so.

For the next two and a half weeks, Grove came to a grinding standstill.

Union meetings were held throughout the company, and when they were not taking place, most of the staff were arguing with one another from morning till evening, words replacing work. Key manuscripts were put on hold, design and production simply shut down, as did every other department to varying degrees. What the horrendous cost overruns on the new building had not quite accomplished, the unionization battle was, I feared, fast bringing us to an endgame.

If Barney had arrived back from Denmark in a state of near apoplexy, the veins of his forehead visibly throbbing, he was nonetheless, most of us felt, secretly pleased. Crises were his forte, he seemed to thrive on them, and this was a doozy. With Rembar to counsel him, he made the decision not to press charges against the invaders. "They'd love nothing more than to be made martyrs," he said. Only Myron disagreed. He was still not happy they were out on their own recognizance. It was clear there was going to be a union vote, however, and on Wednesday we had a war council to assess the situation. The first act of business was to try to figure, from the Grove personnel list, who would vote which way. Surprisingly, as we ticked off the list, Barney's initial fury softened, and he began to joke, acidly, to be sure, when we came to a name he particularly disliked.

On Friday the seventeenth, a meeting was held in Rembar's office, where it was agreed both that an NLRB-supervised election would be held "as soon as possible" and that we would submit to binding arbitration the nine fired employees' request to be reinstated.

So far all the propaganda had been one-sided. Now, with Jules calling most of the shots, we began a counteroffensive, issuing our own broadsheets that detailed the liberal benefits already extant at Grove and compared them, point by point, with the union alternatives, which looked far more restrictive. We pointed out some painful truths: unions were no longer what they used to be twenty years earlier; they had consistently supported the Vietnam War; they discriminated against blacks, especially in the building trades; they failed to support students who went to Mississippi to fight segregation. As for women's rights, "when and where did they fight for equal rights for women?" We also wondered, in print, what the Amalgamated Meat Cutters and Butcher Workmen—or their Fur, Leather, and Machine Workers division—knew about or could contribute to publishing.

Finally, on April 30, the vote was held on the second floor of the Grove offices, from 3:00 to 5:00 p.m. When the votes were counted, the union was, as Jules had predicted, roundly defeated, by a vote of 86–34, with another 29 votes discarded as unqualified. In subsequent arbitration, we were obliged to rehire the nine employees. Their presence, especially Robin's, was poisonous, but, thank God, blessedly brief.

55 ❧

Retreat to Eleventh Street

ITHIN THE NEXT SEVERAL MONTHS, with income falling like a shooting star in summer, almost half the remaining staff was let go, and it became increasingly clear that we would have to sell our wonderful new building.

Battered and bruised, but still standing, we began repacking our boxes barely a year after we had moved into these sumptuous quarters. In my twelve years at Grove, we had had times that were daunting, dangerous, discouraging, depressing. But they had all—well, most—been leavened by moments of pleasure, of gratification, even of triumph as a key court case was won or a book you had labored over and worried about—had you done your best for the author? would the reviewers like it? would it sell enough to justify the effort?—exceeded expectations. Now, close to broke, we bantered little as we gathered old manuscripts, correspondence, piles of dead matter that once had been so alive, filling large black plastic bags for the sanitation men who would come tomorrow, hoisting these paper treasures into their bulging trucks without so much as a wild thought of what marvels they were carting to oblivion. How many precious relics were we tossing, which in later years might have brought thousands—tens of thousands?—from rare-book dealers? But there was no recourse. As Napoleon had learned so bitterly, when you were retreating in disarray, you jettisoned whatever it took to save not your soul, hell, no, but your life. Even at an Irish wake they sang and drank. Here, today, it was the silence that hurt. Where was the bonhomie of yesteryear?

Barney had been adamant: everything nonessential goes. At Eleventh Street, he warned, there will be barely room to turn around. In place of these spacious top-floor offices, we'll often be two or three in a room. It was as though the clock had been turned back ten years. Maybe twelve. Even 64 University Place had been larger, lighter. I tried to think of something positive. Nothing. No, no: there must be something. Flinging a long galley of Anonymous, one of the Victorian gems, in the general direction of the shiny black garbage bag (it missed), I had an epiphany: Beckett. There was still Beckett, our North Star. Then in a rush a dozen others followed: Henry Miller, Octavio Paz, Bill Burroughs, Jean Genet, Eugène Ionesco, Malcolm X, "Cubby" Selby, John Rechy, Harold Pinter, Tom Stoppard, Robert Coover, Frantz Fanon, Alain Robbe-Grillet, Marguerite Duras . . . To raise morale—mine—I felt like shouting out their names, to share the good news. But somehow I could not.

Boxes all packed, taped, and stacked, the guilty black plastic bags lolling by the door, I took one last look around my office. Would I miss it? Not really. You have to have lived in an office for a long time, absorbed its light and smell, imparted yours, to truly regret it. My office, with its impressive desk, its posh leather easy chairs, its generous windows looking west over the Village, light streaming in as the sun dropped slowly behind the rooftops that lay between us and the Hudson, suddenly struck me as foreign. I closed the door behind me, made my way down the broad corridor, glancing left and right into the other offices for signs of life, but all my colleagues had already fled. Only Barney was still there, staring out the window. His face, when he swiveled at the sound of my footsteps, was stricken. Somehow he managed a smile, wan but true, and I raised my hand in a short salute.

"See you tomorrow," I said.

He nodded.

"Life goes on," I said, only half believing.

He nodded.

"How about a drink at the Cedar Tavern?" I tried.

He shook his head.

"Okay, then. Tomorrow." And as I turned and walked for the last time down the dreamworld hallway to the executive elevator, the great divider, catalyst at least to some degree of all the ills that had beset us these past several months, I had a sinking feeling that my days at Grove were num-

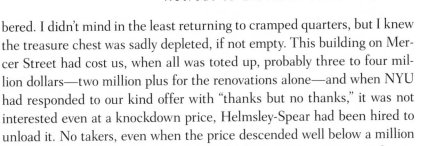

bered. I didn't mind in the least returning to cramped quarters, but I knew the treasure chest was sadly depleted, if not empty. This building on Mercer Street had cost us, when all was toted up, probably three to four million dollars—two million plus for the renovations alone—and when NYU had responded to our kind offer with "thanks but no thanks," it was not interested even at a knockdown price, Helmsley-Spear had been hired to unload it. No takers, even when the price descended well below a million dollars. Meanwhile, we were stuck with the several mortgages—five in all—without the income to cover them. And to think that only months before, *Architectural Record* had showcased the building in its January issue, honoring us with a 1970 Interior Design Award. *Interiors*, equally admired among professionals, featured the building in its November 1970 issue. Belated awards, cold comfort as the mighty ship was slowly (or not so slowly) sinking beneath the Mercer seas.

If, in 1969, 80 University Place—to which we had moved several years before when 64 became impossibly overcrowded—with its roughly ten thousand square feet had been far too tight for us, East Eleventh Street at half that size was a pressure cooker, with hallways turned into offices and offices meant for one shared by two or three. Fortunately, Barney owned the building, so the burden of rent was lifted, at least temporarily. When we had moved to Mercer Street, the former Evergreen Theater in the same building had been leased to a movie distributor, so there was a bit of income from that end. But money, or the lack thereof, was only part of the problem. Personal animosities, banked, if not buried, by flush times, resurfaced. Jules Geller and Myron Shapiro, who till now had scarcely concealed their dislike for each other, now openly feuded. Barney, however he disdained the mad accusations and demands of the movement headed by Robin Morgan, was deeply wounded by all that had happened these past few months, especially since he had always considered Grove's stands in liberating the country from its still Victorian attitudes and restrictive censorship, and its taking on daring works like Malcolm X, Frantz Fanon, LeRoi Jones, and Julius Lester in the area of black studies, put it in the forefront of innovative book publishing. Shaken to the core, Bonaparte on Elba, he brooded and plotted, itching to rescue Grove, and himself, from looming defeat. Even worse, his image as an enlightened liberal had been stained, if not shattered, as members of our own profession, suddenly emboldened by our weakened position, had taken up arms against us. Now sequestered in his second-floor office, prowling the premises in search of some internal misdemeanor, he was his own worst enemy. And ours. He was not just fighting the newly emerged demons who had fomented the needless strife; he was fighting for survival, as the multimillion-dollar real estate mistake was compounded by a sudden downturn in the publishing business itself. Even pared to the core, the company was having trouble paying its bills and meeting payroll. The Hudson Street warehouse had to be shut down, and an arrangement was made, just in time, for Random House to handle our distribution. Not without pain, for as part of the deal we had to give up the rights to a dozen of our solid backlist moneymakers, from *Games People Play* to *Malcolm X*. Days now were grim, all the hijinks gone. Still, after twelve years on the battlements, I felt it my bounden duty to weather the storm. Nat and Morrie and Jules and Fred all felt more or less the same: we would not go out looking for other jobs as long as there was even a glimmer of light at the end of the Grove tunnel.

Then one night all that changed. Barney called me at home to say he planned to fire Nat Sobel, but before he did, he wanted to inform us and get our assent. Why? I asked. Because he wasn't pulling his weight, Barney said, which was nonsense, for Nat was a superb sales director. Further probing resulted in the blunt "We simply can't afford him." I started to say something, but Barney hung up without saying goodbye.

"You've got to get out of there," Jeannette said. "And the sooner the better."

"You mean, leave Beckett behind, and all those authors I brought in and love? Not all that easy, darling." Yet I knew she was right. In fact, she'd been saying as much for almost a year. I was genuinely torn. I had loved my job most of the time and through thick and thin had never kowtowed to Barney or his whims, had always tried to tell him the truth as I saw it, no matter how unpleasant, no matter how he might fulminate and disagree. Ultimately, I felt sure, he respected me for my candor.

Morrie was the next of the old gang to go, the justification being that much of his time and energy had been spent promoting the films, and now that they were—momentarily?—moribund, there was little for him to do. Besides, "we simply can't afford him." Jules, meanwhile, was lend-leased to Random House, to liaise and oversee the new distribution—more to the point, one less burden for the Grove Press payroll. Still, both Fred and I were paid considerably more than any of the three now gone.

"The problem is," Jeannette advised, "Barney will never fire you. It'll be *Kind Hearts and Coronets*, with you both holding your swords aloft as the ship slowly sinks beneath the waves . . ." She paused. "The difference is, *you* can get another job." But could I? The whole endless Grove debacle had demoralized me, filled me with self-doubt.

One day I came back from lunching with an agent—still, fitfully, looking for books—to find my desk had been completely trashed. Yes, trashed. To be fair, holding down three or four jobs, including editorial and production, I had allowed my cubbyhole to degenerate into a mess, a cloaca, with correspondence, manuscripts, and galleys covering not only every last centimeter of the desktop but both chairs to boot. Apparently, Barney, not for the first time, had pointed out the mess to Fred, who always agreed with him, and together they had done a surgical strike while I was at lunch. I looked at the clean desk, started to turn, sure I had landed in the wrong office, realized I had not, turned back, and like a blind man began sifting through the wastebaskets and bins corralled for the occasion, kneeling to empty first one, then another. I felt violated. That Barney had taken this route infuriated me, but that Fred had joined in struck me as unspeakable betrayal.

I stormed upstairs and let Barney have it with both barrels. Did he have any idea what he had done? There were precious manuscripts ready for copyediting, galleys ready for proofing, submissions I had read and was ready to report on—there was even a new Beckett translation he had tossed God knows where. He listened, head bowed, whether chastened or silently chortling I had no idea. "You should be fucking ashamed of yourself" was all I could muster as I turned to leave the room, then, an over-the-shoulder parting shot: "You've never had a more faithful employee. Or friend. And you never will."

Downstairs, I called Alan Williams, a friend at Viking whom I greatly respected, and announced I was leaving Grove. "Seriously? Let me call you back." Against my better judgment, I decided not to clear out my desk, but used a Magic Marker to write on all the bins and wastebaskets a bold DO NOT REMOVE UNDER PENALTY OF DEATH!

It was with heavy heart and Sahara-like mouth that I left the office very late that afternoon. Home, Jeannette seemed elated. "You should have left years ago," she crowed. "And the kids agree with me.

"You'll find something, I am certain of it," she insisted. "Anyway, it's a cause for celebration." With which she headed toward the kitchen and reemerged with a bottle of champagne.

Next morning, as I was quietly reconstituting my desk to its former mayhem, the phone rang. Alan Williams. Was I free for lunch next day? Of course. "I'd like you to meet Mort Levin," he said. I'd never heard of the man, who turned out to be the general manager of Viking, the publisher Tom Guinzburg's trusted second-in-command, a man I sensed as soon as I met him was decent, gentle yet firm, and very knowledgeable about the book business. I expected him to ask why I was leaving, but he did not, spending most of the time talking about Viking, its past, present, and especially its future. At two thirty on the dot he looked at his watch, thanked me for having come uptown, and said he had a three o'clock meeting. Thinking back to the last time I had ventured outside the office for lunch and the repercussions thereof, I was fully prepared for anything as I stepped back into my Eleventh Street lair. To my practiced eye, not a hair had been moved; the paper clip I had planted at precisely a forty-five-degree angle was still there, intact and untouched.

Only two people were aware of what had happened—the violation of my desk—dear Marilynn Meeker and a relative newcomer, Rusty Porter, a young, buxom blonde I had hired as production manager, not for her looks (though they may, I must confess, have played a part), but for her boundless energy, past production experience, and loyalty. Both women, who had seen the sad results of the office invasion, had come to me openly and commiserated. Marilynn, who had been at Grove longer than I, tried to make excuses for Barney. "He's under such pressure," she said. "But," she added, "that Fred went along is unforgivable. Have you talked to him since?"

I shook my head. "I told Barney what I thought, but not Fred."

"But please don't leave," she said. "Please!"

I went over and took her frail body and hugged her. She let her head rest on my shoulder, and I felt a shudder pass through her before she pulled away, her eyes bright with tears.

A week later Mort Levin called and asked if I could come next morning to the Viking office at 625 Madison Avenue. He came out to meet me and take me into his relatively modest office, next door to the Big Man, Tom Guinzburg. There was no editorial opening at Viking itself—the letdown must have been visible despite the forced smile—but what Tom and he were proposing was an imprint, similar to that of Kurt and Helen Wolff at Harcourt, Brace. I would have an acquisition budget to be determined, a monthly draw against future profits, and full editorial control, unless an intended acquisition reached a certain figure, at which point I would have to consult him or Tom for approval. The smile was no longer forced. To start when? I asked. Mort shook his head. "We'll need to work out the details, then you'll need a lawyer to meet with ours, but that shouldn't take more than a few days. Which leads me to ask you: When would *you* like to start?" "Let me talk to my wife tonight, and I'll get back to you tomorrow." "Fine. Now, let me introduce you to Tom Guinzburg."

He led me to the next-door office, one of the most bizarre adult play-pens I had ever seen. Tom, tall, angular, and uncommonly awkward, rose from his throne behind a gilded desk and shook my hand firmly. His smile was broad but, I felt, forced, as if one of many facial gestures his position obliged him to make, perhaps daily, in which he did not really believe. His father, Harold Guinzburg, had founded Viking in 1925 and, from all re-ports, was a consummate diplomat, whose charm and charisma had en-abled him to build, in a mere three decades, one of the premier publishing houses of his time. His son Tom, using his name and fortune, had, after graduating from Yale, opted for the fast lane, soon an intimate of the rich and famous. His close friends included young Jacqueline Kennedy and Grace Kelly, whose wedding to Prince Rainier of Monaco he had attended, to judge by the enlarged photographs prominently displayed in his office.

No doubt concerned about the playboy path his son's life was taking, Harold had brought him into the business some years before, but instead of making it clear to all and sundry that Tom was his automatic successor and moving him routinely from mail room to senior executive in rapid suc-cession, the usual nepotistic route, Harold made Tom earn his stripes. From that initial encounter I got the distinct feeling that Tom had never recov-ered from his father's dictates. In any event, he had had his filial revenge, for Harold keeled over one day, and suddenly Tom was in charge, ready or not. He hired Mort Levin, a soft-spoken, self-effacing, rabbi-like man of great charm and utter common sense, held in the highest esteem by every-one, to be his alter ego in the house.

Jeannette wanted to know my candid opinion of Tom, for, however in-dependent the new setup sounded, a boss was a boss, and she wondered if, exchanging Barney for Tom, I was going from the frying pan into the fire. "He was extremely nice and welcoming," I said, "but I've never met anyone who seemed so . . . uncomfortable. He can't seem to sit still, as if he's not in control of his own body." "Your own list, independent editorially but with all Viking's apparatus to make it work? For God's sake, *take* it!"

That night we moved from sparkling California to Veuve Clicquot. As our glasses clinked, Jeannette said simply: "I knew you'd find something else. But I didn't think it would be this soon."

———

Next day, I walked up to Barney's office to find him unshaven, a bottle of beer in hand. An all-nighter, no doubt. He gestured me to sit, and his smile was genuine. I had to admit I still liked the bastard. I said I was leaving Grove—regretfully, but I thought it better I did, both for him and for me. He listened impassively. "Have you really made up your mind?" I nodded. "I hope it wasn't that incident the other day," he offered. "I felt bad afterward . . ." "That was a factor," I said. "The message was pretty clear, no?" He said nothing, rolling the slim neck of the half-empty bottle between thumb and forefinger. "It's been a rough couple of years," he began, then his voice trailed off. "You simply can't afford me," I said, "and I had the feeling you couldn't bring yourself to fire me. So I had to take matters in my own hands." That brought a smile. "Where will you be going?" he asked. "Not sure," I lied, but only partially, for nothing had yet been settled, and I knew how often things could fall apart at the last minute. "Don't worry," I said, "I'll clean up that damn desk before I leave." At which he got to his feet and, with all his 130 pounds, gave me a bear hug worthy of someone twice his size and weight. A hug as hearty as any I'd ever had.

Was it relief I felt as I left his office for the last time, or regret? A chapter of my life had been closed, a very important chapter. Would the new chapter be as challenging? As daunting? As fun filled? As crazy? As debilitating? As rewarding? I doubted it. Only time would tell . . .

Epilogue

AFTER HIS TWELVE INSPIRING AND EXCITING YEARS at Grove Press, Dick carried on his sterling publishing career for more than five decades. He always maintained close ties with literary France and with European writers. One of a handful of old-school book editors, Dick nurtured and worked hands-on with his authors, line by line, paragraph by paragraph; the editing process was something he approached with passion and great care.

In 1971, Tom Guinzburg, the head of the Viking Press, invited Dick to form his own imprint, Richard Seaver Books. After being trained by him, I joined him at the imprint. William Burroughs, Octavio Paz, Emil Cioran, Eugène Ionesco, Samuel Beckett, and many more followed him there, and Dick happily continued in his tradition of seeking and introducing new, often provocative literary voices from around the world. Dick became head of Penguin USA in 1975 and I took over the imprint, which became simply Seaver Books, and would continue in its original mission for the next fourteen years.

In 1979, Holt, Rinehart and Winston, one of the oldest American publishing houses, recruited Dick as its president and publisher, a position he held for ten years.

In 1989, Little, Brown and Company, another distinguished house, then a division of Time, Inc., asked the Seavers to create and head a new division, Arcade, the primary goal of which was to attract international authors to Little, Brown's already robust American list. Shortly thereafter, when Time merged with Warner and Little, Brown became part of the Time Warner Book Group, Dick and I initiated a management buy-out.

In 1993, Arcade Publishing became ours, and over the next two decades we published more than five hundred books from more than thirty countries, thriving as one of the last independent literary houses.

Throughout his life, Dick also translated more than fifty books from the French (it was only after his death in 2009 that he was officially revealed to be Sabine D'Estrée, the translator of *Story of O*). In 1996, we were both awarded medals of the Ordre Chevalier des Arts et des Lettres—Knights of Arts and Letters—by the French government.

JEANNETTE SEAVER

Acknowledgments

I thank my invaluable friends Jill Jakes, Joanne Turnbull, Dan Okrent, Toby and Dan Talbot, and Steven Lipstitz for generously taking the time to read the nine-hundred-plus manuscript pages of Dick's memoir. Your important notes helped and encouraged me at a time when it was most needed. Leon Friedman, thank you for stepping in with your sound advice, shepherding Dick's manuscript into the publishing world and astutely targeting the right publisher. I can't imagine a better place than Farrar, Straus and Giroux for Dick's writing. Jonathan Galassi, your enthusiasm, high standards, and devotion made my and Dick's dream come true. Thank you. I very much enjoyed our collaboration, Sean McDonald. Your excellent editorial hand made all the difference in how the book was shaped. A big hug to Charlotte Strick for creating such a happy book cover. And to Abby Kagan, who had in earlier days worked with Dick at Holt; this serendipitous reunion of designing Dick's book turned the whole experience into something quite special. Nathalie, Alex, and Nicholas, without your love and unwavering support—editorial and otherwise—the task of editing the work of one of the best editors would never have happened. To all, thank you.

INDEX